INTRODUCING ANTHROPOLOGY

SIXTH EDITION

INTRODUCING
ANTHROPOLOGY SIXTH EDITION

An Integrated Approach

Michael Alan Park
Central Connecticut State University

Mc
Graw
Hill
Education

INTRODUCING ANTHROPOLOGY: AN INTEGRATED APPROACH, SIXTH EDITION

Published by McGraw-Hill Education, 2 Penn Plaza, New York, NY 10121. Copyright © 2014 by McGraw-Hill Education. All rights reserved. Printed in the United States of America. Previous editions © 2011, 2008, and 2006. No part of this publication may be reproduced or distributed in any form or by any means, or stored in a database or retrieval system, without the prior written consent of McGraw-Hill Education, including, but not limited to, in any network or other electronic storage or transmission, or broadcast for distance learning.

Some ancillaries, including electronic and print components, may not be available to customers outside the United States.

This book is printed on acid-free paper.

1 2 3 4 5 6 7 8 9 0 DOC/DOC 1 0 9 8 7 6 5 4 3

ISBN 978-0-07-803506-7
MHID 0-07-803506-6

Senior Vice President, Products & Markets: *Kurt L. Strand*
Vice President, General Manager, Products & Markets: *Michael Ryan*
Vice President, Content Production & Technology Services: *Kimberly Meriwether David*
Managing Director: *Gina Boedeker*
Brand Manager: *Courtney Austermehle*
Executive Director of Development: *Lisa Pinto*
Managing Development Editor: *Penina Braffman*

Marketing Specialist: *Alexandra Schultz*
Director, Content Production: *Terri Schiesl*
Lead Project Manager: *Jane Mohr*
Buyer: *Jennifer Pickel*
Cover Designer: *Studio Montage, St. Louis, MO*
Cover Image: *(c) Goodshoot / Fotos*
Compositor: *Aptara®, Inc.*
Typeface: *10/12 Sabon*
Printer: *R. R. Donnelley*

All credits appearing on page or at the end of the book are considered to be an extension of the copyright page.

Library of Congress Cataloging-in-Publication Data
Park, Michael Alan.
   Introducing anthropology : an integrated approach / Michael Alan Park. —Sixth edition.
      pages cm
   ISBN-13: 978-0-07-803506-7 (alk. paper)
   ISBN-10: 0-07-803506-6 (alk. paper)
   1. Anthropology. I. Title.
GN25.P293 2014
301—dc23
                                                              2013015524

The Internet addresses listed in the text were accurate at the time of publication. The inclusion of a website does not indicate an endorsement by the authors or McGraw-Hill Education, and McGraw-Hill Education does not guarantee the accuracy of the information presented at these sites.

www.mhhe.com

In memory of her companionship many years ago
as I conceived, researched, and wrote
my first book, this one is for:
Joyce
(1982–1996)

And the patches make the goodbye harder still.
—CAT STEVENS

Contents

Preface

Modern anthropology has become extraordinarily diverse, with a wide variety of schools of thought and theoretical models within the discipline. Not surprisingly, this breadth in the field has led to a range of approaches to thinking about and teaching those courses traditionally called four-field introductions to anthropology. In short, we anthropologists each have sometimes very different answers to the question, What *is* anthropology?

The ideas about the nature of anthropology that have guided this book's organization, discussions, and selection of topics center on the field's identity as scientific, humanistic, and holistic:

- **Anthropology can be, should be, and is scientific.** That is, it operates by inductively generating testable hypotheses, which are then deductively tested in an attempt to derive working theories about the areas of human biology and behavior that are our focuses. This is not to say that applying science to cultural variation or the abstract aspects of cultural systems is easy or particularly straightforward, or that science has even come close to satisfactorily answering all the major questions anthropologists ask about our species. Far from it. I simply believe that—if it is to be truly scholarly—the *process* of anthropologically investigating humankind is a scientific one.

- **Anthropology can be, should be, and is humanistic.** A scientific orientation and focus does not preclude nonscientific investigations and discussions of human behavior, or humanistic applications of anthropology. We are, after all, dealing with human beings who have motivations for their behaviors that fail to respond to fixed laws as do chemicals or subatomic particles. Moreover, because we deal with people, we cannot help developing a concern for the welfare of our fellow humans. Indeed, this is what leads many to choose anthropology as a career in the first place. It becomes, then, only natural—if not morally incumbent on us—to apply what we have learned about humans and human behavior to give voice to those without one and to lend our knowledge to the agencies and governments that administer, guide, and, sometimes, compel and manipulate social change.

■ **Anthropology can be, should be, and is holistic—*because its subject is holistic.*** Thus, affiliation with one of the traditional subfields of anthropology should be no more than a starting point to the scholarly investigation of the nature of our species. In short, despite the enormous breadth of anthropological subject matter and approaches to studying those subjects, there *really is* a field called anthropology that has a distinctive viewpoint and methodology that make it uniquely valuable.

FEATURES

The assumptions that guided my writing have been concretely applied through the following features:

■ To convey the holism of the discipline, the traditional subfields are not used to divide the text into major parts, nor are they titles of chapters. The standard subfields are described and defined in the first chapter, but subsequently, the methods and contributions of each are interwoven throughout the book. In other words, the text is organized around the unique subject matter of anthropology—the human species in its holistic entirety—rather than being organized around the current subfield structure of anthropology itself.

■ To convey the multidimensional holism of the field at the introductory level requires choosing a theme that can act as a common thread tying all the parts together. Just saying that anthropology is holistic and giving a few specific examples is not enough. There are, of course, any number of themes that would be equally useful as such a pedagogical device. The one I have chosen is that of adaptation, broadly defined. I am not using the term in just its biological, ecological sense, although, of course, this definition does apply to human biological evolution and to the direct responses of cultures to their environments. But even abstract aspects of culture are adaptive responses to *something.* In other words, to paraphrase the title of an old anthology, my theme is that "humans make sense." Even if we have a hard time making sense of some of our behaviors, my central integrative assumption is that behaviors have *some* explanation within their cultural contexts.

- I've assumed that student readers have little or no familiarity with anthropology. I am introducing them to the field from the ground up, starting from scratch, and having in mind courses whose goal is to truly *introduce* rather than supply an encyclopedic survey. For the introductory student, none of the detail about models, paradigms, or current theoretical debates makes a bit of sense unless and until that student has a basic knowledge of the general approach, subject matter, methodology, history, and facts of our field. Although I do briefly discuss the area of anthropological theory and note several current debates, a text that focuses on that subject or that is written from just one perspective would fail to do justice to the field. And it would certainly fail to convey to the introductory student the basic identity of anthropology, the basic facts that anthropology has discerned about the human species, and the richness of our subject matter, our scholarly worldview, and our contributions to knowledge and human welfare.

- To get students to feel that I am talking to them personally, I have mixed an appropriate level of informality with the more formal style that must be used to convey the ideas of anthropology and the seriousness with which we approach our subject. I want the students to feel that I am taking a journey through anthropology with them, not that I have just given them a map and guidebook and left them on their own.

- Because a common misconception of our field is that we only study old dried-up fossils and exotic living peoples with their bizarre behaviors, I have tried to emphasize that anthropology studies the world's peoples in all their guises—ordinary and extraordinary, next door and in remote places. I have used as many examples and analogies as possible from North American cultures, groups, and situations. Students should know that anthropology doesn't stop the moment they walk out the classroom door; they should know that they too can do anthropology and that they too are anthropological subjects.

- To really understand anthropology, students must apply it to thinking about their own lives. To further encourage this, the text includes a "Contemporary Issues" box at the end of each chapter that specifically applies the topic of the chapter to some question about the contemporary world, with a focus, where possible, on America and American culture.

- Stories have worked well for most of human history as a vehicle for transmitting facts and ideas. They are more memorable than lists. I have written this text keeping in mind the narrative approach. There are a few literal stories, such as the one about my fieldwork that begins the book. But narrative in a more general sense refers to a causal sequence of events, and I have tried to show how the various topics within anthropology connect with one another in this manner. The student readers should be able to navigate their way through the book and know where they are within the broad and diverse field of anthropology. I have provided signposts in the form of part, chapter, and subheading titles that logically and descriptively divide the subject as I have ordered it. The number of cultures used as examples is limited so that the same groups may be referred to throughout the book in different contexts.

- A true introduction should be short and to the point. Achieving brevity while trying to introduce such a broad field is a challenge. I have tried to include every major topic within mainstream anthropology while managing the amount of detail presented. I think it is more efficient, at this level, to convey a sense of a topic through one clear, interesting, memorable example rather than four or five. One's own favorite example can always be discussed or more detail added in class.

- Finally, the text is as accessible, attractive, straightforward, and uncluttered as possible. Important terms are boldfaced where they first appear and defined briefly in a running glossary in the margin. These terms are also listed alphabetically in a glossary at the end of the book. Also included is a standard bibliography. The text itself is not interrupted with specific references and citations. These are listed in a section at the end of each chapter called "Notes, References, and Readings," along with other references to the topics covered and to some specific studies or facts for those interested in pursuing a subject further. A chapter summary precedes this section, as well as "Questions for Further Thought," which help students explore the real-world ramifications of the chapters' topics. Photographs and line art are in color where possible, and captions add information rather than simply label the illustrations.

NEW TO THIS EDITION

The book has been updated where needed, and the discussion of many topics has been clarified. Highlights include the following:

- The major new feature is the addition of new subheadings in the chapters. This is to help the readers navigate through the more complex topics and, if they study this way, to provide them with a built-in outline of the chapter contents.

- The text has been further streamlined. No subject has been deleted, but I have tried to include only central ideas and related concepts that lead to and follow from them.

- Topics have been updated throughout to reflect new data, research, and ideas.

- Chapter 2, "How Anthropology Works," has an improved discussion of the scientific method.

- Chapter 3, "Themes of Anthropology: Evolution," includes simplified discussions of genetics and the processes of evolution, to better prepare students for the applications of those topics to come later.

- Chapter 4, "Themes of Anthropology: Culture," has a revised discussion and diagram relating to the methodology of studying cultural systems.

- Chapter 5, "Our Place in Nature: Humans as Primates," returns to the use of *hominid* to include only humans and our direct ancestors. I briefly account for this in the context of a simplified and improved discussion of taxonomic schemes.

- Chapter 6, "Evolution: The Bipedal, Large-Brained Primate," contains updates on the fossil record, including the new evidence for interbreeding between "modern" humans and Neandertals.

- Chapter 7, "Reproduction: The Sexual Primate," and Chapter 8, "Human Variation: Biological Diversity and Race," have been considerably streamlined to more clearly make their important points.

- Chapter 13, "Culture Change: Theories and Processes," now does a better job of discussing the processes that bring about culture change.

- Chapter 14, "The Evolution of Our Behavior: Putting It All Together," simplifies the discussion of the biblical food laws so as to better set up the topics that follow.

- Chapter 15, "Anthropology in Today's World: Problems and Contributions," updates material on the societies discussed.

ANCILLARIES

Visit our Online Learning Center Web site at www.mhhe.com/park6e for robust student and instructor resources.

For students: Student resources include self-quizzes (multiple-choice and true or false), Internet links, and chapter study aids.

For instructors: The password-protected instructor portion of the Web site includes the instructor's manual, a comprehensive computerized test bank, and PowerPoint lecture slides.

ACKNOWLEDGMENTS

I want to thank all the hardworking people at McGraw-Hill who have turned my ideas, words, and doodles into a real book. These include Courtney Austermehle, brand manager; Penina Braffman, managing editor; Jane Mohr, project manager; Nicole Bridge, developmental editor; Alexandra Schultz, marketing specialist; and Jennifer Pickel, buyer.

Special thanks also to the sponsoring editor of the first edition of this book, Jan Beatty, who encouraged me to try something different and whose influence will always be a part of this and all my other books.

Thanks as well to my friend, colleague, and ofttimes coauthor, Ken Feder, for his help in many important ways. Roger Lohmann provided a detailed set of suggestions, comments, and corrections that were helpful throughout the book and particularly so in the religion chapter. Laura Donnelly provided advice for and posed for the sign-language photos. For those times when I ventured into the physical sciences, Bob Weinberger checked my facts, and Fran Weinberger kept me on my toes regarding the facts of the biblical dietary laws; both these people, of course, remain innocent of any final transgressions. And for forty years my students at Central Connecticut State have been my "guinea pigs" for teaching ideas covered in this text; they have also been my most candid, most vocal, and most helpful critics.

The manuscript was reviewed by the following people: Anthony Tessandori, Bellevue College; Benjamin Arbuckle, Baylor University; Pam Sezgin, Gainesville State College; Wanda Clark, South Plains College; Cassandra Kuba, California University of Pennsylvania; Karla Davis-Salazar, University of South Florida; Elizabeth Peters, Florida State University; Catherine Fuentes, University of North Carolina; R. A. Halberstein, University of Miami; Cindy Isenhour, University of Kentucky; Manouchehr Shiva, Bellevue College; and Jim Wanner, University of Northern Colorado–Greeley. I thank them all for their helpful and insightful contributions. Any errors, of course, remain entirely my responsibility.

To My Readers

I've always appreciated knowing something about the authors of the books I read, and so I think you should know something about me—especially since you are relying on me to introduce you to anthropology.

I started my college career at Indiana University as a biology major, then switched two or three times to other majors. I took my first anthropology course because it sounded interesting—and because it fulfilled a general education requirement and met at a convenient time. But soon I was hooked. Once I learned what anthropology was all about, I realized it was the perfect combination of many subjects that had always interested me. I went on to get my undergraduate degree in anthropology and stayed at Indiana for graduate work, specializing in biological anthropology—first human osteology (the study of the skeleton) and forensic anthropology and later redirecting my interests to evolutionary theory and evolutionary processes as they apply to the human species. This, as you'll read about in Chapter 1, was the focus of my fieldwork and research among the Hutterites. I received my doctoral degree in 1979.

In 1973 I started working at Central Connecticut State University, where I've been ever since, teaching courses in general anthropology (the topic of this book), human evolution, human biocultural diversity, forensic anthropology, the evolution of human behavior, and human ecology. I have also taught courses in the biology department and the university's honors program. I consider myself primarily an educator, so it was a natural step from classroom teaching to writing textbooks. This one is my sixth.

In addition to my personal and professional interest in anthropology, I'm also concerned about the quality of science education and about public knowledge and perception of scientific matters. I have written and lectured on such things as teaching evolution, scientific investigations of palm reading and psychic detectives, and environmental issues.

On the purely personal side, in case you're interested, I live in rural Connecticut with my wife, two Labrador retrievers, and two cats. When I'm not doing anthropology, I enjoy reading (although most of what I read seems to have something to do with science) and travel (although our trips nearly always include museums and archaeological sites). And since you may wonder when you get to Chapter 3, I've never followed up on my tropical fish experiments.

PRACTICAL STUDY TIPS

Most Importantly: Establish Your Own Style and Stick to It.

What works for one person won't for another. I always needed peace and quiet to study and still do, but I know some of my students like to study while listening to their iPods. Some people highlight passages in the text, others make marginal notes, still others write an outline of the material. Of course, you'll have to adjust your study style to the text in question and to your instructor's format, but for the most part, you can do this around your basic approach. Don't be too inflexible, though; try some of the following suggestions. If they work, fine. If not, forget them.

Read the Text as a Book.

It may sound strange, but this *is* a book. It is not a Web site on paper nor a guide to using other resources. Very simply, it should be read as a *book*, as you would a novel, for example. I wrote it in a "narrative" style. That is, the contents of the chapters and the order of the chapters themselves are meant to convey a story, where one idea leads to the next and each idea follows from previous ideas. Stories are how humans have shared information since time immemorial. And because this book is structured as a story—a causal sequence of ideas—it is much easier to retain than is a list of facts.

Don't Highlight Everything.

I've seen some of my students' textbooks with virtually every sentence glowing yellow, pink, or green. This is not helpful, just as it's not helpful to try to write down everything your instructor says in class. Notes and highlighting should be *clues to jog your memory.* Here are two examples taken from the previous edition of this text—of what not to do and of what would help you actually learn the material:

FIGURE 9.6
A San healer (*left*) in a trance tries to discover the cause of the other man's illness.

in polygynous marriages are healers, men possessing special powers that allow them to cure illness (Figure 9.6). This is one of the few symbols of differential status seen among the San. Women, by the way, may also be healers, but these women do not seem to have any special privileges.

San religion recognizes multiple supernatural beings, including two very important, powerful gods who are largely responsible for the creation of the world and for keeping it running. There are also lots of individual spirits, as well as the ghosts of deceased people, who tend to be malevolent. The healers are thought to possess a substance, or healing power, that they can invoke through a dance. It causes them to go into a trance during which they are able to cure illnesses and speak with the ghosts of the dead.

The last trait of foragers I noted earlier is their lack of a concept of land and resource ownership. This is true for the San. It's not that each band of San roam wherever they want. Each band has an area in which it normally hunts and gathers, and this area is acknowledged by other bands. If, however, the home range of one band runs out of a resource—say, if its water hole dries up or becomes contaminated—that

See the difference?

FIGURE 9.6
A San healer (*left*) in a trance tries to discover the cause of the other man's illness.

status

religion

ownership

in polygynous marriages are healers, men possessing special powers that allow them to cure illness (Figure 9.6). This is one of the few symbols of differential status seen among the San. Women, by the way, may also be healers, but these women do not seem to have any special privileges.

San religion recognizes multiple supernatural beings, including two very important, powerful gods who are largely responsible for the creation of the world and for keeping it running. There are also lots of individual spirits, as well as the ghosts of deceased people, who tend to be malevolent. The healers are thought to possess a substance, or healing power, that they can invoke through a dance. It causes them to go into a trance during which they are able to cure illnesses and speak with the ghosts of the dead.

The last trait of foragers I noted earlier is their lack of a concept of land and resource ownership. This is true for the San. It's not that each band of San roam wherever they want. Each band has an area in which it normally hunts and gathers, and this area is acknowledged by other bands. If, however, the home range of one band runs out of a resource—say, if its water hole dries up or becomes contaminated—that

Use the Ancillary Material as Support.

The text in the book, with the illustrations and captions, is the main part. The running glossary entries (in the margins), opening questions, material at the ends of chapters, the main glossary, and the Online Learning Center Web site are all there to help you *make sense of and learn* the material in the book. Use all these things to help you define words and test your knowledge of the material, but don't start with them or rely on them. The text I had when I took introductory anthropology had *none* of these things. They are helpful but not necessary.

Organize Reviewing and Studying for Exams.

For this book, I'd suggest first rereading the opening questions and then the summary for each chapter. These will remind you of the themes of the chapter, the general ideas that the facts are supporting. Then, review your highlights and notes. Finally, see if you can answer the opening questions.

Ask Questions!

If you miss one idea, you may well miss many ideas that follow from it. Write down questions that occur to you, or make notes in the margins of the book. Then get answers to them as soon as you can. And while it's a cliché, it's true: No question is stupid. Someone else in the class may well have the same question. And if you would like my input, feel free to email me at: ParkM@ccsu.edu.

PART ONE

Anthropology: The Biocultural Study of the Human Species

DOING ANTHROPOLOGY

Defining the Discipline

CHAPTER CONTENTS   In the Field • The Hutterites • Anthropology • Contemporary Issues: What Responsibilities Does the Anthropologist Have When Studying Other Cultures? • Plan of the Book • Summary • Questions for Further Thought • Notes, References, and Readings

If you asked ten people to define **anthropology,** you would probably get ten answers, each partially correct but not covering the entire definition of the field. This is understandable. Anthropology is such a broad discipline that many people—including me when I took my first anthropology course—conceive of the field in terms of the one or two aspects they are familiar with.

In this chapter, we will define anthropology as a whole, discuss the major subfields of the discipline, and then show how all these subfields interact and work together. Then I will briefly describe how the rest of the book is organized. But first, because I think fieldwork is perhaps the best-known aspect of all areas of anthropology, I will begin with a brief description of one of my own fieldwork experiences and the people and society I studied. This introduction will also help you become familiar with a cultural system that we can examine throughout the book.

AS YOU READ, CONSIDER THE FOLLOWING QUESTIONS:

1. Who are the Hutterites, and why did the author study them?
2. What is the general definition of anthropology?
3. What are the major subfields of anthropology, and how do they integrate with one another?

IN THE FIELD

We had left behind the spacious wheat fields surrounding the small town in western Saskatchewan, Canada, and were now driving a straight, flat, two-lane road through the open, rolling plains. Lyrics of old songs came to mind as I saw mule deer and pronghorn antelope playing in the "amber waves of grain." In fact, on that June day in 1973, I was desperately trying to think about anything other than where I was going.

I was on my way to meet my first real anthropological subjects, a colony of people belonging to a 450-year-old religious group called the Hutterian Brethren, or Hutterites. Up to this point I had not felt much anxiety about the visit. My situation was quite safe. Whereas other anthropologists had contacts with Amazon rain-forest warriors and highland New Guinea headhunters, I was in an English-speaking country, preparing to study an English-speaking people of European descent who practiced a form of Christianity that emphasized pacifism and tolerance.

anthropology The holistic, scientific study of humankind.

Such thoughts, however, were of no help. Nor was the fact that I was accompanied by the wife of a local wheat farmer who was well known and liked by this Hutterite community. I had that unnamed syndrome that affects many anthropologists under these circumstances.

The road turned from blacktop to gravel and then to dirt. After about 10 miles, it curved abruptly to the right, ran through an authentic western ghost town, and crested a hill. I saw below me, at the literal end of the road, a neat collection of twenty or so white buildings surrounded by acres of cultivated fields. This was the Hutterite colony, the *Bruderhof*, or "place of the brethren" (Figure 1.1).

As we drove into the colony, I became more anxious. There was not a soul to be seen. My companion explained that it was a religious holiday, requiring all but essential work to cease. The colony minister and the colony boss, however, had agreed to see me.

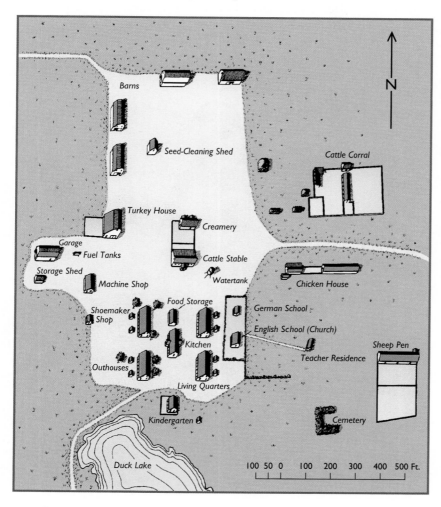

FIGURE 1.1
Diagram of a typical Hutterite colony. The variety of buildings and their functions are indicative of the Hutterites' attempt to keep their colonies self-sufficient and separate from the outside world. (In reality, there would be many more buildings designated as living quarters.)

We knocked at the door of one of the small buildings I assumed was a residence. We were greeted formally but warmly by an elderly man dressed in the Hutterite fashion—black trousers and coat over a white shirt—and with a full beard. The room we entered, clearly a living room, was darkened in observance of the holiday. That darkness, combined with my nervous excitement, has erased all impressions of the next few minutes from my memory.

My recollections of that day resume moments later, with my bearings straight and introductions made. I explained the reason for my visit to the man who had greeted us, a younger man, and a woman. The older man was the colony minister; the other man, who happened to be his son, was the colony boss. The woman, the minister's wife, was also dressed in the conservative style of the Hutterites. She wore a white blouse beneath a nearly full-length sleeveless dress with a small floral pattern on a black background. Her head was covered by a polka-dot kerchief, which they call a shawl (Figure 1.2).

FIGURE 1.2
Hutterite women in typical dress.

The three listened in silence as I went through my well-rehearsed explanation. My contacts, the wheat farmer and his wife, had briefed them about what I wanted to do, and I had already written them a letter introducing myself. But I realized that if they didn't like me or my explanation, they could still decline to cooperate. So I started from the beginning, reviewing that I wanted to take their fingerprints—which are partially influenced by genes—and collect genealogical data to document genetic changes between populations and across generations.

When I had finished, they asked me a few questions: Was I from the government? (They apparently knew about fingerprints only in the context of law enforcement and personal identification.) Did I know Scripture? (My equivocal answer seemed to create no problem.) What would I use this study for? Was I going to write a book? Did I know Dr. Steinberg, who had been there two years earlier collecting medical data? (I had taken a course from him.)

When they had exhausted their questions, I expected that they would confer with one another or ask me to come back when they had decided. Instead, the minister, who was clearly in charge, simply said, "Today is a holiday for us. Can you start tomorrow?" And so, for the next month I took part in my personal version of the anthropological fieldwork experience—taking fingerprints, recording family relationships, observing colony life, and befriending the Hutterites of this and a related Bruderhof in Alberta.

What exactly had brought me 1,300 miles from the university where I was doing graduate work to this isolated community of people whose way of life had changed little over nearly half a millennium and whose lifestyle and philosophy were so different from that of North American culture in general? Essentially, it was the same thing that takes anthropologists to the savannas of East Africa, the outback of Australia, the caves of southern France, and the street corners of New York City: the desire to learn something about the nature of the human species.

In my case, I was pursuing an interest I had developed early in graduate school. I was curious about certain processes of evolutionary change and how they operate in human populations. To examine them and their roles in our evolution, I needed to find a human group with a few special characteristics. First, the group had to be fairly genetically isolated, meaning that most members found their mates from within the group. The group had to be fairly small as a whole, but with large individual families. I was also looking for a group that had knowledge of their genealogy and in which family relationships reflected genetic as well as cultural categories. (As we will see in Chapter 10, all societies have systems of family relationships, but few of these coincide completely with biological relationships.) Finally, I was hoping for a community in which individual units within the group were created through the splitting up of existing units.

The Hutterites fit this description very well. I had learned of them through library research on genetically isolated populations. My opportunity to study them was greatly enhanced by a stroke of luck: a fellow graduate student was the daughter of the wheat farmer and his wife who became my contacts. Let's briefly look at the Hutterites, whom we will use as one example of a cultural system throughout this book.

THE HUTTERITES

The Hutterian Brethren is a Christian religious sect founded in Moravia (part of the present-day Czech Republic) in 1528 by peoples from southern Germany and Austria. They were part of the Anabaptist movement, whose doctrines shunned the idea of infant baptism and advocated a church free from the control of the state. Because of their doctrines, the Anabaptist groups were disliked by the mainstream Catholics and Protestants of their time. Many Anabaptist sects formed during this period, but only three remain today: the Hutterites; the Mennonites; and a Mennonite branch, the Amish. All now live mainly in North America.

One additional aspect of some of these groups' nonconformity was their belief in communal living and ownership. The biblical passage that forms the basis of the Hutterite lifestyle is Acts 2:44, which reads in part: "And all that believed were together, and had all things common."

But the nonconformity of the Anabaptists also led to persecution. Many members of the various sects were imprisoned, and some were tortured and burned at the stake. One of those executed was Jacob Hutter, an early leader of the group that, after his martyrdom, took his name. This persecution resulted in the demise of most Anabaptist groups, but through continual migration and sheer persistence, the Hutterites managed to survive. Over the next 300 years they lived in Slovakia, Romania, and Russia, coming finally in the 1870s to the United States. Later problems connected with taxes and with the military draft (the Hutterites, remember, are pacifists) led many Hutterites to move again, this time to Canada. Today there are over 45,000 Hutterites in 462 colonies located in the Canadian provinces of Manitoba, Saskatchewan, Alberta, and British Columbia; the rest are in Montana, North and South Dakota, Minnesota, and Washington (Figure 1.3). (We'll cover more of Hutterite history in Chapter 12.)

The sect is now divided into three subsects descended from the three original colonies founded by the Hutterite migrants to North America. The subsects have been genetically isolated from one another since World War I; that is, members find mates only from within their subsect. The differences among the subsects include degree of cultural conservatism, which is manifested in, for example, clothing styles.

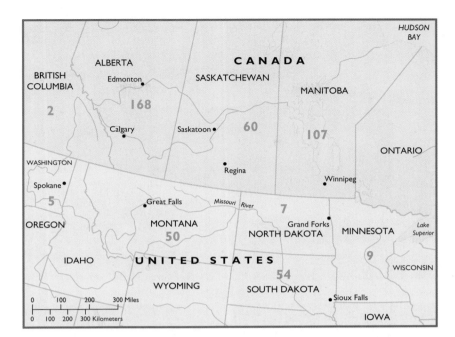

FIGURE 1.3
Map showing the number of Hutterite colonies in each state or province as of 2012.

The Hutterites live in Bruderhofs, colonies of around 100 people. The lifestyle is communal in almost every sense of the word: all land, resources, and profits are colony property. An individual's personal belongings are all contained in a hope chest. Decisions concerning the colony are made by elected officials headed by the colony boss. The colony minister, in charge of the group's religious welfare, is also elected. Work is divided along sexual lines and among a number of specialists—chicken men, teachers, cooks, and so on—but the division is not absolute. The community views the completion of required tasks as a community responsibility; when work needs to be done, there is someone to do it.

The Hutterite economy is basically agricultural, and the specific crops and animals raised depend on the geography and economy of the area occupied. Although the Hutterites (like the better-known Amish) have traditionally shunned such worldly items as television, radio, and personal ornamentation, they will readily accept any modern technology or any contact with outsiders that aids them as farmers. Because of this attitude and the relative wealth of most colonies, the members of a Bruderhof look like people who have stepped out of the past but who use modern tractors, milking machines, fertilizers, antibiotics, telephones, and computers (Figure 1.4).

Traditionally, children have been educated at the colony in the "English school" by a state or provincial teacher until the legal age at which they can leave. The most important schooling, however, given

FIGURE 1.4
Scenes of colony life. *Top:*
A kindergarten for young
children after they no longer
spend all day with their
parents and before they
begin regular schooling—
a Hutterite invention.
Bottom: A young woman
packaging eggs in a colony
that specializes in this
product. Note the
mechanized equipment.

by the colony teacher in the "German school," transmits the ways of
Hutterite life and religion, which are one and the same. In addition,
practical education is given in the form of an apprenticeship in one
of the jobs vital to the colony's existence. This training prepares the
child to become a working member of the community when schooling
is completed.

The Hutterites are almost completely isolated in genetic terms. Few
Hutterites ever permanently leave the group, and converts entering their
communities have numbered only a few dozen since the original colonies'

migration to North America. Moreover, on average about half of all Hutterite marriages take place between members of the same colony. The rest involve members from another colony of the same subsect.

Hutterites restrict marriage to individuals who are second cousins or more distant relations. In fact, because individuals within a subsect are all fairly closely related, the most common unions involve second cousins. The average age at marriage is twenty-four years for men and twenty-two years for women. Only about 2 percent of Hutterite men and 5 percent of women never marry.

An interesting phenomenon within the Hutterites' breeding structure is the frequency with which siblings (brothers and sisters) marry other sets of siblings. In one sample, 20 percent of all marriages were "double sibship" marriages (two brothers marry two sisters or a brother and sister marry a sister and brother), and 8 percent were triple or quadruple sibship marriages.

Hutterite families are large, but family lines are relatively few. There are only twenty surnames among all Hutterites, and five of these belong to a small percentage of families. The average family has ten children, the highest substantiated per-family birthrate recorded for any population. Hutterites maintain a great interest in their genealogies, and they have kept family records with great accuracy. It is thus easy to trace degrees of biological relationship among individuals, even back to the sixteenth century, a fact that has been important for much research on the group, including my own.

Completing the match of the Hutterites to my ideal research population is their practice of regularly dividing their colonies, or "branching out" as they call it. When, after fifteen or twenty years, a colony becomes so large (about 130 to 150 people) that social and administrative problems arise and there is increasing duplication of labor specialists, a colony will purchase a new tract of land and divide its population. Usually the minister simply makes two lists, each with about half the colony's families. Family units, of course, are never broken up. The ministers do manipulate the lists to equalize age and sex distributions and to ensure that each new colony has the required specialists. At last, lots are drawn to determine which group of families will remain and which will move to the new land as founders of the new Bruderhof.

The two Hutterite colonies I visited in the summer of 1973 were the results of a branching out that had taken place in 1958. Enough time had elapsed for a new generation to be born. Using fingerprint patterns as genetic data (these were the days before so-called DNA fingerprinting), I was able to estimate degrees of genetic relationship within and between the colonies and, most important, to trace changes in genetic makeup from generation to generation. These analyses would help me answer some of the questions I had posed about specific evolutionary processes and their role in human evolution.

ANTHROPOLOGY

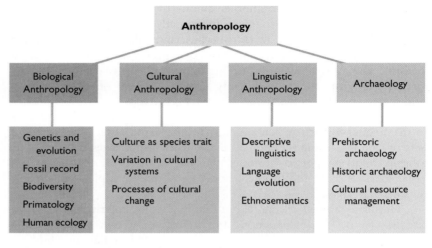

biological anthropology
The subfield of anthropology that studies humans as a biological species.

physical anthropology The traditional name for biological anthropology.

species A group of organisms that can produce fertile offspring among themselves but not with members of other groups.

cultural anthropology The subfield of anthropology that focuses on human cultural behavior and cultural systems and the variation in cultural expression among human groups.

culture Ideas and behaviors that are learned and transmitted. Nongenetic means of adaptation.

When many people think of anthropology—when *I* think of anthropology—the image that first comes to mind is the sort of thing I've just been describing: the fieldwork experience, when the anthropologist visits a land or a people usually very different from his or her own. This is the romantic and exciting part of the discipline that shapes the public image and makes for interesting films (dramatic as well as documentary). It is also the part that brings out the humanism of anthropology—the need to understand, to get to know, to communicate with other peoples from *their* perspective.

Fieldwork is certainly one of the things that attract people to anthropology as a career. And fieldwork *is* important. It is the part of the science of anthropology where basic observations are made, data are collected, and ideas about humans are tested. But does it tell us what anthropology is really about? Does it define the field?

The first problem in trying to define anthropology is accounting for the great variety of activities that anthropologists engage in. In fact, the field is so broad it is traditionally divided into four subfields (Figure 1.5).

Biological (physical) anthropology. Biological anthropologists focus on humans as a biological **species** and study such topics as human genetics, human evolution, the fossil record, and the biology of living populations. Some even study nonhuman species such as our close relatives, the monkeys and apes (Figure 1.6).

Cultural anthropology. Cultural anthropologists focus on our species' unique ability to create ideas, behaviors, and technologies that we share with one another—that is, our **culture.** They study the nature of culture as a characteristic trait of our species and how and why cultural systems differ among human societies (Figure 1.7).

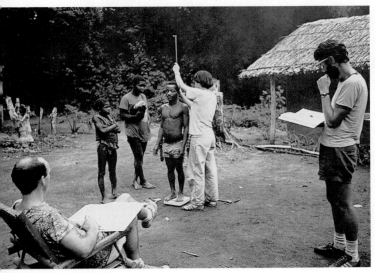

FIGURE 1.6
Biological anthropologists at work. *Clockwise from top left:*
The author identifies bones from an early New England grave,
excavated at the family's request. A macaque on Gibraltar is
observed by primatologist Agustín Fuentes. Paleoanthropologist
Bill Kimbel uses dental tools, a small drill, and a microscope to free
fossil fragments from the surrounding stone. Richard Wrangham
and Robert Bailey watch Elizabeth Ross measure the stature of an
Efe man from the Democratic Republic of the Congo.

FIGURE 1.7

Cultural anthropologists at work. *Clockwise from top left:* Raymond Hames uses a battery-powered computer to collect data about settlement patterns among the Yanomamö of Brazil. Marjorie Shostak talks with two San men, members of a foraging (hunting-gathering) people of southern Africa. As part of her research on the Nuer, a pastoral society of Sudan, Sharon Hutchinson studies some of their cattle.

Linguistic anthropology. Linguistic anthropologists study language as a human characteristic and attempt to explain the differences among the 3,000 or so existing human languages. They also look at the relationship of specific languages to their cultures.

Archaeology. Of all the cultural systems that have ever been, most are no longer in existence. And because for most of human history there were no written languages, all that these extinct cultures have left behind are their material remains, often literally their garbage— broken pottery, abandoned dwellings, used tools, and the like. Archaeologists study the relationships between such **artifacts** and the cultures that manufactured and used them and then expand their findings to reconstruct past cultural systems. Archaeology might be seen as the anthropology of the past. Archaeology also develops the techniques for locating, recovering, dating, and preserving the often fragile remains of past cultures (Figure 1.8).

In addition to the topics listed under each subfield in Figure 1.5, the data and concepts within each subfield have certain practical applications— social welfare concerns, legal and crime-related matters (forensic anthropology), preservation of cultural resources, and health issues, to name a few. Such activities are referred to as applied anthropology, and we will discuss them in more detail in Chapter 15.

Now, how can these sorts of studies all be anthropology? What is the common theme that ties together such things as the fingerprints of Hutterites, the behavior of chimpanzees, a 3-million-year-old fossil, the culture of a highland New Guinea society, the languages of the Eskimo, and the material culture of ancient peoples of southern New England?

The answer to that question reveals what anthropology is all about. What all anthropologists do is try to answer questions about the human species. All anthropologists want to know why we humans behave as we do, how we evolved to look like we do, why we don't all look the same, and why there is such variation in our cultural behaviors. We may start answering these questions from points as different as ancient fossils and modern Hutterite farmers, but if our goal is scientific knowledge about the human species, then we're doing anthropology.

Thus anthropology, as its name indicates, is the study of humankind. But, you might be wondering, don't history, political science, sociology, and even mathematics all study something about humans? What makes anthropology different?

The answer is that anthropology is the **holistic** study of humankind; it searches for interrelationships among all the parts of its subject. Primary among those relationships is what we term the **biocultural** perspective. Humans are a complex species. Like any species, we have an anatomy, a physiology, a set of behaviors, an environment, and an evolutionary history—all of which are interrelated. But unlike any other species, we also have culture. We can consciously invent and change our behaviors, and

linguistic anthropology The subfield of anthropology that describes the characteristics of human language and studies the relationships between languages and the cultures that speak them.

archaeology The subfield of anthropology that studies the human cultural past and reconstructs past cultural systems.

artifact Any object that has been consciously manufactured.

holistic Assuming an interrelationship among the parts of a subject.

biocultural Focusing on the interaction of biology and culture.

CONTEMPORARY ISSUES

What Responsibilities Does the Anthropologist Have When Studying Other Cultures?

Living peoples are not chemicals in a test tube or electrons in a particle accelerator. When anthropologists visit, observe, and eventually analyze the behaviors of another culture, we have important ethical responsibilities that go beyond those of the chemist or physicist. There are three overlapping and interrelated areas we must be aware of. We have a responsibility to our subjects, a responsibility to the science of anthropology, and a responsibility to ourselves.

Any time scientists observe a subject, they risk affecting that subject. With people, the changes can be profound. When anthropologists visit another society, we may introduce its people to new technologies that may bring about subtle changes in their culture. For example, offering a previously unknown or unavailable tool—say, a metal knife or a cigarette lighter—to one individual but not another may cause jealousies or even alterations in the community's power structure. Likewise, new behaviors introduced by anthropologists, if adopted by some of the people being studied, could disrupt the harmony of the cultural system. We may also inadvertently introduce new diseases, with obvious potential consequences. Some influence from our presence is unavoidable, but we must be conscious of the possibilities and try, as much as possible, to limit them.

At the same time, we should not withhold knowledge that could be of use to the people we study. When, for example, anthropologists and medical researchers visited the Yąnomamö of the Amazon rain forest, they discovered that previous contact with outsiders had started a measles epidemic. Never having been exposed to measles before, the Yąnomamö had no natural defenses. The scientists brought in a vaccine to try to fight off the disease. A controversial book published in 2000 accused these scientists of unintentionally *causing* a measles epidemic among the Yąnomamö through their use of a certain vaccine. It also blames anthropologists specifically for disrupting Yąnomamö economy by introducing goods and for mischaracterizing the group as violent and thus fueling abuses by outsiders. The charges regarding the measles vaccine and ethical violations were eventually discredited by, among others, the American Anthropological Association.

As this example demonstrates, we have a responsibility to treat and respect our subjects as equals. This sounds obvious, but some anthropologists have a tendency to think of their subjects, especially if they are from a less technologically complex culture, as childlike and in need of almost paternalistic protection. Such an approach is patronizing and insulting, not to mention counterproductive. A scientist who is able to gain the respect of his or her subjects stands a greater chance of conducting a fruitful study. When I arrived at one of the Hutterite colonies, for example, I found the colony leaders suddenly reluctant to let me conduct my study, despite a previous arrangement, because they had been interviewed by a journalist whose subsequent

we can think about those behaviors and even about our own consciousness. Thus, all the other academic fields I mentioned, and more, are necessary in order to fully understand every aspect of human biology and culture. However, also necessary is a field that seeks to understand how all the aspects of our species are related—how our biology and our culture interact; how our past has influenced our present; how one facet of

magazine article was inaccurate and somewhat demeaning. My initial inclination was to simply back off and quietly leave. Instead, I decided to argue for my position, indicating that I was not a journalist but a scientist and educator and, as such, that my job was to present their culture accurately and from their point of view. Although they said no several times more, I persisted. In the end, they agreed, we got along fine, and they provided me with important information.

We also have a responsibility to anthropology itself. As I just noted, we must describe another society from its point of view, without imposing our own cultural values on our description and analysis. We call this **cultural relativity.** While we may not agree with everything another culture believes and does—and may even be repulsed by it—we are obliged as scientists to assume that the behaviors of others fit somehow into their cultural systems, that is, are acceptable *relative to* their cultural beliefs. We may, for example, find the ritual warfare and killing by the Dani of New Guinea (see Chapter 14) abhorrent by our cultural standards, but we understand that within *their* cultural system, it makes sense. We can only understand human culture and human cultures if we study them objectively.

Still, we have a responsibility to ourselves, in two basic ways. First, in the process of practicing cultural relativity, we need not shun or deny our own beliefs and standards. A culture persists because its members adhere to certain standards and, indeed, take them on faith. While one benefit of anthropology is the opportunity to learn about alternative ways of thinking, we anthropologists

should not simply jettison the beliefs that make us part of our own societies. Moreover, by acknowledging reactions to the behaviors of others—even repulsion—it is easier to set these reactions aside for the purposes of objective science.

Second, the concept of cultural relativity has limitations. While certain behaviors may make sense within specific cultural systems and while we must practice cultural relativity in order to understand those systems, the nature of the contemporary world as a global village suggests the presence of and need for widely accepted universal standards of behavior. Not everything every society does is universally morally acceptable, and we have a responsibility to try as best as we can to speak out about such practices in the hopes of changing them. For example, the subsistence farmers who are burning large areas of the world's rain forests may have perfectly sound personal reasons for their activity but lack the big picture in terms of its effect on our global ecology. We should be trying to provide these farmers with other, less destructive ways of pursuing their livelihoods. Another example is a society that denies its women equal medical care simply because they are women. The reasons for doing so may be culturally consistent and long-standing, but such a practice is contrary to basic, widely accepted human rights.

Considerations like these make anthropology a difficult profession, fraught with debatable and even contentious issues. But they also make anthropology—the discipline that possesses the broad perspective needed to make these considerations—a very important science.

culture, such as economics, is related to some other facet, such as religion. Trying to understand these relationships is what anthropologists do.

Think of it this way: If you were a zoologist interested in, say, honeybees, you couldn't possibly understand that insect fully unless you understood its anatomy, its physiology, its behavior, its environment, and its evolutionary history. You might specialize in one aspect of its

cultural relativity Studying another culture from its point of view without imposing our own cultural values.

FIGURE 1.8

Archaeologists at work. *Clockwise from top left:* Ken Feder shifts soil and examines potential artifacts at an excavation near the Farmington River in Connecticut. Connecticut State Archaeologist Nick Bellantoni excavates an early New England grave (see Figure 1.6). Margaret Conkey, a specialist in prehistoric European art, examines an ancient painting at the cave of Le Reseau, France. Terry del Bene studies ancient toolmaking techniques by producing replicas.

life—say, its complex communication system—but to know just what a honeybee *is,* you would have to understand the interrelationships among *all* aspects of its life.

Anthropology is much the same—but with the important distinction that what sets humans apart from all other living creatures is our cultural behavior. Culture adds a dimension to our species that is beyond the purely biological. A bee can't change its behavior at will. We can. Thus the biocultural focus of anthropology.

PLAN OF THE BOOK

This chapter has given you a brief and basic introduction to anthropology. In the next chapter, we'll delve deeper into the nature of anthropology as a scientific and humanistic discipline. In the rest of Part 1, we'll examine the two major themes of anthropology: evolution and culture.

Part 2 will focus on how anthropology studies and defines its subject, the human species. We will see where humans fit into the world of living things, with particular attention to our identity as one of the living species of primates. We will then examine how we evolved from our earliest apelike ancestor to become the unique large-brained, cultural primate we are today. A key aspect of our identity is our sexual behavior—which not only is how we reproduce and thus perpetuate our species, but also is a perfect example and reminder of the biocultural perspective of anthropology. Finally, another major characteristic of our species, and one with many social implications, is our biological diversity and the categories into which different societies organize that diversity based on cultural precepts—in other words, the thorny issues of race and racism.

With the biocultural perspective as our organizing principle, in Part 3 we will look at the categories into which anthropologists typically divide our cultural behavior and show how the subfields of anthropology interact in pursuit of that perspective. We'll look at how we obtain and distribute our food and other economic resources, how we organize our families and societies, how we share knowledge through language, and how we maintain order through religious and secular rules. We'll then examine some of the various ways anthropologists try to organize the data on human societies and to explain how behaviors change over time—how they evolve.

In Chapter 14, using several specific examples, we'll merge all the aspects we've covered into a coherent theoretical framework. Remember, what anthropologists are attempting to accomplish—no matter where their individual research begins—is to understand how and why the human species looks, thinks, and behaves the way it does.

We will end with a chapter on anthropology in the modern world, showing how anthropology can be applied to real-world issues and what the anthropological perspective has to tell us about our lives today and in the future.

SUMMARY

Anthropology can be defined as the biocultural study of the human species. Its central focus is the feature that is unique to humans—our cultural behavior. Culture is the way we as a species deal with our world and with one another. Understanding a species' behavior— even when that behavior is largely cultural—necessarily requires an understanding of all aspects of that species' identity, from its biology to its environment to its evolutionary past to the cultural behaviors that come in many different forms.

QUESTIONS FOR FURTHER THOUGHT

1. What specific responsibilities do you think I had to take into account when planning and conducting my research among the Hutterites? Consider another culture, and imagine what particular responsibilities would be involved in studying that culture as an anthropologist.

2. Because of anthropology's wide range of interests and its overlap with other scholarly disciplines, anthropologists have sometimes been characterized as "jacks of all trades and masters of none." Do you agree? Explain.

3. Think of a real-life example of a society with a practice entirely antithetical to your cultural beliefs but quite consistent with and integral to *that* society's cultural beliefs. How would you deal with this, both as an anthropologist doing fieldwork there and as an individual?

NOTES, REFERENCES, AND READINGS

Perhaps the most complete work on the Hutterites is John A. Hostetler's *Hutterite Society*. (All references and reading suggestions are listed, with complete information, in the Bibliography at the back of the book.) See also the Hutterites' Web site, www.hutterites.org/index.html, and "Solace at Surprise Creek," by W. A. Allard, in the June 2006 *National Geographic*.

There are many good descriptions of anthropological fieldwork. Among my favorites are Nigel Barley's *The Innocent Anthropologist* and Katherine A. Dettwyler's *Dancing Skeletons: Life and Death in West Africa*. If you like novels, try *Return to Laughter*, by Elenore Smith Bowen (the pseudonym of anthropologist Laura Bohannon).

Among the most famous descriptions of fieldwork is *Studying the Yąnomamö*, by Napoleon A. Chagnon. Chagnon's research is also at the center of the controversy about the scientific study of that group. The book that makes the accusations noted in the Contemporary Issues feature box earlier in the chapter is *Darkness in El Dorado: How Scientists and Journalists Devastated the Amazon*, by Patrick Tierney. For an update on the issue, see "Chagnon Critics Overstepped Bounds, Historian Says" by Charles C. Mann in the September 11, 2009, issue of *Science*, p. 1466. For more discussion, read "Guilt by Association," by Thomas Gregor and Daniel Gross, in the December 2004 issue of *American Anthropologist*.

2

HOW ANTHROPOLOGY WORKS

Methods of Inquiry

CHAPTER CONTENTS The Scientific Method • Belief Systems • Anthropology as a Science • Contemporary Issues: Are Science and Belief Inherently in Conflict with One Another? • Anthropological Methodology: Fieldwork • Summary • Questions for Further Thought • Notes, References, and Readings

From books, movies, and television comes our popular image of the scientist as a walking encyclopedia of facts. Science, indeed, is often understood as a process of fact-collecting. Yet while it's fair to say that scientists certainly need to know a lot of facts, so do a lot of other people. Champions on the TV quiz show *Jeopardy* are seldom professional scientists.

Facts are the raw material of science, the data scientists use. But what scientists really do is *explain* facts, not simply collect them. **Science** is *a process of inquiry, a way of answering questions about the world.*

AS YOU READ, CONSIDER THE FOLLOWING QUESTIONS:

1. How does science work?
2. Is science the only valid method of explaining the world around us? How does science differ from other methods of inquiry?
3. Can science and other methods of inquiry operate in harmony within a cultural system?
4. How is anthropology—the study of human culture and biology—a scientific discipline?

THE SCIENTIFIC METHOD

The world is full of things that need explaining. We might wonder about the behavior of a bird, the chemical composition of a star in the night sky, the identity of a fossil skeleton, the social interaction of students in a college classroom, or the rituals of a society in the Kalahari Desert of southern Africa. As people, we strive to understand such phenomena, to know why and how these things occur as they do. As scientists, we must try to answer these questions according to a special set of rules—the **scientific method**.

The "Rules" of the Scientific Method

science The method of inquiry that requires the generation, testing, and acceptance or rejection of hypotheses.

scientific method The formal process of conducting scientific inquiry.

The central rule of science is that a scientific idea must be empirically testable. That is, one must be able to gather tangible evidence in support of, or in opposition to, a proposed idea. It works like this:

We normally begin with a question we wish to answer about observed facts, or something we wish to explain about patterns of phenomena we see. Charles Darwin, for example (as we'll see in the next chapter), was trying to explain the nature of the fossil record and the patterns of variation he saw in living species.

We then attempt to generate a *general* explanatory principle that will account for the *specific* patterns of real data we observe. Such a general explanation is called a **hypothesis,** and this process of reasoning, from the specific to the general, is called **induction.**

It is important that the inductive process of generating a scientific hypothesis fulfills two criteria. First, data must be real and tangible (not imaginary), and a hypothesis must be built on *existing* data (not data that might *someday* show up).

Second, the hypothesis that develops must be *testable* using real, tangible data. Put another way, a hypothesis must be *disprovable* and be an *answerable* question. Darwin spent a whole chapter of *The Origin of Species* detailing the data that could refute his hypothesis. (Obviously, he successfully disputed those data!)

Testing a scientific hypothesis uses the process of **deduction,** which goes from the general to the specific. It asks: *If* my hypothesis is correct, *then* what specific things should I find? We look, for example, for:

- *Repetition:* Does the same phenomenon occur over and over?
- *Universality:* Does the phenomenon occur under all conditions? If we vary some aspect of the situation, will the phenomenon still occur? How might different situations change the phenomenon?
- *Explanations for exceptions:* Can we account for cases where the phenomenon doesn't appear to occur?
- *New data:* Does new information support or refute our hypothesis?

Our ultimate goal in science is the development of a **theory.** Popularly, the term is used as a synonym for hypothesis, or even a guess. But in science, *theory* is a positive term. A theory is a general concept—made up of interacting and well-supported hypotheses—that coordinates, explains, and interprets a wide range of factual patterns. The theory of gravity, the theory of relativity, and the theory of evolution are called theories because they do just that. All facts of biology, for example, make sense only within the general theory of evolution (which we'll examine in the next chapters).

Some Common Misconceptions about Science

"Science Proves Ideas for All Time"   We try to avoid the word *prove* in science. Rather, our approach is to determine the degree of support for hypotheses and theories, and, ideally, we always look for new evidence and are always open to and, indeed, inviting of change. This is how scientific knowledge progresses. The best science can do is paint the *most accurate* picture of the world possible at any time.

That said, there are some scientific theories so well supported over time that they are, for all intents and purposes, proved. They have become *fact*. Darwin's natural selection—which at first was a

hypothesis A proposed explanation for a natural phenomenon.

induction The process of developing a general explanation from specific observations.

deduction Suggesting specific data that would be found if a hypothesis were true.

theory A general idea that explains a large set of factual patterns.

hypothesis requiring evidence—is now observable fact. So, for that matter, is the theory of evolution (the common ancestry of all living things, changing over time).

"Once We Have a Theory about a Particular Topic, We Don't Need to Do More Science"   No theory is complete. The theory of gravity, for example, establishes that such a force exists, and we know a great deal about its effects. But we still debate how it works and how it originated in the early universe. We still debate details of evolutionary theory. The process of science, even with regard to theories so well supported they are *facts*, never ends.

"Science Studies Only Visible, Tangible, Present-Day Things"   Gravity is not visible or tangible. We can't touch it. But we know it exists, and we can measure it and predict its actions because we can deductively test its effects. We see it at work constantly. We logically predict that if gravity is the property of objects with mass, then the bigger the object, the more gravity. We saw this clearly when we watched the astronauts walk on the moon; they were literally lighter there (about one-sixth their earthly weight) because the moon is smaller than earth. On the other hand, very massive objects have more gravity (Figure 2.1). We can even explain exceptions *within the context of the theory of gravity:* The reason a helium-filled balloon seems to violate gravity is because the helium

FIGURE 2.1

Light bent by gravity. Einstein predicted that a strong gravitational field could bend light. His prediction was verified when light from stars that should have been blocked by the sun could be seen during a solar eclipse. The effect is greatly exaggerated in this drawing.

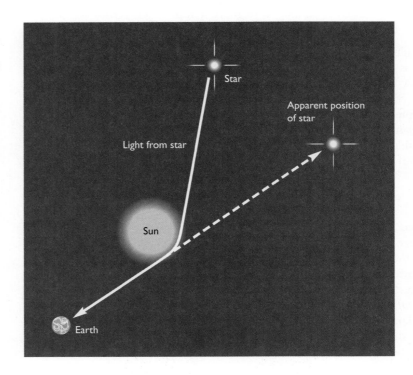

trapped in the balloon is less dense than the surrounding air and so responds relatively less to the earth's gravity; the balloon floats on the air as a boat (filled with air) floats on the denser water.

Similarly, past events can't be directly seen or touched. They can't be directly experimented on or repeated. The evolution of living organisms is an example. But again, we know that evolution occurs because we see the results, which can only be explained by the theory of evolution (which we'll detail in the following chapters).

Science Is Conducted in a Cultural Context

Don't scientists search for truths that are objective and not influenced by preconceived notions or prejudices? Ideally, yes. But keep in mind that scientists are members of their societies and participants in their cultures, and science is always conducted within the context of a particular culture at a particular point in time. Thus, science—as objective as we try to make it—is always affected by what we already know, by what we still don't know, by the technology available to us to gather and test data, and even by certain influential social or cultural trends.

For example, I remember my elementary school teacher back in the mid-1950s pointing out that the east coast of South America and the west coast of Africa seemed to fit together like pieces in a giant jigsaw puzzle (Figure 2.2). Of course, she said, there's no way the continents could move around, so it must just be a coincidence. In fact, she was reflecting the scientific knowledge of the time. There was plenty of geological and fossil evidence that the continents had moved around, and the idea of continental drift had been proposed in 1912, but there was no mechanism to explain it. Beginning in the 1960s, however, new technologies gave us new evidence that explained such a mechanism. We now have a well-verified theory of continental drift by the process of plate tectonics.

Let's consider an example of one influential cultural period that generated a hypothesized explanation for a famous historical event—the Salem witch trials of 1692, when a group of young girls in Massachusetts accused some adults of witchcraft, resulting in the execution of twenty people. The hypothesis suggested that the people of Salem had consumed bread made from grains tainted with ergot, a fungus that contains alkaloids, some of which are derivatives of lysergic acid, which in turn is used in the synthesis of the hallucinogenic drug LSD. In other words, maybe the young girls who made the witchcraft accusations were inadvertently having an "acid trip." Not surprisingly, this explanation arose and found popularity in the 1960s, a period associated in part with the so-called drug culture. Although the idea showed up as recently as 2001 on a public television documentary, there is no evidence to support it. It's not even logical: Why would only those girls have eaten the tainted products?

FIGURE 2.2
Topographic map of the Atlantic Ocean floor showing the correlating outlines of the edges of the Eastern and Western Hemispheres. Also shown is the Mid-Atlantic Ridge—evidence for the plate tectonics that pushed the once-connected continents apart.

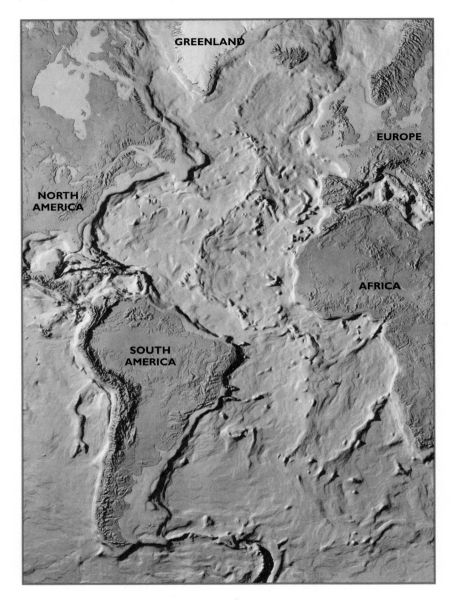

So, science answers questions about our lives and about the world in which we live. For an answer to be defined as scientific, however, it must be testable—and must be tested. For an answer to be accepted, it must pass all those tests and be refuted by none.

Thus, science tells us what the world is really like and how it really works. In contrast to science are belief systems. They tell us how we think the world *should* be. Belief systems are also a topic studied by anthropology.

BELIEF SYSTEMS

Some questions about the world, even in a technologically complex society like ours, remain beyond the scope of science. Scientific inquiry, as powerful and important as it is, doesn't answer everything. In our society, for example, we treat medical matters scientifically. But science does not, and cannot, inform us how best to apply medical knowledge. Who should practice medicine? How are medical practitioners trained and administered by society? How should they be compensated? What should their relationship be with their patients? Is everyone equally entitled to medical care? Society answers these questions through traditions, laws, and regulations—formalizations of beliefs. For example, one version of the Hippocratic oath taken by doctors says in part, "I will not permit considerations of religion, nationality, race, party politics or social standing to intervene between my duty and my patient."

And then, there are questions that can never be answered by science—matters like the meaning of life, the existence of a higher power, the proper social relationships among people within a society, or the purpose of one's own life.

All these sorts of questions are addressed by **belief systems**—religions, philosophies, ethics, morals, and laws. Belief systems differ from science in that the answers they provide cannot be tested and cannot be disproved. They are taken on faith, and that, of course, is the source of their power. They provide stable bases for our behaviors, for explanations of what is beyond our science, and for the broad, existential questions of life. Belief systems change, but they only change when *we* decide to change them, either as a society or as individuals.

The existence of a supreme being is an example of an idea held by a belief system. Two of us with opposite views on the subject could debate the issue endlessly, but no scientific test could support or refute either view. If I were to change my mind on the matter, it would be a matter of personal faith, not reason. The supreme being is not to be found in a test tube or seen through a telescope.

Belief systems don't apply only to these big questions. I had a friend in graduate school from a West African society in which men could have several wives. That tradition is normal for his society, whereas in mine, one wife (at least, one at a time) is the norm. We discussed the pros and cons of these two systems at length one day but never, of course, arrived at any "answer." His belief was right for his society, as was mine for my society. We each took it on faith that this was so.

Although we often perceive science and belief systems as being eternally and inevitably at odds with one another, nothing could be further from the truth. Conflicts between the two realms do arise, most commonly when a belief system makes a statement about the real world that is not supported by empirical evidence. But it should be apparent

belief systems Ideas that are taken on faith and cannot be scientifically tested.

that for a society to function, it needs both scientific knowledge and beliefs. Neither, by itself, addresses all the questions. (See the "Contemporary Issues" box for this chapter.)

Understanding the distinctions and the interrelationships between science and belief systems is important for each of us as members of our own culture. It is particularly important for us as anthropologists, because among the things we study are the belief systems of other people. Scientific knowledge and beliefs are a part of every culture, but their identity and interaction may well be different from what we are used to in our culture. Furthermore, we need to be aware of the influences of our own cultural background on the science we conduct as we study other societies and their cultures.

To use a metaphorical statement once made by Galileo, while science tells us "how heaven *is*," belief systems tell us "how to *get* to heaven." Or, in the words of biologist John Maynard Smith, science tells us what is "possible," and beliefs tell us what is "desirable." No culture can function without both.

ANTHROPOLOGY AS A SCIENCE

Given anthropology's wide range of topics, including such complex areas as human culture and cultural systems, some may wonder how anthropology can be defined as a science. Some facets of our field, of course, are clearly scientific—my study of evolutionary changes among the Hutterites, for example, or what we now understand about the distribution of skin color among **indigenous** populations (see Chapter 8). Less clearly scientific at first glance are other areas of anthropology.

Studying the Past

Many anthropologists deal with the past—some biological anthropologists study extinct species and premodern forms of humans, and archaeologists study past human societies and cultural systems. How can we examine something that we can't directly observe and can't replicate? As noted earlier, we can still collect data related to those things past and extinct, data from fossils of extinct species, often found in datable layers of soil; comparative studies of the anatomy and genetics of living species that have descended from previous forms; the material remains of past cultures, sometimes complete and well preserved enough to present us with a picture frozen in time (Figure 2.3); and our knowledge of how living peoples exist and create and use material culture.

We also look for repeated patterns in our evidence from the past. For example, we might note some similarities among the cultures that

indigenous Native; refers to a group of people with a long history in a particular area.

first began to grow food instead of collecting it. From these similarities, we can generate ideas to explain *why* people made this transition (see Chapter 9).

All these sorts of data, and more, can be used to deductively test the hypotheses we have generated to explain the past. It is really no different from our ability to scientifically examine things we cannot see directly, like gravity or subatomic particles. We know they exist, and we know a lot about them because we can observe the results of their existence.

Studying Culture

Culture is not a *thing* like a chemical in a test tube or an electron or even an ancient fossil. Culture is the result of the decisions and actions

FIGURE 2.3
A moment frozen in time. Natural casts of victims of the eruption of Mt. Vesuvius in A.D. 79 that destroyed the Roman cities of Pompeii and Herculaneum.

CONTEMPORARY ISSUES

Are Science and Belief Inherently in Conflict with One Another?

The simple answer is that, no, they are not. As we discussed, any society, in order to function, needs both rational knowledge of the world *and* beliefs. But the assumption that generates the above question is not without foundation; there are conflicts between science and belief systems. These conflicts most often arise when someone tries to address scientific questions with concepts or approaches from belief systems. This is known as a **pseudoscience.**

The term has several working definitions, but here I use it to refer to a scientifically testable idea that is taken on faith even if there is no evidence to support it—and even if it is tested and shown to be false. The idea is treated as a tenet of a belief system.

Let's consider a simple example. Some people believe that the lines in the palms of my hands and on my fingertips hold information about my personality, talents, and even my future. This is the pseudoscience called palmistry. Why does it qualify as a pseudoscience? Because there is no empirical,

scientific evidence in support of this testable idea, and yet proponents (palm readers and their clients) accept the idea, take it on faith, and apply it as if it were valid. Other pseudosciences include astrology, crystal power, and mental telepathy. This is not to say that there is *no* potential validity to these ideas, just that *at present* there is no scientific evidence in their support, either in terms of objective data and testing or even in terms of a theoretical context. In other words, so far as we know, palmistry *couldn't* be valid *given what we understand about the nature of anatomy, genetics, and personality.*

Now, while the above examples may seem relatively harmless, other ideas—in the guise of religious scholarship—call into question some of the most basic principles of science. Sometimes the idea in question comes directly from an established, mainstream belief system. For example, there are people who still seriously think the earth is flat, despite copious amounts of evidence to the contrary. The major source for this belief

pseudoscience Scientifically testable ideas that are taken on faith without scientific evidence to support them or even when tested and shown to be false.

of people. Are there scientific theories to account for the behavior of groups of people any more than there are scientific theories for our own personal behavior? A cultural system, after all, is an incredibly complex web of relationships. And this web is the creation, conscious and unconscious, of real people making decisions, responses, and actions for all the complex reasons people do such things.

Some actions of groups of people have obvious explanations. People, for example, have certain direct responses to their natural environments. They eat what foods their environments provide, and they build their shelters from available materials in designs that make sense for a given set of climatic conditions (Figure 2.4). But many aspects of culture are related to something other than the natural environment. People in Beijing and Philadelphia, for example, have very different cultures despite living at the same latitude

is a very literal interpretation of several biblical passages, for example Matthew 4:8: "Again, the devil taketh him [Jesus] up into an exceedingly high mountain, and sheweth him all the kingdoms of the world." How, the "flat-earthers" ask—ignoring the metaphorical intent of the passage—could Jesus have seen all the kingdoms of the earth unless the earth were flat?

Here's another example. On a certain Web site, physicist D. Russell Humphreys is quoted as claiming that the new data in support of the presence of water in the past on Mars is "evidence . . . for a global flood on Mars. Many creationist scientists, including myself, think the Genesis flood on earth was part of a catastrophe which affected the whole solar system." Not only is there no evidence for a global flood on either Earth or Mars, but a flood affecting the *entire* solar system is simply inconceivable; it *couldn't* have happened given what we understand about astronomy, physics, and chemistry. But, as with the flat-earth idea, this idea comes from one literal interpretation of the Bible, specifically the book of Genesis; the Web site in question is, in fact, called *Answers in Genesis* and

represents a point of view that considers the creation story and those that follow in the first book of the Bible to be literally true, despite a total lack of evidence for the empirical parts—the simultaneous creation of everything in the universe, the great flood, and so on.

The concern here, relative to our topic, is that both science and religion suffer when thrown into conflict as a result of such ideas. Proponents of these ideas ignore modern science (only when it suits them, of course; I'm sure they still fly on airplanes, whose designs are based on modern, mainstream physics, and make use of modern medical techniques based on mainstream biology). At the same time, they seem to make adherence to a *belief system* dependent on the veracity of their scientifically unsupported claims. Little wonder that these claims leave many people confused and thinking that they have to choose between their religious beliefs and science. It is a choice they do not have to make.

Science and belief are both vital for the functioning of any society, but they are *not* equivalent. As discussed in the chapter, they address different types of knowledge in different ways. There is no inherent conflict.

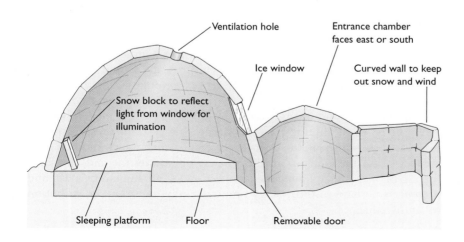

Ventilation hole

Entrance chamber faces east or south

Ice window

Curved wall to keep out snow and wind

Snow block to reflect light from window for illumination

Sleeping platform   Floor   Removable door

FIGURE 2.4
The well-known igloo of the Inuit, made from the only material readily available in the Arctic winter and including many ingenious features that make it remarkably adapted to life in a harsh climate.

and having similar climates. Languages, beliefs, clothing styles, political systems, family organizations, and so on obviously require complex explanations. Such complexity may lead us to wonder if any scientific explanation is possible at all. Theories of culture may be more elusive than theories about concrete entities such as fossils and genes.

This doesn't mean, however, that we should not try. Remember that an important step in the scientific method is to look for patterns, associations, and repetitions. We do find these when we gather data about cultural systems—a process called **ethnography.** For example, in Chapter 4 we'll discuss an observed connection between a culture's subsistence pattern (how a group of people acquires food) and the number of supernatural beings (gods, spirits, and ancestors) it recognizes. Such a connection holds true often enough to allow us to make a generalization and to propose a reason for it—to generate a hypothesis. We can then test our general hypothesis by seeing if *all* cases show the same association or, if there are exceptions, seeing if we can make sense of the exceptions *in terms of our hypothesis*.

Now, we may discover—at least for some aspects of culture—that such hypotheses don't pan out, that no overall idea explains all cases and exceptions. But when we *do* find generalizations, we consequently learn more about our own behavior and the behavior of other societies and are able to at least make educated predictions that might help us cope with all the changes and challenges that the modern world imposes on human societies and their ways of life.

It should be pointed out that although anthropology is a science, it is also a humanistic endeavor. Indeed, this is what draws many into anthropology as a profession, and in fact, many anthropologists see humanism, rather than the scientific approach, as the major focus of at least cultural anthropology. (See the "Contemporary Issues" box in Chapter 13.) For in the process of observing, learning about, and trying to understand culture in general and other cultures in particular, we come to better understand humanity as a whole. We appreciate our species' unique position in the world. We better understand our own society, and perhaps most important, we come to understand other societies, other cultures, and other people. We see that despite all the striking differences among us, there are deep similarities in those things that really matter—the needs, desires, potentials, and limitations shared by all people. We may have our different ways of thinking and of doing things—and these certainly can lead to unfortunate and even tragic misunderstandings and conflicts—but the goals of all these behaviors are, in the end, the same for all of us. The fundamental connection of all humanity, past and present, is perhaps anthropology's most socially important contribution to knowledge.

ethnography A description of a cultural system based on fieldwork within that culture.

ANTHROPOLOGICAL METHODOLOGY: FIELDWORK

Data Collection

Obviously, the four major subfields of anthropology (see Chapter 1 and Figure 1.5) have different specific methods of conducting their science. Even though anthropology is holistic, the starting points for a biological anthropologist, cultural anthropologist, archaeologist, and linguistic anthropologist are different and require different skills, have different problems, and use different technologies. Particularly important are the ways in which anthropologists collected their primary data. These are their field methods.

As my colleague Roger Ivar Lohmann nicely points out, there are five methodological categories that all anthropological field research falls into: (1) material observation, (2) biological observation, (3) behavioral observation, (4) direct communication, and (5) participant-observation.

Material Observation   This is the collection of information about "objects and settings." For a biological anthropologist, it might include the basic material factors of an ecosystem, or human-made objects that have some impact on human or nonhuman primate biology. For the cultural anthropologist, artifacts, architecture, natural and manufactured landscapes, and spatial relationships in a village would fall into this category. The linguistic anthropologist might be interested in written records.

For the archaeologist, material observation is sometimes the only record of past societies and their cultures, so archaeological methodology is focused on the locating, recovery, preservation, dating, and analysis of material remains. Here, the utmost care is required because once an archaeological site is excavated, the context of the materials is lost, so the science of archaeology is far more precise than as often depicted in television and movie stereotypes. (We'll talk more about archaeology in Chapter 4.)

Biological Observation   Clearly, observation is important for the biological anthropologist, who collects and analyzes data on human anatomy, genetics, and physiology; on primate fossils; and on the biology of living nonhuman primates. Foods eaten by us and the other primates, as well as biological pathogens, also fall into this category. The fossil record is one area where this category and that of material observation overlap, because many of the specific methods of the archaeologist are applied to paleontological research. The cultural anthropologist and the archaeologist will, of course, also collect biological data—about food, interacting species, disease-causing organisms, and so on.

Behavioral Observation   Obviously, whether studying nonhuman primates or other humans, observing behavior is vital. As we will discuss in Chapter 3, behavior is *how* organisms adapt to their environments, whether those environments are natural or cultural. The trick, of course, is to observe behaviors without your presence influencing them; this is a constant concern for the anthropologist.

Direct Communication   This includes surveys, formal and informal interviews, and focus groups, but perhaps the best form is simply the *conversation* between anthropologists and their sources of information, known as *informants*. An informal conversation can best bring out the *informants'* ideas and emotions, his or her *worldview* (see Chapter 4). This is why learning the language of one's subject society is so important. There are also nonlinguistic communications—gestures and body language—and this is also how the primatologist gathers some data on nonhuman primates.

Participant-Observation   The anthropologist's participation in the cultural activities of the group he or she is studying is the norm for cultural anthropological research because it gives the anthropologist the best, most intimate insight into the minds of another society and its culture. There are limits, of course—not having grown up in that culture, an anthropologist cannot possibly truly understand all that is going on, and, of course, the anthropologist is participating for the reason of gathering data and so will not be a participant in the same way natives are. Yet, by even attempting to be part of another culture, one can gain a depth of understanding not possible by more objective, remote study. This category usually applies to humans, but in some ways one can also gain insight into the lives of nonhuman primates this way. Jane Goodall, for instance, made and slept in a chimpanzee nest and ate termites, a favorite chimp food!

Some Other Considerations

In the "Contemporary Issues" box in Chapter 1, we discussed some of the ethical concerns involved in fieldwork—the care that must be taken not to have the mere presence of the anthropologist unduly affect the subjects and their culture; the need, at the same time, however, to use our knowledge to help our subjects, in the case of medical treatment, for example; and the need to practice *cultural relativity,* that is, to not let our cultural prejudices influence the objective science of our analysis.

But as Lohmann also points out, some *subjectivity* is also important, because first, it helps us understand our own prejudices and biases and, second, it can "deeply enrich the humanistic engagement of the researchers with the topic or people under study."

Studying people cannot be the same as studying chemicals or subatomic particles. We'll return to this topic in the "Contemporary Issues" box in Chapter 13.

SUMMARY

Science is the method of inquiry that generates testable hypotheses to explain the real world and then tests those hypotheses with the goal of deriving theories—broad explanatory principles. Belief systems are another method of inquiry. Beliefs are taken on faith. They are not open to testing in a scientific way, though many of us regularly test our beliefs on a personal level.

Although it may seem that belief and science are eternally at odds with one another—and while conflicts between the two do arise—both methods of inquiry are essential for the smooth operation of any cultural system. Any culture requires both scientific knowledge (what

is possible) and belief (what is desirable) in order to function and survive.

Anthropology is a science in that it attempts to explain observed phenomena of human biology and culture, and it does so by generating and testing hypotheses. In the process, we achieve a better understanding of ourselves and others, and we become more likely to learn how to cope with the numerous and rapid changes that confront us in the modern world. At the same time, the humanism of anthropology provides us with a better personal and philosophical understanding of our species, its nature, and its wealth of diversity.

QUESTIONS FOR FURTHER THOUGHT

1. We sometimes forget that much of what we accept as "fact" was generated by the scientific method and that it is the scientific method, still, that supports it. For example, we "know" the earth revolves around the sun and not the other way around. But *how* do we know? List some pieces of evidence for this fact and some ways you could test it scientifically.

2. The famous Shroud of Turin is another example of a perceived clash between science and religion. Do some research on your own regarding the two sides of the supposed debate. Start with two Web sites: http://www.csicop.org/sb/show/john_calvin_and_the_shroud_of_turin/ and www.shroud.com. Do you think there's a real conflict here?

3. Science and belief systems are different, and yet they are both aspects of culture and, thus, necessarily have some influence on and interaction with one another. Consider some current ethical debates—abortion, euthanasia, stem cell research. What points of view do science and belief bring to these debates? Do you think it's possible to reconcile some of the seeming differences of opinion on how to deal with these issues in the "real world"? Does our discussion in this chapter help answer this question?

NOTES, REFERENCES, AND READINGS

One of the best complete discussions of the scientific method is chapter 2 in Kenneth Feder's *Frauds, Myths, and Mysteries: Science and Pseudoscience in Archaeology,* seventh edition. This book also, as the title indicates, describes and scientifically examines various claims within archaeology, clearly showing how science works and how it can be misused and misunderstood. Another good discussion

of the scientific method is in chapter 1 of *The Sciences: An Integrated Approach,* by James Trefil and Robert M. Hazen.

The quote from John Maynard Smith appeared in the November 1984 *Natural History* in an article titled "Science and Myth," which nicely discusses the differences and relationships between science and belief systems. Anthropology as a science is the topic of "Science in Anthropology," by Melvin Ember and Carol Ember, in *The Teaching of Anthropology,* edited by Conrad Kottak et al.

For objective scientific examinations of pseudo-scientific ideas, see the articles in two popular journals, *The Skeptical Inquirer* and *Skeptic.* Specifically, for more on palmistry, see my "Palmistry: Science or Hand-Jive?" in the winter 1982–1983 *Skeptical Inquirer.* The flat-earthers are examined by Robert Schadewald in "Scientific Creationism, Egocentricity, and the Flat Earth" in the winter 1981–1982 *Skeptical Inquirer.* See also www.theflatearthsociety.org.

The Web site with the statement about a solar-system-wide flood is www.answersingenesis.org/ docs2/4412news12-6-2000.asp. For a discussion of the biblical flood, with more references, see the Feder book noted above.

Sam Harris provocatively addresses the issue of the conflict between science and religion in *The End of Faith: Religion, Terror, and the Future of Reason* and *Letter to a Christian Nation.*

The discussion of fieldwork is elaborated on in the entry "Field Methods" by Roger Ivar Lohmann in *Encyclopedia of Anthropology* edited by H. James Birx.

3

THEMES OF ANTHROPOLOGY

Evolution

Each of us lives in a world made up of our society and of that society in interaction with all the societies on earth. We live, in other words, in a social and cultural environment. In addition, even with all our technological achievements, we humans are still part of another world—the natural world. We are, after all, a type of animal. Even though we sometimes forget it, we, like all life on earth, interact continuously with the natural environment. We affect it, it affects us, and we are dependent on it. The actions of the natural processes that have affected every other living organism have also affected our **evolution**. Our species has descended from nonhuman ancestors, has changed over time into modern *Homo sapiens*, and is still changing—in other words, we are still evolving.

AS YOU READ, CONSIDER THE FOLLOWING QUESTIONS:

1. What is the cultural context of the history of the theory of evolution?
2. What are the basic concepts of modern genetics and inheritance, and how do these contribute to our understanding of evolution?
3. In what way is adaptation at the heart of evolutionary theory?
4. What is the evidence for biological evolution, and what are the major processes of evolution?
5. How do new species evolve from existing ones?

THE EVOLUTION OF EVOLUTION

The idea that biological species, including humans, have changed over time and have given rise to other species can be traced all the way back to the ancient Greek philosophers. Our present-day understanding of evolution, however, begins in Europe in the late 1700s.

Before Darwin

The Biblical Context   Before the 1700s, the study of biology was limited by two assumptions, derived in part from literal interpretations of the Bible, in part from ancient philosophical ideas, and in part from a simple scarcity of data. First, living things were thought to have undergone no change since they were divinely created. They were thought, in other words, to be "fixed" or "essential" in terms of both their appearance and the number of existing kinds of

evolution In biology, the idea that species change over time and have a common ancestry.

organisms. Moreover, the variety observed among living things was thought to represent a *great chain of being,* a hierarchical organization leading from simplest and least perfect to most complex and most perfect—with the Supreme Being, of course, as the last link in that chain.

Second, the earth was thought to be very young. This idea was formalized in 1650 by Irish Archbishop James Ussher (1581–1656), who calculated—using passages in the Bible as well as some historical records—that the biblical creation had begun on Sunday, October 23, in the year 4004 B.C. Thus, Ussher calculated that the earth was less than 6,000 years old.

The Evidence for Change Accumulates   By the latter half of the eighteenth century, however, ideas began to change. Scientists were beginning to recognize **fossils** as the remains of creatures that once existed but existed no longer, or at least not in that particular form. Previously, they had interpreted fossils as everything from the remains of deformed individuals of existing species to mere "tricks of nature."

The nature of the geological record was also becoming clear, and scientists realized that the earth itself had undergone enormous change over what must have been more than 6,000 years.

The evidence came from the recognition of the layers of rock and soil beneath the earth's surface. These layers are **strata** (singular, *stratum*), and their study is **stratigraphy.** The idea is that the strata represent a sequence of events, the lower layers earlier and then higher layers later. The nature of the rock and soil of each stratum, as well as its fossil contents, shows the natural conditions at the time the layer was deposited (Figure 3.1). It was clear that neither the earth nor its inhabitants were stable and unchanging.

Catastrophism Offers an Explanation for Change   The fossil and stratigraphic records are imperfect. They seldom record the usually slow change that we now know characterizes the history of the earth and its life. Rather, the record of the fossils and rock layers seems to show abrupt changes. Look at Figure 3.1 and the seemingly distinct layers, with sometimes distinct fossils. A number of scientists of the eighteenth and early nineteenth centuries, most notably the French naturalist Georges Cuvier (1769–1832), felt the obvious explanation was that the earth had undergone a series of worldwide cataclysms—floods, earthquakes, volcanoes, changes to the crust—that changed the surface of the earth and brought about the mass extinction of life forms. New life forms then appeared.

Cuvier probably would have accepted that some divine creation produced those new life forms, but this was not a part of his model. Indeed, he thought many of the new forms seen in subsequent layers migrated from other areas. So **catastrophism** was *not* a religious idea,

fossils Remains of life-forms of the past.

strata Layers; here, the layers of rock and soil under the earth's surface.

stratigraphy The study of the earth's strata.

catastrophism The idea that the history of the earth and its life is accounted for by a series of global catastrophes.

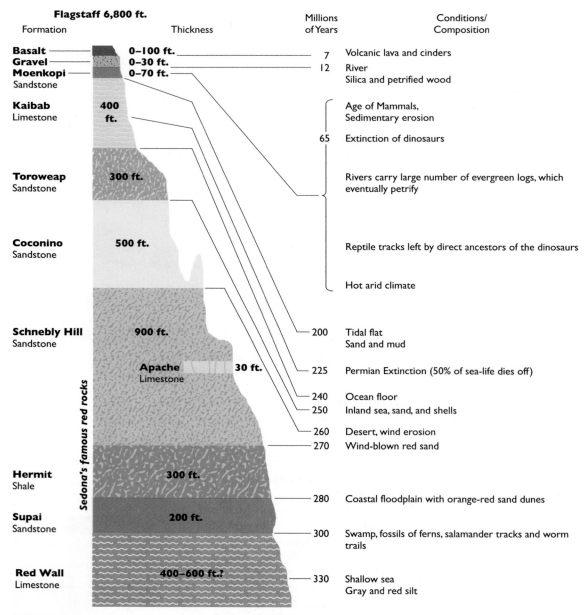

Flagstaff 6,800 ft.				
Formation	Thickness		Millions of Years	Conditions/ Composition
Basalt	0–100 ft.		7	Volcanic lava and cinders
Gravel	0–30 ft.		12	River
Moenkopi Sandstone	0–70 ft.			Silica and petrified wood
Kaibab Limestone	400 ft.			Age of Mammals, Sedimentary erosion
			65	Extinction of dinosaurs
Toroweap Sandstone	300 ft.			Rivers carry large number of evergreen logs, which eventually petrify
Coconino Sandstone	500 ft.			Reptile tracks left by direct ancestors of the dinosaurs
				Hot arid climate
Schnebly Hill Sandstone	900 ft.		200	Tidal flat Sand and mud
	Apache Limestone	30 ft.	225	Permian Extinction (50% of sea-life dies off)
			240	Ocean floor
			250	Inland sea, sand, and shells
			260	Desert, wind erosion
			270	Wind-blown red sand
Hermit Shale	300 ft.		280	Coastal floodplain with orange-red sand dunes
Supai Sandstone	200 ft.		300	Swamp, fossils of ferns, salamander tracks and worm trails
Red Wall Limestone	400–600 ft.?		330	Shallow sea Gray and red silt

Sedona's famous red rocks

Sedona 4,500 ft.

FIGURE 3.1
Geological cross section of the area around Sedona and Flagstaff, Arizona, showing the variation in composition and thickness of the strata and some of the events represented in those strata.

as it is often said to be. It was, in fact, scientific, posing a logical model for a literal interpretation of what the fossil and geological records appeared to show. The religious connection comes from the idea that the most recent in the series of catastrophes was Noah's Flood as depicted in the Bible, which was still taken as a literal, but perhaps incomplete, record of earth history. The catastrophists thought that history went back in time far beyond 6,000 years.

We know now, it should be added, that in fact five times in the history of the earth, there *have* been major and worldwide catastrophes that have, indeed, changed the face of the earth and brought about mass extinctions. A prime example is the asteroid impact 65 million years ago that wiped out, among other life forms, all of the dinosaurs. But most change is less dramatic, slower, and more steady over spans of geological time.

Uniformitarianism Answers Catastrophism   It was another French scholar, Comte de Buffon (1707–1788), who first coined the term **Uniformitarianism.** He said that catastrophes are rare and localized and that earth's history is mainly explained by "operations *uniformly* repeated, motions which succeed one another without interruption" (emphasis mine). In other words, earth's geological history could be explained by normal, everyday processes such as erosion and deposition of sediments in water. All you needed was enough time and the recognition that the fossil and geological records are imperfect, that they don't record every step along the way. It was the Scotsman Charles Lyell (1797–1875) who formalized this concept and made the idea seem sensible and applicable to the history of life as well. Even so, by the beginning of the 1800s, what was at issue was not *whether* change had occurred in the earth and its life, but *how* it had occurred.

Lamarck Explains Biological Change   Numerous models were proposed to account for the fossils and for the obvious lack of fixity in species that they demonstrated. One of the best-known models was proposed by French biologist Jean-Baptiste de Lamarck (1744–1829). Lamarck said that living things are adapted to the environments in which they live. Since the geological record, as well as simple observation, shows that environments continuously change, it stands to reason that living things must change over time in order to survive. No problem there.

But Lamarck went on to propose a mechanism to explain how animals and plants change in response to changing environments. His idea, which he refined from earlier, similar proposals, is called the **inheritance of acquired characteristics** (Figure 3.2). Species, said Lamarck, have a "will" that enables them to recognize that some environmental change has taken place and to carry out the proper adaptive actions. The organs necessary for these adaptations then change accordingly. Species can even develop new organs if needed. These new or changed traits are then passed on, in their new form, to the organism's offspring, thus the "inheritance" of characteristics "acquired" during an individual organism's lifetime. Furthermore, Lamarck proposed that this evolution was progressive, always working toward producing more-complex and

uniformitarianism The idea that present-day geological processes can also explain the history of the earth. Can be applied to biological change as well.

inheritance of acquired characteristics The incorrect idea that adaptive traits acquired during an organism's lifetime can be passed on to its offspring.

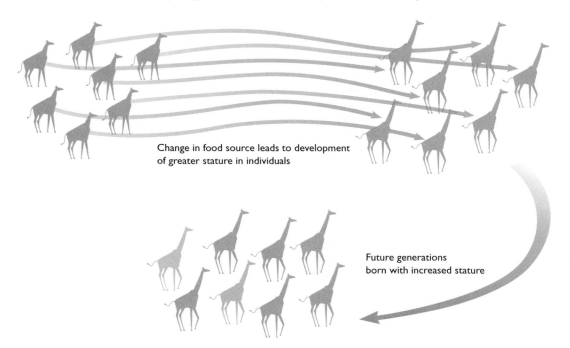

Change in food source leads to development of greater stature in individuals

Future generations born with increased stature

FIGURE 3.2
Lamarck's model of inheritance of acquired characteristics applied to the evolution of long necks and tall bodies in giraffes. In the past, giraffes were short, but environmental change altered their food source, placing the foliage they ate high up in the trees. Confronted with this problem, *each giraffe* was able to stretch its neck and legs enough to reach the leaves. This greater height was automatically passed on to the giraffes' offspring, which had to make themselves even taller, and so on, giving rise to the 18-foot-tall giraffes of today. (Compare with Darwin's model, Figure 3.4.)

thus more-perfect forms. You can guess what species he thought the most complex and perfect.

Lamarck's model, or something like it, maintained some acceptance, both within science and among the general public, into the twentieth century. There was, after all, a certain comfort in his idea. If we had to accept that living things have changed over time, at least they changed in a particular (and human-oriented) direction, and they changed by a process dependent on something within the organism itself—Lamarck's "will." It was also a process that was unfailing. There was, in other words, no extinction. Creatures represented only by fossils were simply creatures that had undergone so much change that they now looked very different.

But Lamarck's model doesn't work. We know of no way in which traits can arise automatically when they are needed, whether through the organism's own will or some action of the environment. Furthermore, traits that are acquired during an organism's lifetime cannot be passed on to its offspring. The blacksmith's strong right arm, in contrast to what Lamarck himself suggested, *will not* be inherited by his sons. It should also be clear that species can't just create new organs as needed.

So, although Lamarck's model was popular, many scientists at the same time searched for a better mechanism for evolution. Enter Charles Darwin (Figure 3.3).

FIGURE 3.3
Charles Darwin in 1869, by
famed photographer Julia
Margaret Cameron.

Charles Darwin

Charles Robert Darwin was born into a prominent British family on
February 12, 1809 (the same birthday as Abraham Lincoln's). As a boy
and a young man, Charles seemed to lack a direction in life, at least
one that pleased his father. Careers in both medicine and the clergy
failed to interest him. Natural history was his passion. It was with some
reluctance that Charles's father gave him permission in 1831 to join the
HMS *Beagle* for its voyage of discovery around the world. The elder
Darwin, unknowingly, changed the history of science.

The story of the voyage of the *Beagle* is itself a fascinating one. For
our purposes here, suffice it to say that the journey provided Darwin
with a perspective, rarely available to men of his time, on the nature
of living creatures. Darwin was able to observe and collect data,
literally from around the world, on geological formations and the
fossils they contained, on the geographic distributions of species, on
the adaptations of various creatures to their environments, and on
how individual populations varied from one another according to
environmental differences (Figure 3.4). The data not only indicated to
Darwin that organisms changed over time (which was generally accepted
by then) but also hinted that species could give rise to other species.
Perhaps it hinted as well at the mechanism that brought about these
processes. In addition, the works of other thinkers, especially geologists

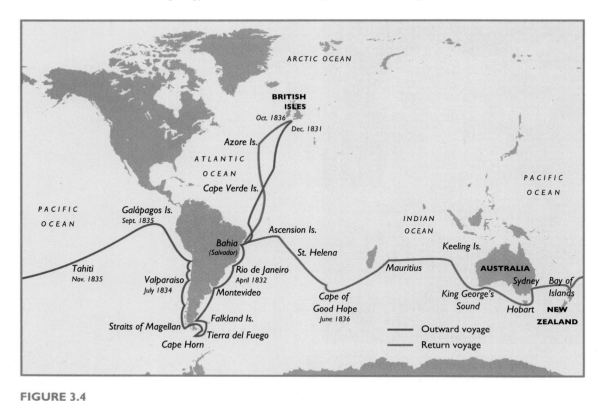

FIGURE 3.4

The route of Darwin's voyage aboard the HMS *Beagle* from 1831 to 1836. This trip provided Darwin with observations and thoughts vital to his formulation of the theory of natural selection. Especially famous and important was his visit to the Galápagos Islands in the eastern Pacific.

like Charles Lyell and social philosophers like Thomas Malthus (see "Contemporary Issues," Chapter 9), contributed to Darwin's thinking by introducing new perspectives on natural and social change.

Oddly, rather than writing about the transmutation of species—as it was then called—on his return from the *Beagle* voyage in 1836, Darwin turned his attention to other scientific subjects. He mentioned what we now call evolution only privately to friends and wrote about it only in his personal notebooks and in two trial essays published in the early 1840s. Darwin's silence can probably be attributed to his fear that science and society were not ready to accept his explanation. He may have felt that the process he had discerned was too dependent on random, fortuitous events. Recall the popularity of Lamarck's idea at the time, which appealed to people because it said that when change was needed, it occurred, and that there was no extinction.

But history was not to leave Darwin alone. In 1858 Darwin received a brief paper from a young, lesser-known British naturalist named Alfred Russel Wallace (1823–1913). Wallace, suffering from a malaria-induced fever during a collecting trip in Indonesia, had glimpsed the basics of a mechanism that might explain, better than had Lamarck, the transmutation of species. Later, working it out in more

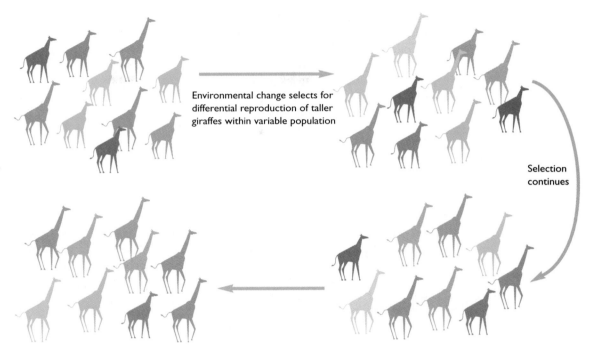

Environmental change selects for differential reproduction of taller giraffes within variable population

Selection continues

FIGURE 3.5

Darwin's model of natural selection applied to the evolution of long necks and tall bodies in giraffes. An environmental change, perhaps in the location of food sources, made the taller giraffes within a variable species relatively more reproductively successful. These giraffes thus passed on their stature to a greater number of offspring, making succeeding generations taller on average. (Compare with Lamarck's model, Figure 3.2.)

detail, Wallace felt his idea had merit, and he decided to check it out with the most renowned of British naturalists, Darwin.

Upon reading Wallace's paper, Darwin's hand was called, for Wallace had described the same idea, in nearly the same terms as Darwin had. Darwin was urged to publish, and in the following year, 1859, *On the Origin of Species by Means of Natural Selection or the Preservation of Favoured Races in the Struggle for Life* hit the bookstores and sold out in a single day. Possibly to Darwin's surprise, the time was ripe for his idea of **natural selection,** which was heralded by most of the scientific community (Figure 3.5). "How extremely stupid of me not to have thought of that!" one colleague is reported to have remarked.

Charles Darwin died in 1882, but not before authoring numerous volumes on various scientific topics, including a second major work on evolution, *The Descent of Man* (1871). In this book Darwin did what he dared not in 1859. He applied his ideas explicitly to humans, and by that time his views were well accepted within the scientific community.

But Darwin died without ever finding the answers to two important questions. First, he did not understand exactly *how* traits in living organisms are passed on. Obviously, the ability of adaptively successful parents to give their traits to their offspring was vital to natural selection. There were, at the time, some vague ideas about a blending of substances from father and mother, but no substantial theory.

natural selection Evolutionary change based on the differential reproductive success of individuals within a species.

Second, Darwin did not know where variation came from. Without variation, selection cannot operate; there is nothing to select *from.* He recognized that variation was always present in a species, even after years of selection to the same environment—even after years of selective breeding. But as to the origin and maintenance of that variation, Darwin had no explanation.

Ironically, the basic answers to both questions were available during Darwin's lifetime, and they came from the same source. At about the time Darwin was writing *Origin of Species,* an Austrian monk named Gregor Mendel (1822–1884), working in a monastery in what is now the Czech Republic, described the basic laws of inheritance. Experimenting with pea plants, no doubt the culmination of many undocumented years of research, Mendel arrived at a number of important conclusions regarding the origin of and passing on of traits.

First, he realized that rather than being carried in some substance (as was then thought), traits are controlled and passed on by individual particles or factors—we now call them **genes.** Moreover, individuals carry these factors in pairs, both members of a pair not necessarily coding for the same expression of a trait.

Of course, if both parents passed on both genes, the resulting offspring would have twice the proper number of genes. What prevents this from happening occurs during the production of the sex cells, or **gametes** (for example, sperm and egg in animals); the gene pairs separate so that each gamete has only one genes from each pair. Then, when fertilization takes place, the new individual will again have a pair of each gene, one allele of each pair from each parent.

Here, then, were the answers to how inheritance takes place *and* to why there is variation within species: traits are controlled by individual factors, and these factors are shuffled during reproduction to produce new combinations.

In 1900, almost twenty years after Darwin and Mendel died, Mendel's work, which had fallen into obscurity, was rediscovered. In that year three investigators, working independently, came upon the monk's obscure paper and realized what they had found. One of the people involved had been trying to explain the rare variations that sometimes appeared in plants and animals—things like a single flower of the wrong color or a plant that was far smaller or larger than other members of its species. (Breeders called these oddities "sports.") He called them **mutations.** Now, with his discovery of Mendel's work, he understood that his mutations were the results of sudden changes in Mendel's factors.

With this, a link in a basic theory of evolution was in place, for mutations explained the source of new variation—where the different versions of factors or genes came from in the first place. The interaction of Darwin's natural selection and Mendel's genetics is known as the *Synthetic Theory* of evolution.

genes Technically, those portions of the DNA molecule that code for the production of specific proteins.

gametes The cells of reproduction, which contain only half the chromosomes of a normal cell.

mutation Any spontaneous change in the genetic code.

FIGURE 3.6
Chimpanzee conservation center. Member of the HELP-Congo sanctuary with three baby chimpanzees. The HELP sanctuary was founded in 1990. It protects and cares for chimpanzees orphaned through illegal poaching and trafficking in the Democratic Republic of Congo (DRC). The center was the first of its kind in the DRC and the first to show that chimpanzees could be reintroduced to the wild. It also campaigns against the illegal trafficking and poaching of these animals. Photographed at the HELP-Congo sanctuary, Pointe-Noire, Congo, in 2003.

SPECIES

Consider two familiar animals (Figure 3.6). Although humans and chimpanzees look different, they are surprisingly similar in other respects. They differ in relatively few genes. Thus, many products of their genetic codes are identical; for example, the ABO blood types. They can contract many of the same diseases. They also share striking anatomical and behavioral similarities. It has been concluded, in fact, that a mere 5 million years ago these two had a common ancestor; that is, they were the same creature. And yet, they cannot interbreed now. They are clearly different species.

A species (notice that *species* is both singular and plural) looks and behaves the way it does because, as Lamarck observed, it is **adapted** to its environment. In other words, it possesses physical characteristics and patterns of behavior that help it survive in a given set of natural circumstances. It is able to find shelter, acquire food, locate mates, produce offspring, keep from being something else's food.

Different species exist because in the continuous process of adaptation, species can and do give rise to new species. Environments to which species are adapted are always changing. Organisms are always moving around. Populations of living things sometimes split up, and the resulting subpopulations become adapted to different environments and, under the right circumstances, evolve into different species. Thus, any two species will have a common ancestor somewhere in the past. How far back in time this common ancestor existed determines to a great extent how similar any two species are.

Here's an analogy: You are biologically related to all members of your family. But you and your sister are very closely related because you

adapted When an organism has physical traits and behaviors that allow it to survive in a particular environment.

both have two immediate ancestors in common—your parents. You and your first cousin, although related, are more distantly related than are you and your sister because the common ancestors—either your father's parents or your mother's parents—are a generation further back. Species of living things are related in the same fashion—like a branching tree. In fact, we often depict biological relationships with a tree diagram, just as we speak of and draw family trees (see Figure 3.11).

When we consider the adaptation of a plant or animal to its environment, we have two basic questions to ask: (1) To *what* is the organism adapted? (2) *How* is it adapted?

To What Is the Organism Adapted?

The science concerned with this question is **ecology.** *Ecology* comes from the Greek *oikos,* meaning "house." It studies the "houses," or habitats, of living things. More technically, it is the science concerned with discovering and explaining the network of relationships among organisms and all the various aspects of the environments in which they reside. Obviously, we need some way of organizing such a study, and the central organizing concept in ecology is the **niche.**

An ecological niche may be defined as all the environmental factors with which a particular species normally comes into contact and the ways in which that species is adapted to those factors. Niches overlap. Even if we are concerned with a particular species, we must learn about the ecology of the other species that make up its ecological niche. Ecology, like anthropology, is a holistic study.

These ideas relate to humans in two ways. First, we are a biological species that evolved from other biological species. We thus have to understand ecological relationships in order to understand our basic nature. Second, this natural model can also be applied to the cultural environment of our species. We can each be thought of as living in a particular cultural niche, which is affected by other cultural niches, which collectively make up the human cultural environment. We are also adapted to these cultural niches and to this general cultural ecosystem.

How Is the Organism Adapted to Its Environment?

ecology The science that studies the network of relationships within environmental systems.

niche The environment of an organism and its adaptive response to that environment.

Each living species has its own unique set of adaptations to its own unique environmental niche, and these can be described. But is there any general concept we can use to study adaptation, any one thing we can focus on?

We tend, both literally in laboratories and figuratively in adaptation studies, to "take organisms apart," to look at and explain their individual traits. But does a list of features fully describe a species' adaptation? Of course not. A species doesn't survive by having anatomical and physiological traits. It survives by *using* them—by doing something, by behaving. And this is true of any organism, even the simplest single-celled animals, even plants. They all function, behave, do something—and this is how they interact with their environments—get food, elude predators, find shelter, reproduce, and so on. Anatomy and physiology make behaviors possible. Thus, behavior is the key to understanding adaptation. Behaviors, like physical features, are the results of natural processes.

How can this idea be applied to humans? After all, we are not programmed to behave in all the ways we do. In fact, we are unique in that we can consciously change certain behaviors if they are not giving us the desired results.

Think of it this way: Our cultural behaviors and the strictly biological ones of other organisms *serve the same function.* They help us adapt and survive in a given environment. Considered that way, the focus on behavior makes sense whether the environment and adaptations to it are natural or are created by the organism. Moreover, our behavior—our culture—is not entirely separate from our biology. We are, in a sense, biologically programmed to have culture in the first place through the structure and functions of our brains. As I'll describe in Chapter 14, there may even be some more direct connections between our biological heritage and some of the general themes of our behavior; and, as I'll point out in Chapter 13, some of the processes of biological evolution may be analogous to those of cultural evolution. So, as long as we keep in mind that there are differences between our cultural adaptations and the instinctive ones of most other animals, a focus on behavior from the biocultural perspective is most appropriate for the anthropologist studying the adaptations of the human species.

MODERN EVOLUTIONARY THEORY

If environments always stayed the same, organisms would not change their adaptive characteristics and behaviors. All living things today would be essentially like the very first living things. This, of course, is not the case. Ecological conditions are in a constant state of flux. In addition, organisms don't stay put. Seeds are blown by wind or carried by birds to new locations. Animals wander or for some reason get pushed into new environments.

When environments change or when populations within species move into new environments, species may change. When a species is split up, with some populations isolated from the parent population and able to thrive under new ecological circumstances, new species may come about.

There are two aspects to this idea that must be considered: (1) the *evidence* for change over time, which exists in ample quantities, and (2) the *processes* that bring this change about. If you think about it, evolution is a bold idea. It says that living creatures are not stable, unchanging entities. Such a broad, important idea requires a good deal of supporting scientific evidence.

Evidence

I've already noted one basic piece of evidence: species are not separate and equally distinct but are, like members of a family, similar to and different from one another in varying degrees. They are like members of a family line that have descended from earlier members. And there's more.

For one thing, despite the great diversity among the earth's living things, there exists a unity of life. All living creatures on the planet are composed of cells, all of which have the same basic structure. All living forms make their proteins from combinations of the same twenty amino acids. All organisms use the same genetic code for building their proteins from amino acids, and this code shows some remarkable similarities across species.

Furthermore, living things do not exist independently of one another. In addition to being biologically related, they are all functionally related. They exist within a complex web of ecological interrelationships, each species dependent on the existence of many other species.

Of course, it's conceivable that all species could have arisen (or could have been created) at the same time, already exhibiting these similarities and connections. The type of evidence for evolution I've given so far is, as they'd say in a courtroom drama, circumstantial. What we need is not only supporting evidence for what *could* have happened, but also evidence for what *did* happen. And we have this too. It's the evidence from the geological and fossil records—the story of the earth's history and life, often literally written in stone. The story these records tell is clearly one of evolution.

We've already discussed the stratigraphic record (see Figure 3.1), a record of change over time. When you consider that in some areas there are hundreds of strata, it becomes obvious that we are dealing with vast spans of time.

Now, if we find fossils in certain strata, we can assume relative dates for them. That is, even if we don't know exactly how old a certain fossil is, we can tell if it is older or younger than some other fossil by noting the number of strata separating the fossils.

Fossils, in their stratigraphic relationships, show us biological change over time in a number of ways. For one thing, the fossil remains of a particular group of organisms show change. As we'll discuss in Chapter 6, there is a nice sequence of fossils showing change within the human fossil record. We have similarly good records of change for the horse and elephant families. At a broader level, we can even see the evolution of one major type of organism from another. It was suggested over a hundred years ago that birds evolved from dinosaurs. We now have fossils that give evidence of forms transitional between these groups (Figure 3.7). Similarly, we have transitional fossils showing the evolution of mammals from early reptiles, of whales from land mammals, and of humans from apelike ancestors.

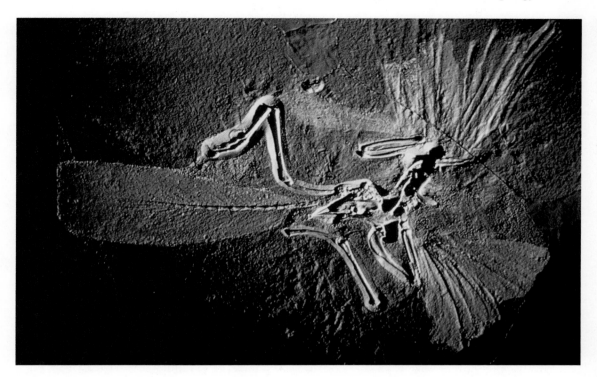

FIGURE 3.7

Fossil of *Archeopteryx* ("ancient bird"), about 150 million years old. This is essentially a small two-legged dinosaur with feathers, clearly showing the evolutionary relationship between dinosaurs and birds.

The fossil record of the earth's life also shows an increase in the range of diversity over time. The earliest fossils are all of fairly simple single-celled organisms, and these remained the *only* kind of organism for over half the history of life. Then, about 1.7 billion years ago, multicellular creatures arose. As evolution accelerated, we begin to see fossils of early plants, animals with hard shells, animals with skeletons, flowering plants, flying insects—all the amazing array of life we now observe around us.

Related to the increase in diversity is an increase in complexity. This does not mean all types of organisms are always evolving to become more complex. Some organisms stay simple. In fact, most species on earth today are bacteria, among the simplest of creatures. Other species may become simpler over time by evolving a smaller size or losing some anatomical structure they once had. But as time goes by, one finds *more kinds* of more-complex living things. This is the progression you would expect: earlier types of creatures giving rise to new, diverse types of creatures. Just as technological innovations gradually become more complex by building on the base laid down by previous inventions, so too living things increase in complexity over time by adding new structures or functions onto already existing ones.

So every individual piece of evidence in the geological and fossil records supports the idea that changes in the earth itself and in its inhabitants have taken place over great spans of time and that living things, including us, are related to one another as in an enormous and complex family tree. Within science these ideas are not an issue today, nor have they been for some time. But precisely how all this happens—the processes by which evolution takes place—is still an important area of research and was the real scientific issue in Charles Darwin's day. The centerpiece of these processes is Darwin's great contribution, natural selection.

Processes

Natural Selection   A good analogy—and one that pointed Charles Darwin in the direction of his theory—is the selective breeding, by humans, of plants and animals (Darwin was particularly interested in pigeon breeding). Here's something from my own experience.

In high school I kept and bred tropical fish. One of my favorites was the swordtail, a live-bearing fish (a type of fish that bears living young rather than laying eggs; Figure 3.8). Not quite grasping all the subtleties of natural selection, I decided to try to breed a bright-red strain of the fish, which didn't exist at the time. I started with a pair of the reddest fish I could find and allowed them to mate. From the

FIGURE 3.8
Swordtails.

first generation of this mating—a dozen or so babies that quickly grew up—I chose the reddest and put them in a separate tank to breed. Then, from the second generation I again selected only the very reddest to breed the third generation, and so on. In this way, I hoped to get redder and redder fish until I had a pure strain of bright-red ones.

Notice that I was making two assumptions. First, I assumed that reddish swordtails were likely to produce reddish offspring, reasoning that children tend to resemble their parents. But second, I knew that not all the offspring of reddish parents would be equally red. In every generation I had to eliminate from breeding the offspring that were not the reddest (don't worry, I just moved them). Any group of organisms shows variation in certain characteristics, within each generation and from generation to generation.

In general terms, I had set up a mini-habitat in which the most important adaptive characteristic was reddish body color. I then selected from the natural variation of the group the individuals in each generation that possessed an acceptable expression of that trait. These were the ones I allowed to reproduce, anticipating that the fish with the favorable expression of the trait would increase in frequency (become a larger percentage of the whole population).

If that makes sense, you need only take one more step to have a basic understanding of natural selection. But it is an important step, and it's the one that causes the most difficulty in understanding this process. The example I just gave is of **artificial selection.** A conscious agent—me—was making choices and taking direct action to implement them. Such an agent doesn't exist in nature.

So, aside from the conscious agent, simply translate all the parts of my example to a natural situation. Wild swordtails from Central America live in a habitat that requires the expression of adaptive traits within a limited range of variation. These traits would include things like body color; swimming ability; vision, smell, and other senses; and instinctive behaviors. Selection starts right away. Each female swordtail gives birth to many more young than can eventually survive, and she helps cut down the number herself by eating any newborn she can catch. Thus swimming speed, protective coloration (wild swordtails are a dull green), and perhaps some sort of fleeing instinct are immediately important. As life goes on, various other traits—the ability to find food, to keep from becoming food, to ward off disease, to find a mate and reproduce—"select" the swordtails better able to thrive. We can call these individuals more *fit*. They are the most successful at producing offspring and thus passing on the characteristics that made them fit. Favorable expressions tend to increase in frequency, unfavorable ones to decrease. That's the essence of natural selection.

The primary result of natural selection is the maintenance of a species' adaptation to its niche. But at some time in the life of every species, some environmental change occurs. At that time, different expressions of

artificial selection Selection for reproductive success in plants and animals that is directed by humans. Also called selective breeding.

certain traits may be more adaptive than they had been previously, and other traits may now be more poorly adapted. Moreover, once-important traits may now be neutral. If sufficient variation exists, natural selection may take a new direction; a species may undergo change over time.

It may seem that selection would be able to work any time it's needed. That's not the case, however. Remember that there is no directing force at work in natural selection. The characteristics of a species do not vary according to what environmental changes may happen in the future. Selection can only operate with variations that are *already present*. It can't make new traits because they are needed or may be needed in the future. I could not *make* bright-red fish by producing the right genetic combination. All I could do was *hope* I had redder and redder fish from which to select my breeding pairs.

Eventually in the life of all species, some environmental change is likely to occur with which the species can't cope. Faced with extreme and/or rapid change, a species' population would decrease faster than its individuals could produce sufficient generations of offspring to adapt to the change. The result would be extinction. This is the norm, not the exception. Estimates indicate that over 95 percent of all species that have ever lived are now extinct. Selection has its limitations. But it is the central process behind all adaptive evolution.

The Other Processes of Evolution Natural selection may be the centerpiece of our understanding of evolution, but it is not the only process involved. Figure 3.9 lists all the processes of evolution and shows how they are related. Use it as a guide as you read this section.

A species is adapted to the environmental habitat in which it lives. This relationship, however, is not static. Environments are constantly changing. Species, if they are to continue to exist, have to undergo change in their adaptations to keep pace. This is accomplished, if it *is* accomplished, by natural selection, the process of evolution that acts to maintain the adaptive balance between a species and its environmental circumstances.

But the species itself is changing as well. There are processes of evolution that bring about genetic change by affecting the **gene pool** of a species, which in turn affects the traits of the species upon which natural selection operates. Evolution is, at its most basic level, genetic change. The first of these processes is mutation. A mutation is any spontaneous error in the genetic code, and it can take place at the level of an individual letter in a genetic word, or it may involve an entire **chromosome.**

Some mutations are caused by cosmic radiation, X rays, gamma rays from radioactive substances, and certain chemicals, but most mutations take place during the two normal but very complex processes when the genes copy themselves during cell division and when the genetic code is read and translated into proteins. Such mutations happen all the time. In fact, some took place in some of your cells as you read this sentence.

gene pool All the alleles in a population.

chromosome Strands of DNA in the nucleus of a cell.

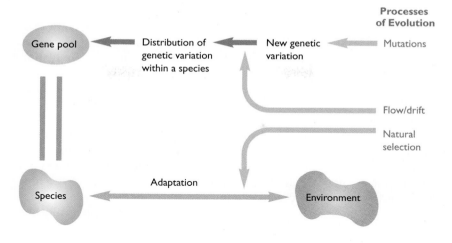

FIGURE 3.9
The processes of evolution. A species is in an adaptive relationship with its environment. This relationship is maintained by natural selection. Environments, however, are constantly changing, so the adaptive characteristics of a species change over time. In addition, the gene pool of a species is always changing, altering the traits upon which selection acts. Mutation provides new genetic variation by producing new genes or otherwise altering the genetic code. Flow and drift mix the genetic variation within a species, continuously supplying new combinations of genetic variations.

Although many mutations are harmful, mutations are the price living things pay for evolution. Without mutations there would be no new versions of genes and therefore no variation. If the first life-forms on earth over 3 billion years ago had always reproduced themselves absolutely without error, nothing would have changed, and the first type of living thing would still be the *only* type of living thing. Thus, mutations are the raw material of evolution, adding new genetic variation to a species' gene pool and giving natural selection new choices to select from.

After new variation has been added to the species' gene pool, it then gets distributed within the species. Think of this analogy: If I have a gallon can of white paint and add a small amount of red paint to it, the red paint will remain in one spot. If I give the paint a couple of stirs, the red will be distributed in a long streak through the white. If I stir the paint well, I will end up with a can of evenly colored light pink paint. How, and how much, the new color is distributed within the existing color affects the color produced by the mixing of paints.

The same thing is true with new genetic variation: how new variation is distributed within the species will affect what natural selection has to work with at any point in time and in any given individual populations within the species. There are two more processes of evolution that affect this distribution of genes.

One process affecting the distribution of variation is called **gene flow**—genetic exchange among populations within a species. (Remember, genes cannot be exchanged between *different* species.) Gene flow may result when (1) populations move to new areas, (2) small groups move from one population to another, or (3) mating takes place between members of neighboring groups. The result is new genetic combinations, new variations, and, thus, new raw materials for natural selection to work with.

gene flow The exchange of genes among populations through interbreeding.

A human example comes from the Hutterites, the group you read about in Chapter 1. On average, half of all Hutterite marriages take place between colonies, and they involve the bride's moving to her husband's colony. The woman thus brings her genes into the population and contributes them to subsequent generations. Changes from one generation to the next in a Hutterite colony are greatly affected by this continuous flowing and mixing of genes among individual populations.

The second process that distributes genetic variation is **genetic drift.** Actually, there are two processes that are usually included under this label. The first is **fission** and its result, the **founder effect.** Sometimes populations split up (fission) and found new populations. When this happens, the two or more new populations are not genetically representative of the old, original population, nor are they genetically the same as each other. In other words, fissioning instantly creates, or "founds," new sets of genetic combinations.

Again, the Hutterites provide an example. Recall that Hutterite colonies split, or branch out, with regularity. I found in my study that branching out can produce marked genetic differences between the original colony, the half that stays in the original location, and the half that founds a new colony.

Fission and gene flow are particularly important for our species as a whole. For most of our history we have been divided into many small populations defined by such things as kinship, religion, and politics. But these populations have always mixed genes, and they have split up to found new populations that have then mixed *their* genes. Over the past few centuries, gene flow has increased enormously as our species' mobility and motivations for moving around have increased. Our history of gene flow and fissioning, then, has resulted in a constant rearranging of genetic combinations and constantly changing distributions of genes throughout the species.

The second form of genetic drift is **gamete sampling.** Just as genes are not sampled representatively when a population splits, they are not sampled representatively when two individuals produce offspring. An organism passes on only one of each of its pairs of genes at a time, with chance dictating which one will be involved in the fertilization that produces a new individual. One gene of a pair, for example, may *never* be passed on.

This process has the most significant effect in small populations, because any chance change in gene variety numbers would have a profound impact on the gene pool. In a large population, a change in one direction might well be balanced by a change in the opposite direction.

Thus all these processes of evolution are continuously in operation—providing new genetic variation, affecting the distribution of that variation throughout a species, and, through natural selection, maintaining, if possible, a species' adaptive relationship with its environment.

genetic drift Genetic change based on random changes within a species' gene pool; includes fission and the founder effect, and gamete sampling.

fission Here, the splitting up of a population to form new populations.

founder effect Genetic differences between populations produced by the fact that genetically different individuals established (founded) the populations.

gamete sampling The genetic change caused when genes are passed to new generations in frequencies unlike those of the parental generation.

THE ORIGIN OF NEW SPECIES

So far in this chapter we've talked about how evolution takes place *within* a species. But how do *new* species evolve? That was the real topic of Darwin's *Origin of Species*—the "mystery of mysteries" he called it.

The evolution of new species—**speciation**—is based, as is the modification of species, on environment and adaptation. To take the simplest case (Figure 3.10), say a species inhabits a wide geographic range with populations at opposite ends of the range having slightly different adaptive responses to their environments. Now, say some environmental change—the alteration of a river's course, the destruction of some important resource, or the advance of a glacier—splits the species,

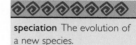

speciation The evolution of a new species.

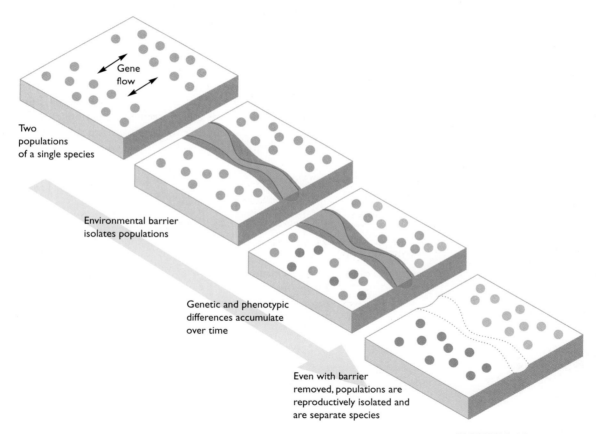

Two populations of a single species

Gene flow

Environmental barrier isolates populations

Genetic and phenotypic differences accumulate over time

Even with barrier removed, populations are reproductively isolated and are separate species

FIGURE 3.10
A simple example of speciation through environmental isolation. The blue arrow represents time.

isolating one portion from the other. Over time, each population will continue to undergo genetic change and to adapt to its environment, but without being able to exchange genes with the other population. There is, in other words, no gene flow. Each population will accumulate different genetic and physical traits. If one or more of these traits, by chance, affects the ability of members of the two populations to reproduce with one another, they would not be able to interbreed, even if at some point in the future the barrier were removed so that the two populations *could* mix. They would be separate species.

There are other, more subtle forms of speciation, but they all involve some sort of isolation of a portion of a species from the whole. The new units then go off on their own, unshared genetic directions, in some cases becoming separate species.

The evolution of new species from existing ones has given rise to all the diversity we see in our planet's living forms, both existent and extinct. Since we assume that life started just once, we may picture the history of life on earth as a giant, complex family tree, with each branch representing a species, and clusters of branches representing groups of related species with shared characteristics (Figure 3.11). In actuality, a depiction of all species, even for a portion of life's family tree, would more closely resemble a dense bush, with countless twigs each standing for one of nature's adaptive experiments—an individual species.

FIGURE 3.11
A family tree for the fourteen species of birds collectively known as Darwin's finches, named for the naturalist who described seeing them in the Galápagos on his famous voyage. Notice that they have all evolved from a common ancestor (a species from South America) and that the species are grouped by general type of adaptation (tree, ground, and warbler-like) and then by shared feeding habits (vegetarian, insectivorous, and so on). (We will take up the process of naming species and building such trees in Chapter 5.)

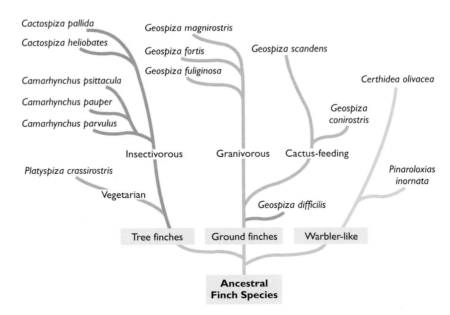

CONTEMPORARY ISSUES

Is Evolution a Fact, a Theory, or Just a Hypothesis?

It may at first be surprising that the answer to this commonly asked question is *all of the above.* Evolution, as a broad topic, incorporates theory, fact, *and* hypothesis. This is because the scientific method is not a nice, neat, linear series of steps from first observation to final all-encompassing theory. Rather, science works in a cycle, and the inductive and deductive reasoning of science is applied constantly to the different aspects of the same general subject. Data and hypotheses are always being reexamined, and each theory itself becomes a new observation to be questioned, tested, explained, and possibly changed.

A theory is a well-supported idea that explains a set of observed phenomena. Evolution is a theory in that all our factual observations of life on earth—fossils, the geological formations in which they are found, and the biology of living creatures—make sense and find explanation within the concept of evolution, the idea that living things change over time and that organisms are related, as in a huge branching tree, with existing species giving rise to new species.

There is so much evidence in support of evolution that this tried and tested theory may reasonably be considered a fact. Analogous to evolution is another concept you were asked to reexamine at the end of Chapter 2—the accepted fact that the earth revolves around the sun and not, as people thought for so long, the other way around. But how do we *know* the earth revolves around the sun? It certainly appears, upon daily observation, to do just the opposite. We accept the heliocentric (sun-centered) theory because there is so much data in its support. It makes so much sense and explains so many other phenomena that we consider it a fact and take it for granted, never

giving it much thought on a regular basis. I would be very surprised to read in tomorrow's newspaper that some new evidence refuted the idea. Similarly, that evolution occurs and accounts for the nature of life on earth is a fact.

But that fact poses more questions. A big one (the one that confronted Darwin) is *how* evolution takes place. The fact of evolution now becomes a new observation that requires explanation through the generation of new hypotheses and the subsequent testing and retesting of those hypotheses. Darwin proposed a mechanism he called natural selection and then, over many years, examined this hypothesis against real-world data. The mechanism of natural selection is now so well supported that we call it, too, a fact.

But an overall explanation for how evolution works—a theory to fully explain the observed fact of evolution—is far from complete. We know that mechanisms in addition to natural selection contribute to evolution. The relative importance of all these mechanisms is still being debated. The broad picture of evolution—the "shape" of the family tree of living things—is a matter of much discussion. We have only a glimpse of the specific genetic processes behind all evolutionary change, as new technologies are letting us look at the very code of life. In other words, we are still examining hypotheses to account for *how* evolution takes place.

Evolution—like any broad scientific idea—involves a complex and interacting web of facts, hypotheses, and theories. It is the never-ending nature of scientific inquiry that can make science so frustrating but that also makes it so exciting and important in the modern world.

SUMMARY

The history of evolutionary theory is the story of the application of the scientific method to the questions of the origin and nature of living organisms, as scientists learned to gradually give up their presuppositions and look to nature herself for the answers. Adhering faithfully to the spirit of the scientific method, Charles Darwin was able to synthesize his observations and thoughts with those of many others to formulate a theory that laid the groundwork for our modern understanding of biological evolution. Basic genetics, as first outlined by Mendel, gives us an explanation as to the origin of phenotypic variation and to the nature of inheritance.

The evolution of organisms is based on the concepts of ecology and the adaptation of species to their habitats. Because environments are always changing, it stands to reason that changes in species' adaptations can account for evolutionary change. The basic process that brings this about is natural selection, which maintains a species' adaptive relationship with its environment and, if there is sufficient variation, alters a species' adaptations in response to changed environmental circumstances.

Change also occurs within a species' gene pool. Mutations supply new genetic variation. Gene flow and genetic drift affect the distribution of genetic variation within a species. Thus, not only do environments change over time, so do species themselves—all this constantly providing natural selection with new and variable sets of relationships between species and environments.

When a portion of a species is isolated from the rest of the species, the stage is set for speciation, the evolution of a new species. If the isolated portion accumulates enough genetic and therefore physical differences over time, it may become reproductively isolated from the original species; that is, it may no longer be able to produce offspring with members of the original group. A new species has evolved.

The diversity of life on earth—the result of countless speciation events—can be depicted as a huge, incredibly complex bush. The main stem represents the single origin of life, but it then begins branching, producing millions upon millions of twigs, each standing for a new species, a new natural experiment in adaptation.

QUESTIONS FOR FURTHER THOUGHT

1. The history of evolutionary thought is often popularly depicted as a battle between science and religion. Do you think this is the case? What *is* the relationship between these areas of inquiry in the history of evolution?

2. Apply the discussion in the "Contemporary Issues" box in Chapter 2 to the topic of evolution. There are those who object to the teaching of evolution on religious grounds, claiming that the theory of evolution violates a literal interpretation of the book of Genesis and, therefore, their religious beliefs. Is there a real conflict here? How should this issue be resolved in terms of public school education in the biological sciences? The National Center for Science Education (NCSE) Web site is a good source for material on this matter: ncse.com.

3. Given that all life is related in a giant family tree, how might this fact influence ethical considerations, especially with regard to our relationships with other species? Should we give greater consideration to species closely related to us? How close is "close"? What criteria should we use—shared biological characteristics? the same branch of the family tree?

NOTES, REFERENCES, AND READINGS

The history of evolution is nicely covered in Ronald K. Wetherington's *Readings in the History of Evolutionary Theory,* which contains numerous selections from original works, and in John C. Greene's *The Death of Adam.* The impact of Darwin's work on modern knowledge in general is the theme of Philip Appleman's *Darwin: A Norton Critical Edition,* second edition. A good biography of Darwin is John Bowlby's *Charles Darwin: A New Life.* A fascinating biography of Wallace is *Alfred Russel Wallace: A Life,* by Peter Raby.

In the past several years, our knowledge of the nature of genetics in general and human genetics in particular has grown at a remarkable pace. The details are beyond the scope and requirements of this book, but for those interested, try Matt Ridley's *Genome* and John H. Relethford's *Reflections of Our Past: How Human History Is Revealed in Our Genes.*

A book about the close genetic relationship between humans and chimpanzees, and much more, is Jonathan Marks's *What It Means to Be 98% Chimpanzee: Apes, People, and Their Genes.*

For examples of animal and plant adaptations to various environments, try three books by zoologist and filmmaker David Attenborough: *Life on Earth, The Living Planet,* and *The Trials of Life.* These each accompany a video series.

There are many good general books on evolution. I especially recommend Edward O. Wilson's *The Diversity of Life* and, for a more technical treatment, Mark Ridley's *Evolution,* third edition.

For a very readable narrative of the whole panorama of the evolution of life, try *Life: A Natural History of the First Four Billion Years of Life on Earth,* by Richard Fortey. Another, somewhat more technical treatment is *The Book of Life: An Illustrated History of the Evolution of Life on Earth,* edited by Stephen Jay Gould.

Another example of natural selection, this one in a human population, can be found in Jared Diamond's article "Curse and Blessing of the Ghetto" in the March 1991 *Discover* or in my *Biological Anthropology: An Introductory Reader,* sixth edition.

For more on the fascinating story of Darwin's finches, see the Pulitzer Prize–winning *The Beak of the Finch,* by Jonathan Weiner.

The nature of evolution as both fact and theory is covered in more detail by Stephen Jay Gould in "Evolution as Fact and Theory," from his *Hen's Teeth and Horse's Toes,* also in my reader.

Evolution, of course, is still considered controversial by small but vocal groups of people, especially the scientific creationists and those who support intelligent design. For more on this aspect of the topic, see the Stephen Jay Gould article noted above, as well as others in the same section of that book.

Visit the Web site of the NCSE: ncse.com. This not-for-profit organization works to support the teaching of evolution and to increase public understanding of evolution and science in general.

4

THEMES
OF ANTHROPOLOGY

Culture

CHAPTER CONTENTS The Concept of Culture • Brains and Culture: The Basic Biocultural Level • A Model for the Study of Cultural Systems • An Anthropological Analysis of the Necktie • Material Culture and the Study of the Cultural Past • Contemporary Issues: Can Anthropologists Study Their Own Cultures? • Contemporary Issues: Who Owns Archaeological Sites and Their Contents? • Summary • Questions for Further Thought • Notes, References, and Readings

Among the most amazing builders in the world are the weaver ants from the Old World tropics. Colonies of these ants construct nests in trees in the form of tents made from the tree's leaves. The ants "sew" the leaves together in the following way: teams of ants serve as living staples, holding the leaves together while other teams of ants gently carry larvae along the "seams," stimulating the larvae to excrete a silk that "sews" the leaves together (Figure 4.1).

A few years ago I decided to build a wall and hang a door to create a new room for my study. Having virtually no knowledge of such matters, my first step was to purchase a book about home improvements and digest all the necessary information about partition building, lumber, drywall, and tools. Then I drew up my plans and materials list. Still unsure of myself, I consulted a colleague experienced in carpentry who looked at my proposed construction site and suggested a few amendments to my plans. Off I went to buy my materials and some shiny new power tools, and a few days (and half a container of plastic wood filler) later, I had my new room, complete with a door that actually swings open and shut.

Both these examples are amazing feats of engineering—well, at least the ants' is—but they are fundamentally different. My project was cultural. The ants' was not. I had to do all sorts of thinking and analyzing to build my wall. The ants didn't think at all about how to build their nest. Indeed, ants don't really have much to think *with*.

It should be obvious, in general, whether a behavior is cultural or not. I've been discussing culture in the preceding chapters, and you've probably had no problem understanding what I've meant. We all know what culture is.

Or do we? My colleagues Emily Schultz and Robert Lavenda offer one definition: *Culture is a set of learned behaviors and ideas that human beings acquire as members of society. We use culture to adapt to and transform the world in which we live.* But culture as a general human characteristic and, especially, as something that varies enormously from society to society in its specifics, is a complex concept. Moreover, some other organisms may not *have* culture as we do, but they exhibit behaviors with some of culture's characteristics. So let's begin by discussing the characteristics of culture, those features that distinguish cultural behaviors from noncultural ones. Then all our discussions to follow will make more sense and can be viewed in a larger context.

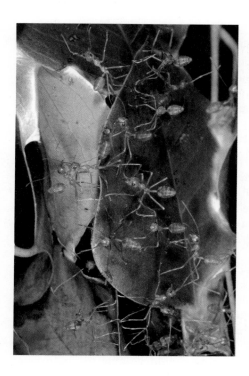

FIGURE 4.1
Weaver ants building a nest. While some of the ants hold the leaves together, others gently carry larvae along the "seam," stimulating the larvae to excrete silk, which "sews" the leaves together.

AS YOU READ, CONSIDER THE FOLLOWING QUESTIONS:

1. What are the characteristics of culture? What differentiates a cultural behavior from a noncultural one?

2. Are humans the only species with behaviors that exhibit the characteristics of culture?

3. How might the structure of the brain be related to our cultural ability?

4. How can we study the vast variety of cultural systems in the world in an organized and logical fashion?

5. How do we reconstruct past cultural systems from their material remains?

THE CONCEPT OF CULTURE

The Characteristics of Cultural Behaviors

Culture Is Learned Perhaps the clearest distinction between the two building behaviors described above is that culture is *learned*. The ants' behavior is built into their genes and is expressed by a complex series of stimuli that elicit a complex set of responses. My accomplishment, on the other hand, was possible only through learning; the skills and information I learned were transmitted by those who learned them from someone else, and so on.

Learning used to be considered the only distinguishing feature between cultural and noncultural behaviors, but a moment's reflection will tell you that learning is not enough. Other creatures learn. My dogs, for example, have learned many things, including, of course, the taboo against eliminating in the house, but such learned behavior would not really be considered cultural. Why not? What other differences are there?

Culture Involves Concepts, Generalizations, Abstractions, Assumptions, and Ideas   The ants are locked into the specifics of their nest-building behavior. It must work the same all the time. If some important variable is different, the ants cannot make specific adjustments. They don't, in other words, know what they're doing. Their behavior is not part of some larger concept.

My wall building, however, certainly involved concepts. No external stimuli elicited a wall-building response in me. Rather, I decided, consciously, to do the project for my own set of reasons. The home-improvement book didn't relate to my wall in particular but gave general ideas about partition building that I adapted to my specific situation. As I ran into unexpected problems, I was able to use my knowledge of the general principles to solve them. I now should be able to apply what I've learned to other, similar tasks—that is, to generalize.

Imagine if you had to learn every specific behavior for every situation you encountered in the course of a day. Life as we know it would be impossible. But because we have learned to generalize from specific data, we can adapt those generalizations to each new situation—more often than not successfully.

But even concepts and generalizations don't absolutely define human cultural behavior. My dogs have some concept of the elimination taboo. When we go to other houses and buildings, I don't have to teach them all over again. Rather, I'm confident that they have generalized from their training in my house the concept that says something like "Don't go to the bathroom in people's buildings." But that still doesn't make their behavior cultural.

Culture Involves Active Learning and Symbolic Transmission   Learning in most organisms is passive. They learn from imitation or from trial and error. For many birds, for example, singing just the right song is impossible unless they've heard another bird sing it. Singing itself is genetic, but the song must be learned.

symbol Something that stands for something else, with no necessary link between the symbol and its meaning.

But learning can also be active, when specific data and general ideas are *transmitted* from one organism to another *extragenetically* (that is, without any direct genetic influence, as in the birdsong example) using **symbols** in the form of images or written or spoken words. The ants' basic information about nest building is solely genetic. The information I acquired about wall building was transmitted to me extragenetically through symbols.

Now, if I adopted a new puppy and put her in the house with my dogs and if I allowed her to leave and enter the house at will, would she learn the elimination taboo? I doubt it. Each dog can learn it independently, but one can't share the information, and certainly not the generalization, with other dogs. ("Hey listen, never, ever go to the bathroom in people's houses, OK?") Dogs can and do learn by imitation, by reinforcement, and by generalizing from external data. Probably, after a while, the new dog would start to behave accordingly. But she would have learned on her own, passively. Thus, her behavior would not be considered cultural. There are no symbols involved.

Culture Requires Artifacts An **artifact** is defined as any object made intentionally. It is, in other words, not natural but "human-made." This book is an artifact. To be sure, the ants made their nest, but that nest is *natural*. The behavioral program for the nest is genetic. In a sense, the nest is like the ants' hormones and bodies—natural and not the result of learned, shared concepts and generalizations.

Although the usual definition of *artifact* limits it to concrete items (tools, houses, books, pottery) I'd like to expand it a bit here to include cultural institutions and organizational systems, such as religions, governments, educational establishments. These too are human-made. Artifacts—both concrete ones and abstract organizing principles—facilitate the realization of cultural ideas, and human culture is dependent on them. Without artifacts, there is no way I could have built my wall, which, of course, is an artifact itself.

So, cultural behavior has these four characteristics:

1. It must be learned.
2. It must involve concepts, generalizations, abstractions, assumptions, and ideas.
3. It must be shared through the extragenetic transmission of symbols.
4. It must be realized through the use of artifacts, both concrete and abstract.

At this point in the discussion of culture, a question naturally arises. If my dog exhibits behaviors that have two of the four characteristics of culture (numbers 1 and 2 above), is it possible that some nonhuman organisms actually do possess behaviors that could be considered cultural? The answer is yes, and it's no surprise that they are the apes.

Culture in Nonhuman Primates

As we will see in Chapter 5, we differ from our close **primate** relatives not in kind but in degree. The same holds true for the mental abilities that make culture possible. And there are some clear examples of cultural behavior, or nearly cultural behavior, among the nonhuman primates.

artifact Any object consciously manufactured. Usually refers to human-made objects but now includes those made by other primates.

primate A large-brained, mostly tree-dwelling mammal with three-dimensional color vision and grasping hands. Humans are primates.

Chimpanzees Make Tools   Perhaps the most famous example was first witnessed by primatologist Jane Goodall in 1960. Goodall has spent over fifty years studying a large population of chimpanzees in the Gombe Stream Reserve in Tanzania. The chimps there have developed a taste for termites. African termites spend most of their lives inside tunnels within large dirt mounds that they construct. For a short period the termites, having sprouted wings, fly around to form new colonies. This period is what most animals must wait for to make a meal of the termites. The chimps, however, have found a way to get a head start. Some of them, mostly females, will break a twig off a bush and strip off the leaves, or pull a long, stiff blade of grass from the ground and tear off any excess length. They will then insert their termite fishing stick into the opening of a tunnel in a termite mound, wiggle it around to cause the soldier termites to attack it, and carefully draw it out and have themselves a termite snack (Figure 4.2). A clever idea, and it fits our criteria for cultural behavior almost entirely.

First of all, this behavior is learned and not programmed in the chimps' genes. Not all chimps perform it, as one would expect with a genetically based behavior. It is shared extragenetically, as chimp offspring learn the behavior by closely studying their mothers doing it. It also clearly involves an artifact: A raw material is purposely modified to perform a specific task.

Most important, fishing for termites uses concepts and generalizations. To accomplish the behavior a chimp must (1) understand a behavior of termites that it can only see the results of (that is, the soldier termites attached to the stick or grass by their long, sharp mandibles), (2) understand how to exploit the insects' behavior to get the termites out, and (3) visualize a tool for that purpose within a plant and conceive of and perform the steps needed to modify the plant to produce the tool. Moreover, chimps don't need the stimulus of a termite mound (where the insects are out of sight anyway) to elicit the chain of behaviors. They have been observed making their tools and *then* going in search of a mound. Different chimps even have different styles of the tool. It is clear that they have a concept in mind. When a young chimp learns from its mother's actions, it could not perform such a complex set of behaviors unless it conceptually understood what she was doing. It is more than just imitation.

Chimps use and make other tools as well. In fact tools are found in all natural populations of chimps that have been extensively studied. Moreover, a recent synthesis of data from seven well-established chimp field sites across Africa, comprising an accumulated 151 years of observation, has shown variation in thirty-nine different behavior patterns, including tool use, grooming, and courtship behaviors. The nature of the variation points to the chimps' ability to invent new behaviors and pass them on socially—in which case the behaviors can be thought of as "customs" and therefore examples of culture. In

addition, chimpanzees hunt, often with other primate species as the main prey. Again, regional and group variations are seen in preferred prey species, favorite parts to be eaten, and whether hunting is solitary or cooperative. We can't deny that these behaviors at least come close to what we call culture. The lack of symbols is really what keeps this behavior from being completely cultural.

Monkeys Use Tools   Another primate example shows that possession of culture is a matter of degree. There is a colony of Japanese macaques (and Old World monkey) on the island of Koshima, Japan, that has been extensively studied for fifty years. The scientists conducting the study put piles of sweet potatoes on the beach to encourage the monkeys to both come into the open and spend time there picking the sand off their food, knowing that the monkeys dislike dirty food. In 1953 a young female they had named Imo began taking her sweet potatoes to a fresh-water pool to wash off the sand (Figure 4.3). Soon, other members of the group picked up the idea. Some even washed theirs in the sea, possibly because they liked the salty taste.

Having been thwarted, the scientists tried to increase their observation time by throwing grains of wheat onto the sand. But Imo simply

FIGURE 4.2
Chimps using tools they have made to extract termites from their mound.

FIGURE 4.3
A macaque washing its food, a behavior that has been termed protocultural because it fulfills most but not all of the characteristics of culture; in this case the behavior does not involve an artifact. The monkey is, however, using the water as an unmodified tool.

ecofact An unmodified natural object used as a tool.

protocultural A behavior having most but not all of the characteristics of a cultural behavior.

picked up a handful of wheat and sand, took it to a freshwater pool, and dumped it all in the water. The sand sank but the wheat floated, and this she scooped out and ate. This behavior, too, spread through the group.

Now, there is obviously one cultural criterion missing here: there were no artifacts. The monkeys were just manipulating unmodified natural objects. But the behavior was learned, it was shared extragenetically, and it did involve a concept (although there were no symbols). And they were using a natural object, the water, for a specific, conscious purpose. Some have termed the water in this case an **ecofact**—a tool that has not been modified. (Another example of an ecofact would be the rocks that some chimps use to crack open hard-shelled nuts, which they sometimes first place on another, flat rock.) The washing behavior of these monkeys might be called **protocultural**. It is important to remember, though, that these behaviors of the Japanese macaques resulted from some degree of human influence.

Apes Can Be Taught the Rudiments of Human Language   A final example deals not with natural behaviors but with behavioral potentials seen under artificial conditions. For some time, researchers tried to see if apes could learn to talk. All attempts failed because apes don't have the vocal apparatus needed to make human sounds (see Figure 11.4).

But they can use a substitute for spoken language such as American Sign Language (Ameslan). Perhaps, scientists reasoned, this might work with apes. At present, there are a fair number of chimps, gorillas, and bonobos that have become amazingly proficient at Ameslan or other substitute forms, and with these they can communicate using the features of a human language (see Figures 11.6 and 11.7).

I'll detail this phenomenon in Chapter 11. For now, however, suffice it to say that these achievements indicate that although apes in the wild don't use a symbolic communication system, they obviously have the mental capabilities that enable them to learn the rudiments of the one cultural trait that we always thought was ours alone.

Humans Are Cultural   If, then, other creatures have behaviors that we consider cultural, *how are we different?* Very simply, in these nonhumans, behaviors that fulfill the criteria for culture are rare and individual. They don't make up the majority of the animals' behavioral repertoire. For us, however, culture is absolutely vital. We are dependent on it for our survival. All our behaviors, even though some may have their origins in our biological past, are learned culturally and performed culturally, for cultural reasons, within a system of cultural behaviors. Moreover, as noted, we live in cultural worlds of symbols. A symbol is something that stands for something else, with no necessary link between the symbol and what it stands for. The words on this page are symbols. In this regard, *everything* in a human cultural system is symbolic, that is, it has meaning beyond whatever practical use it may serve. Without symbols, human cultural systems could not attain the level of complexity that characterizes them, nor could their elements be shared among members and across generations. Other species may *have* cultural behaviors, but our species *is* cultural.

Of course, the ability to have culture in the first place is dependent on a biological phenomenon—the structure and function of our brains. Just what is it about our brains, and to a lesser extent the brains of apes, that makes the cultural ability possible? How did this evolve?

BRAINS AND CULTURE: THE BASIC BIOCULTURAL LEVEL

The topic of brain structure and function is, obviously, complex and not yet completely understood, especially with regard to the origin and nature of conscious thought. It is important, however, to try to understand something about the brain in general to get a glimpse into how it makes our cultural behavior possible.

A useful model for picturing the brain, and one that has an evolutionary theme, was devised by Paul MacLean of the National Institute of Mental Health. He calls his model the triune (three-part) brain, and it refers to three evolutionary stages seen in the mammalian cerebrum (see Figure 5.5). It describes three different functions of the brain that are interrelated in complex physical and functional ways.

The deepest and oldest part is the **R-complex** (for reptilian). It is shared by all vertebrates and deals with such basic self-preservation functions as aggressiveness, territoriality, mating, and social hierarchy. Above this is the old mammalian brain, the **limbic system.** This appears to be the area that controls strong emotions such as fear, rage, altruism (self-sacrifice), and care and concern for the young. Also part of the limbic system are areas dealing with basic sexual functioning and with the sense of smell. Some aspect of memory also seems to be housed in the limbic area. Surrounding these two parts is the new mammalian brain, or **neocortex.** This is where we think. Various parts of the neocortex are concerned with perception and deliberation, spatial reasoning, vision and hearing, and the exchange of information between the brain and body.

So, we humans have inherited the basic survival behavior of reptiles, the emotional responses of mammals, and the thought processes that became more elaborate during mammalian evolution. And all these operate together, influencing one another in a complex feedback system. Take, for example, the aggressive actions of a soldier at war or a police officer in the line of duty. Their actions are not simply automatic stimulus-response functions but also the results of logical deliberations and emotional reactions. At the same time, their taking aggressive action in the first place may have nothing directly to do with their own survival but, rather, may be related to abstract concepts of law, patriotism, group identity, or ideology. In other words, when all these evolved areas of the brain work together this way, we have the basis for the complex abilities of consciousness, reasoning, and, eventually, culture.

Moreover, within the neocortex all the information acquired by the senses is stored and accessed through a highly cross-referenced retrieval system. Our brains can store massive amounts of information; we retain not just memories of whole events but of the individual pieces of those events and we can associate our mental pieces of information with related pieces or even with unrelated pieces if we wish. When we retrieve information, we can use only those pieces of information that we deem relevant, and we can put pieces from various events together in all sorts of combinations to create scientific hypotheses, philosophical ideas, generalizations, solutions to problems, and so on.

Put another way, what we can do is experience events in our nervous systems. That is, our mental experiences are not limited to what our senses are sensing at the moment but to what they have sensed in the past, what they may sense in the future, and even what they would sense in hypothetical situations. Only humans can make up stories. Only humans have philosophies. Only humans are good liars.

R-complex A primitive portion of the brain involved in self-preservation behaviors such as mating, aggressiveness, and territoriality.

limbic system A portion of the brain involved in emotions such as fear, rage, and care for the young.

neocortex A portion of the brain involved in conscious thought, spatial reasoning, and sensory perception.

Keep this model in mind as we move on in subsequent chapters to talk about human culture and cultural adaptations. Note how these would be impossible without brains that work in the manner described.

In addition, this model helps us understand how some animals can exhibit a degree of cultural ability. Apes, for example, have relatively large neocortexes. Their brains have the same basic structure and function as ours, only less complex. After all, we both evolved from a common ancestor in the relatively recent past. The conscious thought, complex social behavior, and tool use of our closest relatives are really no surprise. In fact, since all mammals possess a neocortex, it's reasonable to attribute some thinking ability to them all. It's clear to any pet owner that dogs and cats can reason. Whales and dolphins are also known to be highly intelligent. We humans are different from them in degree, not kind (although the difference in degree is a large one).

This difference in degree can be accounted for evolutionarily. In conjunction with other trends we will discuss, there was also selection at some stage of our evolution for individuals who had larger neocortexes and who could reason at a more complex level. This would have enhanced the conscious controls over social and psychological relationships and over the problems posed by the environment. We see the results of this evolution in the gradual but steady improvement in tool technology and in the successful expansion of humans into new geographic locations and diverse environments.

This, then, is the story of culture as a species characteristic shared by us all. But there's another level, the level of *individual cultures*—the specific systems that characterize each **society** within our species. How do we study, describe, and explain all the world's cultural systems? Why do we find such enormous variation from one culture to the next?

A MODEL FOR THE STUDY OF CULTURAL SYSTEMS

If we think of culture as our adaptive mechanism, it's easy to understand some of the cultural variation we observe around the world. Important aspects of people's cultures are geared to the conditions of their habitats. The Netsilik people of the Canadian Arctic have cultural ideas and technologies for hunting seals but not for hunting kangaroos. For Native Australians it's just the opposite. Living in New England, I own clothing and heating devices to keep me warm during the winter. Native Americans in the tropical rain forests of Brazil, however, have very few concerns about keeping warm.

But what about peoples who live in almost the same environment but whose cultures still differ? As I noted in Chapter 2, Philadelphia and Beijing, being at the same latitude, have very similar climates, but the cultures of those two cities differ in everything from language to

society A group of organisms living together in an ordered community. In the case of humans, a group with a shared culture.

economics to clothing styles to eating habits. The climate of highland New Guinea is fairly homogeneous, yet that area is home to hundreds of similar yet distinct cultures. How can we explain these differences in terms of the adaptive theme we've been following?

The Cultural "Filter"

Culture has two identities. It is our major adaptive mechanism for coping with our basic biological needs. But at the same time, it is such an important, pervasive part of our lives that it has actually *become* our environment. Look around you. Everything you come in contact with, everything you're concerned about, all the solutions to your concerns—they are all cultural. And in that light we can see that most cultural adaptations (once we've taken care of basic biological needs) are adaptations to culture itself. Most changes in a cultural system are responses to other changes in that cultural system. So, as we collect data through ethnographic fieldwork or library research, we must look within cultural systems and view them as their own unique, integrated environments in order to understand just how they work and why we see such great variation from society to society.

There are as many specific ways of going about this as there are anthropologists, and there are, as we'll discuss in Chapters 13 and 14, several major schools of thought about the nature of culture and how to analyze it. The following discussion represents my way of looking at these issues. I think my model reasonably captures the basic biocultural approach of anthropology and so is useful for examining cultures and explaining cultural variation (Figure 4.4).

We begin, naturally, with the biological characteristics of humans. We should never lose sight of the fact that despite the power of culture, we are still limited by our biological structure, function, and needs. However, because part of our biology includes a brain capable of culture, there are various specific ways we can fulfill our basic needs. There are many possible behavior patterns, and our task as anthropologists is to figure out why, from all the possible patterns, each society exhibits and practices its unique combination, its specific cultural system.

I like to visualize all the potential behavioral patterns going into a metaphorical filter, like the filter in a drip coffeemaker. All the unwanted behaviors are filtered out. Those that are wanted, that work for the society in question, pass through and are combined and integrated to form the specific cultural system. The problem now becomes what to label the filter.

Worldview

I think the best label is **worldview**. A worldview is, as someone once put it, "a set of assumptions about the way things are." What sorts of "things"? Well, as vague as this sounds, just about anything: the nature

worldview The collective interpretation of and response to the natural and cultural environments in which a group of people lives. Their assumptions about those environments and values derived from those assumptions.

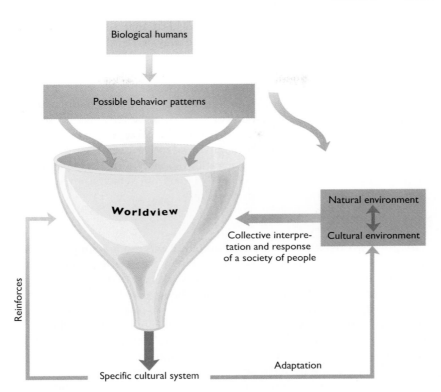

FIGURE 4.4
A model for the study of cultural systems as described in the text.

of the world and its living creatures; the place of humans in the natural world; the proper relationships between humans and nonhumans, between individuals and groups of people; the explanations for why all these are as they are—these and many more are the "things" with which the worldview of a culture concerns itself.

But why do I prefer the label *worldview* and not *environment* or *conscious choice*? Simply because those alternatives, while partially accurate, are incomplete explanations. As noted, not every aspect of a cultural system can be explained as a direct adaptation to the environment. Moreover, claiming that culture is directly determined by environment is too mechanistic. It makes culture sound like an entity, a tangible thing like some chemical in a test tube. It leaves real people out of the equation. And to claim that all aspects of a cultural system are the results of conscious, rational choice is to say that there are no generalizations we can make about human culture, no trends or tendencies that make some sense out of cultural history. That point of view would mean that every cultural system is idiosyncratic, making sense only in terms of the minds of the people who created it.

Worldview, as the term implies, must be a view of the world that a group of people knows. It encompasses their natural world and their cultural world, that is, their cultural world at that point in time and across its history—how it got to be the way it is. These two factors interact as people move around, encounter other peoples, and develop new and different ways to cope with their environments.

Worldview, then, can best be thought of as the collective interpretation of and response to the natural and cultural worlds in which a society of people lives. All aspects of a cultural system may be seen as derived from, linked to, and supportive of this view of the world. Such a model takes into account both direct adaptive responses that make logical sense as well as the idiosyncratic responses of real people, which may or may not make logical sense to others but which are reasonable and consistent to the people in question.

Some Examples

First, two words of caution. The examples I will use are simplifications. I will try to narrow things down as much as possible in order to show what we mean by *worldview* and how it serves as a label for our imaginary filter. In real life, much more would be involved. A cultural system is a complex, integrated whole. All aspects of a cultural system interact with each other and with all the facets of a society's natural and cultural environment. You will see this clearly as we examine specific aspects of cultural systems in the following chapters, and we will address some of the questions you may have about these examples.

Second, we must appreciate the difficulty of trying to understand and describe another culture's worldview. Remember, worldview is not a thing. It is an abstraction, a term we use for the totality of the collective interpretations and responses of a society of people. One cannot ask members of another culture what their worldview is. It is not something people articulate, because it exists in the background. (In a bit, we'll see how this is so by trying to describe an American worldview.)

The Role of Religion   We can, however, open a window onto another group's worldview by looking at their religious beliefs. Note, however: *Religion is not the same as worldview.* Religion is merely one aspect of a cultural system. But one function of religion (which we will examine further in Chapter 12) in all societies is to allow people to **codify** their worldview—to talk about, share, and pass on those assumptions about the way things are via symbols. Most, if not all, religions include a creation story (how the world and its people began); the history of a people; stories about the people's relationship to the supernatural, to each other, to the other species on earth, and to the earth itself; and basic rules of behavior.

So with those cautions in mind, let's compare the worldviews of groups from two distinct geographic regions and times—the recent peoples of the Arctic and Southwest Asia (also called the Near East or Middle East) starting 10,000 years ago.

codify To arrange systematically. To put into words and other symbols.

The Arctic   The peoples of the Arctic live in one of the harshest environments of any human group. It's not that they are poorly adapted. On the contrary, even before acquiring modern technological items, they were known for their clever and effective use of natural resources to satisfy their needs (see Figure 2.4). They saw themselves not as separate from the land and its life, but as one with it. As writer Barry Lopez puts it, their relationships with animals, even those they hunt, are "local and personal," and those animals are "part of one's community." Their lives are, he says, "resilient, practical, and enthusiastic."

But this intimacy with nature comes at a price. The Arctic has never been an easy place to live, and the people there see that world as one over which their control is limited, tenuous, and unstable. They live, says Lopez, with "a fear tied to their knowledge that sudden, cataclysmic events are as much a part of life, of really living, as are the moments when one pauses to look at something beautiful."

How is this view reflected in Arctic religions? In other words, how did they codify this worldview? Note that there are many different Arctic peoples, in both North America and Asia, and so there are many specific individual cultural systems. But we may look at a few aspects of one and, because there are certain similarities among all peoples of this region, apply them as a generalization.

The Netsilik ("people of the seal") live in the Hudson Bay region of Canada (Figure 4.5). Seal hunting in the winter is a major focus of their lives, although they also hunt caribou and fish for salmon in the spring, summer, and fall. In the Netsilik view, the natural world, the supernatural world, and the world of human moral order are one integrated whole. But the natural world is under the control of the spirit world, and important natural phenomena—as well as all humans and animals—have personified spirits or souls with approximately equal power. There are other spirits with various degrees of control over the world as well. The Netsilik, like many hunting peoples, recognize multiple supernatural beings, or souls.

The control these souls have over the physical world helps explain why things are as they are, especially why things can go wrong. Souls are seen as, at best, unreliable and are generally considered evil or capable of becoming evil. Souls that have been wronged can cause misfortunes, and thus there are many rules about how they should be treated. A newly killed seal, for instance, must be placed on fresh snow rather than the dirty floor of the igloo. The hunters beg the forgiveness of the spirit. Water is poured in the dead seal's mouth because its soul is still thirsty. Caribou souls are especially sensitive, and no work on caribou hides can be done in sight of living caribou. If they see and are offended, their souls will not allow them to be caught. By adhering to these rules the Netsilik have gained at least some sense of influence over their difficult lives. Thus, not only the technology of the Netsilik but more abstract aspects of their culture can be linked to their interpretation of and response to the real world in which they live.

FIGURE 4.5

An Inuit hunting for seals. Because the seals are below the ice, the hunter must harpoon them sight unseen. He has placed a bit of swan's down in what he hopes is a seal's breathing hole, which had been located by his dogs. When the seal uses the hole, the disturbed air between the water's surface and the ice will move the swan's down, and the hunter will thrust his harpoon down the hole. If he strikes the seal, he must then enlarge the hole to pull it out.

monotheistic Refers to a religious system that recognizes a single supernatural being.

Southwest Asia   Contrast the Netsilik with various societies in Southwest Asia prior to about 10,000 years ago. These people also lived as hunters of wild animals and gatherers of wild plants. They did not have, perhaps, as hard a life as that of the Arctic peoples, but they were still dependent on naturally occurring resources in an environment where humans were pretty much at the mercy of nature. Religions in the area probably also recognized multiple supernatural beings that controlled important natural phenomena.

But about 10,000 years ago, a major cultural event occurred in Southwest Asia—the invention of farming (which we'll discuss in greater detail in Chapter 9). The farming peoples of Southwest Asia had direct control over a most important natural resource—food (Figure 4.6). That one cultural change gradually altered their world, their feelings about their world, and their place in it. As the long history of farming influenced the physical and cultural worlds of Southwest Asia, three important religious traditions—Judaism, Christianity, and Islam—arose, reflecting a shift in worldview.

All three of these religions are **monotheistic,** that is, they recognize one supreme supernatural being. According to these religions, that one

FIGURE 4.6
A farmer in Egypt uses techniques that are essentially unchanged from thousands of years ago to grow crops that were among the first domesticated plants.

being, whom we can refer to as God in all three cases, brought about and has control over all natural phenomena, including human affairs. But things are not entirely out of human hands. First, humans are said to have been created in God's image, so humans have a closer connection to the supernatural than do any other living things. In the Judeo-Christian tradition, for example, humans are given dominance over the other creatures of the earth (Gen. 1:28); it is the first human, Adam, who names the animals (Gen. 2:19–20); and humans are enjoined to multiply and subdue the earth (Gen. 1:28, 8:17).

Second, humans are no longer at the whimsical mercy of the supernatural as they are in Eskimo tradition. In the Judeo-Christian-Islamic tradition, humans may petition God through prayer and action. They may ask God for favors and, if God is pleased and willing, stand a chance of having those requests granted. Humans have some sense of personal control in their dealings with the supernatural, even with an all-powerful being.

Beginning with the invention of farming, the history of Southwest Asia clearly reflects the articulation of a worldview in which people came to see themselves as having an ability to know and understand their world and to use that knowledge to exercise some control over their world for their own benefit. As these peoples now had some dominion over the natural world, so God had dominion over humans. As they began to view the world as clearly divided into the human and the natural, so too a division was drawn between humans and a single, omnipotent supernatural entity. Their belief in one God supplanted their belief in the multitude of spirits and souls that previously controlled aspects of the real world at will with only minimal influence from people.

Thus, worldview is a useful focus around which we may describe the other aspects of a society's natural and cultural worlds. Doing so allows us to take into account both the practical and the more abstract connections within the integrated whole we call a cultural system.

The American Worldview

As an exercise, try putting into words some important facets of a modern American worldview. Remember that worldview is not the same as religion; it's far more abstract. When I give my classes this assignment, students often mention individualism. Think about our "heroes," those larger-than-life individuals—past, recent, real, and fictional. Daniel Boone, Harriet Tubman, Helen Keller, Martin Luther King, Superman, Rosa Parks, Will Rogers, Muhammad Ali, César Chávez, and (my personal favorite) Indiana Jones, to name only a handful, all embody in their own ways the rugged individualism we Americans so admire.

Other students have said that we Americans expect, value, and embrace change. Our clothing styles, automobile designs, and musical trends change annually. We place term limits on those who run our government. We focus intently on some news event and then quickly move on.

Still another aspect of the American worldview might be our love of big things. We've always seen our country as big. The early history of the United States is full of stories of the explorers and pioneers (more rugged individuals) setting off into the unknown expanses of a huge continent. There's always been room to grow. We've built, at one time or another, the tallest building, the biggest sports stadium, even the largest shopping mall. We even admire physical size in people. Studies have indicated that taller men are more likely to be hired for some jobs than shorter men, even if height is irrelevant to the work.

For the sake of introducing the concept of culture and my model of cultural systems, the above examples barely scratch the surface of an extremely complex topic. To even begin to fully analyze a cultural system one would have to include data about every aspect of that system and every aspect of the natural and cultural environment to which it is a response. We will do a more complete job with some other examples in Chapter 14. For the moment, however, to show that this model can apply to all sorts of human matters, I give you the following.

AN ANTHROPOLOGICAL ANALYSIS OF THE NECKTIE

In class several years ago, after I had presented the model you've just read about, one perceptive student raised her hand and asked, a bit sheepishly but with a touch of a challenge in her voice, "What about your tie? It doesn't have a practical purpose for survival. Can you explain *that* with your coffee filter?"

"Well," I faltered, "sometimes certain cultural practices are so obscure and indirectly related to whole systems that it's nearly impossible to explain them in this perspective. Oh look, time to go!"

Overnight, though, I gave it some thought, and in the next class I proudly presented my analysis. The origin of this specific item—a colored piece of cloth tied around the neck of males—is obscure. It seems to have originated during the reign of Louis XIV of France, when, called a *cravat* (from the French word for Croatian), it was worn as part of the uniform of Croatian soldiers as a sign of rank. The French, always on the cutting edge of fashion, liked the idea and adopted it as a normal item of clothing.

But what does the tie *mean* to us? Although not as regularly worn as it once was (my father would even wear one shopping or attending sports events), the tie is still a symbol of status. It is worn in certain situations to display one's social status, socioeconomic position, and attitude about the situation. For example, certain jobs require a necktie. A man nearly always wears one to job interviews, even if the job itself doesn't require one. We wear ties to court, whether we're defendant or plaintiff. We wear them to weddings, funerals, bar mitzvahs, and christenings to acknowledge the importance of the event. When worn in a less formal setting, a tie is a sign of one's relative socioeconomic status. For example, I have been treated very differently by clerks in the same store depending on whether I'm wearing a suit and tie or jeans and a sweatshirt. This useless and often uncomfortable item lacks any practical purpose but is obviously full of meaning.

This relates to our general discussion when we realize that not all cultures recognize the concept of differential status and wealth that something like a tie symbolizes. Among traditional hunters and gatherers, it might prove detrimental if some people had more wealth than others. In such societies (which we will discuss in detail in Chapter 9) wealth is distributed equally among members, and there are no recognized differences in social status. To be sure, some people are better hunters than others or are more adept at decision making, but these differences are not institutionalized or formalized. Such societies can't afford to have anything but a group of people working together as harmoniously as possible for the common good. As a result, there are no symbols of status or wealth differences, such as different clothing for those of higher position.

In societies that farm, however, we find a new phenomenon: surplus products. At least when things are going well, a family can produce more than they need to feed themselves. The excess can be traded to someone else for some other resource that that person has a surplus of. Or it can be traded for a service that person may perform, which might include leadership activities. With all that wealth changing hands, all those surpluses, and all the specializations in labor, it is inevitable that some people are going to have more than others—both more wealth and more status, with the two generally going hand in hand. Status differences arise, and symbols of those differences develop, including, of course, items of personal adornment.

Western civilization can trace much of its cultural heritage back to farming societies of Southwest Asia and early Europe. Our cultural tradition has long had the concept of status differences built into it. So, the necktie has a history of its own, but its use as a symbol denoting differential wealth and power can be linked to worldview.

Cultural artifacts are important not only for their function but also, perhaps more, for their meaning. And this leads to another question: Since most of human cultural history took place before written records, how can we understand past cultural systems? The answer is that by using the theory and techniques of archaeology we can deduce the meaning of material culture and gain insight into societies of the past.

MATERIAL CULTURE AND THE STUDY OF THE CULTURAL PAST

Of all the subfields of anthropology, archaeology is perhaps the most distinct. Anthropologists specializing in this subfield tend to identify themselves first as archaeologists. The general public has a good idea what an archaeologist does, but it has a hard time defining anthropology. This is in part because archaeology is the oldest formal specialty within the field, going back as far as the European Renaissance, when "antiquarians" began excavating the remains of the classical civilizations of Greece and Rome.

The most important reason for the distinct status of archaeology, however, concerns the unique problems archaeologists face in collecting and analyzing their data. Those data, the material remains of past cultures, must usually be dug up—literally. They're most often underground because they're so old and have been buried over the years by flooding, windblown dust and sand, volcanic eruptions, soil buildup, and so on. To just find and recover ancient artifacts requires a very specialized set of technical skills. Other techniques and theories are then needed to identify, analyze, and interpret the artifacts.

But don't think this makes archaeology different from anthropology in general. Archaeology is not just finding interesting old stuff in the ground and putting it in museums (although it used to be). The archaeologist uses the recovered artifacts and knowledge of the relationship between artifacts and cultural systems (that is, their meaning, as in the case of the necktie) as data to answer the same types of questions as any anthropologist—questions about the nature of the human species and its behaviors. *Archaeology is the anthropology of the cultural past.* Let's see how this works in practice.

Material Culture and Cultural Systems

Living in New England, I have on hand a very good example of the connection between artifacts and the practical and abstract parts of culture. The artifacts are gravestones carved from the mid-1600s to the mid-1800s. The original research on this topic was conducted by archaeologists James Deetz and Edwin Dethlefsen.

If you explore old New England cemeteries and look at the stones from that period, you begin to notice that although there are numerous designs carved into the markers, the majority fall into three broad patterns: death's heads, cherubs, and urns and willows (Figure 4.7).

FIGURE 4.7

An example of each of the three major styles of gravestones in New England from the mid-1600s through the mid-1800s. *From top:* death's head, cherub, urn and willow. These are from cemeteries in Connecticut.

What sorts of things can we tell from these stones? We can certainly tell how old they are. The dates are right on them. And from each epitaph we can find out about the person buried beneath: name, sex, age at death, sometimes the cause of death, and maybe something about the person's occupation, family, standing in the community, and personality (although, given the context, information on the latter might be biased).

Using historical records, we can sometimes find out who carved the stones (there seem to have been a limited number of gravestone carvers in the area), where the carvers traveled in New England, and even the price paid for the markers. The prices are, in a few cases, carved into the stones themselves.

But the stones can tell us even more. The designs were not carved at random, and they do not exist outside a cultural context. They are symbols that relate to attitudes toward death and the afterlife—in other words, to religious beliefs as practiced in a given cultural environment. As attitudes changed, so did the statistical frequencies of the designs (Figure 4.8).

The death's head—a grim, grinning skull—symbolized a pessimistic view of life and death. It reminded the living of human mortality, of everyone's inevitable end. The epitaphs on these stones usually read "Here lies buried the body of . . ." The death's head is associated with the period of orthodox Puritanism from the 1600s to the mid- to late-1700s, depending on the region. The famous witch trials at Salem Village, Massachusetts, in 1692 coincided with the peak in popularity of this design.

As orthodox Puritanism declined beginning in the mid-1700s, attitudes about death changed. The emphasis shifted to resurrection and the rewards to be enjoyed in heaven. This change is reflected in the replacement of the death's head with the cherub—a smiling baby-faced angel with wings—and in epitaphs that are more positive. "In memory of . . ." began to replace "Here lies the body of . . ." These new ideas, and the adoption of the new design, seem to have begun in the urban intellectual center of Cambridge, Massachusetts, the site of Harvard College, and spread from there. Moreover, the cherub design in this area was associated with graves of upper-class, educated individuals. So we see a connection here between artifacts, religious beliefs, and the nature and status of intellectual influence in early New England culture. The gravestone designs themselves, it should be noted, originated in England—a further connection that could be explored.

By the late 1700s, religion had taken on a less emotional nature than it had under Puritanism. This, in association with a trend toward Greek Revival architecture, gave rise to the classical-looking urn-and-willow design. "In memory of . . ." had now completely replaced references to the buried bodies, and some stones simply carried the person's name and dates.

By the mid-1800s, gravestone designs began to show more variation. This was the result of a combination of factors: greater variety of religious expression, a trend toward more individual freedom, and the immigration

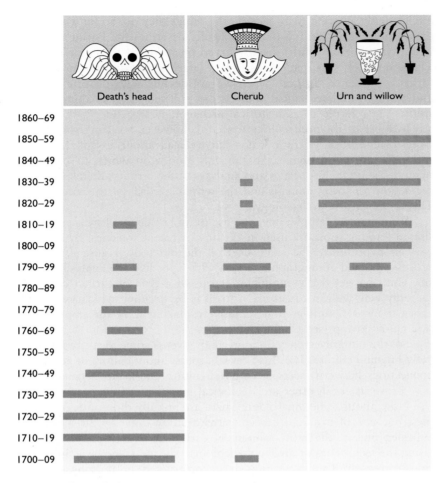

FIGURE 4.8
A graph, called a *seriation graph*, showing the changes in statistical frequencies of the three gravestone styles in central Connecticut for the years shown. Such a statistical pattern of design replacement is typical for many artifact types analyzed by archaeologists. A seriation graph could also be constructed for more recent artifacts such as automobiles or clothing styles. (K. Feder)

■ = 10% of the stones in a ten-year period

of peoples from diverse parts of the world. But in New England during that earlier period, we see clear connections between the gravestones—an artifact—and other facets of culture, even ideological ones.

Archaeological Analysis

Now, you're probably thinking that these gravestones are historic, that there's little scientific analysis going on since the basic information is written right on the stones and all the historical and religious context is recorded. Where's the archaeological analysis?

There are several responses to that logical question. First, as surprising as it may seem, there are things we don't know even about cultures with written records, including colonial New England. People don't write everything down. As we've discussed, people are not always

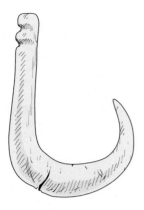

FIGURE 4.9
No archaeologist ever saw this item in use, but it doesn't take much imagination to figure out what it was used for in second-century-B.C. Japan. The artifact is depicted in approximately actual size.

historical archaeology The archaeology of a society that has written records.

prehistoric archaeology The archaeology of a society prior to written records.

ethnographic analogy Interpreting archaeological data through the observation of analogous activities in existing societies.

intellectually aware of why they do the things they do. So far as I know, there's nothing in writing that specifically describes the Puritans' motivations for having death's heads carved on many of their gravestones. The connection was made by scholars later on, looking at the various forms of evidence. So even when we are dealing with historic periods and cultures, archaeological analysis can still tell us some things. Such studies are referred to as **historical archaeology.**

In most of the archaeological record, however, we can't see all the facets of culture in operation, nor can we read about any of them. We find *only* material remains. So the only things on which to base our hypotheses are the properties and analyses of the artifacts themselves and the actions of living humans and the written records of the recent past. This is **prehistoric archaeology.**

We can, for example, infer the use of an ancient tool by seeing how similar-looking tools are used in existing or recent societies. By analogy we can hypothesize the same use for the old tool (Figure 4.9). This process is called **ethnographic analogy.** It's a lot like the analysis of fossils. Until we get really complete records of a type of extinct creature, the only way we can categorize a fossil is by deciding which living category it most resembles and tentatively placing it in the appropriate taxonomic group (see Chapter 6).

So, the old gravestones do more than give us some ideas about early New England culture. They also reveal aspects about culture in general—connections between facets of material culture and abstract belief—that may prove useful in other archaeological investigations.

How about something older? There are literally thousands of examples, but one of my favorites concerns a study done by Sir Mortimer Wheeler, one of the most famous of early Old World archaeologists. Using the techniques of archaeological analysis and some basic information from early Roman writings, he reconstructed, in amazing detail, a battle that took place around A.D. 47. In that battle, the Roman commander (and later emperor) Vespasian attacked and conquered a Celtic hill fort, now called Maiden Castle, in southern England (Figure 4.10).

Wheeler was able to tell, for example, that the eastern side of the fort was attacked, what sorts of weapons were used, and that the Romans attacked with arrows first, followed by an infantry charge. He could tell that some huts near the entrance to the fort were burned and that the attackers, possibly because they encountered more resistance than expected, massacred women and children as well as adult male defenders. And when the Romans had won, they proceeded systematically to destroy the fort, tearing down fighting platforms, taking apart gates, and toppling stone walls alongside the entrances.

Soon after the battle (perhaps the next night), the conquered people of Maiden Castle buried their dead in the area of the burned huts. The burials were hasty (perhaps because the Romans were still around), but the survivors remembered in most cases to include food and drink

FIGURE 4.10
An aerial view of the Celtic hill fort of Maiden Castle, showing the outline of its bank-and-ditch defensive system. The fort was built on a site that had been occupied since about 6,000 years ago. At the height of its importance, during the second century B.C., Maiden Castle had timber and stone walls, circular houses, streets, and underground silos for grain storage. Because the silos were so extensive, it is thought they stored grain for more than just the fort's inhabitants. Maiden Castle was perhaps the capital of a large territory.

in the graves for the journey to the next life. Probably the following day, when the Roman soldiers had moved on, the people began cleaning up and putting things back in some order. Eventually they built a new road across the ruins of their old fortifications. They continued to live there under Roman rule for about twenty years, when Maiden Castle was finally abandoned and its remaining walls torn down.

How could Wheeler tell all this? For details, I refer you to his fascinating book *Maiden Castle*. But briefly, Wheeler found such evidence as iron Roman arrowheads clustered on the eastern side of the fort. He could tell the order of events by the stratigraphy of the artifacts and other features. For example, the graves were clearly dug *through* the ashes of the burned huts. The skeletons in the graves were not found in any particular position or orientation, and grave goods varied, indicating hurried burials. The bodies showed signs of the wounds that killed them. The brutal nature of the multiple wounds led Wheeler to use the term *massacre*. Finally, it was clear that at least one stone wall was pulled down when the people abandoned the site, sometime in the 60s of the first century A.D., since the remains of that wall are on top of the other features and even block one of the roads built some time after

CONTEMPORARY ISSUES

Can Anthropologists Study Their Own Cultures?

Anthropologists can and do study the cultures in which they have grown up, but doing so involves a somewhat different approach from that used to study a culture foreign to us. When we study another people, our goal is to understand their worldview so we can then understand how all the features of their culture interrelate to each other and to the world that the people observe, live in, and interpret. When we seek to anthropologically understand our own culture, we need to begin by stepping away from our worldview.

By definition, one's worldview is not something one is aware of on a daily basis. Worldview is an abstraction; it is the name anthropologists give to the complex web of interpretations and responses of a society to its natural and cultural environments. Everything we do as members of our culture is linked to our worldview. Indeed, trying to describe components of one's worldview can be difficult, because we don't think in those terms. My motivations for my daily behaviors

are fairly basic. I do many things simply because I've always done them or they're expected of me or they fit the immediate situation. Rarely do I acknowledge that I do things because they relate to my society's worldview. So a first step in making your own culture an anthropological subject is to try to view it from the outside, as an objective observer.

How does one accomplish this? First, simply start thinking about your society's behaviors and ideas in the same anthropological terms you would apply to a foreign society. In 1956 Horace Miner wrote a piece in *American Anthropologist* called "Body Ritual among the Nacirema" that described and analyzed the meaning of various behaviors related to the human body performed by an exotic culture. It included passages like the following:

> The daily body ritual performed by everyone includes a mouth-rite. Despite the fact that these people are so punctilious about care of the mouth,

---

forensic anthropology A subfield of anthropology applied to legal matters. Usually involved in identifying skeletal remains and assessing the time and cause of death.

experimental archaeology The process of understanding ancient skills and technologies by reproducing them.

the battle. So, using knowledge of such things as stratigraphic relationships, weapon types, architecture, technology, **forensic anthropology,** and some pottery types and Roman coins, Wheeler was able to paint an amazingly clear and detailed picture not only of the way of life of the people of Maiden Castle but also of a particular event that took place nearly 2,000 years ago.

But are those written Roman records bothering you? How about another example from even further back in time? Something *really* old.

Archaeologist Nick Toth has examined some sites in East Africa of early stone tool manufacture dating back millions of years (see Chapter 6). Based on his analysis of these places where our early ancestors produced stone tools, he has determined that the stones were often transported from their natural locations for use later on. Using a technique known as **experimental archaeology,** Toth has made thousands of similar tools and thereby deduced what a manufacture site would have looked like. Noting that some of the actual sites show evidence of only partial stone modification, he has determined that the tools were worked

this rite involves a practice which strikes the uninitiated stranger as revolting. It was reported to me that the ritual consists of inserting a small bundle of hog hairs into the mouth, along with certain magical powders, and then moving the bundle in a highly formalized series of gestures.

Miner is obviously describing how Americans (look at the word *Nacirema* closely) brush their teeth. (Toothbrushes used to be made with hogs' hair bristles, and tooth powders rather than pastes were common in 1956.) The article is humorous and clever, but it also illustrates for many people (including me as a young anthropology student) how our culture is as much a subject for anthropology as any other.

Second, to understand your own culture in anthropological terms, focus on a specific subculture. Each such subculture has its own unique set of beliefs and behaviors—indeed its own unique worldview—but is still a variation on the worldview, beliefs, and behaviors of the larger culture of which it is a part. A geographically large, populous, multicultural, pluralistic society like ours contains many groups worthy of study

as subcultures. For example, there are anthropological descriptions and analyses of religious isolates (such as the Hutterites and Amish), urban street gangs, inner-city ethnic communities, baseball, business corporations, the health food movement, hospital operating rooms, cocktail waitresses, retirement communities, the public school classroom, courtrooms, prisons, tattooing and body piercing, motorcycle societies—I could go on and on. Understanding one or more of these subcultures or practices sheds light on the larger society that gave rise to them and in which they exist.

Knowledge of one's own culture is important simply because all anthropological knowledge helps us understand our species and its behaviors. Such knowledge is also especially valuable on a personal level. There is certainly a satisfaction in seeing one's own culture from a new perspective and understanding something about the origins and meanings of its components. And, for those who wish to contribute to their culture and effect change within it, an anthropological understanding and context is, I think, vital.

on over a period of time. Moreover, by comparing his own with those from actual manufacture sites, he has concluded that some of the variation in tools was the result of specific methods used to produce them. By actually trying out his tools, he has found that some types of tools are better for certain important tasks, especially animal butchering.

So using these and other techniques of archaeology, we can reconstruct events from several hundred, to 2,000, to 2 million years ago. The three examples above, however, are all about rather specific situations— gravestone design, an ancient battle, and very ancient stone tool manufacture. These are just aspects of larger social and cultural contexts. The ultimate goal of archaeology is to reconstruct past cultural *systems* out of such specific pieces of data and analyses. I chose these three stories because they're interesting and memorable and give a general picture of the science of archaeological investigation.

We will see how the basis of archaeological theory—the reflection of cultural systems in material artifacts—has provided us with insight into past cultures and culture in general in some of the following chapters.

CONTEMPORARY ISSUES

Who Owns Archaeological Sites and Their Contents?

Visit any natural history or art museum in a major Western city such as New York, London, or Paris, and you will encounter thousands of cultural artifacts and even human biological remains that were originally found in other countries. In some cases, these items were taken from those countries with permission. In many other cases, the justification for taking them was the cultural dominance of a Western country or the idea that the scientific nature of the museum somehow gave it the right to have, study, and display the items. Recently, many countries have requested the return of such artifacts and remains, and many institutions have complied. It is now generally felt that paleoanthropological and archaeological objects are the possessions of the countries in which they are recovered. In many cases, such objects in fact remain in the appropriate country and must be studied there by foreign scientists.

An example is the famous Ice Man found in an Alpine glacier in 1991—an almost perfectly preserved freeze-dried mummy of a man, along with many of his artifacts, dated to 5,300 years ago. He was found close to the Austrian-Italian border, but because the border was not well marked up in the mountains, it took a while to establish national ownership. The mummy remained for seven years in an Austrian lab, since it appeared at first that he was found in that country. In 1997, however, surveyors determined that he had in fact been located inside the Italian border—by a mere 93 meters (305 feet). He now resides in a museum in Bolzano, Italy.

The situation becomes murkier when debates over ownership involve not geopolitical boundaries but biological and cultural descent. For example, for years in North America, otherwise well-meaning scientists enjoyed the freedom to recover, study, and store or display the skeletal remains of the remote and not-so-remote ancestors of living peoples. Many of the thousands of Native American skeletons and related artifacts housed in museums and at universities were literally exhumed from the graves into which they were placed by members of their societies.

Although these remains have provided much information about the original inhabitants of this continent, Native American groups began to object, for obvious reasons. In 1990 Congress passed the Native American Graves Protection and Repatriation Act (NAGPRA). It says that lineal descendants have a right to the remains of their buried ancestors housed in institutions or discovered on federal or tribal territory. This has led to

SUMMARY

A cultural behavior involves a concept or idea that is shared among members of a population, transmitted extragenetically through learning using symbols, and made possible through artifacts. Culture is the major adaptive mechanism of our species, which we absolutely depend on for our survival. The rudiments of culture can be observed in some other organisms, especially the nonhuman primates. Indeed, chimpanzees who manufacture tools are clearly engaged in cultural behaviors, though these behaviors are not vital to the continuation of their species.

the removal of large collections of human remains and associated artifacts from museums and labs and has made new excavations of Native American remains difficult, if not impossible. Indeed, before naturally shed remains were excluded from NAGPRA regulations, two local tribes demanded the return of some 10,000-year-old human hair found at a site in Montana, hair that could have provided information on the DNA and, thus, on the biological relationships of early Americans.

A well-known example involves the skeletal remains discovered in 1996 in Washington State and commonly known as Kennewick Man. A coalition of Native American tribes from the area laid claim to the 9,000-year-old bones under the terms of NAGPRA. Debate continues but as of this writing, the bones are available for study.

Is there a compromise between honoring the cultural laws and heritage of peoples and providing science with important data—data that may even shed light on the histories of the peoples in question? In the end, each case must be examined and judged on its own merits. Much evidence of early America is in the form of abandoned and naturally covered-over objects and bones, not intentional burials. Such findings cannot be reasonably affiliated with any specific living group and should be freely open to scientific investigation. On the other hand, scientists should no longer go into

clearly identified burial areas armed with shovels and trowels. When ancient bones are uncovered by natural processes or accident (say, during a construction project), the group with which those bones are affiliated may allow scientific information to be gathered before the bones are reburied.

This occurred with the well-known African Burial Ground in New York City. In 1991 construction workers unearthed the graves of some 400 African Americans buried between the late 1600s and 1796. (The whole cemetery, most of which is still under the present city, may contain over 10,000 burials.) Because of the wealth of information that could be gathered from the skeletons and the associated artifacts about an otherwise poorly documented group of people, scientists thoroughly studied the remains. The remains were then reburied with appropriate ceremony.

Whatever the legalities of the individual cases, however, there is one overriding ethical consideration that should guide our actions in these matters: no matter how old (or even from what species) they are, bones were once integral parts of living, breathing, feeling creatures. Artifacts were once important parts of living cultures. Even when we use these things as scientific specimens, they deserve respectful treatment, as do the living peoples and cultures associated with them.

The human brain—the organ that enables us to have culture—may be pictured as having different functional levels, the results of different stages of our evolutionary history. All these levels operate together to produce our basic behavioral repertoire. The thinking part of our brain, our cerebral cortex, is a complex, highly cross-referenced system that allows us to store

data from our memories and experiences and to manipulate those memories to produce the ideas that make culture possible.

Culture is a species characteristic, but individual cultural systems differ greatly. To explain, understand, and analyze a given cultural system requires that we see each system as an integrated set of ideas and behaviors, all of which are related directly or indirectly to the abstract assumptions we call worldview. Worldview in turn may be defined as the collective interpretations of and responses to the natural and cultural environments in which a group of people lives.

The relationship between material culture and the cultural system that designs and uses it is the basis of the specialized area of anthropology called archaeology. By understanding this relationship, archaeologists are able to reconstruct past lifeways and cultural systems and, thus, further expand our knowledge of the evolution and behavior of our species.

QUESTIONS FOR FURTHER THOUGHT

1. Does learning that chimpanzees exhibit behaviors with nearly all the criteria of culture change your view of them? How so? Does your change of view have any practical applications, for example, in terms of using chimps for medical experimentation?

2. My necktie analysis might be rather outdated. Try the same sort of exercise with some other aspect of modern-day culture. What about tattoos, body piercings, or other fashion statements?

3. Think more about the American worldview. What other ideas might describe a typically American worldview? Do you think any aspects of our worldview—perhaps our ideas about size—have changed since the 9/11 attacks on the World Trade Center and the Pentagon?

4. Few, if any, societies are entirely homogenous culturally but instead have regional, class, ethnic, and other subcultures. What subcultures exist in the United States? Do these subcultures have distinct worldviews, or are they variations on a general American worldview?

5. Looting is a major problem in archaeology. In this context, *looting* is defined as the acquisition by amateurs of artifacts for financial gain or for personal collections. But from the perspective of the people who left archaeological remains (and who sometimes *purposely* placed items, as in graves), is there any difference between scientific acquisition and looting? How would you, as an archaeologist, respond? What can archaeologists *do* to clearly distinguish their scientific work from looting?

NOTES, REFERENCES, AND READINGS

The definition of culture at the beginning of this chapter comes from *Cultural Anthropology: A Perspective on the Human Condition*, by Emily Schultz and Robert Lavenda. A nice discussion of the definition of culture appears in *Introducing Cultural Anthropology*, by Roberta Lenkeit.

The emergence of culture from the basic primate behavioral repertoire is the topic of Jane Lancaster's *Primate Behavior and the Emergence of Human Culture*. The question of the presence of culture among the nonhuman primates is addressed in "The Cultures of Chimpanzees," by Andrew Whiten and Christophe Boesch, in the January 2001 *Scientific*

American, and in W. C. McGrew's "Culture in Nonhuman Primates?" in the 1998 *Annual Review of Anthropology*. See also "The Cultured Chimpanzees" by Gayathri Vaidyanathan in the August 18, 2011, issue of *Nature*. More on the behavior of chimpanzees is in Jane Goodall's *Through a Window*.

Carl Sagan won a Pulitzer Prize for his *Dragons of Eden: Speculations on the Evolution of Human Intelligence*. It includes more detail on the structure and function of the human brain and McLean's triune brain model. Another, and more recent, approach to the relationship between the mind and its products is Steven Mithen's *The Prehistory of the*

Mind: The Cognitive Origins of Art, Religion, and Science. I also recommend *How Brains Think,* by William H. Calvin.

Material on the Netsilik can be found in Asen Balikci's *The Netsilik Eskimo.* On the Arctic and Arctic peoples in general, see Barry Lopez's *Arctic Dreams.* The quotes I used are from pages 180 and 181 of that book.

For a good treatment of the history of archaeology, see Brian Fagan's *The Adventure of Archaeology.* For one example of an archaeological adventure, try Nicholas Clapp's *The Road to Ubar: Finding the Atlantis of the Sands.* It's about the discovery of a fabled ancient Arabian city using a combination of old-fashioned archaeology, high-tech satellite imagery, and, maybe, just a touch of Indiana Jones.

The original research and analysis of New England gravestones is in Edwin Dethlefsen and James Deetz's "Death's Heads, Cherubs, and Willow Trees: Experimental Archaeology in Colonial Cemeteries" in *American Antiquity,* volume 31. A popular presentation is Deetz and Dethlefsen's "Death's Head, Cherub, Urn and Willow" in the March 1967 *Natural History.* See also *Gravestones of Early New England and the Men Who Made Them: 1653–1800,* by Harriette Merrifield Forbes. Another example of historical archaeology is Ken Feder's *A Village of Outcasts,* about the archaeology of a remote settlement in Connecticut inhabited by Native Americans,

African American slaves, and European outcasts from 1740 to 1860. Again, the story of Maiden Castle is in the book of the same name, by Sir Mortimer Wheeler.

The analysis of toolmaking by early *Homo* is from Nick Toth's "The Oldowan Reassessed: A Close Look at Early Stone Artifacts" from *Journal of Archaeological Science,* volume 12.

For more detail on the methodology of Archaeology—locating, excavating, and dating sites—see Tom Hester et al., *Field Methods in Archaeology,* seventh edition; Robert Sharer and Wendy Ashmore's *Archaeology: Discovering Our Past;* and Ken Feder's *Linking to the Past.* An excellent collection of thirty-two articles on various aspects of archaeology is Ken Feder's *Lessons from the Past,* and his *Past in Perspective: An Introduction to Human Prehistory* recounts the panorama of human evolution and the evidence used to reconstruct it. The most modern technologies applied to the ancient past are the topic of *Virtual Archaeology: Re-creating Ancient Worlds,* edited by Maurizio Forte and Alberto Siliotti. It uses three-dimensional computer reconstructions of ancient sites as well as striking photographs and diagrams to bring the past to life.

A humorous yet thought-provoking look at what an archaeologist of the future might think of the remains of our culture is David Macauly's *Motel of the Mysteries.*

PART TWO

The Identity and Nature of the Human Species

OUR PLACE IN NATURE

Humans as Primates

CHAPTER CONTENTS Naming the Animals • Into the Trees • Summary • Questions for Further Thought • Contemporary Issues: Should Nonhuman Primates Have Rights? • Notes, References, and Readings

Entomologists study insects. Ichthyologists study fishes. Herpetologists study reptiles. Anthropologists study humans. Although we approach our study of humans in the same general way these other scientists study their organisms, anthropologists are limited by their focus on just a single species, at least just a single living species, *Homo sapiens*. To be sure, humans are a complex enough species to warrant a whole discipline. But to do the job right, we anthropologists need some perspective. We need to see where humans fit in the overall biological scheme of things. We need to be able to compare and contrast humans with other organisms. We need to answer the question of just what the human animal is.

Because all organisms are related on that giant family tree of evolution, there are many groups to which we could compare ourselves. But to narrow it down to the level that will elucidate humans' identity, we should see what group of organisms makes up our local cluster of twigs on that tree. The group of organisms to which humans belong is the primates—the approximately 200 living species that include monkeys, apes, humans, and some other animals you may be less familiar with.

How best to organize this comparison? There are many ways to categorize the features that identify a species, but these seem most relevant and useful to our focus on adaptation in the next four chapters:

1. *Place in nature*—where a species fits into the kingdoms of living things and how it is related to other organisms.
2. *Evolution*—how a species looks and behaves and how those features came to be.
3. *Reproduction*—how a species perpetuates itself (which, as you recall, is what distinguishes and separates one species from another).
4. *Variation*—the nature of a species' biological diversity.

Using these categories, we can then identify our species as the large-brained primate and the sexual primate, and then look at the nature of our biological diversity and the cultural interpretations of that diversity. As you will see, all these topics are intertwined into a single, holistic evolutionary story.

AS YOU READ, CONSIDER THE FOLLOWING QUESTIONS:

1. How does our taxonomic system of classifying and naming species work? How does the Linnaean system differ from the cladistic system?

2. What traits define the primate order?

3. What are the different types of primates, and what traits distinguish them? What is their geographic distribution?

4. What are the characteristics of the human primate?

NAMING THE ANIMALS

Recognition of some relationship among living things is not new. But formalizing this recognition was not always seen as important, even to the emerging science of biology at the beginning of the eighteenth century. After all, plants and animals were then thought to be the unchanging products of divine creation, and an understanding of the evolutionary implications of biological relationships was many years in the future.

Linnaean Taxonomy

One eighteenth-century biologist, however, thought that a formalized view of the relationships was important, even though he thought species were specially created and forever fixed. This was the Swedish botanist Carl von Linné (1707–1778), known to us by his Latinized name, Carolus Linnaeus. Linnaeus sought to devise a system of names that would reflect the relationships among all the plants and animals on earth. The system he came up with is still used today, and it carries more meaning than Linnaeus dreamed it would.

Linnaeus created a system of nested categories of increasing specificity. The largest category contains within it many smaller categories, and so on, down to the most specific, which contains one group—the species. Such a classification system is known as a **taxonomy,** and Linnaeus proposed his taxonomy for living organisms in his *Systema Naturae,* published in final form in 1758.

This system, based on Linnaeus's original scheme, uses seven (and more when needed) basic categories: kingdom, phylum (plural, *phyla*), class, order, family, genus (plural, *genera*), and species. Each organism classified is given a name indicating its place within each of these categories and, thus, its relationship to other organisms. Table 5.1 shows a taxonomy of five familiar species.

taxonomy A classification using nested sets of categories of increasing specificity.

TABLE 5.1 Linnaean Taxonomy of Five Familiar Species

	Human	Chimpanzee	Bonobo	Gorilla	Orangutan
Kingdom	Animalia	Animalia	Animalia	Animalia	Animalia
Phylum	Chordata	Chordata	Chordata	Chordata	Chordata
Class	Mammalia	Mammalia	Mammalia	Mammalia	Mammalia
Order	Primates	Primates	Primates	Primates	Primates
Family	Hominidae	Pongidae	Pongidae	Pongidae	Pongidae
Genus	*Homo*	*Pan*	*Pan*	*Gorilla*	*Pongo*
Species	*sapiens*	*troglodytes*	*paniscus*	*gorilla*	*pygmaeus*

phenetics A classification system based on existing phenotypic features and adaptations.

cladistics A classification system based on order of branching rather than on present similarities and differences.

TABLE 5.2 Linnaean Taxonomy of Humans (with defining criteria)

Kingdom	*Animalia*
	Ingestion
	Movement
	Sense organs
Phylum	*Chordata*
	Internal skeletons
Class	*Mammalia*
	Hair
	Warm-blooded
	Live birth
	Mammary glands
	Active and intelligent
Order	*Primates*
	Arboreal
	Developed vision
	Grasping hands
	Large brains
Family	*Hominidae*
	Habitual bipeds
Genus	*Homo*
	Toolmaking
	Omnivore
Species	*sapiens*
	Brain size 1,000–2,000 ml

All these are obviously members of the animal kingdom and share inclusion in phylum Chordata (essentially, animals with internal skeletons, especially backbones; Table 5.2). All are also obviously mammals, and all are primates (the group we'll describe in detail below). But then, as you can see at a glance, they divide into two intuitive groups: one group comprises humans; the other is made up of the apes, who all share some common phenotypic features. Thus, they separate at the family level. The chimp and bonobo share a genus but differentiate at the species level. So, even if you didn't know these animals, you could tell how they are related, phenotypically, to one another.

Linnaeus thought he was describing a static, divinely created system of living things. We now know that a taxonomy also reflects evolutionary relationships, because the degree of similarity between two organisms is a direct result of the amount of time they have been evolutionarily separated. So, although a taxonomy can't tell us specific dates for branchings, we can infer from it the relative times of these evolutionary events.

Figure 5.1 is a tree showing the relative times of branching for the five primates in the table, inferred from their taxonomic categories. Each taxonomic difference is reflected by a branching point on the tree.

This method of classification is called Linnaean or **phenetic** (for phenotype). There is another system that, in a sense, works the opposite. It is called **cladistics** (clade means branch). Using fossil evidence as well as genetics, it establishes the actual pattern of branching—which may be different from the inferred pattern (Figure 5.2)—and then names the various groups that result from this pattern. Debate continues over which method most accurately reflects biological reality, but that is beyond the scope of this book. Here we will use a phenetic taxonomy of the primates because it best captures the focus on adaptation that we are employing.

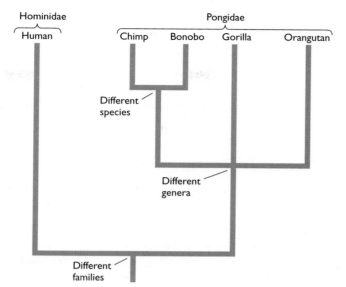

FIGURE 5.1
Evolutionary tree based on phenetic analysis. We infer the evolutionary relationships from the taxonomic classifications.

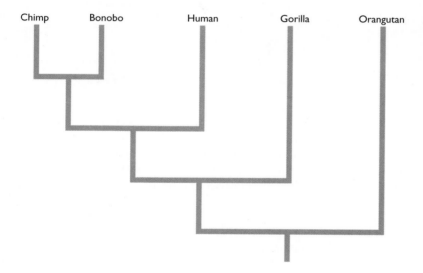

FIGURE 5.2
A tree that is closer to the actual order of branching. Note that the categories of "ape" and "human" disappear here.

A Primate Taxonomy

Now, let's look at a family tree for the primates (Figure 5.3). Notice that we've had to add categories—in this case, suborder and infraorder. We do this to better capture the various actual relationships among organisms. (As an extreme example, look at a taxonomy for insects—it's even more complex.)

Members of the primate order come in two basic types, the two suborders Prosimii and Anthropoidea. The latter suborder has a major

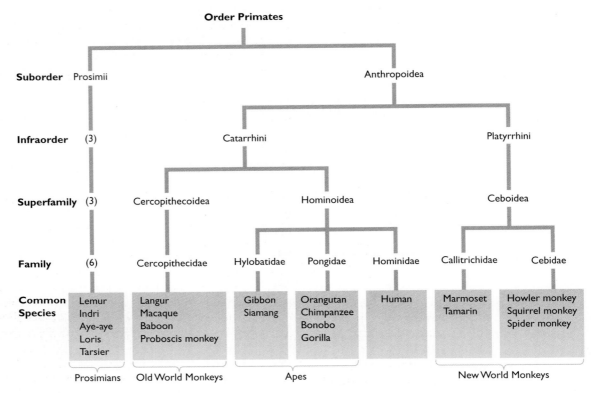

FIGURE 5.3
A primate taxonomy. The numbers in parentheses refer to the number of groups in that category.

division along geographic lines (Figure 5.4): some of these primates, Platyrrhini, inhabit the New World (Central and South America), and the rest, Catarrhini, live in the Old World (Europe, Africa, and Asia). Humans are Old World primates, because that is where our ancestors first evolved and where our evolutionary line has lived for 99 percent of our history. Such a major geographical separation is of obvious evolutionary importance, and thus taxonomic categories must reflect it. Finally, there are groups of families that arrange themselves into larger categories, called superfamilies, based on some shared adaptive characteristics.

Figure 5.3 doesn't include genus and species names for the sake of simplicity. It lists some common names of a few examples in each family. There are, as noted, 200 to 300 living species of primates, classified into about 60 genera. These are not evenly distributed. Family Cercopithecidae has about 15 genera, while Hominidae has only one genus, us, of course, genus *Homo,* the **hominids.**

Now that you understand the mechanics of the taxonomy, let's move to the primates and the definitions of some of those primate taxonomic categories.

hominids Modern humans and African apes and their direct ancestors.

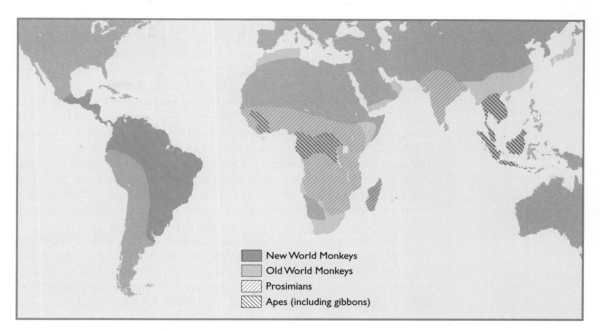

FIGURE 5.4
Distribution of the living
nonhuman primates.

INTO THE TREES

> The organization of the anthropoid *Quadrumana* [four-footed apes]
> justifies the naturalist in placing them at the head of brute creation,
> and placing them in a position in which they, of all the animal
> series, shall be nearest to man.

That statement appeared in the December 1847 issue of the *Boston
Journal of Natural History* in an article containing the first scientific
description of a gorilla. What is interesting is that even twelve years
before Darwin's *Origin of Species,* scientists recognized the similarity
between humans and the apes. In fact, that recognition had been formalized by Linnaeus a hundred years before, when he placed both
humans and the apes and monkeys in the same order, Primates.

So just what is a primate? Why are humans included in this group?
How are humans similar to the other primates? In what ways are we
different?

Primates are members of kingdom Animalia. We have sense organs
and nervous systems, we ingest our food, and we are capable of intentional movement.

Primates are members of phylum Chordata because we have a bony
spine, the evolutionary descendant of a notochord, a long cartilaginous
rod running down the back to support the body and protect the spinal
chord. Chordates with a bony spine are grouped into a subphylum,
Vertebrata. All the species in Table 5.1 are vertebrates.

Primates are mammals because they have hair, can maintain a constant body temperature (commonly called "warm-blooded"), give birth to live young and nourish their young with milk from mammary glands (the characteristic that Linnaeus used to name the group), have an extended period of parental care, and have relatively large, complex brains.

Notice that the items on this list are *not* exclusive to mammals. Birds are also warm-blooded, as are, believe it or not, great white sharks. This trait has also been attributed to some dinosaurs. Some sharks, some bony fishes (like my swordtails), and some snakes give birth to live young. At the same time, some mammals lack this important mammalian trait; the duckbill platypus and the spiny anteater, both from Australia, lay eggs. But otherwise, these two are perfectly good mammals, while snakes, dinosaurs, and birds are not. Only mammals possess that list of traits indicating a certain general type of *adaptation*.

Class Mammalia contains about nineteen existing orders, including bats (which make up one-quarter of all mammalian species); whales and dolphins; seals, sea lions, and walruses; two orders of hoofed mammals; rabbits and hares; rodents; meat eaters; insect eaters; the pouched marsupials; and a group of large-brained tree dwellers with three-dimensional vision and dexterous hands. These are the primates.

The Primate Traits

Comprising 200 to 300 species, the living primates exhibit a great deal of variation in anatomical and behavioral features. Using the following categories, however, we can make some generalizations and point out some of the range of variation.

1. **The Brain.** The two words that describe the primate brain are *large* and *complex*. *Large* is used in a relative sense. A sperm whale, for example, has a brain that weighs 20 pounds and is ten times the size of the average human's. A sperm whale's body, however, is over *five hundred* times larger than ours. Humans have bigger brains than a whale relative to the size of our bodies. Larger *relative* brain size is true of the primates in general.

In addition, the primate brain is complex, especially in the neocortex, the part of the brain responsible for memory, abstract thought, problem solving, and attentiveness (Figure 5.5). In short, primates are intelligent, which may be defined as the relative ability to acquire, store, retrieve, and process information.

2. **Vision.** Vision is primates' predominant sense. Most primates in suborder Anthropoidea see in color. The prosimians, members of the other primate suborder, generally do not see colors; most of them are **nocturnal** (Figure 5.6). All primates, however, have **stereoscopic** vision; that is, they have true depth perception, made possible because the eyes face forward and see the same scene from a slightly different angle.

nocturnal Active at night.

stereoscopic Three-dimensional vision; depth perception.

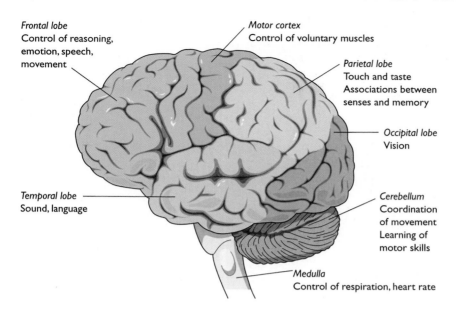

Frontal lobe
Control of reasoning,
emotion, speech,
movement

Motor cortex
Control of voluntary muscles

Parietal lobe
Touch and taste
Associations between
senses and memory

Occipital lobe
Vision

Temporal lobe
Sound, language

Cerebellum
Coordination
of movement
Learning of
motor skills

Medulla
Control of respiration, heart rate

FIGURE 5.5
The human brain and its
major parts and their functions. The lobes and the
motor cortex are all part
of the neocortex.

FIGURE 5.6
The southern lesser bush-baby, or galago, a prosimian primate from Africa. Note the large eyes; large, mobile ears; and moist,
naked nose—all adaptations to a nocturnal way of life.

FIGURE 5.7
Stereoscopic vision. The fields of vision overlap, and the optic nerve from each eye travels to both hemispheres of the brain. The result is true depth perception.

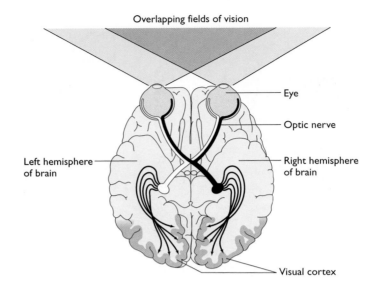

When processed by the brain, this becomes true three-dimensional vision (Figure 5.7). The delicate nerves and muscles of the primate eyes are enclosed and protected within bony sockets. The area of the brain that processes vision, the occipital lobe, is greatly expanded in primates over most other mammals.

3. **The Face.** Primates' faces, as viewed from the side, are relatively flat. Most lack the long, protruding snout of a horse or a dog. As such, primates have a relatively reduced sense of smell. Primates have traded smell for sight. There is, however, some variation here: most nocturnal prosimians have a better sense of smell than the **diurnal** primates. This is reflected by their moist, naked outer nose (see Figure 5.6), as dogs and cats have. Primates tend to have a smaller number of teeth than other mammals and a more generalized dentition; that is, they are geared toward a variety of foods rather than just one type (Figure 5.8).

4. **The Hands and Feet.** Besides stereoscopic vision, the second notable trait of the primates is the grasping ability of their hands and, in many primates, feet. Grasping hands and feet are said to be **prehensile.** The hands of primates also have **opposability,** that is, the thumb can touch, or "oppose," the other fingers on the same hand. There is variation in the dexterity of the hands, but these traits still apply in general to our order. Primates also have nails instead of claws on the tips of their fingers and toes, although some prosimians have retained a grooming claw on a couple of fingers or toes, which is used for cleaning or acquiring food (Figure 5.9).

diurnal Active during the day.

prehensile Having the ability to grasp, especially by wrapping the hand or foot around an object.

opposability The ability to touch the thumb to the tips of the other fingers on the same hand.

FIGURE 5.8
The generalized primate dentition, here in a De Brazza's monkey from Africa. The different tooth forms allow the processing of a variety of foods. As in humans, all Old World monkeys and apes have two incisors, one canine, two premolars, and three molars in each quadrant of the mouth. New World monkeys and prosimians have three premolars in each quadrant.

FIGURE 5.9
The slender loris from India and Sri Lanka, another nocturnal prosimian. The primate prehensile hands and feet are clearly visible. Note also the grooming claw, a prosimian trait, on the toe in the upper part of the picture.

FIGURE 5.10
A tufted, or brown, capuchin monkey from South America, breaking open dead twigs in search of insects. He is gaining extra support from his prehensile tail, which has a hairless patch of skin on the inside surface to enhance friction.

Some species of New World monkeys have a fifth grasping organ, a prehensile tail. Monkeys hanging by their tails have become a stereotyped image of this group of primates, but this is not a general primate trait (Figure 5.10).

5. **The Limbs.** The arms and legs of primates are characterized by great flexibility. The acrobatics of a **brachiating** gibbon or the grace and power of a gymnast on the rings or uneven parallel bars clearly demonstrate this. For primates that clamber about in the trees using both hands and grasping feet, the legs as well are strong and flexible (Figure 5.11). To help support the stresses placed on the arms and shoulders, primates have a well-developed clavicle, or collarbone, that acts as a brace between the shoulder girdle and center of the body. (Feel your own as a perfect example.)

Nearly all primates are **quadrupedal,** that is, their locomotion uses all four limbs, either on the ground or in the trees. Many primates can also stand or even walk on two legs for brief periods, a locomotion pattern called **bipedal** (Figure 5.12).

6. **Reproduction.** Most primate species give birth to one offspring at a time, though some of the South American monkeys and some of the Madagascar lemurs normally produce twins and triplets. As is typical of mammals, primate parents (only the mothers in most species) take an active role in protecting, nurturing, and socializing their young (Figure 5.13). Because of their large, complex brains and because of the importance of learning, young primates are dependent on adults for a long time; just how long depends on the size of the species. The primates, relative to size, have the longest period of **dependency** of any mammal.

brachiating Moving using arm-over-arm swinging.

quadrupedal Walking on all fours.

bipedal Walking on two legs.

dependency Here, the period after birth during which offspring require the care of adults to survive.

FIGURE 5.11
White-handed gibbon from
Southeast Asia suspended
by one arm. Notice the
long, hooklike fingers and
the grasping feet.

7. **Behavior Patterns.** Most primate species live in groups. So do many organisms, but primates are different because they recognize individuals. A primate group is made up of the collective relationships among all individuals who are members. As physical evidence of this, primates are among the most colorful of mammals, and most of the color patterns appear on their faces. One primate species even purposely enhances the colors on its face (see Figure 7.7). So the attention of one primate to another is drawn to the face, to the primate's identity as an individual.

In some primates, each individual may have a rather specific status within the group. Some have more social power and influence than

FIGURE 5.12
A bonobo standing bipedally. He is collecting and carrying stalks of sugarcane in his hands, now freed from locomotor activities.

dominance hierarchy Social ranking based on individual differences.

others. They are said to be dominant, and a structure based on the relative power and influence of a group's individuals is called a **dominance hierarchy.**

Primates maintain their social groups through communication. They have large repertoires of vocalizations, facial expressions, and body gestures. Touch is also an important form of communication and often

FIGURE 5.13
A gorilla female and her young. Primates have an extended period of dependency, and thus parents (usually the mothers) take an active and long-term role in the care and nurturing of their offspring.

FIGURE 5.14
Chimps grooming, an activity that rids them of dirt and parasites and, more important, helps maintain group unity and harmony.

takes the form of **grooming**, an activity that serves the practical purpose of removing dirt and parasites but also acts as a means of reassurance to maintain group harmony and unity (Figure 5.14).

Given this general set of characteristics, and keeping with our theme of adaptation, what can we say about the adaptation of the primate

grooming Cleaning the fur of another animal, which promotes social cohesion.

TABLE 5.3 The Features of the Human Primate

Brain	Vision	Face	Hands/Feet	Limbs	Reproduction	Behavior
1,000–2,000 ml	As in anthropoids	Flat	No prehensile feet	Arms most flexible	Longest period of dependency	Culture
3 times expected size			Most dexterous hands	Habitual bipedalism	Differences in sexuality*	

*See Chapter 7.

order? The basic primate environment is **arboreal**—adapted to life in the trees. To be sure, several species—gorillas and baboons—spend more time on the ground, and we humans are thoroughly terrestrial. But most primates spend most of their time in the trees, and the primate traits we just described all evolved as responses to an arboreal environment. Even the partially and completely terrestrial primates possess features that are variations on this arboreal theme. Thus,

> A primate is a mammal adapted to an arboreal environment through well-developed vision, manual dexterity, and large, complex brains that rely on learned behavior. The latter is aided by the birth of few offspring and the direct and extensive care of those offspring during a long period of dependency while they are socialized into groups based on differential relationships among individuals.

The Human Primate

Each species of primate has its own version of the basic primate adaptive theme. What is ours? Let's repeat the seven categories we used above (Table 5.3).

1. **The Brain.** The human brain is the largest primate brain, both absolutely and relatively. Brains are measured in cubic centimeters (cc) or milliliters (ml). The brain of an average gorilla, the largest living primate, is about 500 ml (about the size of one and a half cans of soda). The average human brain is 1,450 ml. In fact, humans have brains three times the size one would predict for a primate of our body weight. Thus, based on our definition of intelligence, we are clearly the most intelligent of the primates.

2. **Vision.** Human eyes are typical for diurnal primates. The world we see is the same as that viewed by monkeys and apes.

3. **The Face.** The human face is among the flattest of primate faces, and human teeth are among the most generalized for processing a variety of foods. Our sense of smell is probably about the same as that of the anthropoid primates.

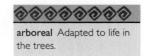

arboreal Adapted to life in the trees.

4. **The Hands and Feet.** The human hand has the longest thumb and thus the most opposability and most precise grip. Our manual dexterity, also involving enlarged areas of the brain, is the greatest of any primate. Our feet, of course, have no prehensile ability whatever because we use them for walking on the ground.

5. **The Limbs.** Human arms are the most flexible among the primates, being entirely freed from locomotor activities and therefore available for a multitude of other purposes. Our legs are less flexible but are longer and stronger than our arms. All this is because humans are *habitually* bipedal, the only primate with this locomotor behavior. In fact, bipedalism was the first human characteristic to evolve (see Chapter 6).

6. **Reproduction.** Humans normally give birth to a single offspring (twins occur in about 1 of every 250 births). Of all the primates, our young take the longest time to mature and so have the longest period of dependency. Chimps, for example, reach sexual maturity in nine years and physical maturity in twelve; for humans, the averages are thirteen and twenty-one. We are born far more helpless than most other primates. In addition, there are important differences in our sexual behaviors, which we will take up in Chapter 7.

7. **Behavior Patterns.** Like most Old World primates, humans live in societies that are based on the collective conscious responses of a group of individuals. The difference is that our groups are structured and maintained by cultural values—ideas, rules, and behavioral norms that we have created and shared through a complex communication system, the topic of Chapter 11 (Figure 5.15).

In the next chapter we will take a look at how our rather odd terrestrial, bipedal, big-brained version of the primate adaptive theme evolved.

SUMMARY

Using the taxonomic system created by Linnaeus in the eighteenth century for classifying living organisms, we may see humans as animals, vertebrates, mammals, and, most important, primates. Primates may be generally defined as large-brained, tree-dwelling mammals with three-dimensional vision and grasping hands that produce few offspring at a time but take extended and direct care of those off-spring, preparing them to live in groups.

Like each of the existing primate species, the human primate exhibits its own unique version of the primate theme. Humans have extremely large brains with the ability to create cultures with complex symbolic communication systems, are completely terrestrial, and, unlike all other primates, are habitually bipedal. We also display some differences in our sexual behaviors that are connected to these other characteristics.

FIGURE 5.15
Renaissance engraving by Albrecht Dürer of the expulsion of Adam and Eve from the Garden of Eden. This engraving shows our species' general physical features, the differences between the sexes, and the importance of symbolic meaning.

QUESTIONS FOR FURTHER THOUGHT

1. All living species have evolved from common ancestors that might have looked quite different. Birds have evolved from dinosaurs. Humans evolved from apes. But does this mean the cardinal at your feeder is a dinosaur? Are humans apes? How far can we take such categories in our popular nomenclature? Do categories that reflect evolutionary history violate reality?

2. The term *animal rights* is often interpreted to mean that advocates suggest such things as giving chimpanzees the right to vote! This, of course, is ridiculous, but what sorts of rights do you think are reasonable? Do these rights apply to all nonhumans equally? What criteria might be used for dispensing rights to different groups of nonhumans? How might rights be applied in some real-world circumstances?

CONTEMPORARY ISSUES

Should Nonhuman Primates Have Rights?

This question concerns one of today's most contentious issues: Do animals share with us any of our basic rights, and do they, consequently, deserve considerations equal to those accorded humans? Opinions on this issue vary enormously. Some animal-rights advocates endorse the view that we should not consider animals as property and so should treat them as independent, autonomous individuals and not in any way exploit them. A letter to my local newspaper represents the other extreme. The writer claimed that animals lack souls and brains and that God put animals on earth, among other reasons, to entertain people at circuses and provide fur coats for women so "men's spirits would be uplifted" seeing them.

Ideas on the subject vary even more when put into actual practice. Many supporters of some form of animal rights adamantly refuse to eat mammals or birds but continue to eat seafood— apparently drawing some sort of ethical line between warm-blooded and cold-blooded creatures. Many who are sickened at the sight of a fur coat still wear leather shoes. Hunters easily justify killing wild creatures for sport while, at the same time, treating their hunting dogs as members of the family. Veterinary researchers, interested in promoting the health of animals in general, will subject some animals to experimentation and surgery. Clearly, this is a complicated issue involving many aspects of a thinking person's moral, emotional, and material life.

The question is perhaps most profound and intense with regard to our closest relatives, the nonhuman primates, especially the apes. These species have always struck us as being very much like our own, probably because, as we've learned in recent years, we share with some apes the vast majority of our genes. The chimpanzee, bonobo, and human share a recent common ancestor. Only 5 million years ago, we and they were the same creature.

Some have claimed that this genetic closeness itself makes obvious the need to extend basic human rights to apes. But this brings up the problem of where to draw the line. *Is* there a line? Chimps and humans are by one measure 98.5 percent genetically similar. The orangutan shares about 96 percent of our genetic material by the same measure. Is that enough dissimilarity to warrant doing things to orangs that we would not do to a human? What about monkeys, which are even less genetically similar? or prosimians? or nonprimates?

The detailed genetic data are, in fact, not relevant to this issue, but there *are* relevant differences as well as similarities that can be considered. Indeed, the intellectual differences between the apes and us are certainly relevant in some regards. No one, for example, would seriously suggest giving bonobos the right to vote. Yet we must take into account our physiological similarities. Experimenting on an ape is the same as experimenting on a human in terms of physical and emotional stress and pain. The reason apes are used as human surrogates in medical experiments— their extreme similarity to us—is the very reason we might consider not so using them. What we know factually about the anatomy, physiology, and behavior of apes supports such a view.

Many people (me included) constantly struggle with the emotional, philosophical, and practical questions involved in this issue. Even those who agree that some human rights should be extended to apes and other animals must still cope with such moral matters as balancing our needs against theirs in such areas as medical research, habitat destruction, and a diet that includes meat. But—especially after considering the question from the point of view of our closest biological relatives—the one thing we cannot do is ignore this issue.

NOTES, REFERENCES, AND READINGS

An excellent book on the primates is Noel Rowe's *The Pictorial Guide to the Living Primates,* a beautifully illustrated, up-to-date, and informative reference to all living primate species. A collection of articles covering primate taxonomy, evolution, behavior, and conservation is *Primates in Perspective,* edited by Christina Campbell, Agustín Fuentes, Katherine MacKinnon, Melissa Panger, and Simon Bearder.

A comprehensive and readable book comparing humans with other primates is Richard Passingham's *The Human Primate.*

For more on the behavior of our closest primate relatives, see Jane Goodall's *Through a Window: My Thirty Years with the Chimpanzees of Gombe,* Dian Fossey's *Gorillas in the Mist,* Biruté Galdikas's *Reflections of Eden: My Years with the Orangutans of Borneo,* and Frans de Waal's *Bonobo: The Forgotten Ape,* featuring Frans Lanting's wonderful photos.

For more on some taxonomic considerations—and the topic of the first question above—see Jonathan Marks's *What It Means to Be 98% Chimpanzee,* especially chapter 2.

Some good references regarding the "Contemporary Issues" topic of animal rights are *Created from Animals,* by James Rachels; *Animal Rights and Human Morality,* by Bernard Rollin; *Animal Experimentation: The Moral Issues,* edited by Robert Baird and Stuart Rosenbaum; and, focusing on the apes, *The Great Ape Project,* edited by Paola Cavalieri and Peter Singer. For a slightly different take, see "Save the Apes from the Ape Rights Activists!" by Jonathan Marks in the December 2006 *Anthropology News.*

EVOLUTION

The Bipedal, Large-Brained Primate

Clearly, the feature that distinguishes humans from our closest relatives, the African apes, is our big brain—three times the size, on average, of theirs and three times the size that one would expect for a primate of our body mass. This fact led the earliest seekers of human fossils, in the nineteenth century, to assume that the big brain was the *first* human trait to evolve and that the first human fossils would be, essentially, apes with big brains. Exploiting this expectation, a famous fraud was committed in Piltdown, England, in the early years of the twentieth century, when someone buried the jaw of an orangutan and some cranial bones of a modern human. The bones were then "discovered" and, because they fit the expectation, were named "Eoanthropus," the "dawn man," and were fairly well accepted. Only forty years later was Piltdown Man shown to be a fake.

In the meantime, however, many real fossils from Africa showed that another characteristic human trait was the first to evolve. This was our habitual upright stance, our bipedal posture and locomotion. Though the details are still under investigation, it's clear that bipedalism preceded the enlargement of the hominid brain by millions of years. The evolution of bipedalism and how it set the stage for the evolution of the large-brained primate are the topics of this chapter.

AS YOU READ, CONSIDER THE FOLLOWING QUESTIONS:

1. What do we know about the evolutionary history of the primates in general?

2. When and under what circumstances do we think the evolution of the hominids began? Specifically, why did bipedalism evolve?

3. What do we currently know about the evolution of the hominids, particularly the members of our genus, *Homo,* the large-brained primate?

OUT OF THE TREES

Primate Evolution

Fossils representing the precursors of the primates may go back before the extinction of the dinosaurs 65 million years ago (mya). Some primatelike teeth and bones found in Montana and Wyoming are dated from 65 to 60 mya, but the first undisputed primates appear about 55 mya. Their fossils are found in North America, Europe, Asia, and Africa, continents that at that time were in different geographic positions than they are today (Figure 6.1).

These early primates, despite the primate arboreal theme, may not themselves have been arboreal. Rather, the primate hallmarks of prehensile hands and feet and stereoscopic vision may have evolved to aid in leaping through dense undergrowth and to promote fruit eating and the hunting of insects. As the primates continued to evolve, these basic traits proved a useful adaptive response to a more generalized life in the trees (and even, of course, set the stage for one group of terrestrial bipedal primates).

It appears the earliest primates comprised three groups, one becoming extinct (Figure 6.2). By 40 mya, early monkeys appeared in the Old World. They expanded and began to outcompete the earlier prosimians, pushing them into marginal areas. Most prosimians now live—as endangered species—on the island of Madagascar (see Figure 5.4).

Later the Eastern and Western Hemispheres (the New World and Old World) became completely separate (see Figure 6.1), dividing the early primates into two geographical groups. Apes appear in the fossil record about 23 mya. At first they were monkeylike but with a few anatomical details that foreshadowed later, more typical apes' larger bodies and larger brains, and no tails. Between 23 and 5 mya, there were an estimated thirty or more types of apes throughout Europe, Africa, and Asia.

We are most interested in the early African apes because it is from one of them that the hominids evolved. Unfortunately, the fossil record of the African apes is scanty until about 7 mya when we find the possible first hominids. The early hominids can be exemplified by one of the most famous hominid fossils, popularly known as Lucy, found in Ethiopia and dated to 3.2 mya (Figure 6.3).

Lucy (named after the Beatles' "Lucy in the Sky with Diamonds," which was playing the night her discoverers examined her skeleton) is remarkable because, as old as her fossilized bones are, she is 40 percent complete, with all parts of the body, except the cranium, well represented. Lucy was a female who stood about 3 feet 8 inches and weighed around 65 pounds. She and other members of her species (over 300 specimens have been found so far, representing individuals of both sexes) had the brain size of a chimpanzee and in many respects resembled chimps. Their faces jutted forward, a trait called **prognathism,** and their canine teeth were pointed like an ape's. There is, in some individuals, the hint of a bony crest running along the top of the skull from front to back for the attachment of a major chewing muscle. Gorillas have such crests. The arms were proportionately

More than 200 mya

180 mya

65 mya

Present

FIGURE 6.1

The relative position of the continents over the past 200 million years. Continental drift occurs as the motion of the molten rock in the interior of the earth causes the individual plates that make up the earth's crust to change shape and location. This in turn causes the continents—those parts of the crust that protrude above sea level—to shift.

prognathism The jutting forward of the lower face and jaw area.

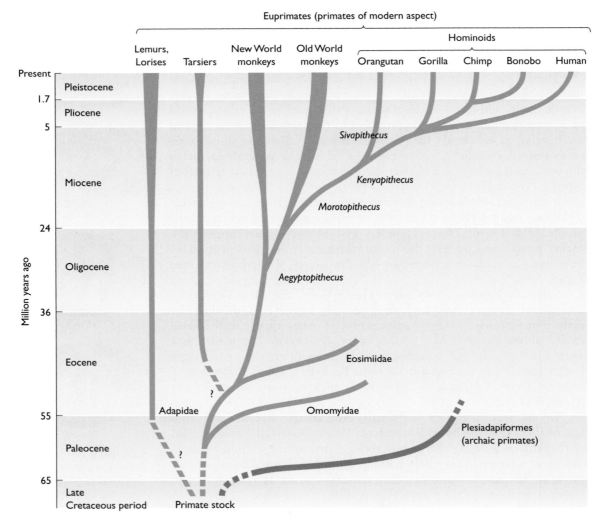

FIGURE 6.2
Simplified evolutionary tree for the primates, with major geological epochs and dates. Question marks and dashed lines indicate insufficient data to establish evolutionary relationships. This tree represents one of several possible interpretations.

longer than in modern humans and the legs relatively shorter. The bones of the arms and shoulders show evidence of heavy musculature. The hands and feet are long and show curvature of the finger and toe bones.

But Lucy and her kin walked bipedally. The bones of the pelvis and legs clearly show this, as does the large hole in the base of the skull from which the spinal cord emerges and around which the top of the spine attaches. This hole is located underneath the skull, rather than in back, and thus indicates a creature that faced forward while its spine dropped straight down. Lucy is therefore considered a

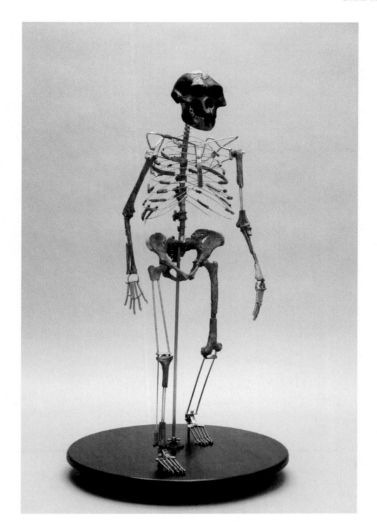

FIGURE 6.3
A reconstruction of the 3.2-million-year-old skeleton of Lucy (technically *Australopithecus afarensis*), the most complete early hominid fossil found to date. Her pelvis and leg bones are those of a biped, but otherwise she was quite apelike (see Figure 6.7).

member of family Hominidae, traditionally the only primate group that is habitually bipedal.

The Evolution of Bipedalism

So, bipedalism was the first hominid feature to evolve—millions of years before our big brains. This leads us to question, then, *why* bipedalism first evolved. What environmental circumstances would

FIGURE 6.4
The climatic zones of Africa today, except for the large deserts of the north and south, were similar when hominid evolution began 5 mya.

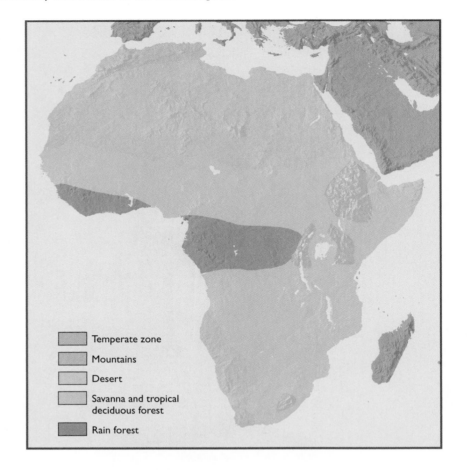

Temperate zone

Mountains

Desert

Savanna and tropical deciduous forest

Rain forest

have selected for that form of locomotion while leaving the other apelike traits pretty much intact?

The Benefits of Bipedalism Early hominid fossils, found in eastern and southern Africa, have long been linked to the **savannas**—the open plains of central and southern Africa (Figure 6.4) that began expanding because of climatic changes about 5 mya. In that environment, it is hypothesized, bipedalism served four functions. *First,* and probably most important, it freed the forelimbs to carry things, including offspring and food. *Second,* by elevating the head, bipedalism aided early hominids' ability to find food and see danger. *Third,* the vertical orientation helped cool the body by exposing a smaller surface area to the intense equatorial rays of the sun and by placing more of the body above the ground to catch cooling air currents. *Fourth,* bipedalism, although requiring a great deal of energy for running, was very

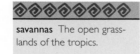

savannas The open grasslands of the tropics.

efficient and required less energy for long periods of steady walking. With food less concentrated on the open plains and with dangerous animals around eager to make a meal out of a small primate, the ability to search for food while possibly carrying one's offspring and to carry the food back to a safe location would certainly have bene-fited early hominids.

Two Problems *First,* if you look back to Figure 5.12, you see that bonobos, one of our two closest relatives, are at least occasionally bipedal and that they live in very dense forests, not vast, open savannas. Notice, too, that the bonobo in the photograph is carrying something.

Second, recent analyses have shown that some of the earliest hominid fossils are from creatures who resided in forests and not on the open plains. And other research has indicated that there was no abrupt change in ancient East Africa from forest to savanna; instead, the change resulted in a mixture (or mosaic) of forest and open areas. Moreover, climatic changes were taking place, beginning 5 mya, in an increasing range of variation, from cool to hot and moist to dry. This led to great fluctuations in water and vegetation.

In conclusion, then, it seems that the evolution of bipedalism—with the retention of long, strong arms and powerful shoulders—was an adaptation to living in an environment of *both* arboreal and terrestrial settings, giving our earliest ancestors great adaptive flexibility. As we will see, when the open plains later became the hominids' main habitat, arboreal adaptations disappeared and bipedalism became our adaptive focus.

The Early Hominids

Beginning with the first evidence of habitual bipedalism, *perhaps* 7 to 6 mya, the hominid fossil record becomes more complete and more complex. Although there is much information, there is really no agreement on how it all goes together. Especially at issue is the question of just how many species of early hominids there were. Some paleoanthropologists (called *lumpers*) group fossils together into a small number of species. Others (called *splitters*) emphasize the dif-ferences among fossil specimens. It is beyond the scope of this book to cover all the details of the debate, but Figure 6.5 will give you an idea of the maximum number of potential early hominid species cur-rently recognized.

The Earliest Possible Hominids There are several candidates for "first hominid," depending on one's interpretation of the existing data. (Figure 6.6 maps the important fossil sites in Africa.) These are the genera to the left in Figure 6.5: *Sahelanthropus, Orrorin,* and *Ardipithecus.* The

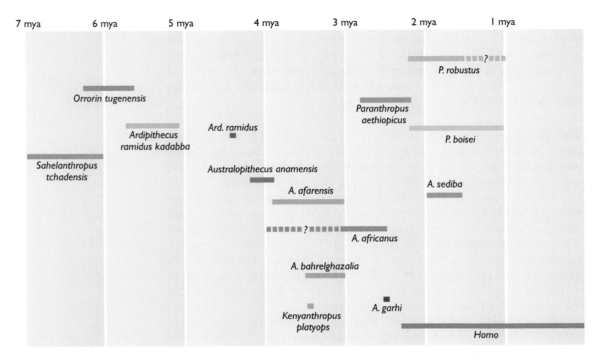

FIGURE 6.5

The maximum number of early hominid species that have been suggested by some authorities. Others lump some of these together or reject some as hominids. (When a genus name has been established, it may be abbreviated. Thus *Ard.* stands for *Ardipithecus,* and *A.* for *Australopithecus.*) Some of these forms are discussed in the text.

first two are still controversial at the moment, with some evidence for bipedalism, but their identity as hominids is not well agreed upon by all authorities. *Aridipithecus* is clearly a biped, and its place in the human family tree is fairly well established.

But consider this possibility: Perhaps all hominids were bipeds but not all bipeds were necessarily hominids. Given the association of bipedalism with a mixed adaptation to a mixed environment, perhaps it evolved, to varying degrees, more than once but persisted only in the line that led to us. Perhaps, then, those early forms are bipedal apes, and are not on our evolutionary branch, as is commonly supposed. One of them is probably a direct ancestor, but not all of them. As we'll see later on, bipedalism comes in different expressions, and the type of bipedalism associated with our genus, *Homo,* is distinct.

More Definite Hominids The earliest *well-accepted* hominid fossils are placed in genus *Australopithecus* ("southern ape") and are often divided into as many as six species. The famous Lucy belongs to this group. *Australopithecus* fossils have been found in Ethiopia, Kenya, Tanzania, Chad, and South Africa and are dated at 4.2 to 2.3 mya. Their bones allowed full upright walking, but their face was apelike,

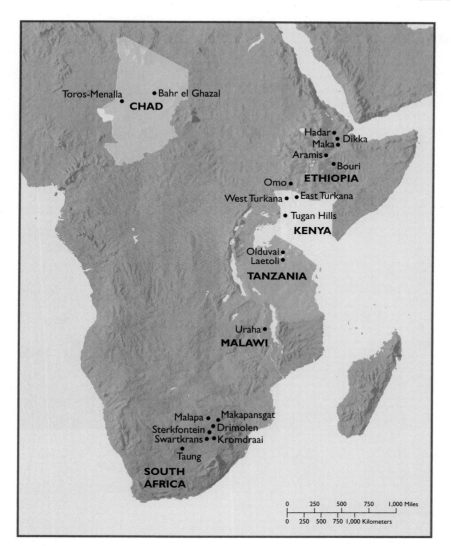

FIGURE 6.6
Map of major early
hominid sites.

their brain size approximated that of the chimpanzee (around 450 ml), they weighed an average of 105 pounds, and their arms were long and heavily muscled (Figure 6.7). They were probably well adapted to both arboreal and terrestrial environments, and microscopic analysis of their teeth indicates a mixed-vegetable diet of fruits and leaves. *Australopithecus* remains the best candidate for the ancestor of later hominids (Figure 6.8).

Around 3 mya there is evidence of a drying trend in Africa that caused further decline of the forests and an expansion of the savannas. The fossil record shows two responses to this environmental change.

FIGURE 6.7
A reconstruction of an australopithecine pair, from a display at the American Museum of Natural History in New York. These figures are based on analyses of the remains of members of Lucy's species (see Figure 6.3). Note the retention of apelike physical features combined with complete bipedalism.

FIGURE 6.8
A generalized evolutionary tree for the early hominids. There are at least six specific models that differ in number of genera, number of species for each genus, and precise evolutionary relationships. Most of them, however, are versions of this basic model.

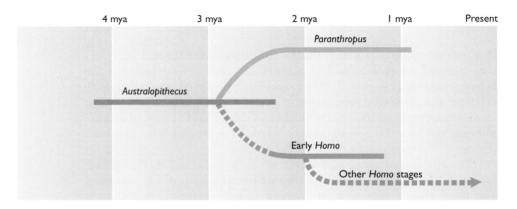

FIGURE 6.9
An example of a robust early hominid often included in genus *Paranthropus*. Note the large crest on top of the skull for the attachment of chewing muscles, as well as the large cheekbones and the broad, dished-out face—all evidence of a diet of tough, gritty vegetable matter. This specimen, from Kenya, shows the most extreme expression of these robust traits.

One comes in the form of the so-called robust early hominids, placed by many scientists in their own genus, *Paranthropus* ("nearly human"). As many as three species have been recognized. Their fossils have been found in Ethiopia, Kenya, Tanzania, and South Africa and are dated at 2.8 to 1 mya. The word *robust* applies not to body size or shape. In these features and their brain size they resemble *Australopithecus*. Instead, *robust* refers to all the features involved in chewing (Figure 6.9). Robust species have crests along the top of the skull for the attachment of important chewing muscles; broad, dished-out faces; large cheekbones; huge lower jaws; and large back teeth. These traits all point to a diet of large amounts of vegetable matter with an emphasis on hard, tough, gritty items such as seeds, nuts, hard fruits, roots, and tubers—the kinds of foods more likely to be found in open areas. Microscopic analysis of tooth wear confirms this. The genus's main adaptation seems to have been to the open plains, achieved by the evolution of chewing features adapted to the kinds of plant foods found there.

The First Members of Genus *Homo*

There was a second evolutionary response among the hominids to the expansion of the savannas (see Figure 6.8). This was the beginning of the genus *Homo*, to which we modern humans belong. Early members of this genus, comprising one or two species, are found in Ethiopia, Kenya, Tanzania, and possibly South Africa and are dated at 2.3 to 1.2 mya. They retain the body size and possibly the long, powerful arms of *Australopithecus* and *Paranthropus*, but their crania show important differences. Their faces are much flatter, their foreheads less sloping, and their brains much bigger. From an average brain size of about 480 ml for all the other early hominids early *Homo* jumps to an average of 680 ml, with a maximum of 800 (Figure 6.10). (For comparison, the modern human range is 1,000 to 2,000 ml.) It is this evidence for the beginning of a trend to increased brain size that prompts us to classify these fossils in our genus.

The First Stone Tools   What were they doing with those big brains? We can speculate that they were better able to perform intellectual tasks—learning about their environment, altering their behaviors to fit specific circumstances and address specific problems, manipulating social situations, and forming more conscious and intimate relationships with other members of their group—some of the attributes of culture (see Chapter 4). Unfortunately, these behaviors do not leave direct remains. We do, however, have archaeological evidence of the brain power of early *Homo* in the form of the tools they made.

FIGURE 6.10

An example of early *Homo* from Kenya. Note, relative to the other early hominid the flatter face, less sloping forehead, more rounded brain-case, and generally smoother contours. The brain of this individual is estimated at about 775 ml, notably larger than that of *Australopithecus* or *Paranthropus*.

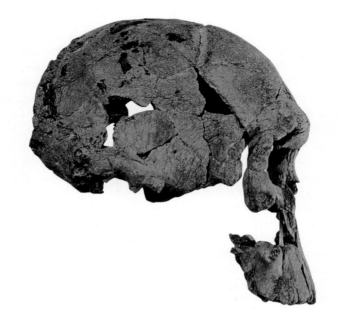

FIGURE 6.11
A sample of Oldowan tools, named after Olduvai Gorge, Tanzania, a famous fossil site. The stone at the upper left was used unmodified. The two at the lower right are flake tools. The rest are core tools, from which flakes have been taken off to create sharp edges. A major use of such tools may have been the quick dismembering of animal carcasses. (For scale, the tool at the upper right is a little larger than a tennis ball.)

It is likely that the other early hominid species also made tools. After all, chimpanzees make simple tools (see Chapter 4). The materials the chimps use, however, would not leave evidence of their use as tools. But early hominids made tools from stone (Figure 6.11). Stone tools last—for millions of years—and provide evidence that they *were* tools.

Stone tools have been crucial to humans, serving as the major type of tool for 99 percent of human cultural history. When they were first invented, around 2.6 mya, stone tools reflected a jump in our ancestors' conceptual and actual control over their environment. There is nothing in an unmodified stone to suggest that sharp edges or points can be found within it. It takes a leap of imagination to understand this and to picture the process needed to produce those edges or points—hitting the stone with another, harder stone at just the right angle and force.

These stone tools are probably a major reason why genus *Homo* persisted while the other hominid genera of Africa became extinct. And they are important to the anthropologist because they are often the only remnant of a past culture that is well preserved. Much of what we know about the adaptations and movement of peoples around the world, and of their cultural systems, is based on our analyses of their stone artifacts. These stone tools come in an incredible array of varieties over space and time. We can, however, make some generalizations about them.

Making Stone Tools   For the most part, stone tools are made of rock that, when struck, shock waves travel through and produce a fracture that splits off a flake. The size and shape of the flakes are determined by how hard, with what, and at what angle the stone is struck. Flint, or chert—a type of sedimentary rock—flakes well and was used extensively for tools, as was obsidian, a volcanic glass.

FIGURE 6.12
Flint knapping—striking a piece of flint with a hammer stone to fracture off a flake of desired size and shape. Notice the flakes on the ground from previous strikes.

To take flakes off a core, you have to hit the core with another hard object, usually another stone. If that sounds simple, it's not. One must understand the nature of the core material and of the tool one is striking it with (Figure 6.12). Manual dexterity is important, and practice, as always, is required for anything close to perfection.

How do we know, especially with these early, relatively simple tools, that they *are* tools? Couldn't they be rocks that were fractured naturally? For one thing, when flint is struck hard enough to detach a flake—something that rarely occurs by chance in nature—the blow leaves a convex surface on the flake called the **bulb of percussion.** Below this there are often concentric rings, like ripples in water, that represent the shock waves. On the core, there is a corresponding concave surface. Naturally fractured stones rarely exhibit these rings, nor do they show a pattern of flakes. Even in some of the simplest stone tools (see Figure 6.11), one can see the plan of the manufacturer, the goal of creating a sharp edge or a point.

As technological skills improved, other implements were used to gain more control over the shape of the flakes being removed. A piece of bone, wood, or antler could be used to make a more precise strike

bulb of percussion A convex surface on a flake caused by the force used to split the flake off. Rarely found in a natural break.

FIGURE 6.13
Pressure flaking by pushing a piece of antler against the edge of a core tool. The core is held in a piece of leather to support it and to protect the toolmaker's hand.

or to **pressure flake** the core, which meant taking off smaller flakes by pushing the tool against the side of the stone (Figure 6.13). Later still, two tools were sometimes used to acquire even more control—a piece of antler or bone became a chisel when struck by a rock used like a hammer. Finally—a feature associated with early farming societies—stones were ground into the desired shape using a rough rock such as sandstone to make a smoother and more durable cutting edge. This practice also allowed people to choose tougher, coarser-grained rocks that did not necessarily have the flaking characteristics of flint.

The Lives of Early Homo   What sort of work were these tools used for? Many of their probable uses—such as sharpening branches for crude spears or sticks for digging up roots, or cutting plant material for food—have left no concrete evidence. But one use *has* left evidence, and it may provide the key to explain why *Homo* survived while the other genera of early hominids became extinct. It appears that stone tools allowed early *Homo* to better exploit a source of food that would have entailed greater difficulty and danger—the scavenged meat and bones from the carcasses of dead animals.

Scavenging the carcasses of large savanna ungulates (antelopes and their kin) would have been difficult. These animals would have been killed by dangerous predators such as lions, leopards, and cheetahs and scavenged by dangerous meat eaters such as hyenas, jackals, and wild dogs. The inherent danger probably made this source of food rare

pressure flake Taking a flake off a core by pushing a wood, bone, or antler tool against the stone.

among early hominids until they had a means to quickly cut up a carcass so they could then carry the parts to a safer location for further processing and eating.

Evidence suggests that scavenging was a major use of stone tools by early *Homo*. Animal bones found at early *Homo* sites in Tanzania were mostly lower-leg bones of antelopes, the only parts left after a large carnivore has finished eating. Such bones, however, are rich in marrow. Scientists reason that early *Homo* cut these parts away from the remainder of the carcass, took them to a safe location, cut off what little meat remained, and then broke the bones open for the nutritious marrow inside. Microscopic analysis of some of the animal bones reveals cut marks from stone tools. Sometimes these cut marks overlie carnivore tooth marks, showing that the carnivores had killed and scavenged the animal first.

So it is a reasonable scenario that early *Homo,* in the face of expanding savannas and shrinking forests, used stone tools—made possible by their bigger brains—to exploit a new and reliable source of food. There were nearly always vast herds of grass eaters around, many of whom would die natural deaths or be killed by predators. Stone tools made the acquisition of this food source quicker, safer, and more efficient.

We picture, then, early *Homo* living in small cooperative groups, maybe family groups, foraging on the savannas for plant foods and always on the lookout for a large dead animal, maybe watching for a group of scavengers gathered on the ground or a flock of vultures circling overhead. Their big brains allowed them to better understand their environment and to manipulate it, making imaginative and technologically advanced tools from stone, which helped provide them with an important new source of food. The adaptive themes of bipedalism, large brains, complex social organization, and tool technology were established in this primate evolutionary line and set the stage for the rest of hominid evolution.

AROUND THE WORLD

The adaptations of early *Homo* proved so successful that hominid evolution seems to accelerate about 2 mya. Within about 800,000 years of the first evidence of stone tools in Africa, fossils of *Homo* are found as far away as Georgia (the former republic of the Soviet Union), China, and Java.

But if there is little agreement among anthropologists about the taxonomy and relationships during the first 2.5 million years of hominid evolution, there is even less agreement regarding the latest 2 million years—the evolution of genus *Homo*. Some suggest a single species of *Homo* during this time. Others see as many as ten species or more. The

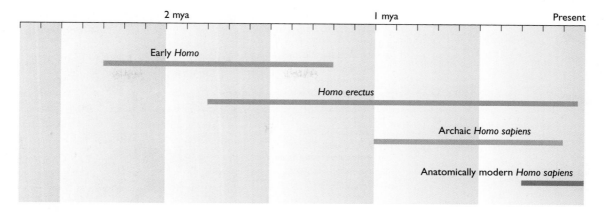

2 mya   I mya   Present

Early *Homo*

Homo erectus

Archaic *Homo sapiens*

Anatomically modern *Homo sapiens*

FIGURE 6.14
The stages in the evolution of genus *Homo*. There are major disagreements as to how many species are represented and how they are related to one another. The branching pattern, in other words, is a matter of intense debate.

debate over these models is at times rather heated, because what is at issue is the very identity of our species, *Homo sapiens.* Under the first model, all the fossil hominids I'm about to describe belong to one 2-million-year-old species that displays variation over time but has always maintained enough gene flow to remain a single species. According to the second model, *Homo sapiens* is only the latest of many products of speciation in the hominid fossil record, with all previous species now extinct. Under this model, we are a young species—around 200,000 years old.

The details of this debate are complex and change with every new fossil find and each new analysis. But in many ways the outcome of the debate will not change the basic story of our genus's adaptive evolution. For this section, then, I will discuss the groups of fossils of our genus as three "stages" defined by physical characteristics, geographical distribution, and behaviors. Figure 6.14 shows a generalized chart of the evolution of genus *Homo.*

The *Homo erectus* Stage

Beginning about 1.8 mya, we find fossils in Africa representing what looks like a fairly sudden jump in our evolution. Body size is now within the modern human range and is essentially modern in shape (Figure 6.15). And there is evidence of a new enhancement of bipedalism. This includes an arch of the foot and a different attachment point of the Achilles tendon; large gluteus (butt) muscles to stabilize the hips; muscle attachments to keep the head steady; and modifications in the balancing mechanisms in the ears. The focus of all these is to facilitate *endurance running,* that is, slow, steady running sustained over long distances. The adaptive significance of this for a savanna scavenger seems clear.

From the neck up, however, the bones reveal the retention of primitive features (Figure 6.16), with one notable exception. Brain size has

FIGURE 6.15
The Turkana Boy fossils from Kenya, dated at 1.6 mya. It is estimated that he was twelve years old when he died. He was about 5 feet 6 inches and, had he lived to adulthood, may have reached 6 feet and weighed around 150 pounds. Although his skull retains some primitive features, from the neck down he was essentially modern.

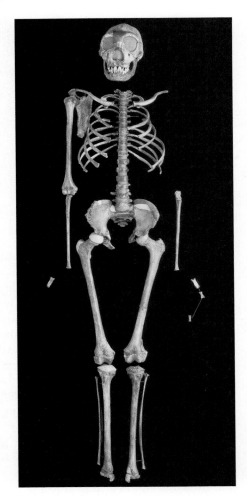

FIGURE 6.16
Cranial features of *Homo erectus* compared with those of modern *Homo sapiens*. The *sagittal keel* refers to a sloping of the sides of the skull toward the top. The *torus* is a bony ridge at the back of the skull to which heavy neck muscles are attached.

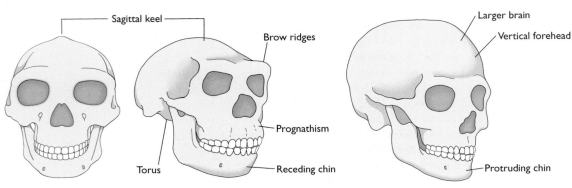

Homo erectus   Modern *Homo sapiens*

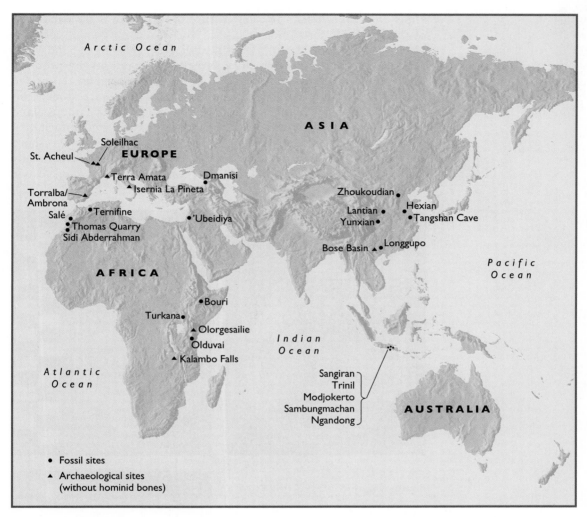

FIGURE 6.17
Map of major *Homo erectus* sites.

now evolved to an average of 980 ml and a maximum of 1,250 ml—overlapping the modern human range of 1,000 to 2,000 ml.

This is the *Homo erectus* stage, so named because when the first of these fossils were found in Java around the turn of the twentieth century, they were thought to be the first humans to walk upright. (We know today, of course, that upright locomotion was achieved millions of years before this.) Often considered a separate species, fossils belonging to the *Homo erectus* stage are dated from 1.8 mya to perhaps as recently as 100,000 years ago (ya) and are found at sites all over the Old World (Figure 6.17).

Tools and Migrations The key feature of this stage is the expansion of the hominids throughout the Old World. Success on the savannas of Africa provided the motivation and the means to expand. This success was made possible by a larger brain and its by-product: more-advanced stone tools. About 1.4 mya, *Homo erectus* elaborated on the earlier toolmaking technique by flaking the entire stone, controlling the shape of the whole tool. This tool is the famous **hand axe** (Figure 6.18), symmetrical, edged and pointed, and **bifacial.** In addition to hand axes, *H. erectus* also made tools with straight, sharp edges called cleavers. In making a hand axe or a cleaver, a great many flakes were produced—as many as fifty usable ones according to one

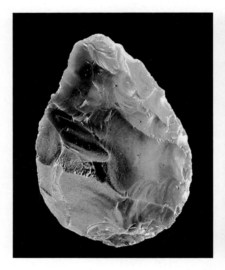

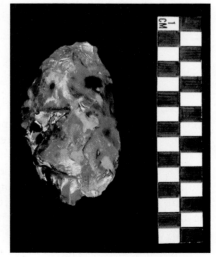

FIGURE 6.18
Bifacially flaked hand axes became one of history's most popular tools. They are found in a variety of sizes showing varying degrees of quality.

hand axe A bifacial, all-purpose stone tool, shaped somewhat like an axe head.

bifacial A stone tool that has been worked on both sides.

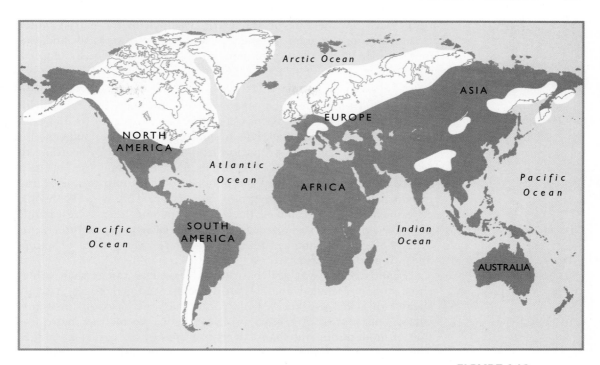

FIGURE 6.19
Maximum extent of the ice sheets during the Pleistocene.

estimate—and these could be further flaked to produce desired shapes for specific purposes.

Expanding on the successful adaptations of early *Homo,* the members of the *Homo erectus* stage may well have rapidly increased their population size, a factor that put pressure on resources as well as social harmony. Groups on the African plains may have subsequently split up and moved away from familiar areas in search of less competition over food, water, and shelter. In search of these resources, then, *H. erectus* wandered the Old World, arriving in the Far East after what appears to be only a few hundred thousand years.

The Ice Ages   But what makes these migrations even more remarkable is the fact that as members of *Homo erectus* were expanding their range, they were coming into contact with the changeable environments of the Ice Ages, technically called the **Pleistocene,** the period, from about 1.6 mya to around 10,000 ya, when a decrease in the earth's average temperature caused great sheets of ice—**glaciers**—to advance from the polar regions and out of higher elevations. There may have been as many as eighteen glacial advances over this time, interspersed by warmer periods when the glaciers retreated. We are not yet sure of the reasons for these fluctuations. Suffice it to say, however, that they caused a great climatic and environmental change (Figure 6.19). One

Pleistocene The geological time period, from 1.6 mya to 10,000 ya, characterized by a series of glacial advances and retreats.

glaciers Massive sheets of ice that expand and move.

result was the lowering of sea levels, as much of the earth's water froze, forming the great ice sheets. Thus, exposed areas of land formerly under water allowed humans to migrate to previously inaccessible places.

Behavioral Traits The other important first normally associated with *Homo erectus* is the purposeful use of fire. Good evidence for this goes back to 790,000 ya in Israel. Fire, of course, provides heat and can also be used for cooking and protection from other animals. According to science writer John Pfeiffer, however, its most important use was as a source of light; fire extended the hours of activity into the night and provided a social focus for group interaction. This is when people experimented, created, talked (in whatever manner they were capable of at the time), and socialized. Fire may also have given *Homo erectus* a psychological advantage, a sense of mastery over a force of nature and a source of energy.

Homo erectus was still basically a scavenger rather than a big-game hunter. Detailed analyses of associated animal bones strongly suggest this. We also know, from reconstructions based on their fossilized bones, that *H. erectus* probably had a vocal tract more like that of modern humans than like that of apes or the earlier hominids. There are also features of their brains (seen in casts made from the insides of their skulls) that hint at language ability. Whether or not they *did* have a complex, symbolic language like ours (see Chapter 11) cannot be determined, but I think that given their ability to make fairly complex tools, to control fire, and to survive in different and changing environments, they certainly had complex things to talk *about*. It is not out of the question that they had a communication system that was itself complex.

Fossils with the traits that identify the *Homo erectus* stage—essentially modern bodies with primitive cranial features and an average brain size just a bit below the modern human minimum—have been dated to as recently as 100,000 ya in Java. The stage—whether a separate species or not—was long-lived.

But meanwhile, back in Africa and southern Europe, a new development was taking place, possibly as long ago as 780,000 years. This marks the next stage of our story.

The Archaic *Homo sapiens* Stage

Traditionally, when the average brain size of fossils reaches that of modern humans, such fossils are given our taxonomic name, *Homo sapiens*. That brain size, and some other detailed features associated with modern humans, appears to have been achieved by some fossils

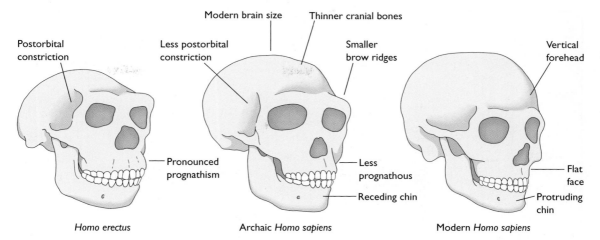

Postorbital constriction

Modern brain size

Thinner cranial bones

Less postorbital constriction

Smaller brow ridges

Vertical forehead

Pronounced prognathism

Less prognathous

Receding chin

Flat face

Protruding chin

Homo erectus

Archaic *Homo sapiens*

Modern *Homo sapiens*

FIGURE 6.20
Cranial features of *Homo erectus,* archaic *Homo sapiens,* and anatomically modern *Homo sapiens. Postorbital constriction* refers to a narrowing of the skull behind the eyes, as viewed from above.

from Spain dated at 780,000 ya and from Tanzania and Ethiopia at 700,000 and 600,000 ya.

These fossils, however, hardly appear completely modern. Their crania retain so-called primitive characteristics but with some changes over those of *Homo erectus* (Figure 6.20). Hence, they are often referred to as archaic *Homo sapiens,* including them in our species but indicating that they are not fully modern in their physical features.

Fossils included in this stage have been found all over the Old World and date from more than 700,000 ya to perhaps 36,000 ya (Figure 6.21). Although the oldest examples come from Spain, those are from just a single site. There are several very old sites of archaics from Africa, and so the traditional model has this new, big-brained hominid evolving on that continent, most likely from a population of the *Homo erectus* stage.

An early achievement of this stage of our evolution, dated to around 200,000 ya and appearing first in Africa, was a new toolmaking technique. It's called the **Levallois,** or prepared-core, technique and essentially allows for the production of a number of predictably shaped flakes off of a single core—history's first example of mass production (Figure 6.22).

The Neandertals Because of a dearth of fossils, we know relatively little about the earliest three-quarters of this stage, but the last quarter includes one of the most famous human fossil groups. As with other archaics they had modern-sized brains and retention of primitive cranial features. They also show a distinctive expression of those cranial

Levallois A tool technology in which uniform flakes are struck from a prepared core.

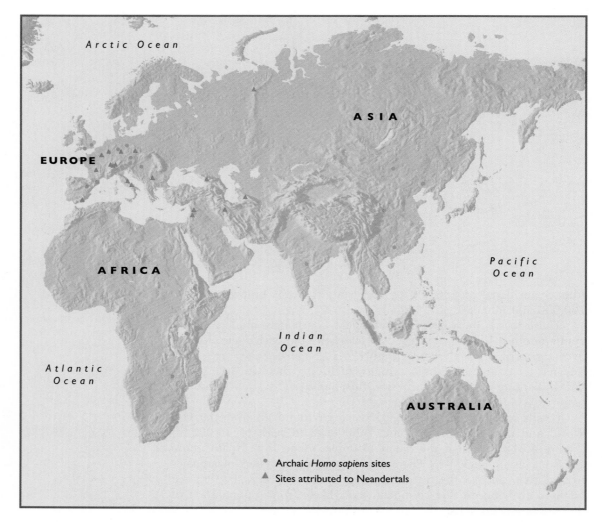

FIGURE 6.21
Map of archaic *Homo sapiens* sites. The sites attributed to Neandertals are indicated by a triangle. For clarity, the names of the sites have been omitted. The stress here is on the geographic range of this stage in the evolution of the human genus.

traits, as well as some differences in the postcranial (from the neck down) skeleton (Figure 6.23).

First discovered in 1856 (three years before Darwin wrote *Origin of Species*) and named after the Neander Valley in Germany, this group of archaics dates from 225,000 ya to 36,000 ya. Their fossils have been found in Europe and Southwest and Northwest Asia (see Figure 6.21). Their brain sizes ranged from 1,300 to 1,740 ml, a larger average than that of modern humans, but their foreheads were still sloping, the backs of their skulls broad, their brow ridges large, their faces jutting forward, and their chins receding.

Side Views   **Top Views**

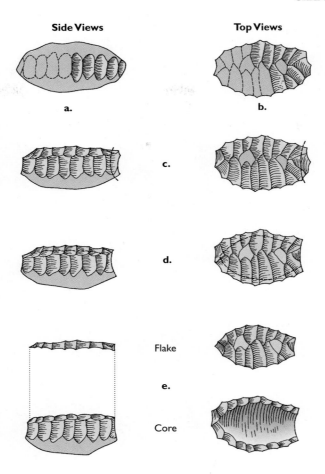

a.   b.

c.

d.

Flake

e.

Core

FIGURE 6.22
The Levallois technique:
(a) produce a margin along
the edge of the core,
(b) shape the surface of
the core, (c, d) prepare the
surface to be struck (the
striking platform), (e) remove
the flake, and return to
step (b) for additional
flake removal.

From the neck down, there are also striking features. The bones of the Neandertals, even the finger bones, were sturdier, with heavier muscle markings than those of modern humans or, for that matter, other archaics. They were stocky, muscular, powerful people, and these traits are even seen in Neandertal children, so they are assumed to be the result of inheritance, not simply a hardworking lifestyle. Their stockiness, as well as their short stature of 5 feet 6 inches for males, might have been an adaptation to the cold conditions of Pleistocene Europe during the glacial advances. Shorter, heavier bodies conserve heat.

Among the well-established accomplishments of the Neandertals was an elaboration on the Levallois technique. Called the **Mousterian** tradition, after the site of Le Moustier in France, it involved careful retouching of the flakes taken off cores. These flakes were sharpened

Mousterian A toolmaking
technology, associated with
the European Neandertals,
in which flakes were carefully retouched to produce
diverse tool types.

FIGURE 6.23

Two Neandertal skulls from French sites, showing extreme expressions of archaic *Homo sapiens* features. Note the large brow ridges, sloping forehead, prognathism, receding chin, bulging rear of skull, and overall rugged appearance. Many European Neandertals had brain sizes larger than the modern human average, although this should not be taken to indicate greater intelligence. Within the modern human range of 1,000 ml to 2,000 ml, there is no evidence of a relation between size and intellect. The Neandertals' large crania match their large, rugged bodies.

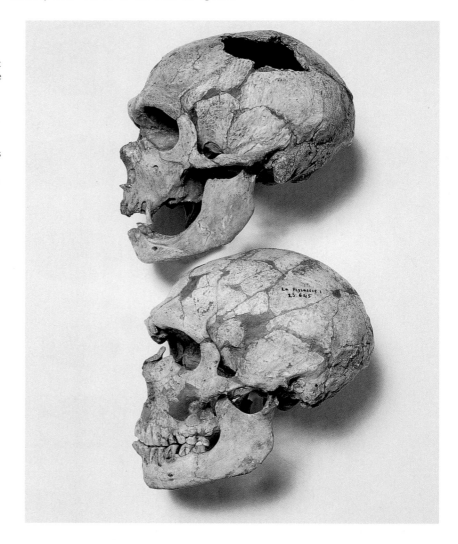

and shaped by precise additional flaking, on one side or both, to make specialized tools (Figure 6.24). One authority has identified no fewer than sixty-three Mousterian tool types.

Several specific uses of Mousterian tools have been inferred from microscopic wear-pattern analysis, which indicates animal butchering, woodworking, bone and antler carving, and working of animal hides. The Neandertals may also have been the first to **haft** a stone point.

Perhaps most striking, at least thirty-six Neandertal sites, dating from 75,000 to 35,000 ya, show evidence of intentional burial of the dead, including special positioning of the bodies, sometimes in a fetal

haft To attach a wooden handle or shaft to a stone or bone point.

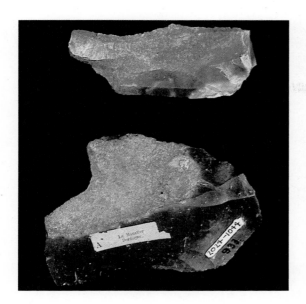

FIGURE 6.24
Retouched Mousterian flakes from the original site of Le Moustier in France. The lower flake is about 4 inches long.

position (Figure 6.25). In about 40 percent of these graves were remains of grave goods—stone tools, animal bones, and, possibly, flowers.

It has also been suggested that Neandertals were among the first to care for their elderly, ill, and injured. That is, they had ideas about the value of individual lives and some sense of social responsibility. A skeleton of a Neandertal man from Iraq shows signs of injuries that resulted in the loss of one arm and possibly blindness. He lived with these conditions for some time, obviously fed and cared for by his comrades.

The Neandertals have been at the center of the controversy over the number of species of genus *Homo* that have existed, with some opinions that they are a separate species from us and others that they are a population of our species, *Homo sapiens*. Recent genetic evidence has shown that a small portion of the DNA of some modern human populations came from interbreeding with the Neandertals. Thus, under the definition of species we are using, we and they *are* members of the same species, and they represent a specialized and localized, and now extinct, population of our species.

The Anatomically Modern *Homo sapiens* Stage

Beginning perhaps as early as 300,000 ya, fossils with near-modern or modern features appear, earliest in Africa and later in other parts of the Old World. We call these fossils *anatomically modern* because they lack

FIGURE 6.25
The Neandertal burial from La Ferrassie, France. The body was buried in the flexed position with the knees drawn up to the chest, perhaps to mimic sleep. (The basket in the background belonged to the excavators.)

some features characteristic of earlier hominids and possess features common to humans today. Gone is the prognathous profile; the face is essentially flat, and there are no heavy brow ridges. The skull is globular rather than elongated and the forehead more nearly vertical. The face is smaller and narrower, and there is a protruding chin (Figure 6.26). The postcranial skeleton is less sturdy.

Fossil data, as well as some fairly new techniques of genetic analysis, suggest that modern-looking humans first arose in Africa, evolving from

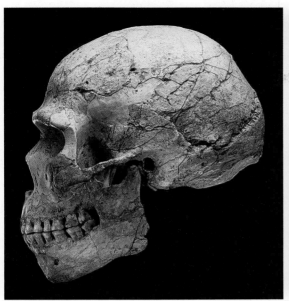 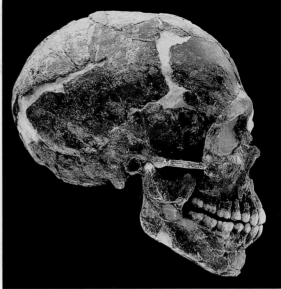

FIGURE 6.26
Two examples of early anatomically modern *Homo sapiens,* both from Israel and dated to around 100,000 ya. Note the more vertical forehead, more rounded braincase, flatter face, and protruding chin (see also Figure 6.20). Although the left skull retains fairly prominent brow ridges, its other features are modern. Indeed, brow ridges are still found in some living populations such as Native Australians.

a population of archaics, and then spread around the world. Whether they replaced the archaic populations they encountered (because they were a different and more successful species) or interbred with them (because they were members of the same species, only different looking) is part of the ongoing debate.

Tools   What we do know is that with modern-looking anatomy came further advances in technology and the expressions of modern behavior patterns. Although much of their tool kit at first resembles that of archaics, artifacts from one of the oldest modern human sites show an important advance. From South Africa, dated to perhaps 120,000 ya, come long, bifacially worked spear points made by hitting a piece of antler with another stone, thus "punching" off a more precise blade. Much later, **microliths,** small stones made from pieces of blades, were attached to handles to make sickles, devices for harvesting grasses (see Figure 9.12).

By about 50,000 ya, modern *Homo sapiens* had spread all over the Old World. This marks an important cultural period called the Upper Paleolithic (Late Old Stone Age), known first through finds in Europe and distinguished by several notable cultural innovations. Blades struck off cores become so precisely and beautifully made as to be virtual works of art (Figure 6.27). In fact, some are so thin and delicate we think they may have been just that. Tools in the Upper Paleolithic were also made from bone, antler, and ivory. Some are practical, such as

microliths Small stone flakes, usually used as part of a larger tool such as a sickle.

FIGURE 6.27
Bifacially flaked Upper Paleolithic spear points, some of the finest stonework ever seen. The middle one is about 5 inches long.

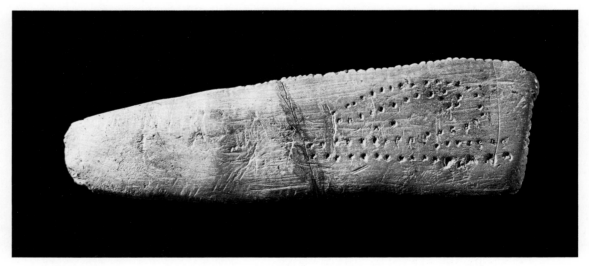

FIGURE 6.28
A 32,000-year-old engraved antler plaque from Abri Blanchard, France, which Alexander Marshack interprets as a record of the phases of the moon.

harpoons, spear points, and shaft straighteners. Some have symbolic significance, and even some of the utilitarian items are decorated (see Figure 6.28).

The final step in stone tool technology, the ground stone tool, is first seen from around 9,000 ya in Europe and Southwest Asia and perhaps even earlier in Japan and Australia. Grinding was accomplished by rubbing an unformed stone, called a blank, on a gritty stone such as sandstone. Using a finer stone with some wet sand on it provided a polish for the finishing touches. The advantages of ground stone were that the smooth surfaces cut better than the rough ones of a flaked tool and that stones less likely to break on impact could be made into tools. The use of stone tools persisted even among peoples who learned how to use metal. And so, for the prehistoric period of our cultural evolution, tools are essential bits of evidence in our reconstruction of past lifeways.

Art Perhaps the best indication of abstract thought is art—items that are not utilitarian but that may carry symbolic meaning or produce aesthetic pleasure. There is some tantalizing evidence for very early art: some collections of natural pigments, possibly for body decoration, a female carving from Morocco 300,000 to 500,000 ya, an amulet made of a shaped and colored mammoth tooth, some shell beads, and an engraved piece of ochre. All these are dated from 500,000 to 75,000 ya. But we see unequivocal examples of art beginning about 40,000 ya. These finds are associated with anatomically modern *Homo sapiens.*

From Australia come painted symbols, handprints, and petroglyphs (designs scratched into rock) dated at 43,000 to 36,000 ya. There is a cave painting in Namibia dated at perhaps 29,000 ya. A carved ivory disk found in a child's grave and a colored pendant in the shape of an animal come from Russia about 28,000 ya.

The best-known and most evocative early art is that from the Upper Paleolithic in Europe. This does not necessarily mean that Europeans at that time were the most prolific artists in the world. It may simply be that archaeology has been carried out longer and more extensively there than just about anywhere else, so we have found more artifacts and thus know and understand the prehistory of Europe better.

Much of the earliest European art is in the form of carvings with strictly symbolic meaning. From France, dated at 32,000 ya, is a piece of antler engraved with a curving line of 69 marks (Figure 6.28). Archaeologist Alexander Marshack interprets these as a succession of lunar phases—the correct shape, order, and number for more than two months. The carving, he thinks, may have been an early lunar calendar.

Among the most famous of the carvings are the so-called Venus figurines found throughout Europe and dating back to as early as 30,000 ya (Figure 6.29, bottom; Figure 6.30). These are commonly interpreted as fertility symbols since many depict women with exaggerated sexual dimorphic features who appear to be pregnant. Others, however, seem to be of women at other stages of life. We may never know just what these figurines meant to those who made them. Clearly, however, they had *some* meaning.

FIGURE 6.29
Carved artifacts, including a shaft straightener with carved animals (*top*), a harpoon carved from antler (*left*), and an example of the famous Venus figurines (*lower right*) that may have served as fertility symbols.

By far the most famous early artworks are the cave paintings, the majority of which are located in southern France and northern Spain and are dated at 32,000 to 10,000 ya. Using natural pigments, the artists rendered accurate depictions of important animals—bison, aurochs, horses, deer, reindeer, mammoth, ibex (an antelope), and even rhinoceros, lions, and bears, all of which inhabited Europe at the time (Figure 6.31). Some of these paintings are fairly simple and sketchy, but many are beautiful, colorful, and show depth and motion (Figure 6.32). Sometimes the shape and relief of the rock of the cave wall were incorporated into the painting, giving it even greater realism. Seeing these paintings in person, as I did a few years ago, is a truly moving experience.

As with the figurines, there has been debate over the meaning of these paintings. They most often depict important game animals—and the more important the animals, the more frequently they were painted. Big, dangerous animals, even if rarely a source of meat—mammoths,

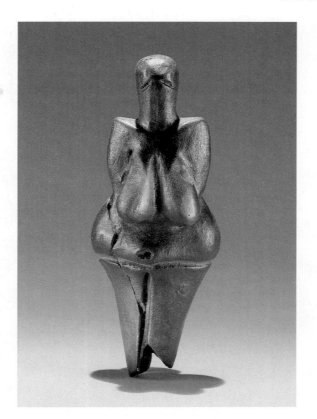

FIGURE 6.30
The Venus figurine from Dolní Věstonice in the Czech Republic.

FIGURE 6.31
This living ox at Le Toth museum near the cave of Lascaux in France has been bred to resemble the aurochs, an ancestor of the modern oxen that was one of the largest mammals of Upper Paleolithic times, weighing more than a ton. The aurochs was hunted for food and was well represented in Upper Paleolithic cave paintings (see Figure 6.32).

FIGURE 6.32
An aurochs and a herd of small horses seem almost to be moving across the cave wall in this painting from Lascaux, dated to perhaps 17,000 ya.

for instance—were also fairly common. In the recently discovered Chauvet Cave near Avignon, France, rhinoceros, lions, and even a hyena—all nonfood animals—were depicted.

The caves in which these paintings were found were not human shelters. Some would have been hard to get to, and the painted areas were often far inside them. Moreover, someone would have had to transport a source of light through the caves to produce the art. There was clearly something special about these paintings.

Anthropologist Patricia Rice and sociologist Ann Paterson have concluded that the cave art served a combination of purposes: "fertility magic, hunting magic, hunting education, and story-telling about hunting."

"Capturing" an animal by painting it may have helped the hunter capture it in reality. Painting a group of animals may have simply helped ensure that they would exist somewhere to *be* hunted. Young men may have been instructed in the hunt with the help of these paintings. And such paintings may also have aided in the recounting of exciting hunting tales (see Figure 9.1). Again, the important fact is that they clearly held meaning of some sort. They stood for and probably helped communicate ideas. It may be no coincidence that these striking cave paintings are found in an area and during a time period that correspond to a maximum advance of the Pleistocene glaciers—a time and place of social and ecological stress.

By at least 50,000 ya, people moved on to present-day New Guinea and Australia, using watercraft but having to cross narrower areas of water than exist today due to lower sea levels resulting from glacial periods. Twenty thousand years ago, and possibly much earlier, humans moved into North America, coming across a land bridge between Siberia and Alaska. They soon moved throughout the continent and into South America. By about 30,000 ya modern *Homo sapiens* had populated every landmass on the planet except Antarctica.

Cultural change then accelerated rapidly, with specific cultural systems geared to the specific ecologies of the areas inhabited. In a few thousand years—a short time when compared to the millions we have been discussing so far—we find in some areas the first traces of farming, metallurgy, cities, and writing.

But before we can discuss the nature of the cultural systems of modern humans, we still need to look at two more identifying traits of our species and see how they evolved and how they affect our nature.

SUMMARY

The primates are one of the earliest of the mammal groups to evolve after the mass extinction that took place 65 mya. They appear to have arisen first in what are now North America and Europe, but the success of their adaptations allowed them to radiate over the Old World and back into the New World after the hemispheres separated. About 23 mya, primitive apes first appeared, and from one group of African apes our family, Hominidae, branched off around 5 mya or earlier.

The habitual bipedalism that marks our family seems to have evolved in response to a fluctuating environment of both forest and open plains. These earliest ancestors were essentially small, bipedal apes.

About 3 mya, a further climate change led to two new hominid adaptive responses. One gave rise to another small, bipedal apelike form with massive chewing bones and muscles adapted to the tough, gritty vegetation of the plains. The other response was the evolution of larger-brained hominids. These hominids, the first members of genus *Homo*, survived by inventing stone tools, which, among other things, allowed them to scavenge the meat of the vast herds of grass eaters.

From this adaptive base, the evolution of our genus accelerated. The *Homo erectus* stage,

CONTEMPORARY ISSUES

How Many "Kinds" of Humans Have There Been?

In this chapter I mentioned the debate over the number of species within genus *Homo* that have existed over the last 2 million years. Opinions range from one species to as many as ten. This debate got some new fuel with the discovery, on the Indonesian island of Flores, of a human skeleton dated to as recently as 13,000 ya. Such a find would not have been remarkable except for the fact that the skeleton is of an adult, probably a female, who stood a mere 106 cm tall (about 3 feet 5 inches) and had an estimated brain size of 380 ml, about the stature and cranial capacity of *Australopithecus*. And yet its physical features seem fairly clearly to assign the specimen to genus *Homo,* with particular similarities to *Homo erectus*. The discoverers have given the specimen the status of a new species, *Homo floresiensis*.

Even for those who propose that there have been multiple species of our genus over the last 2 million years, this find is astonishing, because, so far as we knew, there have been *no* humans other than us—that is, *Homo sapiens*—on earth for at least 27,000 years. And for those of us who feel that only one species of *Homo* has existed, the implication of this find and its interpretation is obvious.

What are we to make of this specimen, sometimes referred to as a Hobbit (a reference to the small characters in Tolkien's *Lord of the Rings*)? Given its body and brain size, could it *be* an australopithecine, indicating that there were populations of this genus outside of Africa? Probably not, since it has phenotypic characteristics that place it clearly in genus *Homo* and it was found in association with stone tools and evidence of hunting and possibly fire and cooking. None of these cultural features are associated with *Australopithecus*. And the game hunted was not small; it included pygmy elephants and Komodo dragons (the world's largest existing lizard). Certainly a high level of cooperation and communication would have been necessary to accomplish such hunting. Moreover, no fossils of australopithecines have been found

with its basically modern bodies and even larger brains, migrated all over the Old World, encountering the climatic changes of the Pleistocene, improving stone tool manufacture, and, at least in some areas, taming fire. Modern-sized brains were reached 780,000 ya, although crania retained some primitive features. These archaic *Homo sapiens,* first seen in Africa and southern Europe, also spread across the Old World, and exhibited such typically human behaviors as burial of the dead and care of the elderly and infirm. The Neandertals are one of the best-known forms of this stage.

The anatomically modern *Homo sapiens* stage, first appearing in Africa around 300,000 ya, is characterized by further advances in tool-making, the clear practice of big-game hunting, and the first expressions of art. Members of this stage entered Australia and nearby islands and reached the New World. Farming, cities, writing, and all the cultural features we associate with modern humanity follow.

outside of Africa, much less as far away as Southeast Asia.

Perhaps this was one individual within a group of pygmy humans or simply a modern human who had an anomalous condition, some form of dwarfism. Again, that seems unlikely, since small humans and humans with anomalous conditions have smaller than average bodies but retain brains within the modern human range (1,000 ml to 2,000 ml). *H. floresiensis* had a brain approximately one-third the modern human *minimum*.

On the other hand, perhaps once evolution achieved a modern human brain complexity, size became less important and a complex brain could develop in a small package. Consider, in a loose analogy, how we can now put hard drives of increasing capacity in smaller and smaller computers, MP3 players, and other devices.

At the moment, my best guess is that this specimen comes from a population of descendants of *Homo erectus* that responded to a phenomenon of dwarfing common to island species, especially mammals. Free from predators and/or restricted in room and resources, species isolated on islands can evolve to be much smaller than their ancestors.

But several questions remain. First, *is* this specimen characteristic of a whole population? The discoverers of the original specimen have reported the recovery of the remains of more individuals with the same features. But until more of these remains are fully described and verified, we can only *surmise* that the original find is representative of an entire group.

Second, even if the original and subsequent finds do represent a population, *is* this population a separate species? We can't, of course, experiment to see if *H. floresiensis* could interbreed with other populations, so there is no definitive way to answer that question. Thus, as noted, opinions on the number of species of *Homo* continue to differ, and there will probably never be a way to resolve the debate for sure.

One thing is certain, however. Unless this individual proves to be just that, one individual with a unique set of physical features, our genus *Homo* is a lot more variable than we once imagined.

QUESTIONS FOR FURTHER THOUGHT

1. People often ask this logical question: If humans descended from apes, then how come there are still apes? How would you respond?

2. There's heated and intense debate over the number of species recognized within genus *Homo*. Why do you think this matters so much? Is there a level of this debate beyond just the issue of scientific interest and accuracy?

3. If evolution in general is sometimes a controversial topic, the subject of *human* evolution is often more so. How would you respond to people who feel that accepting human evolution is antithetical to religious beliefs?

NOTES, REFERENCES, AND READINGS

A detailed account of the Piltdown fraud can be found in Kenneth Feder's *Frauds, Myths, and Mysteries,* seventh edition.

An expanded discussion of the story of human evolution is in my *Biological Anthropology,* seventh edition. For a sense of the excitement of paleoanthropology, even though the details in the book are now outdated, I recommend *Lucy: The Beginnings of Humankind,* by Donald Johanson and Maitland Edey, and its sequel, *Lucy's Child: The Discovery of a Human Ancestor,* by Johanson and James Shreeve. A beautifully illustrated treatment of the subject, based on an exhibit at the American Museum of Natural History in New York, is Ian Tattersall's *The Human Odyssey: Four Million Years of Evolution.* See also Tattersall's *The Fossil Trail,* second edition. These are all somewhat outdated, but they convey the excitement of this subject. For a very readable overview, see *The Complete Idiot's Guide to Human Prehistory,* by Robert J. Meier. Don't let the title fool you; this is a very accurate work by a noted authority.

A *National Geographic* series, "The Dawn of Humans," appears in the following issues: September 1995; January and March 1996; February, May, July, and September 1997; August 1998; and May, July, and December 2000. And see the November 2006 issue for an article about the latest early hominid find, "The Origin of Childhood" by Christopher Sloan. The photographs and graphics are, as usual for that magazine, superb.

For more on the debate about the evolution of genus *Homo,* I shamelessly recommend chapter 11 of my *Biological Anthropology,* or, for the two treatments by the proponents of the extreme views on the subject, *Race and Human Evolution,* by Milford Wolpoff and Rachel Caspari, and *African Exodus,* by Christopher Stringer and Robin McKie.

For more on human endurance running, see "Endurance Running and the Evolution of *Homo,*" by Dennis Bramble and Daniel Lieberman, in the November 18, 2004, issue of *Nature.*

James Shreeve's calculations about the migration of *Homo erectus* from Africa to Java are in his article "*Erectus* Rising" in the September 1994 *Discover.* For the latest on *Ardipithecus,* see the October 2, 2009, issue of *Science* or, for a more popularized article, "A Long Lost Relative" by Michael Lemonick and Andrea Dorfman in the October 12, 2009, issue of *Time.*

John Pfeiffer's idea on the importance of fire can be found in *The Emergence of Humankind.* For a more recent treatment of the importance of fire, see *Catching Fire: How Cooking Made Us Human,* by Richard Wrangham. A lengthier discussion of Upper Paleolithic art can be found in Ken Feder's and my *Human Antiquity,* which also includes a detailed discussion of the origins and early history of domestication. Pat Rice and Ann Paterson's conclusions about the meanings of cave art are in their "Cave Art and Bones: Exploring the Interrelationships," from *American Anthropologist,* volume 87, pages 94–100. Try also the January 1975 issue of *National Geographic* for an article called "Exploring the Mind of Ice Age Man," by Alexander Marshack.

For more on the "Hobbit" from Flores Island, see "The Littlest Human," by Kate Wong, in the February 2005 *Scientific American;* and "*Homo floresiensis* from Head to Toe," by Daniel Lieberman in the May 7, 2009, issue of *Nature.*

The Neandertal genome has been much in the news and hotly debated. For a nice summary, see "Tales of a Prehistoric Human Genome," by Elizabeth Pennisi in the February 13, 2009, issue of *Science.*

7

REPRODUCTION

The Sexual Primate

CHAPTER CONTENTS Sex and Human Evolution • Vive la Différence • Sex and Gender • Sex and Cultural Institutions • Summary • Contemporary Issues: What Causes Differences in Sexual Orientation? • Questions for Further Thought • Notes, References, and Readings

The part of the brain that governs the reproductive function is the cerebellum or little brain. It is located in the lower back part of the head. The cerebellum also constitutes the organ of amativeness, which, according to the teachings of phrenology, "gives love" for the opposite sex. Other things being equal, the strength of the cerebellum is proportionate to its size. . . . You will never find the most popular and successful men and women with a small and weak cerebellum, nor a weak, narrow, retreating chin, because they do not have enough love for the opposite sex to form an incentive to be gallant, polite, attentive, winning, etc.

The above was written in 1895 by V. P. English, MD, in his book *The Doctor's Plain Talk to Young Men.* The book seems quite humorous to us today, for it is filled with all manner of outdated information and nineteenth-century attitudes toward sex. For example, we know now that the cerebellum (see Figure 5.5), the part of the brain concerned with the learning of motor skills and the coordination of movement, has no such direct connection with reproduction. We also know that phrenology—the pseudoscience of determining personality and mental traits from the shape of one's head—doesn't work. And we realize that contrary to what Dr. English implies, human ideas about attractiveness, love, manners, and so on are not species characteristics controlled by the brain but rather cultural norms that vary from society to society.

We humans *think* about sex. Instead of automatically responding to external stimuli, we decide when, where, with whom, and how to have sex. We decide, as members of a particular culture and as individuals, what is sexually attractive and stimulating. And what is attractive and stimulating is tied up with our personality traits, emotional responses, and learned attitudes. To put it bluntly, it matters to us with whom we have sex. And the ability to think about sex not only makes us different from other organisms, but it may also be the result of important changes that took place early in our evolution, perhaps when habitual bipedalism was also evolving.

So, as naïve as this may sound, we must ask just what sex is, how our sexual behavior is different from that of other animals, and what this has to do with our evolution and behavior, both biologically and culturally.

AS YOU READ, CONSIDER THE FOLLOWING QUESTIONS:

1. How does human sexual behavior differ from that of most mammals? How did this difference evolve?

2. How do human males and females differ, and how might these differences be explained evolutionarily?

3. What is the difference between sex and gender?

4. How is our sexual behavior an example of the biocultural interaction that is a focus of anthropology?

SEX AND HUMAN EVOLUTION

Primate Sex

To understand why I call humans the sexual primates, we need to understand how mammals in general reproduce. In most mammals, sexual activity takes place only when it can do what it's supposed to do—make baby mammals. This is because sex is geared to the reproductive cycle of the female. The eggs of female mammals mature and can be fertilized only at certain intervals. These intervals may be regularly spaced throughout the year, or they may be seasonal to ensure the birth of young during times of abundant resources.

Egg maturation, called **ovulation,** has two results sexually. It triggers hormonal changes that make the female sexually receptive to males, and it initiates signals that stimulate the males. During this period, the female is said to be in **estrus** (popularly, "in heat"). This is when sex takes place. At other times, when there is no egg to be fertilized, mammals have much better things to do.

This holds true for most primates. Female primates ovulate and are in estrus at certain intervals specific to the particular species. During estrus, the females give off automatic signals that cause sexual stimulation among males. These signals are **olfactory** (based on smell) as in most mammals and, in some primates, visual, involving the swelling and coloration of the skin in the genital area. Those primates you see in zoos with what look like large, painful growths on their rear ends are females in estrus (Figure 7.1). During estrus, mating may involve a number of males as in chimpanzees, a dominant male that has exclusive mating rights to a particular female, as in some baboons, or a single bonded male, as in gibbons.

The link between sexual activity and ovulation is an adaptive mechanism to give a species the greatest possible chance to produce offspring without wasting time and energy on sex when it will do no biological good. Primates have more than enough to do just trying to stay alive.

ovulation The period when an egg cell matures and is capable of being fertilized.

estrus In nonhuman mammals, the period of female fertility or the signals indicating this condition.

olfactory Referring to the sense of smell.

FIGURE 7.1
A baboon in estrus. The skin around her genital area is swollen, a clear visual sign that she is fertile and sexually receptive. In baboons and some other primates, this area may also be brightly colored.

Human Sex

Loss of Estrus, and Sexual Consciousness You can see right away the key feature in which we humans differ: we have lost the signals of estrus. To be sure, female humans ovulate at regular intervals—about once every twenty-eight days, producing an egg that can be fertilized over a period of three to five days. But there is no outward sign of this. No signals tell a male that a female has ovulated. Women can tell when they are ovulating, sensing physiological or hormonal changes or a rise in body temperature, but men can't tell. In other words, rather than having an estrus cycle with its automatic signals, we humans have what has been called *nondetectable ovulation*.

Now, this seems a pretty inefficient way of perpetuating our species, since it means we don't necessarily know the best time for having sex. But what our species has evolved to take care of this is, in a sense, *continuous estrus*. We have replaced unconscious, innate sexual signals with sexual consciousness. Sexuality has become part of our conscious thought, taking place in our neocortexes (see Figure 5.5) and thus interacting with all the other reactions and attitudes and emotions we have toward other members of our species and toward ourselves.

We thus express ourselves sexually as individual personalities and as members of particular cultural systems. We respond sexually to individual personalities and according to culturally determined standards of behavior and attractiveness. We find a person sexually stimulating not because of a set of automatic signals but because of that person's appearance, personal traits, intelligence, socioeconomic status—all the

FIGURE 7.2
An image of French swimming champion Yannick Agnel stands on an ad for energy corporation EDF, one of the Olympic sponsor partners in the Olympic Park during the London 2012 Olympics. Young women stand to admire him and have their photos next to his athletic figure outside the EDF corporate pavilion. EDP is clearly using sex to attract attention to an item not related to sexual matters.

factors by which we judge and respond to individual people as members of our society.

As further evidence for the psychological and social context of human sexuality, note that we create and recognize symbols for sex. Clothing styles are more than utilitarian; they also become expressions of our sexuality. In this society, the automobile has taken on sexual connotations. Athleticism is often linked with sexual prowess. Advertisements on television and in magazines hype various products through sexual images. Although the products themselves may have nothing to do with sexuality, the ads subtly imply that the use of them will enhance one's sexual attractiveness (Figure 7.2).

Antecedents and Evolution of Human Sexuality   As with other traits we've discussed, there is no *absolute* difference between our expression of sexuality and that of all other animals. Some other species show a degree of sexual consciousness and a similarity in expression to that of humans. Not surprisingly, we find this in our closest relatives, the chimpanzees and, especially, the bonobos.

Chimps engage in sex at times other than a female's estrus, and they use sexual postures as signs of dominance and submission. Some aspect of sex is conscious for them and is separate from purely reproductive functions. But the sexual behavior of the bonobos is strikingly humanlike. Perhaps to phrase it with more evolutionary accuracy, our sexual behavior is bonobo-like.

For the bonobo, sex is not reserved for reproduction alone; it also plays a role in interpersonal relationships and group cohesion. Especially when feeding, bonobos constantly posture sexually toward one another, rubbing rumps or presenting themselves as if initiating sexual activity. When sex does follow, it is often face-to-face, unlike the position of

FIGURE 7.3
Bonobos often engage in sex in a face-to-face position.

other primates and like that of humans (Figure 7.3). Sexual activity is not limited to opposite-sex partners. Females commonly rub genitalia with other females, and males will mount each other and even engage in oral sex. Moreover, the signs of receptivity, the estrus swelling and coloration, are present for about 75 percent of the female's cycle (as opposed to 50 percent for the female chimpanzee's cycle), and there is at least circumstantial evidence that female bonobos experience orgasms.

Sexual activity in bonobos occurs on a conscious level. The motivation for sex seems as much psychological and social as it is reproductive. Primatologist Frans de Waal lists several functions of sexual behavior: the promotion of sharing food and other things of interest (play items, for example), the negotiation of favors, the resolution of social tensions, and reconciliation after aggressive episodes. The nearly constant awareness of sexuality among bonobos also leads to female bonding and mixed (male-female) social units.

Now, can bonobo sexual behavior shed any light on the evolution in humans of continuous receptivity and conscious sexuality? Conscious sexual interest, it is thought, could have helped bond males and females together and would have thus assured the male that the female's offspring were his. Then, with this adaptive relationship in place, any variation that promoted bonding—greater sexual consciousness and concealed ovulation—would have been selectively advantageous.

The Importance of Development and Child Care

Reproduction, of course, doesn't end with the birth of an infant. The infant must successfully reach adulthood and its own reproduction to be considered an evolutionary success. There are also some distinct differences in how humans care for and provision their offspring that have clear implications for the course of human evolution.

Human infants are born particularly helpless and mature slowly. They are born earlier in their development than the infants of other primates because bipedalism produces a pelvis that makes childbirth more stressful and a larger brain requires earlier birth so as not to make the situation even worse. After birth, the larger brains of humans simply take longer to develop, so the period of dependency on the parents is longer.

Thus it becomes harder to successfully raise children, especially in difficult environmental conditions. Anthropologist Sarah Blaffer Hrdy argues that "intersubjective engagement"—care about what others intend and feel—was greatly enhanced in early humans, and that this led to "cooperative breeding . . . shared parental . . . care and provisioning of young," or, as she calls this, **alloparenting**. This is seen in some other primates, particularly in some South American monkeys, but is a feature of many human groups, where the alloparents are often older female relatives (even grandmothers) who have lived past reproductive age. Hrdy hypothesizes that the change took place in *Homo erectus* times, when more, and more varied, food was required to supply larger bodies and brains. Shared parenting would become a necessity and would set the stage for the mutual cooperation among our families and our societies that characterizes our species.

VIVE LA DIFFÉRENCE

All sexually reproducing species display differences between the two sexes, if for no other reason than that the sexes need different anatomical features for their respective reproductive functions. But in some species, unless you look really closely at their anatomies, it's hard to tell male from female—take a familiar bird, the robin, for example. Other species, however, show clear distinctions between the sexes in traits not directly related to reproduction. Such species are said to display **sexual dimorphism**. Another familiar bird, the cardinal, is an example; males and females are easily distinguishable. The same is true with humans (Figure 7.4). And the nature of our dimorphism is most interesting.

alloparenting Shared caring and provisioning of the young by other group members.

sexual dimorphism Physical differences between the sexes of a species not related to reproductive functions.

FIGURE 7.4

Two sexually dimorphic species—the northern cardinal and *Homo sapiens*. Males and females are clearly distinguishable using only external nonreproductive phenotypic features.

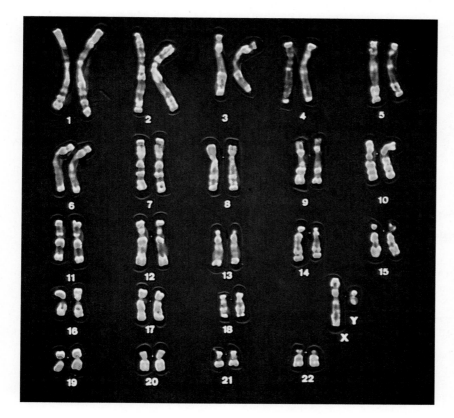

FIGURE 7.5
All twenty-three pairs of
chromosomes typically
found in a human being.
This set of chromosomes
came from a man—note
the last pair has an
X chromosome and a
Y chromosome. A woman
would have a pair of
X chromosomes.

The differences between human males and females begin at the genetic level. Two of the human chromosomes are called the sex chromosomes because they include genes that code for our sexual characteristics (Figure 7.5). The X chromosome is the female chromosome. It is a large chromosome that carries genes for nonsexually related traits as well. The male chromosome, the Y chromosome, is the smallest of the chromosomes and appears to carry only genes related to male sexual characteristics. Each female has twenty-three pairs of chromosomes, including a pair of X chromosomes. Each male has twenty-two pairs of chromosomes, and an X chromosome inherited from his mother and a Y chromosome inherited from his father.

What are the physical and physiological results of the genes on these chromosomes? Can we make any adaptive sense of them?

Human males are, on average, larger and more heavily muscled than females (see Figure 7.4). In this humans are like the apes and some of the monkeys, although the differences are less pronounced in humans. This size difference is most pronounced in the more terrestrial primates, those that spend a lot of time on the ground. Danger from predators seems to have led to selection for larger size in males as a means of

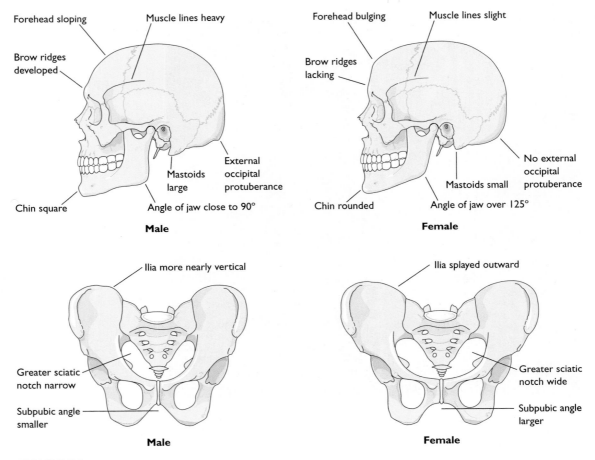

FIGURE 7.6
Sex differences in the skull and pelvis of humans.

helping to protect the group. In some of the savanna baboons, males are twice the size of females. We hominids became established on the savannas of Africa, and our sexual size differences may well represent the same original function. We can, in fact, see this basic dimorphic difference in early hominids as well. For both the early hominids and modern humans, males' bones are generally larger and show heavier muscle markings. There are other skeletal differences too, especially in the pelvis. Nearly everything about the female pelvis is wider, an obvious adaptation to carrying and giving birth (Figure 7.6).

Males have relatively larger hearts and lungs, a faster recovery time from muscle fatigue, higher blood pressure, and greater oxygen-carrying capacity. But males are more susceptible than females to disease and death at all stages of life. During the first year of life, one-third more males die, mostly from infectious disease. Males also are more likely to have speech disorders, vision and hearing problems, ulcers, and skin disorders.

Females have a greater proportion of body fat than do males. They mature faster at almost all stages of life, most notably exhibiting earlier puberty and an earlier growth spurt at adolescence. They are less likely than males to be thrown off normal growth by disease and other factors, and they recover from such problems more quickly than males. Although females appear to have a greater tendency than males to become obese, males suffer more from the effects of being overweight—strokes, for example. Females seem to be more sensitive to touch and pain and, perhaps, to higher sound frequencies, and they are said to be better at locating the sources of sound. Smell sensitivity is about the same in both sexes, but females seem better at identifying smells.

These dimorphic features are not completely understood, and there is a great deal of overlap in the range of variation of these traits. But the above tendencies suggest an adaptive explanation. Many of the characteristics of the human male are aimed at sustained, stressful physical action at the expense, however, of overall health and longevity. Females' overall better health, earlier maturity, and greater sensitivity to stimulation of the senses might be geared toward their reproductive and child-rearing roles. Again, perhaps some basic themes of terrestrial primate sexual dimorphisms were retained and others selected for among our early ancestors as their small, cooperative bands confronted the challenges of life in the changing environments of Africa.

Are there any sexually dimorphic traits or, for that matter, traits shared by the sexes that might be linked to our sexual behavior as described above? One example is hair. We are, as biologist Desmond Morris describes us, the "naked ape." The loss of hair was probably an adaptation to allow more efficient sweating to cool the body as we were doing all that bipedal walking and running around the savannas. But we have retained hair in a few places, and sexual differences exist in this trait as well.

Males have more facial and body hair than females. Consider the location of this hair—the front of the body (male chest hair) and on the face. As primates, we recognize one another as individuals. Primate color patterns focus attention on the face, on the individual (Figure 7.7). As humans, with even more conscious, more specific, more variable relationships with one another, and with our sexual consciousness, it seems reasonable that the dimorphic feature of facial hair, or lack of it, would have evolved to clearly draw attention to and announce to others our individual identities as males or females. The same is true with chest hair—another area of color patterning in some primates.

Along the same lines of logic, it has also been suggested that human lips, which are everted (pulled outward) with translucent skin showing the color of the muscle underneath, may also be signals, a splash of color drawing attention to the face. It is not irrelevant, in addition, that the lips are rich in nerve endings involved in sexual arousal. Nearly all cultures practice kissing, and women in many cultures enhance the color difference of their lips.

FIGURE 7.7
Some colorful primate faces, including that of one primate that purposely enhances facial color. Colorful faces are evidence of the importance of individual recognition within primate societies. *Clockwise from upper left:* Chinese white-handed gibbon, mandrill, human, bald uakari.

But what about the places where both sexes have retained body hair—in the axillary (underarm) and pubic regions? Both these regions have specialized sweat glands that discharge a secretion that decomposes to generate a musky odor. In many mammals these secretions are important **pheromones** that transmit information about, among other things, the olfactory signals of estrus. It has been speculated that they serve, or may have once served, similar functions in humans. After all, humans in many societies use odors as sexual attractants—although in many places artificial perfumes are applied after washing off the odor nature may have given us.

To be sure, all these traits and our attitudes about them are manipulated by culture. Different cultural systems have different standards of physical beauty and normalcy. Facial hair in males is the norm in some cultures, such as in several Islamic societies or among the Hutterites, where beards are a sign of marriage. In the 1960s, many of us college students grew beards—some pretty scruffy looking—as a sign of our nonconformity. In other societies, beards have certain negative associations and the majority of men shave. Facial hair is seldom without some meaning as are all of our physical features associated with our sexual identity.

SEX AND GENDER

There is strong evidence that our basic sexual behavior is something that was selected for and established early on in our evolution. This behavior has been translated from the purely biological to the cultural as our species evolved that aspect of its identity, so that now there are all sorts of variations with regard to "normal" sexual behavior. What may we say in general, then, about this transition from biological themes to cultural interpretations with regard to sex?

The Definitions

We rarely have any difficulty telling the sex of any other human being. *Male* and *female* are two biological categories that are objectively real and common to all human groups. As these two categories are incorporated into various cultural systems, however, differences arise. The identities and roles of males and females under different cultural systems vary depending on the nature of those systems—the complex interactions of economics, politics, family organizations, and abstract beliefs. Thus, *males* and *females* of the human biological species become the *men* and *women* of a particular society practicing a particular culture. We refer to the cultural interpretation of biological sex categories as **gender** (Figure 7.8).

There is an incredible range of variation in gender identities and roles among the world's cultures. The variable factors include such things as the roles of each gender in economic activities, differences in political and other decision-making power and influence, and expected norms of behavior.

pheromone A chemical substance secreted by an animal that conveys information and stimulates behavioral responses.

gender The culturally defined categories and characteristics of men and women.

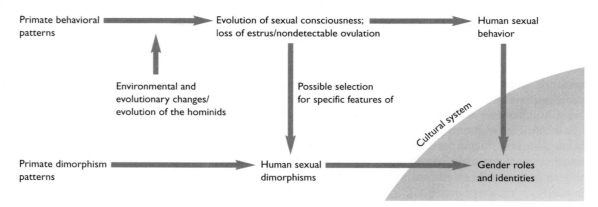

FIGURE 7.8

The evolved sexual identities and roles common to all members of the human species are translated by individual cultural systems into gender identities and roles.

For example, among the Hutterites, women are generally believed to be inferior to men and do not formally participate in colony decisions. They cannot even vote for the head cook, who is traditionally a woman. There is also a strict division of labor; that is, there are men's jobs and women's jobs. However, as I pointed out in Chapter 1, if work needs to be done, a man may perform a woman's task, and vice versa. In one colony I visited, the official "chicken man"—literally a man's job—was a woman. Moreover, women can and do voice opinions and have, I was told, a good deal of unofficial influence, through their husbands, in colony business.

In the United States only a century ago, men were seen as the gender that properly had political, economic, and social power and that, therefore, should be educated. Women were far less likely to receive a college education, seldom held any sort of management position (if they did any work outside the home at all), and, until 1920, were not even allowed to vote. Women were thought of as the literally weaker sex. Obviously, things are different now, at least to a degree. As our culture has changed, our gender roles and identities have changed to fit our evolving cultural system.

Gender as Folk Taxonomy

folk taxonomy A system of classification based on the relationships among cultural categories for important items and ideas.

The relationships among a culturally constructed set of categories, such as those for gender, are collectively called a **folk taxonomy,** or cultural classification. A society orders its world in ways that reflect objective reality as its people see and understand that reality, and that also meet its particular cultural needs and fit the totality of its cultural system.

For example, American society has a scientific viewpoint about the causes of disease. We classify and compare diseases by the nature of their causes—genetic, bacterial, viral, parasitic, environmental, nutritional, congenital, emotional, and so on.

By contrast, the Fore, a farming people of Papua New Guinea (whom we will discuss in more detail in Chapter 14), also classify diseases by their causes, but the causes are very different. The Fore believe that all diseases are the result of the malicious intent of sorcerers or spirits. Life-threatening diseases are thought to be caused by sorcery—the malevolent action of one person against another. This reflects the political and economic and social tensions, rivalries, and jealousies that have become prevalent aspects of the Fore culture.

Folk taxonomies for gender differ widely among the cultures of the world, even though most recognize basically two sexes and two gender categories. Biological sex is, however, not always unambiguous. There are people born with underdeveloped sexual characteristics or with characteristics (including genitalia) of both sexes. In addition, there are those who are ambivalent toward their own sexual identity. As a result, some cultures recognize more than two genders.

A striking example is the *hijras* of India. The word means "not men," and, indeed, hijras are men who have been voluntarily surgically emasculated. They are recognized as a third sex and make up a third gender, and they have very specific identities and roles within the culture of Hindu India. Although often mocked and ridiculed because of their exaggerated feminine expressions and gestures, they are also in demand as performers at important rituals such as marriages and births (Figure 7.9).

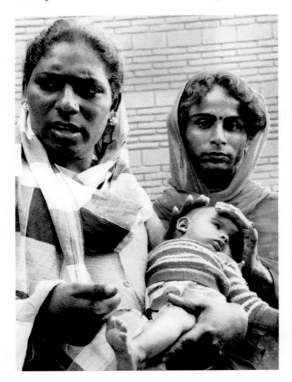

FIGURE 7.9
Hijras, emasculated men who dress and behave like women, make up a third gender category in India. These hijras are blessing a child, one important ritual function they perform.

How may we explain the hijras in cultural terms? According to Serena Nanda, the anthropologist who has studied them extensively, hijras identify with figures in Hindu mythology and Indian culture who are, in various ways, of ambiguous or changing sexual and gender identity: "Indian culture thus not only accommodates such androgynous figures but also views them as meaningful and even powerful." There is also a sense in Hinduism that people should act according to their own inclination, especially in matters of love and sex.

Another example comes from a number of traditional Native American cultures where some men dressed as women and assumed the occupations and behaviors of women. Such men have been referred to by the term *berdache* (a French term with derogatory implications but still in common use). In some cases, they engaged in sexual relations with other men, and certain rituals could be performed only by them. In the cultures in which they were found, berdaches were not considered abnormal, but they were thought of as another gender.

Some societies acknowledge that certain of their members are, or think of themselves as, ambiguous with regard to the two standard sex categories. These societies have evolved third or even fourth gender classifications to accommodate such individuals, and these classifications have come to define identities and roles within the societies' cultures. The categories of sex are biological. The categories of gender constitute a folk taxonomy—a cultural interpretation of the biological reality with implications for and connections with all aspects of a society and its cultural system.

SEX AND CULTURAL INSTITUTIONS

Has our evolved sexual behavior—and its cultural interpretations—had effects on other aspects of our cultural systems? In other words, can we expand on the biocultural interactions already described?

Among the most interesting of cultural phenomena, and sometimes the most puzzling, are cultural universals—behavior patterns found in all societies. Because we humans have the ability to invent our behaviors and change them at will, and because most behaviors show a good deal of variation from culture to culture, it's noteworthy that some behaviors are found everywhere. These behaviors demand explanation. There are two that may well be explained by our identity as the sexual primate.

Marriage

Marriage is a set of cultural rules that bring together a man and a woman (or more than one of either) to create the **nuclear family** and to define their behavior toward each other, their offspring, and their

marriage A set of cultural rules for bringing together a man and a woman (usually) to create a family unit and for defining their behavior toward one another, their children, and society.

nuclear family The family unit made up of parents and their children.

FIGURE 7.10
A marriage in India. Although the specifics vary greatly, every culture recognizes marriage and celebrates the beginning of such unions with a ceremony.

society. Nearly all cultural systems we know of now or have knowledge of from the past have some form of marriage. Of course, there is a great deal of variation in such things as the number of marriage partners one may have, whom one may marry, how property is owned, and so on (we'll cover some of these in Chapter 10). But almost every society, from every level of complexity and part of the world, recognizes a need to culturally define and acknowledge some sort of marriage unit, nearly always male-female (Figure 7.10).

Marriage seems only natural. But that's because it *is* universal. It's what we're used to. Is there, however, any reason for the universality of this institution, especially today when, for many societies, the nuclear family is no longer the center of social and economic organization?

In our own culture, for example, nearly half of all families are single-parent families, some of which have always had only one parent, and this often indicates that someone other than a parent is taking a major role in the care and raising of the offspring. A union of male and female is certainly needed to conceive a child, but after that, anybody can raise and nurture the child to become a functioning member of the group. But with few exceptions, all cultures recognize marriage or some version of it as serving, among other functions, the purposes of procreation and child rearing.

Can the universality of marriage be explained by saying that it is such a good idea that every culture invented it or chose it from among all the possible alternatives? It doesn't seem likely, especially when there *are* other, perfectly viable alternatives. Rather, it seems more likely that it can be explained in much the same way we accounted for sexual dimorphisms—that they had a biological origin and were then translated into a variety of cultural interpretations.

If some sort of male-female bond was crucial to the success of our early ancestors, as I have proposed, and if the social, psychological, sexual, and emotional aspects of this bond became something that was normal and vital for our survival for millions of years, the universality of marriage may be as much a part of our biological heritage as our bipedalism and our sexual dimorphism. In a manner of speaking, we're stuck with being bipedal and sexually dimorphic, and so any cultural variations regarding these features must necessarily take them into account. As a simple example, clothing—no matter what sort—has to be made for bipeds, and clothing that is tailored to any extent must vary somewhat depending on which sex it is for.

Similarly, we had little choice but to base our reproductive units, and, indeed, the basic units of our societies, on the unit formed by the cooperative bond and commitment between males and females that evolved biologically in our ancestors. We have created all sorts of variations in the specific ways we have done this, but they are always variations on this theme.

The Incest Taboo

A taboo (from the Polynesian *tabu*) is a negative rule; it tells you not to do something. The Jewish and Islamic prohibition against eating pork, for example (which we'll discuss in Chapter 14), is a taboo. The incest taboo is a rule that says one cannot have sex with or marry persons to whom one is too closely related. Just who these people are varies enormously from culture to culture, in many cases (as we'll see in Chapter 10) not even corresponding to biological relationships. But every society does include under the incest taboo the prohibition against sex and marriage within the nuclear family between siblings and between parents and offspring. That part is the cultural universal.

incest taboo A cultural rule that prohibits sexual intercourse or marriage between persons defined as being too closely related.

To be sure, sex and marriage are different matters; sex is certainly not practiced exclusively between married couples. But with regard to the cultural norms in question, there is a connection. As anthropologists Emily Schultz and Robert Lavenda put it, "marriage is a formal prerequisite for becoming sexually active." So while the incest taboo may relate directly to sex and while the rules of who one can marry refer to a cultural institution, they amount to the same thing relative to this discussion.

As with all "rules," there have been a few limited exceptions to the universality of the incest taboo. Among certain royal family lines, most notably among the ancient Incas, Egyptians, and Hawaiians, the preferred marriage partner was someone in the family, often a sibling or parent or offspring. This rule was an attempt to maintain the purity of the royal lines, which were considered divine. But most everyone else in these societies lived by the common incest prohibition.

Why is the incest taboo a universal? One obvious result of close inbreeding is the potential for the expression of defective genetic conditions. Each of us carries several deleterious, even lethal recessive genes that are not expressed because they are hidden by normal dominants. Such deleterious genes are rare *because* they are deleterious. Therefore, it's unlikely for any two random people to carry the same rare deleterious genes. But who else in the world is most likely to share your particular hidden genes? Your parents, siblings, and offspring, of course. So a child produced by you and one of these people would stand a chance of having two of the same gene, thereby expressing the defective trait involved.

That's a good reason to institute a parent-offspring and brother-sister incest taboo, and that's the stated reason for such prohibitions in many cultures. But not every society has seen such results happen often enough to make such a generalization. Many societies lack the scientific knowledge to do so. (Our society has had a scientific understanding of this concept for only about a century.) It seems unlikely, then, that the incest taboo originated as a cultural invention to prevent genetic defects.

Another possible function of the incest taboo would be to prevent sexual conflicts within the nuclear family. Having siblings, parents, and offspring competing with one another over sexual access to family members would be disruptive emotionally and economically. Having to seek sexual and marriage partners outside the basic unit would limit this conflict potential. But again, could every single society we know have invented the taboo for this reason? After all, as cultural beings we can come up with all sorts of rules of behavior. To be a bit facetious, there's nothing to stop a society from saying, "You can marry your sister, but just don't fight with your brothers about it." But, except for those few royal lines, no one does.

Finally, many societies require marriage outside a specific group for the purpose of creating social, economic, or military alliances with other groups. But, again, can this explain the universality of the taboo?

Many nonhumans have a "biological incest taboo" that must necessarily be somehow built into their genes. Many of the nonhuman primates, as well as some other social creatures such as wolves, lions, and some birds, seem to have a mechanism that prevents mating between siblings or between mother and son. (The identity of the father is often unknown in many species, so father-daughter matings stand a chance of taking place.) The adaptive significance of such inborn behaviors is probably the first two factors described above: preventing both the expression of deleterious genetic combinations and the disruption of the main economic and social unit. The behaviors were naturally selected for. The same may have been true for our ancestors. As with marriage, then, the explanation for the universality of the incest taboo and the related requirement to marry outside a specific group may lie in a biological norm becoming translated into a set of cultural rules.

Is there any evidence that the incest taboo may, underneath its cultural expression, have a biological basis? Some compelling evidence comes from studies conducted among Israeli *kibbutzim*—communal agricultural settlements (Figure 7.11). In these communities, children of similar age are raised together in day-care centers while their parents are working. Until about twelve years of age, both sexes play, eat, sleep, bathe, and use the bathroom together. They grow up, in other words, as familiar with one another as real siblings, even

FIGURE 7.11
Children in an Israeli kibbutz. Marriage between people who have grown up together in the same age group on the same kibbutz are extremely rare, although no cultural regulations prohibit them.

though they come from different families. Israeli anthropologist Joseph Shepher found only 6 marriages within the same age groups out of nearly 3,000 kibbutz marriages. This is despite the fact that such marriages are not at all prohibited and in some cases are even encouraged. It seems as if the social situation in the kibbutzim has, in the words of an old TV ad, "fooled Mother Nature." The close proximity and familiarity of age-group kids is apparently siblinglike enough to activate some biological mechanism that turns off sexual attraction between real siblings and between parents and offspring, thus eliminating this motivation for marriage.

We can and do make up cultural incest rules that cover many different groups of people, and this variation, as we'll discuss in Chapter 10, has *cultural* explanations. But the fact that there are incest rules at all and that the brother-sister and parent-offspring taboo is universal seems to be explained by delving into our biological past and then finding the biocultural interactions. And, as in the case of the kibbutzim, sometimes even culture can't overcome the remnants of the original behavior.

From our remote beginnings, then, through some of our more obvious anatomical and physiological features, to some cultural institutions so basic we take them for granted, we are indeed the sexual primate.

SUMMARY

Sexual behavior in humans differs from that of most other mammals, including most other primates, in that we have nondetectable ovulation and sexual consciousness. Sexual attraction, norms, and attitudes are tied up with cultural concepts of personality and standards of beauty as well as individual psychologies.

This difference may have evolved early in hominid history as a mechanism to increase and strengthen the direct involvement of males in the care and raising of offspring. Sexual interest would add to the motivations for forming a personal, emotional, and economic bond between parents. Connected to this was the evolution of bipedalism, which helped facilitate mobility and the acquisition and sharing of resources that were part of this bond.

Humans are a sexually dimorphic species, and many of our dimorphic features may be understood in the context of the different roles that would have been played by males and females among the early hominids. Other features make sense as clear, visible signs of one's identity as an individual male or female.

Sex refers to the biological characteristics of and differences between males and females. These differences are translated by cultural systems into the identities and roles of men and women. We refer to these categories as gender. Gender categories differ widely from culture to culture and from time to time.

The universality of two cultural phenomena—marriage and the parent-offspring and brother-sister incest taboo—may be explained as cultural translations of biologically based themes.

CONTEMPORARY ISSUES

What Causes Differences in Sexual Orientation?

In the fall of 1998, a young Wyoming college student was beaten and left hanging on a fence in the cold to die. The young man was gay and the tragic victim of a hate crime. Clearly, a difference in sexual orientation still troubles many people, even to the point of violence, and even the majority who don't feel violent toward homosexuals still tend to ascribe attributes to a person based on that sexual orientation. We have our stereotypes of gay men and lesbian women.

Science has shown an interest in this topic. Over the years, a fair number of explanations for homosexuality have been proposed, including hormonal imbalances, early childhood imprinting, and early sexual abuse. More recently, with new technologies that allow us to peer into our genetic code and generate electronic images of brain activity, genetic differences and differences in brain anatomy have also been offered as connections, if not causes.

While any or all of these factors could be related to aspects of one's sexuality and sexual behavior, it makes sense that no single factor can account for all cases of a preference for members of one's own sex. Sexual preference is a far more complex phenomenon than that.

Consider exactly what is being categorized by the terms *homosexual* and *heterosexual*. Despite all the connotations of those terms, all they really refer to is the sex of one's partner in a given instance. One is having sex either with a member of the opposite sex or with a member of one's own sex. Because the vast majority of people are unambiguously biological males or females, there are really no other choices but those two. So the physical, tangible situation generates the dichotomy we make. In anthropological terms, we have created a fairly obvious folk taxonomy with regard to the sex of one's sexual partners.

But does it follow that the sex of a person's sex partner predicts other things about that person? Does it follow that other factors of one's personality and life also fall into two neat, discrete categories? Consider this: If you know that someone is heterosexual, can you make *any* other inferences about that person other than the sex of his or her sex partners? Hardly. Persons who classify themselves as heterosexual vary widely in every other factor of their lives, including their attitudes and behaviors regarding sex. Two heterosexuals will probably find different features attractive in

QUESTIONS FOR FURTHER THOUGHT

1. Examples of the conscious and cultural dimensions of human sexual behavior abound. As an experiment, the next time you settle in to watch TV, count the advertisements that use sex as a hook. Take note of how many are for products that have nothing to do with sex.

2. For better or worse, TV is a reflection of our culture. Watch a current show, perhaps a sitcom, and then find a rerun of a sitcom from the 70s, 60s, and even 50s. How do they compare relative to their treatment of sexuality and gender?

members of the opposite sex, will prefer different sexual activities, and will have different philosophies and moral outlooks regarding sex. Why should the situation be any different for homosexuals?

Indeed, one finds the same degree of variation in all these factors among homosexuals as among heterosexuals. And this is because attitudes toward sex partners are expressed as a continuum, not as two all-encompassing taxonomic categories. At one end of the continuum are those for whom the only norm regarding sexual activity involves members of the opposite sex. At the other end are those whose focus is exclusively on members of the same sex. In between is everyone else, with enormously varying attitudes about the emotional, physical, and moral considerations involved in the sex of one's partner as well as about all the other complex components of human sexuality. (Think about the complex and varying factors that must motivate the men who become hijras.) That our categories are artificial and limited is evidenced by the fact that for people in the middle range of that continuum, we have created yet another category—bisexual. All the wide range of variation in human sexual attitudes and ideas is forced into three categories because the physical expression of those attitudes and ideas must necessarily be limited by our two biological sexes.

Why does this range of variation in attitudes and ideas exist? To ask a related question in evolutionary terms, why do some people prefer sexual activity that cannot conceivably lead to conception and thus to the perpetuation of the species? The answer is simply that, as we detailed in the chapter, during the evolution of our species the components of sex have been extended from the deeper, purely instinctive parts of our brains into the conscious parts. All the components of our sexuality and sexual behavior are now tied up with all the other aspects of our personalities. Since, obviously, our personalities differ in as many ways as there are people on earth, it stands to reason that our sexual personalities will differ to a comparable degree. And our personalities are influenced by our cultures. There are cultural systems that have encouraged homosexual relationships, for example, the ancient Greeks and several societies from Melanesia. Thus, it also stands to reason that there is no one factor that gives rise to our sexual attitudes, including our choice (or choices) of sexual partners. There is, therefore, no single *cause* for homosexuality. Indeed, given our nature as the sexual primate, a wide range of variation in what gives people sexual pleasure is to be expected.

3. Read "The Five Sexes" and "The Five Sexes Revisited," by Anne Fausto-Sterling (see below). What do you think about "intersexuals," people who do not unambiguously fit either the male or female category? Are they "abnormal," or do they, as Fausto-Sterling suggests, deserve their own category or categories? If so, how would this affect various aspects of our society?

4. Issues of sexual orientation have been very much in the news lately. Consider the issue of so-called gay marriage. Does the information in this chapter shed any light on this contentious question? Has it perhaps changed your mind on the matter?

NOTES, REFERENCES, AND READINGS

More information on the bonobos is in Frans de Waal's delightful *Bonobo: The Forgotten Ape,* which includes Frans Lanting's wonderful photographs. The quote I used is from pages 105–106. But for an update, see "Swingers" by Ian Parker in the July 30, 2007, *New Yorker.* The term "nondetectable ovulation" was suggested by primatologist Agustín Fuentes, whose latest book, with Christina J. Campbell et al., is *Primates in Perspective.*

More on alloparenting can be found in "Meet the Parents" by Sarah Blaffer Hrdy in the April 2009 issue of *Natural History.*

More details on our various sexual dimorphisms are in *Sex Differences,* edited by Michael S. Teitelbaum, and in several chapters of *Female of the Species,* by M. K. Martin and B. Voorhies. The latter also covers variation in sex and gender categories and the var-

ious roles of men and women in different societies. This book is out of print but is well worth looking up in the library.

For more on the hijras see Serena Nanda's *Neither Man nor Woman,* second edition, and "Hijras: An 'Alternative' Sex/Gender in India" by Gayatri Reddy and Serena Nanda. The quote is from Serena Nanda and Richard L. Warms's *Cultural Anthropology,* sixth edition, page 207. For more on intersexuals, see two pieces by Anne Fausto-Sterling, "The Five Sexes" and "The Five Sexes Revisited," in the March-April 1993 and July-August 2000 issues (respectively) of *The Sciences.*

The quote from Schultz and Lavenda is from their *Cultural Anthropology: A Perspective on the Human Condition,* page 303.

Joseph Shepher's study of the kibbutzim is included in his *Incest: A Biosocial View.*

8

HUMAN VARIATION

Biological Diversity and Race

CHAPTER CONTENTS Why Are There No Biological Races within the Human Species? • What, Then, *Are* Human Races? • Anthropology and the Study of Race • Race, Racism, and Social Issues • Summary • Contemporary Issues: Are There Racial Differences in Athletic Ability? • Questions for Further Thought • Notes, References, and Readings

The 6 billion human beings on earth today come in an amazing variety of shapes, sizes, colors, appearances, beliefs, and behaviors, but there is still much misunderstanding about just what our species' diversity means. There are now, and always have been, conflicts—from the ideological to the bloody—based on different interpretations of the origin and meaning of biological and cultural differences.

In Chapter 4 we examined the nature of cultural differences, which we will discuss further throughout the book. But what about biological differences? Where do those come from? What do they mean? How are they connected to differences in behavior? The search for answers to these questions is, I believe, one of anthropology's most important contributions.

Let's begin with one of my favorite photographs (Figure 8.1). It shows European American *National Geographic* photographer George Steinmetz and some Yali men from the highlands of New Guinea. I need not point out who is who. In fact, if I hadn't said anything about their nationalities, you probably could have guessed from what parts of the world they come, even without the cultural cues of clothing. Steinmetz looks European. The Yali men look like people from the interior of New Guinea. (Compare their features with those of the people in Figures 9.13 and 14.8.)

This photo beautifully represents the wide range of phenotypic variation within the human species. Such variation led, for example, the first Europeans who encountered peoples from the New Guinea highlands to assume they were a different species.

We know now, of course, that all the men in the photo are members of the same biological species, *Homo sapiens*. We can provide detailed evidence of their genetic similarities, and the ultimate test of species identity—the ability to produce fertile offspring—has been demonstrated many times.

But look at them! They are distinct in a number of striking physical features. Surely they must represent definable, nameable groups *within* the human species. And so, by implication, there are surely other definable, nameable human groups. In other words, surely the human species is divisible into a number of biological **subspecies,** or, to use a more common term, **races.**

subspecies Physically distinguishable populations within a species; the concept is falling from use.

races In biology, the same as *subspecies*. In culture, categories that classify and account for human diversity.

FIGURE 8.1
A European American photographer, who is 6 feet 2 inches tall, with a group of Yali people from the highlands of West Papua (the western half of New Guinea). There is little doubt as to who is who, nor that members of our species can display a striking degree of phenotypic variation. The major question then becomes: Does this degree of variation mean that there are distinguishable human races?

I'll address that assumption right away. It is now a well-established fact that, *biologically, human races do not exist.* There is no scientifically valid way to divide us up into any number of biologically meaningful groups within the species. But this area of human biological diversity is rife with social, ethical, political, historical, philosophical, and personal implications. And it's a subject in which wishful thinking is sometimes allowed to stand in for rigorous science.

So, it pays to articulate *why* there are no biological races. It's not enough to assume it's the case, no matter how noble the concept makes us feel. We need to be able to explain it, to present the *evidence* for it.

AS YOU READ, CONSIDER THE FOLLOWING QUESTIONS:

1. What scientific evidence refutes the existence of biological human races?

2. What, then, *are* human races?

3. How can anthropology contribute to our understanding of some of the problems surrounding the concept of race?

WHY ARE THERE NO BIOLOGICAL RACES WITHIN THE HUMAN SPECIES?

There are four areas of evidence that we can examine to address this question. As we discuss them, we need to be as objective as possible, to try not to argue to a predetermined conclusion. In the end, this will make our conclusion all the more meaningful.

The Concept of Race within General Biology

Since we humans are a biological species, major theoretical conclusions that apply to other species should apply to us. We may ask, then, what evolutionary biologists in general say about the categories of subspecies or races.

Subspecies names—that is, taxonomic names following the genus and species names, indicating distinct groups—have been in common use for years. Figure 8.2, for example, shows the ranges of four named subspecies of caribou, a large North American member of the deer family (Figure 8.3). The problem here is obvious: since all populations of caribou compose a single species and maintain that species' identity through the flow of genes among their populations, these subspecies distinctions are rather artificial. In reality, the dividing lines shown on the map in Figure 8.2 don't exist. The caribou at the extremes of the range may look quite different (in size, color, and branching pattern of antlers), but one doesn't step over one of these geographical lines and find the caribou suddenly looking completely distinct. Rather, their variable traits, although they may cluster in certain areas, will grade into one another over geographical space. This gradation is called a **cline,** or clinal distribution.

Let's consider another example. Figure 8.4 shows the size variation (based on sixteen skeletal measurements) of the common house sparrow. Northern and higher elevation sparrows tend to be larger, an adaptation to the cold. But, again, the categories are artificial. In no case would those categories deserve formal names.

I sampled recent texts in evolutionary biology and found that the concept of subspecies, or race, is formally recognized less and less.

cline A geographic continuum in the variation of a trait.

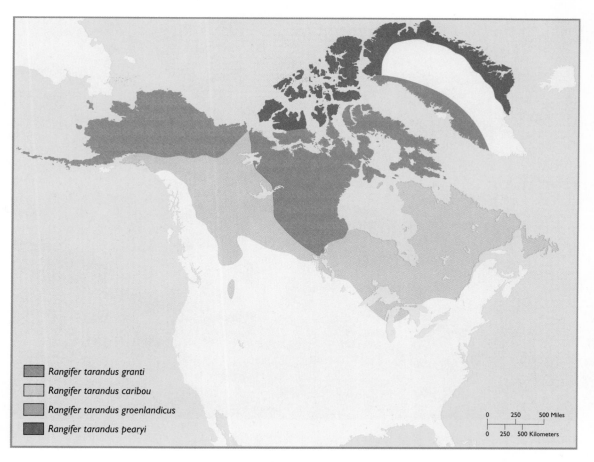

Rangifer tarandus granti

Rangifer tarandus caribou

Rangifer tarandus groenlandicus

Rangifer tarandus pearyi

FIGURE 8.2
North American populations of caribou are considered by some to represent subspecies, or races.

In one major text, for example (*Evolution,* by biologist Mark Ridley), neither term appears in the index or glossary, nor is either formally used in the discussions of species variation or species formation.

The terms *are* used in another book (*Population Genetics and Evolution,* by Mettler et al.), but race is said to be "a subjective convenience," and in place of *subspecies,* the authors suggest **semispecies** to indicate groups within a species that have become isolated and distinct enough to be at an intermediate stage toward becoming actual separate species. An example would be the caribou of North America and the reindeer of Eurasia. Members of these two groups—although they do show phenotypic differences—can interbreed under artificial conditions (in zoos, for example), so they are technically the same species; but they don't interbreed in nature because they've been isolated in separate hemispheres for about 10,000 years (since the last glaciers receded and a rising sea level inundated the Bering Land Bridge).

semispecies Populations of a species that are completely isolated from one another but have not yet become truly separate species.

FIGURE 8.3
The caribou, *Rangifer tarandus.* This woodland caribou of Alaska and Canada is sometimes classified as subspecies *Rangifer tarandus caribou.* Well adapted to a wide range of environments, the caribou has such traits as hollow outer guard hairs, which give it extra buoyancy for swimming and extra insulation for warmth. This feature makes caribou hides a favorite material among some Arctic peoples for making parkas.

Today, evolutionary biology tends to formally recognize biological groups within species only on such relatively rare occasions. Otherwise, variation within species is distributed clinally, making the naming of meaningful subspecies or racial groups impossible.

The Distribution of Human Biological Variation

How, then, does the human species compare with other species as regards races or subspecies? Could we—like caribou and reindeer—come in distinct enough groups to be considered semispecies, thus deserving formal third names after *Homo sapiens*? Or—like the populations of house sparrows or the North American caribou—are we a large, widely dispersed, physically variable single species in which variable traits are distributed as clines such that no truly distinct biological populations exist? Let's look at some of our variable biological traits and their distributions.

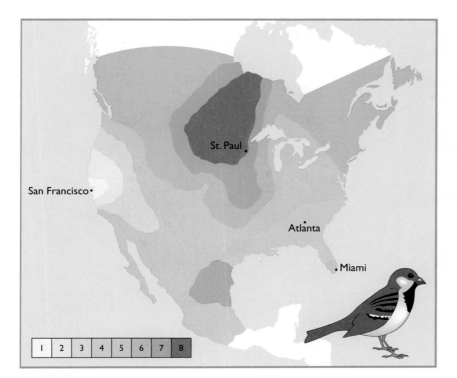

FIGURE 8.4
The distribution of size variation in male house sparrows, determined by sixteen skeletal measurements. The larger the number, the larger the sparrow. The classes, however, are arbitrary. If a line is drawn from Atlanta to St. Paul or from St. Paul to San Francisco, the size variation is distributed as a cline, a continuum of change from one area to another.

Skin Color   One obvious and important example is skin pigmentation—a criterion used for racial classification the world over. Skin color is the result of several pigments, the most important of which is **melanin,** produced by specialized skin cells called **melanocytes.** A function of melanin is to absorb the sun's ultraviolet (UV) radiation. Too much UV radiation can break down folate, a chemical necessary for normal embryo development and rapid cell division, such as in sperm production. It can also cause skin cancer. Under the influence of increased UV radiation, a person's melanocytes increase their melanin production and darken the skin. This, of course, is known as tanning, and even dark-skinned individuals exhibit this response.

Ultraviolet radiation varies with latitude. Sunlight strikes the earth more directly at the equator and at more of an angle the farther one gets from the equator. Hitting at an angle, the solar radiation also travels through more atmosphere, and thus more UV is absorbed by ozone. Not only do humans have the ability to tan in response to increased UV levels, but, as is obvious to us all, populations are genetically programmed for differences in skin color, and these differences also vary by latitude. In general, peoples that live closer to the equator have darker skin. Skin color gradually gets lighter in populations farther

melanin The pigment largely responsible for human skin color.

melanocytes Specialized skin cells that produce the pigment melanin.

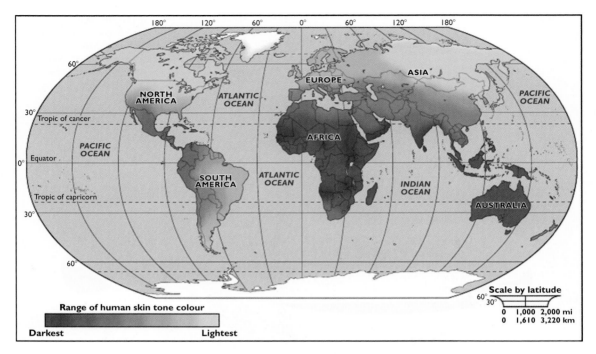

Range of human skin tone colour

Darkest **Lightest**

Scale by latitude

0 1,000 2,000 mi
0 1,610 3,220 km

FIGURE 8.5

Skin color distributions. Darker skin is concentrated in equatorial regions.

away from the equator (Figure 8.5). (These generalizations refer to indigenous populations, those with a long history in an area. The average skin color of people in a cosmopolitan city—say, New York—would obviously be meaningless.)

It is generally agreed that the relationship between dark skin and high levels of UV radiation is an example of an adaptive response. Because of the damaging effects of UV, peoples in or near the equator have undergone selection for permanently higher levels of melanin production. Darker-skinned people do not have more melanocytes than lighter-skinned people, just more melanin. By implication, dark skin was the original human skin color, since our species first evolved in equatorial Africa.

Why, then, did populations that moved away from the equator evolve lower melanin production and therefore lighter skin? It has to do with vitamin D production. Vitamin D can be synthesized in lower layers of skin when a precursor of the vitamin is activated by UV radiation. Vitamin D is important in regulating the absorption of calcium—necessary for bone manufacture—especially during pregnancy and lactation. A deficiency in vitamin D can also lead to a skeletal deformity known in children as rickets. (There is an adult version of the abnormality as well.) Bones with rickets are also more prone to breakage, and deformity of the pelvis can make childbirth difficult.

As populations moved away from the equator, those with darker skin could not manufacture sufficient vitamin D for normal bone growth and maintenance. Those with lighter skin, therefore, were at an adaptive and, thus, a reproductive advantage. Over time, lighter skin became the normal, inherited condition in these groups. Thus, skin color may be seen as a balancing act—dark enough to protect from the damaging effects of UV and light enough to allow the absorption of vitamin D and its related benefits.

Now, look back at Figure 8.5. Although skin color varies by latitude and ranges from the very dark to the very light, in no way does this variation assort into distinct geographical groups. Skin color, like sparrow size, is distributed as a cline, gradually getting lighter or darker across geographic space. So, dark skin, often associated with Africa, is in fact an equatorial expression and is also found—as you have seen—halfway around the world in New Guinea. It does not correspond to one particular population.

Skin color is, however, a trait of continuous variation; that is, the trait itself does not come in nice, neat categories but ranges from light to dark with all shades in between. What about traits that come in discrete, either-or categories? Maybe these could be used to divide our species into subspecies or racial populations.

Blood Type   The well-known ABO blood types are a good example. Everyone on earth is type A, type O, type B, or type AB—there are no other categories and no intermediates. The variation is the result of four variants of a single gene that codes for a protein on the red blood cells. How is this trait distributed?

Figure 8.6 shows the distributions for type A and type B blood. There is no correlation to any obvious environmental factor such as latitude or climate. Type A is totally absent in some indigenous South American groups but is found in over 50 percent of some northern European and indigenous Australian populations. Type B, found in very low frequency among Native Americans, comes in high frequencies in Asia—where Native Americans originated.

It has been suggested that this trait is adaptively neutral, that is, that blood type is not related to health or reproductive success but is just a matter of the random processes of evolution, gene flow, and genetic drift (see Chapter 3). The great apes also have these blood types, so the variation could go well back into our evolutionary history. Others have proposed an association between blood type and susceptibility or resistance to various diseases. There is some statistical evidence for this but no well-established cause-and-effect relationships.

The point here is that, as with skin color, the distribution of blood types is of no help in defining human races. The categories on the maps are arbitrary. I could have divided the range of frequencies into more or fewer groups. The maps then would have looked quite different. But

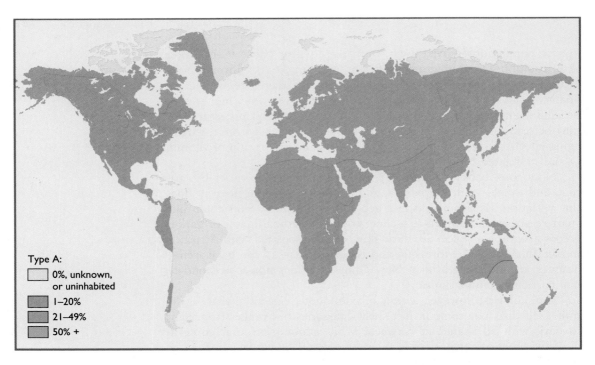

Type A:

☐ 0%, unknown, or uninhabited

▨ 1–20%

▨ 21–49%

▨ 50% +

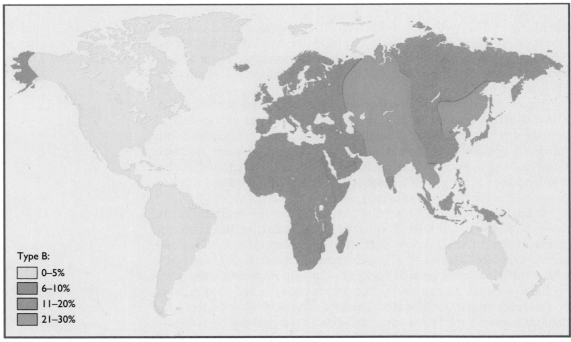

Type B:

☐ 0–5%

▨ 6–10%

▨ 11–20%

▨ 21–30%

FIGURE 8.6
Approximate frequency distributions of type A and type B blood, demonstrating the lack of a pattern in the distribution of this variable trait.

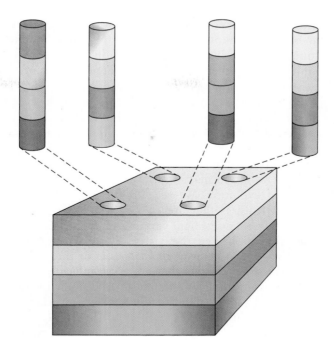

FIGURE 8.7
A diagram of discordant variation. Each layer represents the geographic distribution of one variable trait. Each "core," or cylinder, represents a sample of individuals from a particular area. Notice that each core is different and that any other four cores are very likely to be different as well. The expression of one trait does not predict a particular expression of another. There are no natural racial divisions based on specific combinations of traits.

again, notice that the distribution of the frequencies is actually clinal. If I assigned more categories, this would be even clearer.

In fact, no matter what traits one uses—and there are many more human variable traits—the human species simply cannot be divided into distinct subgroups based on biological differences. Nor will such division work when using combinations of traits, because the distributions of traits are discordant—that is, a particular expression of one trait does not necessarily predict a particular expression of another (Figure 8.7). The nature and distribution of human traits, then, is like that of most other species. Our variable traits are distributed as clines, with no clear-cut boundaries.

Human Genetics

Phenotypic features can be deceptive, influenced as they are by multiple genes, environmental factors, and natural selection. For the past several decades, we have had the ability to look at aspects of the genetic code itself. Some have thought that perhaps this type of research could provide better data for determining the identity of subspecies groups of *Homo sapiens*.

From the beginning, however, it was clear that genetic data did more to refute the concept of biological race than did phenotypic data. When scientists genetically compared samples from traditional racial groups, they determined that there was actually little genetic difference among the groups. Most diversity in genes, around 95 percent, was found between *individuals,* even individuals within the same "racial" affiliation. In other words, only around 5 percent of genetic variation exists between major population groups.

This means that diversity on the genetic level is not clustered into any definable subspecies divisions but is instead fairly evenly distributed and all the phenotypic variation that we try to assort into race is the result of a virtual handful of genes.

Of course, the nature of the genetic variation that does exist is such that the variation may well show a geographic pattern due to the processes of evolution. We see this in skin color, blood type, and other physical features that are characteristic of certain areas. But interestingly, only a few genetic variants (about 7 percent) are unique to any one population, and these are rare in those populations. This means that they are in no way *characteristic* of those populations. Moreover, although some clusters that are geographically distant or isolated by a barrier are statistically different for the studied variants, the frequencies of those change gradually across space; in other words, they are distributed as clines.

And, finally, when we look at an overall pattern of genetic variation for our species, we find something very interesting. The genetic variation within sub-Saharan Africa is greater than that for the entire remainder of the human population. Moreover, the variation in the rest of the world is, for the most part, a subset of that of sub-Saharan Africa (Figure 8.8). Thus, on a broad genetic level, our familiar racial designations don't make sense. "African" is not a genetic race because there is almost no set of African genetic variation not shared by some other populations in the world. Nor do groups such as "European" or "Native American" have any genetic racial identity, because their sets of genetic variants are found somewhere in Africa, the acknowledged geographic home of the species.

FIGURE 8.8
Comparative genetic diversity. Circle (*a*) represents the genetic diversity of humans from sub-Saharan Africa and (*b*) the genetic diversity of the rest of the world's peoples. Note that African diversity is much greater and that most of the diversity of the rest of the world is a subset of African diversity. (Circles are not drawn to scale.)

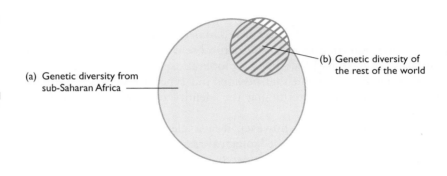

(a) Genetic diversity from sub-Saharan Africa

(b) Genetic diversity of the rest of the world

Thus, as with phenotypic features, variation and regional differences in genes do not translate into support for biologically meaningful racial groups.

Evolutionary Theory and the Nature of the Human Species

Let's look at the question of biological race from a more general perspective. We could ask whether—given the nature of our species and what we know of the workings of evolution—groups distinct enough to be semispecies *could* exist within *Homo sapiens*. After all, semispecies have developed in 10,000 years in *Rangifer tarandus* (reindeer and caribou), and even by the most conservative estimates, our species is ten times as old.

Moreover, we are a populous species; we live in vastly diverse environmental conditions, sometimes in fairly isolated areas; and we further isolate our populations through cultural boundaries. These would seem the perfect circumstances for creating definable groups.

Mobility and Gene Flow   One noteworthy feature of our species for its entire biological history has been mobility. We evolved first in Africa—whether that was 2 million or 200,000 years ago (see Chapter 6)—and then spread with amazing speed all over the Old World, despite mountains, large bodies of water, and other barriers. And when we reached the far corners of Africa and Eurasia, we did not stay put. We continued to move around in search of resources and space. As we evolved, we acquired increasing ability to move around (with the domestication of the horse and with inventions such as boats and navigation instruments), and we found increasing motivation for doing so. Such mobility leads to extensive gene flow, and it's fair to say that humans tend to exchange genes at nearly every opportunity.

What about our cultural rules about marrying within one's own society? Don't they genetically isolate populations at certain times? Recall the Hutterites, who have been largely **endogamous** for over 480 years. Such rules change, and the political, ethnic, and religious populations they define change over time. The Hutterites' nearly half a millennium history is not all that long in evolutionary terms; not much genetic variation could arise in that period, especially in a species with a long generation time. Moreover, rules of endogamy are not always fully upheld. Biological isolation through the cultural institution of endogamy is a temporary condition.

Gene flow, then, is the norm for our species, and, as widespread as we are, we still manage to exchange enough genes—through intermediary populations—to prevent any group of humans from being isolated long enough to evolve the distinct differences sufficient for semispecies status.

endogamy Marriage within a specified unit of people.

Culture   Finally, what about all the different environments our species inhabits? Couldn't natural selection have led to differentiation of some populations? Certainly, the variation and distribution of some of our variable traits—skin color, for example—can be attributed to natural selection. But our major adaptive mechanism is culture, with its values, social systems, and, especially, its technologies that, to a great extent, have increasingly buffered us against the constant editing of natural selection. Adaptively, we change less biologically than we do culturally. Culture and the big brain that makes culture possible are species characteristics, shared by all humans. They are the basis of our modern identity. Culture, in a sense, *is* our environment, and we may say that for some time our species has experienced little of the kind of environmental variation that would lead to the development of distinct, isolated subpopulations, even among such groups as those from Australia, New Guinea, and Tasmania that have been relatively isolated for perhaps tens of thousands of years. As anthropologist C. Loring Brace puts it, we all have undergone the "same selective pressures" leading to essentially the "same lifeway."

WHAT, THEN, *ARE* HUMAN RACES?

Having said all the above, we are still left with the fact that races *are*, indeed, real. We talk about them. We identify ourselves as belonging to one race or another. We identify one another as belonging to a particular race. We are asked on various forms to identify our race. Decisions about our lives are made according to our race. And, certainly, we can't open the newspaper without reading some story related to race. So, if not a biological category, what *is* race?

The answer is that race is a folk taxonomy, a cultural classification (see Chapter 7). All cultures have folk taxonomies for the human variations they are aware of. Isolated societies may have a very simple racial classification: us and them. And often their word for *us* also means something like "human" or "the people," while *them* may imply, well, something other than "the people." Societies having more contact with other groups will, obviously, have more complex folk taxonomies for race and more complex attitudes, reflected by the implications of their names and categories.

The racial categories we are familiar with in the United States are no less a folk taxonomy than those of other cultures. Our basic scheme of categories is something we all are aware of. I once gave a class a weekend assignment: to find ten people—preferably of various ages, both sexes, and different ethnic backgrounds—and ask them two questions: How many races are there? What are they? Some came back with odd responses, such as "three races: black, white, and Polish." Jewish was a race according to some informants. Some listed

Native Americans. But the majority gave some form of racial classification that corresponded to our familiar categories—Caucasian, black, Asian; or African American, white, Oriental. They used different terms depending on their own age and background, but the similarity of responses indicated that some basic taxonomy is shared among members of our society.

Now, since these are cultural categories, we should be able to trace their origins historically. At the risk of oversimplifying European and American history, I will surmise that our racial categories can be traced back to European knowledge and attitudes first acquired during the Age of Exploration. European explorers used mostly water transportation and so were limited in the range and distribution of human variation they could observe. They sampled points along the continuum of human biodiversity. Because these points could differ greatly from one another, it appeared that human variation fell into a small number of relatively discrete categories (Figure 8.9), generally by continent.

In addition, the Europeans didn't see these indigenous peoples as merely different; they compared them to and rated them against European peoples and cultures, usually unfavorably. After all, they looked different, spoke differently, had different cultures, often were less technologically complex, and were not Christians, Jews, or Muslims. In addition, the motivation for exploration was often less to acquire knowledge than to acquire spices, precious metals, territory, and labor. An attitude of profound difference and dominance was built into European relationships with these indigenous peoples. (Notice in Figure 8.9 the men erecting a cross to claim the land for Spain.) A racial folk taxonomy naturally developed to organize this variation and these attitudes.

These folk taxonomic categories were formalized in 1758 by Linnaeus. His species *Homo sapiens* was divided into five varieties: *Homo sapiens ferus* (wild men, possibly to accommodate tales of abandoned children supposedly raised by animals), *H.s. americanus, H.s. europaeus, H.s. asiaticus,* and *H.s. afer.* (Interestingly, despite his obvious biases, he doesn't place Europeans at either the beginning or end of the list, as one would expect.) His descriptions of these races—and this is typical of racial folk taxonomies all over—are blends of biological generalizations, perceived cultural traits, and what anthropologist Stephen Molnar calls "personality profiles." For example, here's his description of *Homo sapiens afer:*

> Black, phlegmatic [sluggish], relaxed. Hair black, frizzled; skin silky, nose flat; lips tumic [swollen]; crafty, indolent, negligent. Anoints himself with grease. Governed by caprice [impulse].

Europeans, by comparison, were "covered with cloth vestments" and "governed by laws."

Because the history of the United States has been so influenced by European cultures, it makes sense that these basic categories would be

FIGURE 8.9
Columbus's first contact with natives of the New World. To the Europeans, the Indians were so strikingly different in physical and cultural features that it was natural to consider them a distinct category of human. Notice the men planting the cross to claim the land as theirs. (From a seventeenth-century Spanish version of a 1594 engraving by de Bry. The Granger Collection.)

carried over to this country and altered by its subsequent history. For example, the reason we distinguish Hispanics from other European Americans is, in part, because of the conflicts between Spain and other European countries over territory in the New World and later between Mexico, a former Spanish colony, and the United States. Notice, too, that in some lists of race, Puerto Rican and Hispanic are separate categories. It's not that some new group of people has arisen; rather, we choose for certain purposes to distinguish people from that U.S. territory—people who, previously and still in other lists, are categorized as Hispanic.

Race is a folk taxonomy—a cultural translation of human diversity, variable across space and over time. But I should offer a caution: having dismissed the idea of biological race and having identified race as a folk taxonomy, let's not relegate the race concept to *just* a folk taxonomy and by doing so imply that the problems inherent in, derived from, and justified by our racial categories are not real. They are. Folk taxonomies are powerful things, not just isolated phenomena of "exotic" cultures. All cultures categorize their worlds with folk taxonomies. Even ours. And even when we are aware of our taxonomies, we still respond to and perceive our world according to them.

ANTHROPOLOGY AND THE STUDY OF RACE

It would be nice to say that anthropology all along has been the discipline that collected real data to support the nonexistence of biological races. But that is not the case. As we discussed in Chapter 2, anthropology is a science conducted, as are all sciences, within a cultural context and so is influenced, even constrained by, cultural trends and limits to knowledge. The fact is, for much of the history of anthropology, into the 1960s, the field acknowledged some racial divisions of humankind and sought to enumerate and define those races.

Going back into the nineteenth century, and earlier—before anthropology was even a named discipline—there was of course scientific interest in explaining human biological and cultural variation, and the existence of biological races seemed as obvious as the existence of different cultural systems. Often, if not most of the time, both these areas of variation were explained as different stages in the evolution from a more primitive to a more civilized state, with the obvious value judgments that implies.

Even after Franz Boas (often called the "father of American anthropology"), in the early part of the twentieth century, challenged the validity of "types" of humans and said that differences in achievement among cultures were the result of historical events, not of differences in mental faculties, the reality of races was still, more often than not, assumed. Museum displays included family trees that showed a branching among the typical races, and popular and scholarly books divided humankind into a usually small number of relatively distinct racial groups.

The virulent and violent racism of Nazi Germany in the Second World War led to a rethinking of the accepted biological reality of race that, if not the cause of such racism, certainly helped facilitate it. As early as 1942, Princeton anthropologist Ashley Montagu wrote *Man's Most Dangerous Myth: The Fallacy of Race,* and in 1964 he edited *The Concept of Race,* a collection of eleven essays that debunk the existence of biological races using the same reasoning—if not all the modern data—of the argument in this chapter.

Still, the idea that races must exist held on in places. My first course in human variation, in 1967, was called "Varieties of Man," the title implying that there *were* varieties. The text we used was *The Origin of Races* (1962) by University of Pennsylvania anthropologist Carleton S.

Coon, a book that not only recognized five original races but claimed that those races could be traced back to *Homo erectus* and had crossed a "sapiens threshold" at different times and in a particular order; thus the races had been "sapient" (it means wise or intelligent) for different lengths of time. (It's almost unnecessary to relate in what order Coon thought they crossed this imaginary threshold.) My class notes for that course include lists of characteristics of the major races, with other lists for hybrid races.

And even as recently as 2004, anthropologist Vincent Sarich and science writer Frank Miele claim in *Race: The Reality of Human Differences* that "race is a valid biological concept" in part because we recognize races culturally. In making this argument, they simply ignore the difference between biological reality and folk taxonomy that we've discussed here. Old folk taxonomies sometimes die hard.

It must be made clear that the claim that biological human races don't exist is not being made because it would bolster moral and ethical precepts of human social equality. That is a separate issue. The fact is, based on good, sound biology, races within our biological species *don't exist*—whether we like that or not. And this has been, despite aspects of our past history, a major contribution to knowledge that anthropology can take almost full credit for.

RACE, RACISM, AND SOCIAL ISSUES

The issue of race is not just a matter of whether or not to apply the biological concept of the subspecies to divisions among humans. Would that it were. Rather, the idea of race can be, and is, used to make prejudgments about people and to determine a person's place in society, often without regard to that person's individual traits, skills, and talents. This is **racism**. The moral dimension of this problem is broad, but we can show how anthropology has examined two claimed connections between racial categories and biological traits and, in the process, remind ourselves just what race is—and what it is not.

Cultural Level

racism Judging an individual solely on his or her assigned racial affiliation, based on the assumption that all members of a "race" possess specific characteristics. Prejudice and discrimination based on such a belief.

One issue is the claim that certain human societies, because they live at a less complex cultural level than most, are somehow less evolved and, thus, less intelligent. There are, sadly, many examples of such an idea and its consequences in human history. One striking example involves the natives on the island of Tasmania, located about 130 miles south of Australia (Figure 8.10).

When first contacted by Europeans in the seventeenth century, the indigenous Tasmanians, numbering about 5,000, lived with one of the least complex technologies of any modern peoples. Their tools were

FIGURE 8.10
Eight of the last native Tasmanians.

simple stone and wood artifacts. They lacked metal, domesticated plants and animals, pottery, and bows and arrows. All these were lacking in Australia, too. But the Tasmanians also lacked things found commonly in Australia, such as boomerangs, dogs, nets, hafted stone tools, barbed spears, and the know-how to fish, sew, and perhaps even make a fire.

The European settlers saw the natives of Tasmania as less than human, perhaps even, some scientists suggested, as missing links between humans and apes. They were enslaved, killed, or relocated to isolated areas. A cash bounty was offered for natives captured alive. Some were hunted for sport. By 1869 there were only three native Tasmanians left, two of whom were further denigrated even in death as their bodies were dissected, some of the pieces used as souvenirs, and their bones put on public display. (Not surprisingly, however, there are still some descendants of Tasmanian women and white settlers.)

Such behavior is, of course, unconscionable, and its immorality needs no discussion. But we can still try to account for the great disparity in technological complexity that the Europeans used to support and justify their ideas about and treatment of native Tasmanians. Was there something profoundly different about Tasmanians themselves that prevented them from inventing some very basic tools and technologies?

The answer is that such differences in cultures are explained not by evolutionary level but, as Franz Boas suggested a century ago, by very practical considerations of geography, environment, history, and mobility. A group of people is adapted to the environment in which it lives. The people can only use what resources their habitat provides. They must contend with the climatic conditions of their area.

Although people have lived successfully in just about every set of environmental circumstances on earth, these variables—resources and climate—can make a big difference. As we will point out in Chapter 9, the first farming occurred where there were wild plants with characteristics that lent themselves to domestication. Similarly, domesticable wild animals must be present for that cultural change to take place.

The movement of peoples with their ideas and technologies is another factor. Societies rely on contact with other societies for the majority of their cultural items, often referred to as their cultural inventory. By some estimates, only 10 percent of a given society's cultural inventory originated within that society. The other 90 percent has been borrowed from other cultures in a process known as **diffusion** (a topic we'll discuss in more detail in Chapter 13). Thus, indigenous populations isolated from contact with others were left very much to their own devices. Societies that inhabited isolated regions changed slowly. On the other hand, societies that lived along major migration routes had contact with various peoples and cultures and had ample opportunity to observe, borrow, and adopt new ideas and items. They changed rapidly.

During the Pleistocene glacial advances, Tasmania was connected many different times to Australia, and Australia itself, while never connected directly to Southeast Asia, was more accessible to that region via a string of islands exposed when sea levels dropped. This is how people got to Tasmania in the first place. But with the last glacial recession 10,000 ya, Tasmania and Australia were separated from one another by a broad strait that the Tasmanians' simple watercraft were incapable of navigating. The hunter-gatherer population of the island was thus almost completely isolated until Europeans arrived in 1642. The Tasmanians changed, to be sure, but slowly, and there is even archaeological evidence that their culture actually lost some items— bone tools and the know-how to fish and sew—that they once had.

Major differences in level of technological complexity between societies can be striking, and we may be tempted to explain them through

diffusion The movement of cultural ideas and artifacts among societies. Cultural borrowing.

differences in biology—evolutionary level or mental facility. But there is no evidence for such biological differences, and there are perfectly sound explanations based on the nature of culture as an adaptive mechanism.

Race and Intelligence

A second claimed connection between race and biology is the idea that human populations differ in intelligence. If one group's goal is to limit the social position and power of another group, it can argue that the other group possesses some unalterable biological difference that inherently limits its abilities and therefore justifies its lower social position. Slavery in the United States was often justified by the claim that the black slaves were less intelligent than the whites and therefore could never hope to attain the dominant race's social, political, and intellectual level.

Such broad statements are so clearly motivated by social and economic agendas as to be at least questionable, if not obviously false. Perhaps more dangerous, however, are the more subtle correlations whose propositions are based on scientific investigation. Ideas that sound scientific are often treated more seriously, especially because, even today, many people feel that science is something so complex and obscure that only a handful can really understand it. Many people take the position that if something sounds scientific and they don't get it, it must be valid.

Such is the case for the claimed connection between race and IQ (intelligence quotient). The most infamous example is the late educational psychologist Arthur Jensen's 1969 article in the *Harvard Educational Review* titled "How Much Can We Boost IQ and Scholastic Achievement?" A more recent work on the same topic is *The Bell Curve,* by R. J. Herrnstein and C. Murray (1994). It is far more complex than Jensen's article but expresses the same basic argument, so a focus on the older work will make the essential points.

Jensen attempted to explain the documented fact that American black children score, on average, 15 points lower on IQ tests than American white children. He wondered why programs aimed at the obvious solution of culturally enriching children's lives had pretty much failed. Hence, the title of his article (this time with emphasis for the right intonation): "How much *can* we boost IQ and scholastic achievement?"

Jensen's first conclusion is that IQ tests measure general intelligence—a biological, inherited entity. Jensen also accepts that 80 percent of the variation in intelligence within a population is explained by genetic differences and that only 20 percent is the result of members of that group having been brought up in different cultural environments.

The obvious conclusion, then, is that the difference in intelligence between the two racial groups must be largely the result of some genetic difference, and thus, all the cultural enrichment programs in the world can have only a limited effect. Jensen's answer to the question in his title is "Not much." He states: "No one has yet produced any evidence based on a properly controlled study to show that representative samples of Negro and white children can be equalized in intellectual ability through statistical control of environment and education."

But Jensen went further. He compared scores from different parts of IQ tests and concluded that the different IQs of blacks and whites result from their having different kinds of intellectual abilities. According to Jensen, whites are better at problem solving and abstract reasoning, while the abilities of blacks are focused on memorization, rote learning, and trial-and-error experience. The former is what IQ tests test.

His ultimate conclusion was that education should be as individualized as possible, taking into account not only individual differences in ability and skill but these racially based ones as well.

As you can imagine, Jensen's article caused great controversy. He was labeled a racist by some. Those with racist leanings embraced his work enthusiastically. Let's examine his argument more scientifically, however.

The idea that IQ tests measure some innate mental ability is fraught with problems. It has been said that IQ tests measure the ability to take IQ tests. This statement is not, as it sounds, just sarcasm. IQ tests, in fact, measure particular knowledge and abilities that are largely learned through one's culture. They are valuable. Relatively low scores may sometimes point out a learning disability that has a biological basis. Because they measure the kinds of skills required by education in our culture as well as by many occupations, they do have predictive value as to one's success within the culture.

We do not, however, even know what intelligence is. How can we—through a test given in a cultural language, in a cultural setting, with cultural problems—apply a single number to such a complex and multifaceted concept? When we do this, we are practicing what is called **reification.** IQ scores reify intelligence—translate a complex idea into a single number, which we then use to assign people to various groups, for example, different learning tracks in schools.

As anthropologist Jonathan Marks suggests, there is a difference between *ability* and *performance*. One's score on an IQ test is a score of one's performance. Certainly some internal factor—innate intellectual ability, whatever that *is*—plays a part in your IQ performance. But that performance is also affected by external factors. In test taking, for example, your cultural background, quality of education, personality, home life, even your mood on the day of the test can all affect your performance. We cannot, therefore, infer innate abilities from a test score any more than we can infer a person's athletic abilities from his or her performance in just one game.

The inherited nature of IQ is a complicated issue, but we can point out a major problem here. Heritability studies—which estimate the

reification Translating a complex set of phenomena into a single entity such as a number.

genetic and environmental components of the phenotypic variation in a population—are done regularly, but they are carried out using organisms like fruit flies, where the genetic mechanisms for phenotypic traits are well known and can be manipulated, and where the environmental variables can be controlled in detail. Numbers may be placed on these genetic and environmental variables, which may then be plugged into a heritability formula. To apply the heritability formula to humans, however, is virtually impossible. What numbers can we place on the environmental variables that affect us? How, in other words, can we reify culture? What number is applied to having a culturally enriched childhood, being a member of a minority group, or having a poor early education?

To further claim that two races have different kinds of intellectual abilities is to ignore the very nature of the modern human species. This claim denies to a large number of people the very abilities—to solve problems, to formulate abstractions and generalizations—that are a hallmark of our species' evolution.

Finally, if you are looking to make biological comparisons between two groups, the groups need to be biologically defined. American whites and American blacks are decidedly not biological races. We have already established that race is not a biological concept for the human species in the first place. The groups are cultural. There's simply not much genetic difference. Indeed, it has been estimated that about 15 percent of all genes in African Americans have come from European Americans as a result of gene flow between the two populations over the last several hundred years.

Our folk taxonomies are powerful and influential. We respond to them often without realizing that they are *our* culture's way of ordering *our* world and are not necessarily scientific universals. The influence of the American folk taxonomy for race can easily be seen in Jensen's work. By understanding what race is and what it's not and by applying what we know about the workings of genetics and evolution, we may see the fallacies of this particular piece of research and adopt a perspective from which to evaluate other such claims.

SUMMARY

Race is one of today's most contentious issues. Anthropology's contribution to this discussion involves the objective examination of the facets of human variation and conclusions about what that variation entails, how it came about, and what it does and does not mean. Armed with such information, we are better able to confront the social, ethical, political, and personal aspects of race.

Scientific data from evolutionary biology, biological anthropology, and genetics show us clearly that while human biological variation exists across geographical space and can be examined and explained, the human species simply cannot be divided into any number of meaningful biological units. In other words, biological races do not exist for our species.

CONTEMPORARY ISSUES

Are There Racial Differences in Athletic Ability?

Nearly 80 percent of players in the National Basketball Association are African American. The figure is 70 percent for professional women's basketball. The National Football League is 65 percent black. In track and field, nearly every men's world record belongs to an African or someone of African descent. In the 2011 New York Marathon, three of the top ten male finishers were from Kenya, including the first and second. Three of the top ten women finishers were Kenyan. In the 2011 Boston Marathon, five of the top ten men were Kenyan, including first and second, and the first, third, and fourth women were Kenyan. These statistics pose an obvious question that we may address by focusing on a controversial book by journalist and TV producer Jon Entine called *Taboo: Why Black Athletes Dominate Sports and Why We're Afraid to Talk about It.* This complex book nicely covers many aspects of the topic of sports and race. Entine wrote it, he says, because "sport remains a haven for some of our most virulent stereotypes" and because he believes "that open debate beats backroom scuttlebutt." And open debate it does.

Our immediate explanation for the disproportionate representation of athletes of African descent in some sports is what might be called social selection. This is the idea that, in this country and others, sports—particularly those not requiring specialized and often expensive equipment—became an outlet for members of minority groups, an achievable goal when access to numerous opportunities such as higher education and careers was limited by social prejudices, poor primary and secondary education, and lower socioeconomic status.

Entine points out that this, in fact, was the case with Jews and basketball in the first half of the twentieth century; basketball (as well as boxing) was a way out of the ghetto and ethnic prejudice. So stereotyped did the association between Jews and basketball become that one 1930s sportswriter made a semibiological connection, claiming that Jews were better at the game because of their "alert, scheming mind" and "flashy trickiness" (quoted in Entine).

But Entine also claims that there are biological explanations and that these are, in some cases, more influential. Specifically, he documents evidence that three regions of Africa— West Africa, North Africa, and East Africa—have populations with physical attributes more common to them than to other populations that make them innately better at sports involving endurance, sprinting, and jumping. These traits include such things as a lower percentage of body fat, a higher proportion of certain muscle fibers, and physiological features related to efficient oxygen use. He says that the reason these traits—of obvious adaptive utility—are more common in Africa is that "while people of African descent have spent most of their evolutionary history near to where they originated, the rest of the world's populations have had to modify their African adaptations after migrating to far different regions and climates."

The arguments in Entine's book and reviews of it are complex and should be discussed and further examined, but for our purposes here we can address two issues. First, is it possible

that there are variable human phenotypic traits, even ones that might show patterns of geographic distribution, that might relate to athletic ability? Of course it is. How many heavyweight boxers could hail from the highlands of New Guinea (see Figure 8.1), where indigenous people are, on average, much smaller than the average European or African? Could the average Inuit compete successfully in a 400-meter sprint against someone built like the photographer in Figure 8.1?

So research into other, less obvious physical differences is perfectly justified. In fact, the Kenyan runners have been studied, with the result that their relative success appears to have more to do with training than with any inherent biological difference.

But for our purposes, a more serious problem with Entine's overall argument—one that relates to a major theme of this chapter—is that he uses exceptional individuals to make generalizations not only about particular populations but about whole racial groups. He starts with the assumption that racial groups exist and that their internal homogeneity (reflected by physiological traits) is the result of how long they have lived in different parts of the world. He says, for example, that "although there is considerable disagreement, the *three major racial groupings—Caucasian, Mongoloid, Negroid*—split from 100,000 ya to as recently as the beginning of the last ice age" [emphasis mine]; he even espouses a minority view that "different races [may not be] modifications of *Homo sapiens,* they were in existence before the emergence of *Homo sapiens.*" In other words, he assumes that the populations he is

examining are races in the traditional, biological sense of that word. This, then, is the basis for his explanation of the dominance of African Americans in some sports, namely as a result of their African heritage. According to Entine, Africans are on average innately better athletes for some skills; therefore, a great number of African Americans have inherited these innate skills.

These are logical leaps with little if any validity. We understand that variation exists and that some is geographically patterned. But clear-cut racial groups do not exist. While a small Kenyan population just might have some features that make them better runners, that in no way means that those features are necessarily more common on the African continent as a whole, because this assumes that Africa is synonymous with a racial group. And it certainly doesn't explain the sports phenomenon in the United States. Among other problems with Entine's conclusions is the fact that the average African American can trace a fair percentage of his or her genes to Europe. This should mean that African Americans would be expected to be worse athletes than West Africans, but this is not the case.

This is a complex issue. Obviously, *both* biological and sociocultural components contribute in different degrees to various aspects of sports. We should not be afraid to examine this issue. But doing so in terms of the demonstrably nonexistent biological races only serves to detract from an accurate understanding of the topic and might further reinforce those "virulent stereotypes" that Entine justly seeks to refute.

Race, of course, does exist, but it is a cultural classification—based on a society's knowledge of human diversity, its history, and its attitudes about various human groups. Just as societies culturally translate sexual differences into gender categories, they also translate human biological and cultural diversity into racial categories.

Political, ideological, and economic motivations have led societies to propose connections between racial categories and biological traits. Differences in cultural complexity have been interpreted to reflect differences in intelligence or evolutionary level. IQ test scores have been said to show differences in intellectual abilities between races. There is no sound evidence for such profound biological differences. Rather, there are logical reasons for differences in test scores and level of technology that are grounded in what anthropological data and theory have shown us about the nature of culture as an adaptive mechanism and about the complex environments in which we, as individuals and members of our societies, live.

QUESTIONS FOR FURTHER THOUGHT

1. The basic concept of this chapter can be a complex one when you confront it in real life. Imagine someone challenged you about the nonexistence of biological races. Suppose this person said, "But, hey, I was just watching the Olympics last summer, and I could *tell* where the athletes were from just by their features. Isn't that race?" How would you respond?

2. Think about the North American categories of race. What specific historic events or sequences may have influenced our commonly understood racial groups? If you are familiar with the racial folk taxonomy of another culture, similarly analyze it.

3. Give some other examples of the "connection" between race and athleticism. For example, are white men and women better golfers? or swimmers? What about the prevalance of Eastern Europeans in gymnastics?

4. On a practical level: suppose it is verified that some populations in Kenya have a disproportionate number of members who possess biological traits that make them better long-distance runners. How would we (indeed, *should* we?) accommodate such an advantage in organized sporting competition?

NOTES, REFERENCES, AND READINGS

The two books in evolutionary biology to which I referred are *Evolution,* by Mark Ridley, and *Population Genetics and Evolution,* by Lawrence Mettler et al.

There are many good books on the nature of human biodiversity. I recommend *Human Variation: Races, Types, and Ethnic Groups,* by Stephen Molnar; *Human Diversity,* by Richard Lewontin; *Human Biodiversity: Genes, Race, and History,* by Jonathan Marks; and *Human Biological Variation,* by James Mielke, Lyle Konigsberg, and John Relethford. The Marks book includes an expanded discussion of race and athleticism and the distinction between performance and ability. For information on the distribution of skin color differences, see "Skin Deep," by Nina Jablonski and George Chaplin in the October 2002 *Scientific American;* and Jablonski's new book, *Living Color: The Biological and Social Meaning of Skin Color.*

For discussions on other human variable traits, see Sara Stinson et al., *Human Biology: An Evolutionary and Biocultural Perspective,* and E. F. Moran, *Human Adaptability: An Introduction to Ecological Anthropology.*

For a collection of articles on the nonexistence of biological races, see *The Concept of Race,* edited by M. F. Ashley Montagu. For a nice treatment of the history of race studies, including a discussion of Linnaeus's taxonomy, try Kenneth Kennedy's *Human Variation in Space and Time.*

Arthur Jensen's article, "How Much Can We Boost IQ and Scholastic Achievement?" is in the Winter 1969 issue of the *Harvard Educational Review.* The quoted passage is on pages 82–83. For a more detailed version of the same argument see *The Bell Curve,* by Richard Herrnstein and Charles Murray. For a rebuttal, see "None of the Above" by Malcolm Gladwell in the December 17, 2007, *New Yorker.*

Perhaps the best book on racism, with an emphasis on scientific attempts to find correlations between race (and sex) and intelligence is Stephen Jay Gould's *The Mismeasure of Man* (revised and expanded). It includes a detailed critique of *The Bell Curve.* For a history of the race concept see *Race Is a Four-Letter Word: The Genesis of the Concept,* by C. Loring Brace, and *Man's Most Dangerous Myth: The Fallacy of Race* by Ashley Montagu.

Two books, separated by forty-two years, that make arguments for the existence of races are *The Origin of Races,* by Carleton S. Coon, and *Race: The Reality of Human Differences*, by Vincent Sarich and Frank Miele.

For more on the race and athleticism issue, see "Taboo: Why Black Athletes Dominate Sports and Why We're Afraid to Talk about It," by John Entine. Passages quoted from that book in the "Contemporary Issues" box are from pages 8, 20, 18, 113, and 116. For the recent research on athletics-related biological variation, see "Peering Under the Hood of Africa's Runners," by Constance Holden in the July 30, 2004, issue of *Science.*

PART THREE

Adapting to Our Worlds

9

FOOD

Getting It, Growing It, Eating It, and Passing It Around

CHAPTER CONTENTS Food and Human Evolution • Food-Collecting Societies • The Food-Producing Revolution • Food-Producing Societies • Which Subsistence Pattern Works Best? • Some Basic Economics • Summary • Contemporary Issues: Is There a World Population Crisis That Is Putting Pressure on Food and Other Resources? • Questions for Further Thought • Notes, References, and Readings

Food is obviously important. No organism can survive without nutrients to build its structure and fuel its functions. For a living creature without enough food, finding shelter and reproducing become secondary concerns. This is as true for humans as for any creature. In many ways, food has been a moving force behind human evolution and cultural history. Indeed, when anthropologists categorize the rich array of human cultures into a reasonable number of meaningful types, we often do it on the basis of food-getting techniques, or **subsistence patterns.** How a society gets its food has important ramifications for all other aspects of its cultural system. What food is available and how it is acquired clearly has a lot to do with worldview, which in turn affects a cultural system.

AS YOU READ, CONSIDER THE FOLLOWING QUESTIONS:

1. What role has food played in the evolutionary history of the hominids?

2. What are the main subsistence patterns found in human societies?

3. What other cultural characteristics of a society might we infer from knowing that society's subsistence pattern?

4. Why and how did some societies make the transition from collecting food to producing food?

5. Is there, in some way, more value in some subsistence patterns than in others?

6. How are some basic categories of economic behavior related to subsistence?

FOOD AND HUMAN EVOLUTION

Food in Prehistory

Once our bipedal version of the primate order was established, environmental changes and adaptations to food sources influenced what appears to be the next major event in hominid evolution. About 3 mya, two new branches diverged from the hominid line of *Australopithecus*, who had a mixed diet of vegetables from the forest and open ground. One new branch, *Paranthropus*, seems to have specialized at least part of the year in the vegetable foods of the open plains. The other branch, genus *Homo*, facilitated by a larger brain and an ability to make stone

subsistence pattern How a society acquires its food.

tools, added large quantities of scavenged meat to its diet. This was an important change, because it provided the early members of our genus with some dietary flexibility that allowed them to continue evolving when further environmental changes brought about the extinction of the other two hominid genera.

This adaptive success was put to the test around 2 mya, when humans began to spread throughout Africa, Europe, and Asia. As they migrated, they encountered new and changing environments—including the advances and retreats of the Pleistocene glaciers—and, thus, new and changing sources of food. In northerly and glacial areas, edible plants were scarce, and so hunting took on an increasingly important role, as we see from the specialized hunting tools associated with anatomically modern *Homo sapiens*. Note, too, that much early cave art had game animals and hunting as a theme (see Figure 6.32).

As important as hunting may have been in our evolution, that importance can be overemphasized. Anthropologists used to think humans *began* as hunters on the savannas—the old "man the hunter" scenario. We have already cited evidence that meat eating was based on scavenging throughout much of our evolution. Scavenging was replaced by hunting only later. And as far as recent **hunter-gather** or **foraging** cultures are concerned, except for Arctic groups, gathering plant foods is usually the more important activity in terms of the relative amount of nutrition it supplies. In indigenous southern African foraging groups, for example, around 75 percent of the food eaten is plant material gathered by the women.

Of course, foraging groups themselves tend to emphasize the hunting part of their subsistence, despite its statistically limited role in their nutrition. This is because hunting is the more precarious of the two activities, the more dangerous, the one less likely to yield results on a regular basis, and the one that causes the most anxiety. There are few rituals related to success in gathering but many that seek to ensure success in hunting. People seldom tell exciting stories about collecting roots, but they enjoy a good antelope hunting tale (Figure 9.1).

There is another possible food-related facet of our evolution. Recall the gradual smoothing out of the facial features and decrease in the size of the teeth that occurred over hominid evolution, including the relatively recent change from the rugged features of archaic *Homo sapiens* to the more delicate ones of modern humans. One explanation for this change is that our teeth and jaws became less important as tools because of advances in stone tool technology, the habit of cooking meat and other foods, and, with the final recession of the glaciers, a shift from an emphasis on big-game hunting to a more mixed diet. It has also been suggested that the invention of eating utensils may have brought about a decreased robusticity in the chewing areas of our crania.

hunter-gatherer A subsistence pattern that relies on naturally occurring sources of food.

foraging Another name for the hunter-gatherer subsistence pattern.

FIGURE 9.1
Two San boys, in Namibia, play a storytelling game. Stories, accompanied by gestures and body language, are often used by the San to tell about hunting adventures, with the storyteller creatively and humorously mimicking the animals involved.

Food in Historical Times

Food has, of course, continued to play an important role in historic events, as countless examples show. The potato, for instance, domesticated in South America and imported to Europe, was suggested as a good, easily grown crop to stave off famine. It later became such an important part of Irish agriculture that when a blight caused the potato crop to fail in 1845 and 1846, the results were the death by starvation and disease of about a million Irish and the emigration of about a million more to the United States.

Food has often been used as a tool to manipulate people and events. During war, the two items that opposing forces try hardest to keep from each other are ammunition and food. Many a battle has been won or lost as a result of the availability of food supplies. "An army marches on its stomach," Napoleon is reputed to have said.

Similarly, a people can best be subjugated by withholding food, as during sieges or blockades.

Food can even supersede arms in importance. Despite the Cold War, the United States and the Soviet Union traded actively with each other. Especially important were shipments of wheat because Soviet agriculture, unlike other aspects of its technology, was not nearly as productive as that of the West. The Soviets relied on this trade to maintain adequate food supplies.

One of the problems with Soviet agriculture is interesting and relevant to several themes in this book. In the 1930s, a Russian agronomist (a specialist in agricultural science) named Trofim D. Lysenko proposed a theory for cultivating plants that was based not on Darwinian evolution and Mendelian genetics but on Lamarckian ideas about the inheritance of acquired characteristics (see Chapter 3). Lysenko thought he could impart the characteristics of winter wheat to spring wheat by refrigerating spring wheat seeds—thus, in his words, "training" them. Lysenko promoted his idea not scientifically but politically and ideologically, claiming it fit Marxist-Leninist social theory better than did Darwin's and Mendel's theories. It was officially accepted as Soviet scientific doctrine in 1948. Needless to say, it didn't work too well, but it wasn't until 1965 that mainstream plant-breeding technology was reinstated in the U.S.S.R. By that time, Soviet agriculture was far behind the West's.

The acquisition of food is a central concern to our species (as to any) and to the individual populations within our species. We can thus use subsistence patterns as meaningful categories to organize our examination of cultural variation and make some generalizations about other aspects of cultural systems within each category (Table 9.1). We will divide subsistence patterns into two main types: food collecting and food producing. Within the latter, there are several more specific types.

These are not mutually exclusive categories. Most societies practice more than one subsistence technique. For example, although I speak of the United States as a food-producing society, we still get some of our food through collecting. Most of the fish served in restaurants, for instance, has technically been collected and not produced. Nonetheless, most societies have one subsistence pattern that supplies the majority of their diet. It is this pattern that becomes the integral part of the society's cultural system and that is related to other features of that system. Thus, we can make *generalizations*. Table 9.1 reflects some of these generalizations that provide us with a starting point for organizing our examination of human societies. I will point out exceptions as we go along.

TABLE 9.1 Subsistence Patterns and Associated Traits This table represents *generalizations* about each subsistence pattern. Exceptions exist, some of which are noted in the text. Traits characteristic of one pattern type may well be found in other types as well. The terms are defined in the text and glossary. Kinship and politics are covered in Chapter 10. Religion is the topic of Chapter 12.

Pattern	General	Social Stratification	Labor Specialization	Resource Distribution	Kinship	Religion	Politics
Foraging	Natural resources Hunting and gathering Small, nomadic	Egalitarian	By sex	Generalized reciprocity	Bilateral Monogamy	Animistic Polytheistic (not hierarchical)	Band
Horticulture	Farming with human labor and simple tools Larger, more sedentary	Rank	Part-time	Balanced reciprocity Redistribution	Unilineal Polygyny	Polytheistic (hierarchical)	Tribe
Pastoralism	Focus on herding Nomadic Highly variable in size	Egalitarian/rank	By sex	Redistribution Balanced reciprocity	Patrilineal Polygyny	Ancestor worship	Tribe
Agriculture	Farming with animal (or mechanical) labor Large, sedentary	Class/caste	Full-time	Balanced reciprocity Market system	Unilineal/bilateral Polygyny/ Monogamy	Polytheistic (hierarchical) Monotheistic	Chiefdom/state

FOOD–COLLECTING SOCIETIES

When I began full-time teaching in 1973 and was preparing notes for my first classes, I recall reading somewhere that there were only 30,000 people in the world who still lived as foragers—approximately the number of full-time students at the university I had attended as a student. I would imagine that at present there are none left, that is, no groups that rely strictly on collecting naturally occurring resources. The modern industrial world has encroached everywhere, bringing its technology, medicine, and education, as well as its problems and abuses. Populations that acquire some food by hunting and gathering still exist, but they also use foods that they or some other people have grown.

Although it is probably impossible today to observe a true foraging culture, there are still people who experienced and remember the way it used to be. Some foraging cultures remained relatively untouched until recently, so we have firsthand anthropological descriptions of them, as well as photographs and films that give us a glimpse into this way of life.

Why is it so important to learn about foragers? Aside from ethical considerations (which we'll take up in Chapter 15), it is important because the foraging way of life is, in one respect, *the* human subsistence pattern. Even if we take a conservative view and say that *human* refers to anatomically modern *Homo sapiens* and is thus at most 200,000 years old, humans were foragers for 96 percent of our tenure on earth. Food producers have existed for only the last 12,000 years. Thus, all of our basic physical characteristics, cultural abilities, and cultural practices arose within the context of foraging. To adopt a common phrase, we might see foraging as "the human condition," at least in an evolutionary sense.

Among the groups that have contributed to our knowledge about this way of life are the Arctic peoples from Greenland to Alaska and into Siberia; peoples (often collectively referred to as Pygmies) from the Central African rain forests; the Bushmen of the Kalahari Desert of Angola, Namibia, and Botswana; Native Australians; peoples from the Andaman Islands in the Bay of Bengal; and some Native Americans such as the Shoshone and Cheyenne from North America and several cultures from Tierra del Fuego at the tip of South America (Figure 9.2).

The Characteristics of Food Collectors

We have already mentioned two characteristics of foraging groups in Chapter 4: a lack of formalized status and wealth differences and religions that generally recognize multiple supernatural beings.

FIGURE 9.2
A Yahgan hunter from Tierra del Fuego, photographed around 1890. Darwin encountered these people on his famous voyage.

social stratification The presence of acknowledged differences in social status, political influence, and wealth among the people within a society.

egalitarianism The practice of not recognizing, and even eliminating, differences in social status and wealth.

polytheism A religious system that recognizes multiple supernatural beings—technically, multiple gods.

animistic The belief in supernatural powers of people, animals, places, and objects.

The first trait—the lack of **social stratification** (from *strata* for layers)—is called **egalitarianism.** Although, obviously, some individuals have skills and talents not shared by others and some have more influence on decision making in certain areas, in foraging societies there are no *recognized, formalized* status differences, and there are most assuredly no differences in access to resources. As explained in Chapter 4, such a society simply cannot afford to have it otherwise. The social order, not to mention the physical welfare of the people, would suffer.

The second trait—that hunter-gatherer groups tend to recognize many supernatural beings with equal or close-to-equal power and influence over the material world—is called **polytheism.** Their religions also tend to be **animistic,** endowing natural phenomena with supernatural powers. This is a direct reflection of the worldviews common to such groups—worldviews that see the environment as predictable yet unstable, with humans pretty much at its mercy.

Foraging cultures as a whole are fairly small, with individual units averaging about fifty persons—although unit sizes vary greatly from society to society and within a society in different locations and during different seasons. Their groups are small because it's difficult to support large numbers of people using only what nature provides. But it's not that such people are—as we tend to visualize them—always on the brink of starvation. Indeed, they can be very successful (after all, we lived like this for most of our species' history). In fact, foraging societies often require methods of limiting their birthrates, including prolonged nursing (because lactation inhibits ovulation), a **postpartum sex taboo,** or, more drastically, methods of abortion or even **infanticide.**

The individual units of a foraging society, called **bands,** are usually made up of several related nuclear families, perhaps including some grandparents, siblings, or cousins. Family relationships are, thus, the basis for social organization. Food, for example, is distributed along lines of kinship. Foraging bands tend to be flexible in their membership. In times of scarce resources, the band may contain only a handful of nuclear families. When times are better, several of these small bands may join together to pool their resources and talents. When important resources, or even a single important resource, are found in great abundance, a foraging society's population may number in the thousands, with individual units of hundreds of people. This was the case for the Kwakiutl of Vancouver Island, British Columbia, Canada (whom we'll discuss shortly). Among other bountiful resources were the great yearly salmon runs that provided them with huge supplies of meat.

With the exception of complex foraging societies such as the Kwakiutl, foragers are **nomadic.** Rather than stay put, they move around, following the animals and plants they rely on for food. The degree of movement depends on the degree of seasonal climatic fluctuation and the response of the resources to it. The Mbuti of the tropical forests of the Republic of the Congo don't have to move around much. There is relatively little seasonal change, and there are many species that can be exploited year-round. The Netsilik of the Arctic, on the other hand, travel great distances as they seasonally hunt for seal, caribou, and salmon.

To maintain their egalitarian social organization, foraging societies distribute important resources equally among their members. Distribution is usually along kinship lines, and the rules for who gives what to whom can be complex. In the end, however, each family receives an equal share. Not every resource is distributed, however. Plant foods are typically used only by the immediate families of the women who gather them. Plants are often a more dependable source of food, so they may be used in this way without adversely affecting the welfare of the whole group.

Although there are exceptions, foraging societies typically display a **division of labor** based on sex, in which men hunt and women gather.

postpartum sex taboo The practice of prohibiting sex for a certain period of time after a woman gives birth for purposes of limiting the birthrate.

infanticide The killing of infants.

bands Small autonomous groups, usually associated with foraging societies.

nomadic Refers to societies that move from place to place in search of resources or in response to seasonal fluctuations.

division of labor The apportioning of a society's jobs to specific individuals, for example, designating men's and women's job roles.

This is a practical arrangement, since hunting is generally the more dangerous and stressful activity and can take hunters away from a home base for extended periods. Since the women carry, give birth to, and care for the society's offspring, it makes sense not to place them and their children at risk or under extreme stress. Beyond this there is no **labor specialization**; there are no full-time leaders, weapon makers, or food preparers. Within the gender roles noted above, each person does whatever he or she is capable of. The society wouldn't work otherwise.

Finally, except in complex foraging societies such as the Kwakiutl, there is no ownership of resources or land. A band may forage in a particular area, but it is not considered their territory. Groups must be able to move around in search of resources. Keeping an outsider off your "property" may someday backfire when your resources fail. Thus there is sharing between bands as well as within bands.

An Example Food–Collecting Society

All the preceding traits of hunter-gatherer societies are generalizations. Because even recent foragers live, or have lived, in such a diverse array of environments, it is hard to pick one group as a typical example. But one society stands out. It has been extensively studied, the people were strictly foragers in the fairly recent past, and they are African, so many of their environmental situations and food resources are similar to those throughout much of human evolutionary history. These are the so-called Bushmen of Angola, Namibia, and Botswana (Figure 9.3).

The term *Bushmen* was applied to these people by the Dutch settlers of South Africa and carries racist connotations. The name San is often used for this group as a whole, referring to a language family noted for its use of click sounds. Perhaps the best-known population within the San has traditionally been called !Kung, also a language-family reference. The ! denotes a click sound, one of four in their language. Among these peoples, the most extensively studied are the Ju/'hoansi ("genuine people") from Namibia and Botswana. The / is another click sound, but an acceptable pronunciation would be *ZHUT-wah-see*. For our purposes here (in part because it's less awkward for English speakers), I'll use San and let the following description, taken largely from studies of the Ju/'hoansi, serve as a generalization for the whole group. I'll also describe them using what we call the **ethnographic present,** speaking in the present tense about their lives as foragers, even though, as we'll discuss later, their lives today are actually much different.

There are about 80,000 San in the Kalahari Desert. There is archaeological and biological evidence that the San and related peoples have lived in this area for about 11,000 years and that they were once more widely spread over the continent.

labor specialization When certain jobs are performed by particular individuals.

ethnographic present Speaking of a society as it was in the past but using the present tense.

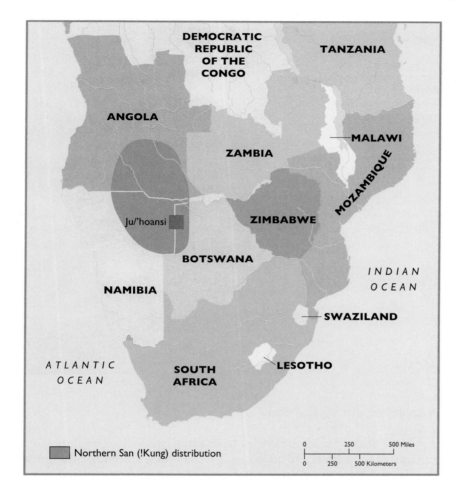

Northern San (!Kung) distribution

0   250   500 Miles
0   250   500 Kilometers

FIGURE 9.3
Map of the San area of southern Africa, with the Ju/'hoansi, one of the most studied groups, indicated. (Data from Lee 1993.)

The San have a characteristic set of physical features (Figure 9.4). They are short people, the men averaging around 5 feet and the women a little under. Their skin is a reddish brown, and their facial features are youthful looking, even those of the elderly. Their hair has been referred to as "peppercorn" because it grows in tightly curled tufts. Most San's eyes are almond-shaped, a trait commonly associated with people from East Asia.

The San live in small bands that average ten to thirty people. Their camps, consisting of grass huts, are temporary because the San are regularly on the move in search of food and, especially, water. The inhabitants of a camp are usually related—a "chain of sibs and spouses," as anthropologist Richard Lee puts it. Membership in a band, however, changes with the seasons and for reasons such as internal conflicts, commonly solved by one family's moving away.

FIGURE 9.4
A San woman and her daughter, showing typical physical features. The mother is instructing the girl in the preparation of mongongo nuts, an important food source.

A camp, as Lee says, is made up of a group of families that "work well together" (Figure 9.5).

Most of the San's food comes from some hundred species of plants recognized as edible and gathered by the women. One of the most popular foods is the mongongo nut, a good source of protein and other nutrients. Game hunted by the men are usually ungulates (hoofed animals), which they bring down with spears or poison-tipped arrows.

While we tend to think of such a way of life as harsh and unstable, the reality is usually quite different. Certainly nature can seem whimsical, and unforeseen environmental changes can mean the difference between life and death. But when things are going as planned, a foraging group actually spends less time than one would imagine in basic subsistence activities. The San, for example, can meet their caloric needs by working 20 hours per adult per week. Not bad when compared to the 35- to 40-hour work week many of us consider normal.

The San are egalitarian. There are, for example, no formal leaders. There are individuals who are more important in terms of such things as settling conflicts or making decisions about where to hunt, gather, or move. But these individuals lead by influence and suggestion rather than by power and command. The San don't consider themselves led by anyone. One San, in response to a request to identify his group's leader, is

FIGURE 9.5
A San campsite among mongongo nut trees with huts used as windscreens and for storage. The people spend most of their time outside.

reputed to have responded that they were *all* leaders. As a logical extension of their egalitarianism, neither sex is seen as superior to the other.

Though plant foods are, because of their relative abundance, generally kept by the gatherer's family, great pains are taken to be sure that meat is evenly shared. Although the hunter whose arrow killed the animal is said to "own" the meat, this merely means that he is responsible for beginning the distribution, which is done according to kinship lines. The concept of sharing meat and even identifying the arrows used to acquire meat is of central importance to the San's social structure.

The idea of equality with regard to meat is so important that the San have a way to ensure that a hunter who has supplied the camp with a fine, meaty animal will not feel in any way superior or even praiseworthy. The people of the camp, rather than showing their joy at the successful hunt, make negative and derisive comments about the quality of the animal killed. Richard Lee calls this "insulting the meat." Some men are bound to be better, more successful hunters than others, and this social leveling device covers up a natural inequality.

As is the general case for foraging peoples, the majority of San men, about 93 percent in one sample, have just one wife. The norm is, thus, **monogamy.** But a small number, around 5 percent from the same sample, have two or three wives. They practice **polygyny.** All the men involved in polygynous marriages are healers, men possessing special powers that allow them to cure illness (Figure 9.6). This is one of the few symbols of differential status seen among the San. Women, by the

monogamy A marriage unit made up of one husband and one wife.

polygyny A marriage unit made up of one husband and multiple wives.

way, may also be healers, but these women do not seem to have any special privileges.

San religion recognizes multiple supernatural beings, including two very important, powerful gods who are largely responsible for the creation of the world and for keeping it running. There are also lots of individual spirits, as well as the ghosts of deceased people, who tend to be malevolent. The healers are thought to possess a substance, or healing power, that they can invoke through a dance. It causes them to go into a trance during which they are able to cure illnesses and speak with the ghosts of the dead.

The last trait of foragers I noted earlier is their lack of a concept of land and resource ownership. This is true for the San. It's not that each band of San roam wherever they want. Each band has an area in which it normally hunts and gathers, and this area is acknowledged by other bands. If, however, the home range of one band runs out of a resource—say, if its water hole dries up or becomes contaminated—that group may use the water hole normally used by another band. They simply ask permission to do so. Permission is always granted—after all, the tables may be turned the next time. This asking and granting of permission has little to do with acknowledging territory; instead, it is more a matter of courtesy, functioning to promote an egalitarianism among the bands as well as within them.

As you can imagine, there is a great deal of variation from one foraging population to the next, depending on each population's specific cultural history and the specific nature of the environment in which it lives. But all exhibit more or less the basic traits listed. The study and understanding of any of these groups give us a picture of how we existed for most of our evolutionary history, keeping in mind that this picture is limited because all the foragers we have been able to study are fully modern. Still, we can say that everything our species is today stems from the foraging lifestyle.

So it was for all our ancestors until about 12,000 ya, when, in a few populations, a "revolution" occurred—not one of riots and warfare, but a peaceful one, a change from within the groups' own cultural systems. This development altered everything that came after. The revolution involved the human *production* of food.

THE FOOD–PRODUCING REVOLUTION

Although we refer to the food-producing *revolution*, the transition was not abrupt. Major changes in cultural history rarely come about instantly. No one simply picked up some seeds, planted them, and invented farming. The shift to food producing came about gradually. But we do have evidence for how and when it occurred.

The Transition to Food Production

Common sense and what we understand about the lives of foragers tell us that this cultural transition must have begun in some populations long before we actually find hard evidence for it. Foragers are intimately familiar with the living things in their environments. They must understand the behavior of animals and the life cycle of plants in order to survive. People probably understood for thousands of years that plants grow from seeds and that some animals can be manipulated. Modern Lapps (move appropriately, Saami) from Arctic Scandinavia and Russia, for example, control wild herds of reindeer but have not actually domesticated them in the sense of conducting selective breeding for desired characteristics (Figure 9.7). Their control is based on an understanding of the behavior of those creatures—an understanding that all foragers possess about the animals they hunt or trap. Human ancestors may well have acted in a similar way with another animal or have experimented with planting seeds or tending an area where an important plant grew.

The real question in evolutionary perspective is not so much how they switched to producing food but *why*. If you were to present the idea of full-scale farming or herding to a real group of foragers, they might

FIGURE 9.7
A Saami with reindeer. The Saami traditionally followed the reindeer herds on their migrations. Sometimes the people captured a male and castrated him to make him more docile and then led him where they wanted to go so that the rest of the herd would follow.

intensive foraging Hunting and gathering in an environment that provides a very wide range of food resources.

find the idea rather strange, if not actually humorous. "Why," they might ask, "should we go to all that trouble when the animals and plants we eat are right out there?" This is a good question, because remember, when things are going normally, foraging populations tend not to spend nearly as much time as we once imagined in their basic subsistence activities.

We are, in fact, still trying to account for the changeover to food producing in those areas where it first occurred. One proposed explanation cites the retreat of the Pleistocene ice sheets and the attendant climatic alterations that occurred around 12,000 ya. Large areas of land underwent substantial ecological change. Where people living in cold areas near the glaciers once subsisted primarily from big-game hunting, now they had access to the greater variety of foods characteristic of habitats not in the grip of the ice. We know from archaeological evidence that people in such areas developed ways of exploiting all the new food sources at their disposal. We call this **intensive foraging**. It may have been in such newly rich environments that people became extremely knowledgeable about the biology of plants and animals and began to use that knowledge for domesticating them.

But wouldn't such a climatic change, with an increase in possible food sources, just make hunting and gathering easier and more reliable? Food producing would seem even less desirable in such an environment. Anyway, glacial retreats were nothing new. They had occurred between glacial advances many times before. What was different 12,000 ya?

One difference was population. As people improved their abilities to find food and deal with environmental pressures, populations increased. Estimates vary, but around 12,000 ya there may have been something like 10 million people in the world, mostly in the Old World. That seems small by today's standards, with over 7 *billion* of us. But twelve millennia ago, considering that people relied pretty much on naturally occurring resources, a large and increasing population could exert a good deal of pressure on some resources in a particular environment. Perhaps such population pressure caused some groups to use their knowledge of plants and animals to gain more control over food resources.

There is a problem with this model as well, at least on the surface. The early centers of farming, such as those in the Fertile Crescent of Southwest Asia, in Southeast Asia, and in Central America, were fairly rich in wild plants and animals. Perhaps, as archaeologist Kent Flannery has suggested, farming began at the edges of these rich areas. Groups pushed out of the optimal areas by a rapidly expanding population found themselves in locations that had marginal wild food sources. One answer to this problem for such groups was to apply their knowledge of wild species to gain control over them and thus enhance their productivity and reliability.

Whatever the specific reasons for the transition to food production— and they probably differed somewhat in each area where it occurred independently—the new idea spread rapidly and brought with it other ecological and cultural changes that altered forever the nature of our relationship with the environment and with one another.

Evidence for the Food–Producing Revolution

In this section we'll look at some specific locations of early food production, some of the specific crops and animals that were domesticated, and some of the specific evidence used by archaeologists in reconstructing this history (Figures 9.8 and 9.9).

Animal Domestication   As you might imagine, the first animal to be domesticated was our "best friend," the dog. Evidence of domestic dogs, descended from wolves, has been found at sites in Iraq and Israel dating from 12,000 ya. (Genetically and reproductively, dogs *are* wolves, although some of the breeds we've created would be incapable of interbreeding with wolves because of their small size.) The Israeli find is the grave of a man whose left hand clutches the skeleton of a puppy—clearly, dogs have held meaning for us for some time. Other

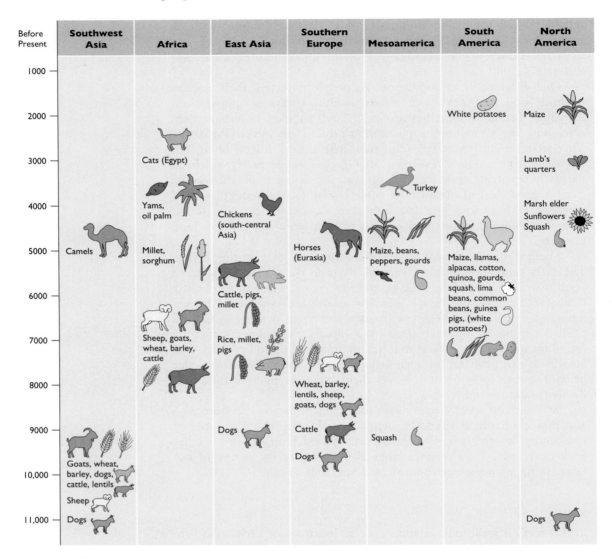

FIGURE 9.8

A chronology of domestication, showing the earliest dates for some important domesticated food sources in different parts of the world. Some species, such as the dog, were domesticated independently in several locations. Others, such as maize, were domesticated first in one location (Mesoamerica) and then spread to other areas.

early dog remains come from Idaho about 8,000 ya. This domestic animal is known worldwide. Dogs now come in all sorts of shapes and sizes, but these early ones, little different from their wolf ancestors, display one telling characteristic: their teeth are crowded together, a result of artificial selection for smaller sizes or, perhaps, a secondary result of selection for more immature characteristics such as docility and subordinate behavior. (Dogs essentially behave like immature wolves.) Although dogs were no doubt used for hunting, another early use was probably as a handy food source. Dogs are still a food source in parts of the world.

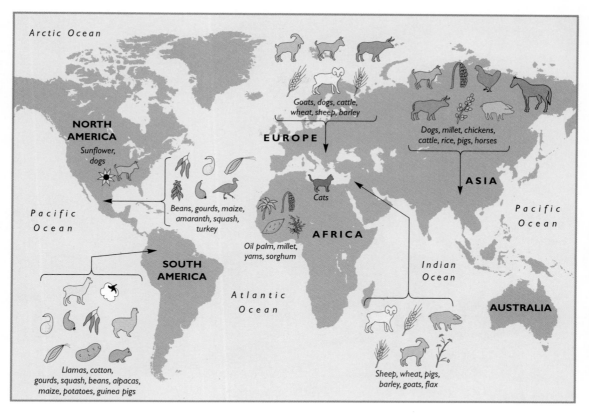

FIGURE 9.9

A map of the apparent hearths of domestication of some important plant and animal species.

As noted before, prior to actual *domestication* (defined as using artificial selection to manipulate the traits of a wild species), people may have learned to exercise some control over wild herds of animals, as modern-day Saami do with reindeer (see Figure 9.7). Evidence for this in prehistory is, naturally, indirect, but sites in Southwest Asia dating back to 18,000 ya show heavy reliance on single species of wild animals—wild sheep or goats, specifically. The inference is that herds were followed and exploited on a regular basis and were maybe even controlled as the Saami do by capturing and castrating a male member of the herd.

Around 10,000 ya, domestic animals begin showing up all over the Old World. Domestic sheep and goats, differentiated from wild ancestors by such things as horn shape and size, appear in Southwest Asia around that time and in southern Europe and Africa a few thousand years later. Domesticated pigs appear in East Asia over 7,000 ya and cattle about 6,000 ya. Cattle were already found in Southern Europe by 9,000 ya. Domesticated camels appear in Southwest Asia about 5,000 ya, and the domestic horse shows up at the same time in Eurasia.

FIGURE 9.10
Llamas, probably the most important animal domesticated in the New World, were used in ancient times as beasts of burden and as food. Here, a packtrain of llamas carries firewood in southern Peru.

Domestication of both animals and plants generally occurred later in the New World and was never as extensive as in the Old World. There are four reasons for this. First, humans didn't enter the New World until later. Second, wild species with characteristics that lent themselves to domestication were not as numerous. Third, some wild food sources, such as the bison, were already found in great abundance. Fourth, in this region populations didn't become large enough to require manipulation of food sources as early as they had in the Old World. The only New World domesticated animals—which come from Central and South America—are turkeys, alpacas, llamas (Figure 9.10), and guinea pigs (yes, they were food).

Evidence for all these conclusions comes in a number of forms. There are the biological differences already mentioned between wild forms and domestic ones. In addition, there are archaeological sites with large numbers of bones of elderly animals, indicating that they were kept, for milk or work, beyond the age at which they normally would have been killed if hunted for meat.

There's cultural evidence as well. From Afghanistan 10,000 ya come small clay tokens, used, it seems, to keep track of trade transactions.

The tokens contain symbols for sheep and goats, animals that were clearly possessions with specific values attached.

Notice that the animals first domesticated in each area are species that were native to that area—the same is true of plants. That may seem obvious, but it's of archaeological significance. We can't, for example, look for domestication of cattle among Native Americans, because there were no wild cattle to domesticate. When searching in the archaeological record, we need to understand what wild species were present and the characteristics of those species.

Plant Domestication The earliest evidence for plant domestication comes from Southwest Asia from about 11,000 ya. The plants involved were wheats called emmer and einkorn. There is also evidence of peas and lentils. Other grains such as barley, millet, and sorghum appear a little later in Southwest Asia, Africa, and Europe. Rice as a domesticate shows up in East Asia around 7,000 ya. At about the same time we find evidence of maize farming in Mexico.

Evidence of plant domestication, as with animals, comes in part from our knowledge of differences between wild and domestic species. Maize, for instance, is thought to have been domesticated from a wild grass called teosinte and shows a number of distinctions from its wild relatives in kernel number, overall structure, and the presence of a distinct cob (Figure 9.11).

It is no coincidence, by the way, that so many early domesticates— wheat, barley, millet, sorghum, rice, and maize—are grasses. Members of this large family of plants grow rapidly and in great abundance, and they grow from the ground up, meaning that they are not killed off by cutting, grazing, drought, or fire. (That's why we have to mow our lawns *every week*.) In addition, many grasses have a high protein content. Maize does not, but in the New World, beans and squash were also domesticated, and they made up the difference; maize, beans, and squash are a very nutritious combination.

Other evidence for early plant domestication is cultural, in the form of tools for planting, harvesting, and storing crops. For example, from several early sites in Southwest Asia and Egypt come remains of sickles (Figure 9.12), presumably used for harvesting plants. These consisted of flint microliths set in a handle of horn, antler, or wood and held in place by mastic (a kind of glue) or bitumen (a natural tarlike substance). One of these was found at the bottom of a 6,000-year-old coiled basket that also contained some wheat and barley grains. Clinching the assessment that these tools were sickles, microscopic analysis of the flint blades showed a luster on their surface like that caused when flint is brought continually into rapid contact with the silica crystals in the stalks of grassy plants. We also have found stones on which grains were ground to make flour, as well as the stones used for grinding. We know what they are because we've seen present-day peoples using similar

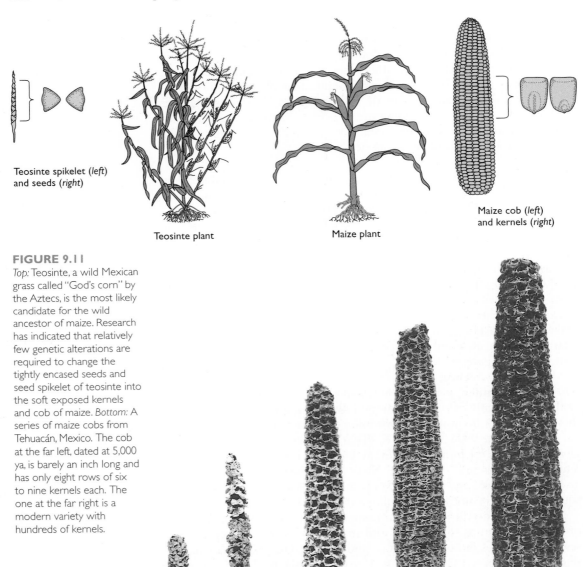

Teosinte spikelet (*left*)
and seeds (*right*)

Teosinte plant

Maize plant

Maize cob (*left*)
and kernels (*right*)

FIGURE 9.11

Top: Teosinte, a wild Mexican grass called "God's corn" by the Aztecs, is the most likely candidate for the wild ancestor of maize. Research has indicated that relatively few genetic alterations are required to change the tightly encased seeds and seed spikelet of teosinte into the soft exposed kernels and cob of maize. *Bottom:* A series of maize cobs from Tehuacán, Mexico. The cob at the far left, dated at 5,000 ya, is barely an inch long and has only eight rows of six to nine kernels each. The one at the far right is a modern variety with hundreds of kernels.

items. Storage pits, baskets, and pottery pieces that hold the remains of grains have also been found, all indicating the presence of farming. Later, of course, we find evidence of more complex farming technology such as plows.

FIGURE 9.12
Flint sickle microliths from the fourth century B.C. in Israel. They were originally set in a horn handle with bitumen.

FOOD–PRODUCING SOCIETIES

Horticulture

There are within the food-producing category three basic subsistence patterns: **horticulture, pastoralism,** and **agriculture.** Horticulture refers to societies that focus on farming and use only human labor and simple tools such as a digging stick or a hoe (Figure 9.13). It does not, in other words, involve animal or mechanical labor or more complex technologies such as plows and fertilizers. As we did for foragers, we will look at some of the general characteristics found among horticultural groups. Examples of horticultural societies include many of the indigenous groups of the Amazon rain forests, the forests of Central Africa and Southeast Asia, and the highlands of New Guinea.

Horticulturalists tend to live in larger groups than foragers. The greater control over at least some of their food sources and the surplus that results allow them to support a greater number of individuals. Their populations are also more **sedentary;** that is, they can stay in one area for longer periods of time since the people can grow food where *they* are rather than having to go where the food is. Population size tends to be more stable than in foraging groups because there is less seasonal fluctuation in resource availability. Although horticultural populations are larger than those of foragers, these groups are still organized around kinship. They are made up of several extended families, most of whom are typically related. A striking feature of many horticultural groups is that their nuclear families are polygynous—men have several wives. (Marriage patterns and other aspects of kinship will be covered in Chapter 10.)

Horticultural groups maintain an essentially egalitarian outlook, but because there is now the possibility of surpluses and because there are more people and thus more need for formal organization, we see in these

horticulture Farming using human labor and simple tools.

pastoralism A subsistence pattern characterized by an emphasis on herding animals.

agriculture Farming using animal or mechanical labor and complex technologies.

sedentary A human settlement pattern in which people largely stay in one place year-round, although some members of the population may still be mobile in the search for food and raw materials.

groups the beginnings of leaders and labor specialists, though these roles are often part-time. For example, a man is not, say, always a leader in battle or always a healer. Most of the time he is a farmer and hunter like everyone else. He takes on his specialized role when needed.

We also see in horticultural societies the beginnings of ownership, on both the family and population levels. Land on which plants are cultivated may be the property of a family or other group of people considered to be related, as are the plants themselves. A herd of animals, for example the pigs ubiquitous to horticultural groups in highland New Guinea, are likewise owned. Despite this limited ownership, though, members of horticultural societies still work for a common good, and the products of their labors, although family owned, are nonetheless shared within the group. The techniques for sharing them, as we will see, are more complex than among foragers.

Horticultural societies also recognize the concept of territory. With growing control over food resources and the increasing *instability* that results (see "Which Subsistence Pattern Works Best?" later in this chapter), there is more need to form intergroup trade networks and, in the face of shortages, to protect one's own resources and, perhaps, to acquire someone else's. Indeed, there is an idea that the advent of farming was a precursor to war (defined as conflict between populations or between groups within a population). Put bluntly, when one society or unit within a society had something another did not, the have-nots tried to take it away and the haves tried to keep it (Figure 9.14).

FIGURE 9.14
A group of Yąnomamö in the Amazon rain forest prepares for a raid against an enemy village to acquire land for farming and hunting and, perhaps, wives.

The association between horticulture and warfare has been illustrated by the societies who live in rain forests. In such areas there are more species of living organisms than in any other land ecosystems on earth, yet rain forests present important limitations to their inhabitants. There are so many species that no individual species is found in abundance. With reference to human food sources, there are few large animals in the rain forests. Moreover, the soil is not particularly fertile. The rain leaches out nutrients fairly quickly, and the abundance of living creatures means that nutrients get recycled quickly and don't have a chance to build up, as they do in temperate climates, where there is an annual leaf fall and where biological processes slow down in winter. As a result, societies in rain forests, especially those that farm and so build up their populations and remain somewhat sedentary, risk overexploiting and depleting the soil's nutrients. This then forces them to shift their areas of cultivation, which can lead to tensions over land and, ultimately, war.

Finally, horticulturalists, like foragers, tend to recognize multiple supernatural beings—that is, they are polytheistic. But unlike the case with foragers, the supernatural beings tend to be arranged in a hierarchy. Some, in other words, are more powerful and important than others. This seems to reflect the people's growing control over nature. They may not see themselves as having mastered nature (as do, for example, modern industrial societies), so natural phenomena are still attributed to the influence of supernatural beings, whom humans must be aware of and propitiate. The most important supernatural beings, however, are often those with direct connections to humans—humanlike deities who gave rise to and control the lives of people or, perhaps, the spirits or ghosts of the dead.

FIGURE 9.15
The Masai of East Africa build *kraals* of thornbush to protect their cattle, goats (*lower center*), and homes from lions and leopards at night. The word *kraal* was possibly borrowed from the Portuguese or Spanish and related to the English word *corral*.

Pastoralism

Pastoralism is subsistence based on the herding of animals. Certainly, nearly all farmers have some domestic animals for food or labor or both, and pastoralists may well do some hunting, gathering, or even farming. But pastoralists are those whose herds are the basis for their subsistence and whose worldview and cultural system are built around this pattern. Examples are the cattle herders of the dry savannas of East Africa (Figure 9.15) and the Indian subcontinent, sheep and goat herders from Southwest Asia, and yak herders on the Tibetan Plateau.

Most pastoralists are nomadic—the people go where there is food for their animals. They are egalitarian with regard to the use of pasture-land within their group but territorial with regard to other populations. Within pastoral societies there is socioeconomic stratification based largely on the number of animals owned. There is some form of leadership, but it is rather vague with regard to how it is achieved and who has it. It is not formalized and so is probably similar to the situation of informal influence found among foragers.

Labor is divided by sex, with the men being largely responsible for the care of the animal herds and the women for handling household tasks and child rearing. In some pastoral societies, however, women

FIGURE 9.16
A farmer with his oxen plowing a field in Egypt. The remains of the Colossi of Memnon are in the background. Agriculture made possible the great civilization of ancient Egypt.

have a say in whether, to whom, and for how much to sell animals. Beyond this, there is no labor specialization.

Pastoralists' religions tend to involve ancestor worship. Their supernatural world is populated by the spirits of the dead. This hints at an emphasis on human control and on a general cultural conservatism. One pleases the spirits of the dead by doing things in a traditional way, the way *they* would have.

Pastoralists are found in areas unsuitable for other subsistence activities, areas where it would be hard to grow anything and where the wild plants are primarily grasses, which don't provide humans with much nutrition but are fine for ungulates that can digest cellulose. The animals turn the plant nutrients into milk products, blood, and, less often, meat for human consumption.

Agriculture

Agricultural societies are so defined because they use animal (or, in recent history, mechanical) labor and more complex tools such as the plow. Agriculture is found in areas that require more complex technologies in order to grow plants in large, concentrated plots and where increased population and more complex social systems necessitate an intensification of subsistence techniques. Remember, any farming involves growing plants under conditions in which they don't normally grow in the wild (Figure 9.16). Thus some farmers need plows to break

235

up compacted, rocky soil and draft animals to pull those plows. Irrigation systems and fertilizers (often the manure of the draft animals) are also often needed to manipulate wild plant species.

Due to even greater control over plant food sources, groups with this subsistence pattern can support greater numbers of people than can horticulturalists. Agricultural populations, quite expectedly, are more stable and sedentary, tied to the land they have cultivated and on which they depend.

With surpluses virtually ensured, there can be full-time labor specialists—not everyone has to devote all their time to getting food. If I'm good at growing wheat, I can concentrate on that and trade my surplus produce (what's left after I've supplied my family's needs) to, say, the family that makes plows for one of their tools. There are also those whose full-time specialty is carrying out religious rituals, healing, or providing military or political leadership. With more than enough food to go around, such specialization is possible, and with larger populations and the increased complexity of social and economic interactions, such specialization is necessary.

And with surplus and labor specialization, some people inevitably accumulate more resources than others. Wealth and power are usually found in the same hands. Thus, agricultural societies exhibit a formal social stratification. Obviously, a central concept in such situations is ownership of one's wealth.

Religion in agricultural societies may still be polytheistic, as with the complex pantheon of ancient Egypt, but if so the deities are hierarchical, some having greater importance than others, and there are usually direct human connections to the most powerful (Figure 9.17). As social situations become increasingly complex, and with a greater sense of control over food resources, agricultural societies tend toward monotheism, a belief in one all-powerful god and, thus, a reflection of the power of humans over nature. This is what we see in Judaism, Christianity, and Islam, all of which arose in agricultural societies in Southwest Asia.

In very complex and very populous agricultural societies, we see one of the important results of the so-called farming revolution. At some point of complexity, there is a need for a centrally located government and a center for economic transactions. In other words, cities develop. The term **civilization**, although often used as a value judgment, literally means "city making," and refers to urbanized societies and their characteristic features (Figure 9.18).

For example, with all the information about trade transactions, ownership, and social and economic positions that such a society needs to keep track of, forms of record keeping arise, evolving eventually into writing. It is no surprise that some of the earliest examples of writing are associated with cities in Southwest Asia, where farming may have first developed (Figure 9.19).

civilization A culture with an agricultural surplus, social stratification, labor specialization, a formal government, rule by power, monumental construction projects, and a system of record keeping.

FIGURE 9.17
Amun-Re, king of the gods (*left*), and Horus, lord of heaven, who shared divinity with the pharaoh. Among the many other gods of ancient Egypt were Thoth, god of the moon, time, and healing; Anubis, embalming; Min, fertility; Seth, violence; Nut, the sky; Geb, the earth; Shu, the air; Ptah, the creator of all things; Hapi, the Nile; and Bes, the household.

There is also a need for public works, such as roads from outlying farming areas into the urban center. Monumental structures are also found early on. Temples, statuary, pyramids, and the like all represent the centralization of political and religious power, and they would not have been possible without the release of large numbers of laborers from basic subsistence activities. Defensive facilities—walls, moats, and fortresses—and standing armies are also associated with urban centers.

Finally, the need to improve the tools on which the success of such systems is based gives rise to another major cultural innovation associated with civilization. This is metallurgy, the extraction and working of natural metals. Cities, centralized governments, writing, monumental and public works, a military, and metallurgy all follow from an economy based on intensive agriculture.

Many anthropologists list **industrialism** as a subsistence pattern. This is generally defined as a system based on mechanical rather than biological power. There are obvious social and economic ramifications of such a system. Populations are very large; there is extreme labor

industrialism Sometimes recognized as a subsistence pattern; characterized by a focus on mechanical sources of energy and food production by a small percentage of the population.

FIGURE 9.18
A New World city, the spectacular ruins of the Inca fortress city now called Machu Picchu (the original name is unknown), 8,000 feet up in the Peruvian Andes. This site was discovered as recently as 1911.

specialization; the emphasis is on the individual, rather than the family, as the unit of labor; governmental systems become very complex; and secular laws supplant religious beliefs as reflections of worldview and behavioral norms.

Industrial societies are different enough from the other types we've examined that they might be considered a separate and unique subsistence pattern. But, for a general overview, I tend to stick with the food theme and categorize societies like ours in North America as agricultural. Despite our industrial base, and despite the fact that under 3 percent of the United States population lives on farms, our subsistence is still based on agriculture. Our society still exhibits the general set of characteristics for agriculturalists. Industrialism is just a *very intensified* form of that subsistence pattern.

FIGURE 9.19
A clay tablet from Mesopotamia dated at about 5,000 ya. The text, written in cuneiform (Latin for "wedge-shaped," referring to the shape of the impressions), records the sale of a slave.

WHICH SUBSISTENCE PATTERN WORKS BEST?

Now, keeping in mind our themes of adaptation and evolution, some questions arise: Why are some people horticulturalists and some agriculturalists? Is agriculture better? Is it a more advanced form and thus a logical evolutionary outcome? Do all horticulturalists eventually become agriculturalists as soon as they acquire the skills?

The general answer is that a group of people uses the subsistence pattern that works for them under existing environmental conditions—keeping in mind from Figure 4.4 that the "environment" to which a society responds includes both natural and cultural factors.

Most horticultural societies live in tropical forests—areas with sufficient rainfall, abundant useful plant species, and year-round sun and warmth. People who cultivate in such areas don't require more complex technology. On the other hand, one tends to find agriculture in areas where natural conditions must be manipulated to grow plants. These are places where the ground must be turned and broken to prepare it for planting, where rainfall is not always sufficient to nourish plants that are not in their natural growing conditions, and where the soil's nutrients may have to be augmented. A society, in other words, does what it must to survive. Doing more would be a waste of energy.

To be sure, societies that acquire the skills and technologies necessary to grow plants in the setting just described are capable of feeding large numbers of people and producing large surpluses. In that sense, agriculture is "better." But there is no inexorable trend toward it. In some areas, such as tropical forests, agricultural techniques would not increase production anyway.

There are negative aspects to agriculture as well, for with such a specific set of circumstances necessary for successful subsistence, more can go wrong. If, for example, something happens to the draft animals, if there is not enough rain to channel through irrigation ditches, if a disease or insect infestation kills off the few species of plants grown—such events can have devastating effects on a society's ability to feed itself (the Irish potato famine being one example). Because societies that practice intensive agriculture have often altered their natural environment, eliminating some native plant and animal species, there may be few alternative sources of food available.

Other problems arise as well. Overall nutrition may be adversely affected by a diet consisting of a smaller variety of foods. Far more energy is expended in agricultural societies than in foraging societies for the same nutritional results. It is necessary to store food, and stored food attracts vermin that may carry diseases. Crowded populations make epidemics possible and pose problems of sanitation and waste removal. Deep socioeconomic differences may lead to class conflicts. Environmental degradation may result from things such as pollution and the importation of desired species and the removal of undesirable ones.

When everything is working well, agriculture allows for larger populations and longer, more stable lives. But it is also more prone to disruption than is subsistence by foraging. So there is no overall better or worse way of obtaining one's food. There is just what works for a particular group in a particular environment at a particular point in its history.

SOME BASIC ECONOMICS

Now, once a group of people has collected or produced the food they need, once they have the tools to get and process that food and to take care of other technological concerns, and once they can provide all the services necessary to maintain their social structure—how do all these resources get to the people who need them? How do societies make sure that the resources are distributed? Does everyone share equally? Is there any correlation between distribution of goods and services and type of subsistence pattern?

Patterns of Exchange

How do *you* go about getting the goods and services you need? Because you provide society with certain goods you help manufacture or services you perform, you receive **money**, a symbolic representation of some value equivalent. This you exchange with other individuals for the goods and services they produce. The quality and quantity of the goods and services you can purchase depend on the amount of money you can spend, which in turn depends on how much society values the services or the goods you help produce. This is all familiar and seems perfectly logical. But are there other systems of exchange?

Reciprocity   Let's assume you live in a family with two working parents and two siblings. Within your family, goods and services are distributed in a different fashion. Your parents bring home the money they earn, which is used to purchase food and pay for housing. Each also performs certain jobs around the household. They certainly don't expect each other, you, or your sibs to repay them in kind or equivalence. No one is keeping a ledger of all the transactions to make sure things balance out. Everyone contributes and receives in return only whatever contributions other family members are capable of providing (depending on their age, health, and occupational status), as well as the physical and emotional security that family membership provides.

This kind of giving and taking of goods and services without expectation of immediate and equivalent return is called **generalized reciprocity**. It's what happens within families—and it's what happens within typical foraging societies. Such societies are, in fact, made up of individual units that are often themselves small family groups. Moreover, since the only efficient way to run a population with a foraging subsistence is to practice egalitarianism, generalized reciprocity is the only method of distribution that makes sense for these groups. Any recognition of what we might call "an imbalance of trade" would break up the equality of wealth and status that is so vital for foraging peoples.

A group may also practice **balanced reciprocity**, the exchange of goods and services with the clear expectation of the return of something of agreed-on equivalent value. In an earlier example, when I traded some of my surplus wheat for a plow someone else made, that was balanced reciprocity. This kind of system tends to be found in horticultural and agricultural societies, with their larger communities, surpluses, labor specialists, and greater need to exchange goods and services in order to survive.

money A symbolic representation of wealth. Used for exchange in place of actual products or services.

generalized reciprocity Giving with no expectation of equivalent return.

balanced reciprocity Giving with the expectation of equivalent return.

An example of balanced reciprocity exists within North American industrial society: gift giving at birthdays and other important holidays. Despite the ethic we profess, that "giving is better than receiving" and "it's the thought that counts," we in fact go through all sorts of mental trauma worrying about how much to spend on so-and-so's gift so it won't be any more or less expensive than the one we last received or next expect to receive from that person. It's neither explicit nor a formal part of our economy, but it's balanced reciprocity just the same.

This also shows that a society may practice several of the resource distribution types we're discussing, depending on the people involved. The Mbuti, for example, foraging peoples of Central Africa, practice generalized reciprocity among themselves, but they also carry on a form of balanced reciprocity when they trade with outside farmers.

Market System   When a society gets so large and the economic transactions within it so complex that the trading of actual items and services becomes difficult, symbolic representations of the value of resources may be used. These can be traded in place of actual products so long as the system is part of the culture as a whole and there is some mechanism for determining and maintaining the value equivalents. This symbolic representation, of course, is money, and a system that uses money is called a **market system**. A market system is, in a sense, balanced reciprocity with symbols and is found in intensive agricultural and industrial societies. A market system operates on a supply-and-demand basis that sets the equivalent values of resources (price, in other words) and involves a profit motive on the part of suppliers.

Redistribution   Between systems that maintain overall egalitarianism and those that recognize and support socioeconomic stratification is a system of distribution that attempts to level out inherent inequalities. This mechanism, called **redistribution**, serves to counteract the unequal distribution of goods and services within a population. Surpluses are collected under the direction of some governing body, perhaps an individual, and then redistributed according to the needs of the recipients. Such a system is common among horticulturalists. The larger number of people in some of these societies and the existence of surpluses mean that wealth is not evenly distributed. At the same time, some horticultural societies are still small enough and closely related enough to want to maintain an egalitarian outlook. A system of redistribution addresses this need, using some social mechanism—a feast perhaps—to gather and dole out surplus wealth. (We'll look at an example from highland New Guinea in Chapter 14.)

Perhaps the most famous example of a large-scale redistribution system comes not from a horticultural society but from a foraging one. (This is also a good example of an exception to the generalizations we've been discussing.) The Kwakiutl of British Columbia, mentioned earlier, were unusual for foragers in that they had a large

market system Where money is used for exchange in place of goods and services; it operates on a supply-and-demand basis with a profit motive for suppliers.

redistribution The central collection of surplus goods and their dispersal to people in need of them.

FIGURE 9.20
In this artist's rendering, guests arrive in their huge, elaborately decorated canoes for a *potlatch*, a feast of extravagant giving that served as a redistribution system for the Kwakiutl.

overall population with large, fairly sedentary communities. Their society was populous due to the abundance of natural resources, especially the annual salmon runs (when, in essence, the food came to *them*). The Kwakiutl would hold periodic feasts called *potlatches*, the immediate point of which was for the host to achieve status by giving away or even destroying more food and other goods than any of his rivals (Figure 9.20). If the host was falling behind in his show of extravagance, he might even burn down his own house as the ultimate display of his wealth. Early anthropologists were puzzled by this seemingly wasteful behavior. Upon closer examination, however, it made sense.

The Kwakiutl, because of their large populations and abundant resources, moved away from the strict egalitarianism of foragers. Still, they were a single, integrated society and were thus concerned about inequalities among their people. In this, they resembled horticulturalists. Specifically, annual fluctuations in the salmon migrations and in the availability of wild plant foods led to some Kwakiutl villages having more food than others. The potlatch, it turns out, was a redistribution system. By giving away surpluses, the haves compensated for the have-nots' deficiencies.

Moreover, the potlatch system was tied up with status seeking (*which was the immediate motivation for it*), so there was continuous pressure to produce as much as possible so one could give away more at the next potlatch. The result, whatever the motivation, benefited the entire population.

You might, of course, be wondering why the Kwakiutl went to such extremes, even if the explanation makes economic sense in the end. Why not just decide that everyone will contribute some of their surplus, which will then be collected by a leader of some sort who then determines who needs it and passes it out? The potlatch is a good example of the complexity of any cultural system. Although the potlatch can be interpreted economically, and although it became a vital part of Kwakiutl culture because it worked economically, the origin of the practice was submerged within the whole of the Kwakiutl worldview, which, you recall, involved not only their present but their history as well. It is probably impossible to reconstruct the origin of the idea, which may have begun for different reasons than those that motivated it when first observed by anthropologists.

A second example of a redistribution system comes from within a market economy and also provides a glimpse into the complexities of cultural systems. In North America we live in a stratified society, but we consider some inequities to be unacceptable and the general welfare to be important. Part of our tax money is used to provide goods and services to those who cannot otherwise afford them and to benefit society as a whole. On the whole it works well, but this redistribution system itself involves inequities, and these inequities demonstrate the power of a whole cultural system and the worldview that generates it.

As a stratified society, we recognize differences in status and wealth and acknowledge them within the system. One way our system supports such strata is through our complex laws of ownership, protecting what we consider the rights of individuals to possess property and wealth and to keep it. So pervasive is this concept that it is difficult to define what constitutes "surplus" to a particular person. Thus, figuring out just what part of a person's wealth goes into taxes, especially income tax, is incredibly complex. In fact, our society places such importance on possession that the ownership of some things can actually reduce the amount of income you contribute to the redistribution pool. Our intent may be in keeping with certain ethical precepts, but this particular mechanism has inconsistencies with regard to our whole cultural system. For example, those who can most afford to give away money can also take advantage of the most loopholes in the tax laws to allow them to keep that money.

Social Stratification

Finally, there are some additional terms for ideas we've been discussing that refer to the degree to which a society is stratified. Egalitarianism— the absence of formalized differences in status and wealth—has been covered at length. Again, it is common to foraging societies. Horticultural societies are often considered **rank** societies. Such groups try to eliminate differences in wealth but do so with a redistribution system that necessarily must recognize differences in status, although temporary ones. That is, persons in charge of redistributing the surplus are those who, at the moment, have the most of it and thus are recognized as having a differential status. From the western Pacific comes the name we use for such temporarily powerful people—"big men." One attempts to become a big man by accumulating wealth, but that status essentially gives one the opportunity and obligation to give away some of that wealth to those who need it.

American society is an example of a **class** system. It recognizes and builds into the system formal differences in both status and wealth. A class system, however, is open. That is, an individual has the opportunity to acquire more wealth and status and move to a higher stratum. Or, of course, one can also lose both and move to a lower stratum.

Another system freezes strata. In these societies, you are born into a socioeconomic layer and stay there. Access to resources, occupational opportunities, and potential marriage partners are all decided by birth as well. This is a **caste** system. The best-known example is perhaps that of India.

The concept of food acquisition and distribution provides us with a basis for discussing all other areas of cultural variation. Let's begin with the following consideration: if you were a San hunter who had brought back to camp a nice fat antelope you had killed, you would distribute the meat according to kinship. That is, you would give some meat to certain of your relatives, who would give some to certain of their relatives, and so on until everyone had their share. Sounds easy enough. Everyone knows who's related to whom and how. Kinship is basic biology. Or is it? In the next chapter, I'll show you how in some societies your uncle is the same as your father, and your cousin is the same as your brother.

rank Refers to a society that strives for equal distribution of goods and services through the use of recognized, often temporary, status differences.

class A system of socioeconomic stratification in which the strata are open and a person may move to a different stratum.

caste A system of socioeconomic stratification in which the strata are closed and a person's membership is determined at birth.

SUMMARY

Perhaps the most important relationships between a species and its environment focus on the processes of food acquisition. For humans, the ways in which societies acquire their food—their subsistence patterns—are so central that we may use them to categorize types of cultures. Thus, we speak of a society as food collecting or food producing. A synonym for the former is foraging. Within the latter are the subcategories of horticulture, pastoralism, and agriculture.

Many, if not most, of the other basic features of a cultural system can be seen as more or less related to subsistence pattern. Generalizations are possible with regard to such things as mobility, population size, basic economics, social stratification, labor specialization, kinship, and religion.

CONTEMPORARY ISSUES

Is There a World Population Crisis That Is Putting Pressure on Food and Other Resources?

A major influence on Darwin's thinking was the English economist Thomas Malthus (1766–1834). In *An Essay on the Principle of Population* (1789), he wrote, "Population, when unchecked, increases in a geometrical ratio. Subsistence increases only in an arithmetical ratio. . . . I can see no way by which man can escape from the weight of this law which pervades all animate nature." Malthus predicted famine and war if humans continued the population increase that even he in his day perceived. If only he knew.

Since Malthus's time, the human population has increased nearly sixfold, and, given the war, famine, and environmental degradation we see around us, we have every reason to believe that Malthus was right. With our current 1.5 percent population increase annually, we will eventually run out of something—most likely food, but possibly also water, land, clean air, or patience with one

another—and our species and its world will be in for some very bad times indeed. The human species has even been likened to a cancer that grows uncontrolled, spreads, and eventually destroys its environment.

So, in theory, it looks as if the answer to the question in the title of this box is yes. But few of us really see this problem firsthand, and so we don't always acknowledge it or respond to it in practical ways.

In fact, it is tempting to those of us in the developed West to place the blame for rampant growth on the developing countries of Latin America, Africa, and Asia, where some fertility rates (the number of children a typical woman has during her lifetime) have been as high as eight. Indeed, nearly every night on the TV news, or in ads for charitable organizations, we are shown starving people in those countries. We tend to

QUESTIONS FOR FURTHER THOUGHT

1. In this chapter we have discussed several examples of the importance of food in human history. Can you think of some other examples? Consider, for example, how food is used as a political tool in parts of the world today.

2. Table 9.1, as noted, makes *generalizations* about societies based on their subsistence patterns. Many societies, however, use more than one subsistence pattern or exhibit traits more commonly associated with a subsistence pattern other than its own. In terms of U.S. society, give some examples of how we practice food collecting and horticulture and how we exhibit generalized reciprocity, balanced reciprocity, redistribution, part-time labor specialization, and so on.

3. The population crisis is a controversial topic. Do you think, as do some, that overpopulation is a key problem in the world today, precipitating other major problems? Or do you think the world can sustain the current and even larger populations. If the latter, how will we deal with such numbers of people in terms of food, water, space, pollution, and intercultural conflict?

see no evidence of a population problem here in North America (the infertility business is booming). The Malthusian predictions, we comfortably assume, must affect only *other* countries. *We* have enough food. If only *they* would change, the problem could be solved.

But in fact, many people *are* changing. In some undeveloped and developing nations, higher birth rates have been traditionally promoted to counteract high infant mortality and high mortality rates in general. But many developing countries are experiencing a fairly rapid decline in birthrates, not as a result of their becoming more like the West but from having better education about and access to contraceptive technology. People in many of those countries realized the problems inherent in overpopulation but lacked the means to address them.

It is rather arrogant to think that *we* are not part of the problem. We do live, as the cliché says, in a global village. All parts of the world are now interrelated in every way imaginable—ecologically, politically, and economically. *Every* new human, no matter where he or she lives, will help use up the world's food, water, and energy resources and contribute to the buildup of waste products (some, such as those of us in the United States, are more responsible for this than others). *Every* new human adds to the population density of the world and encourages the further spread of people, with its resultant alteration of environments.

Aspects of the population problem are still being debated. There are arguments as to how many people the planet could ideally support, as well as arguments as to how best to (or if it is even possible to) bring about those ideal conditions. It has been argued, for example, that there *is* enough food but that, for various reasons, it does not get equitably distributed. Nonetheless, that there *is* a population problem, and thus a resource problem, is undeniable. And to think that it is not *everyone's* concern is complacent at best.

NOTES, REFERENCES, AND READINGS

For more on the anthropological significance of food, see the articles in *Nutritional Anthropology*, edited by Alan Goodman, Darna Dufour, and Gretel Pelto.

Information on the San can be found in Richard Lee's *The Dobe Ju/'hoansi*. It includes his famous and delightful article "Eating Christmas in the Kalahari," about the practice of "insulting the meat." Also included is an annotated list of films about the San. One of the most famous of these is "The Hunters," by John Marshall, an excellent look at San life but one that also overemphasizes hunting and gives the impression that foraging life is unstable and that the people are often on the verge of starvation.

For more on Lysenko see "A Hearing for Vavilov," by Stephen Jay Gould, in *Hen's Teeth and Horse's Toes*.

Hypotheses on the origins of farming and civilization are discussed at length in Ken Feder's *The Past in Perspective*, fourth edition.

A good look at horticultural society, and one characterized by warfare, is Karl Heider's *The Grand Valley Dani: Peaceful Warriors*. This society is a major topic of Chapter 14.

The Kwakiutl potlatch is described and interpreted by Marvin Harris in his famous and provocative book

Cows, Pigs, Wars and Witches: The Riddles of Culture. A more traditional interpretation is in Ruth Benedict's *Patterns of Culture.*

For a discussion of the adverse effects of agriculture, try "The Worst Mistake in the History of the Human Race," by Jared Diamond. It appeared in the May 1987 issue of *Discover* and can also be found in Feder's *Lessons from the Past.* See also Diamond's Pulitzer Prize–winning *Guns, Germs, and Steel: The Fates of Human Societies* for a longer discussion of the domestication of plants and animals and their historical ramifications.

Three good articles on the population crisis are "Ten Myths of Population," by Joel Cohen, in the April 1996 issue of *Discover;* "The Fertility Decline in Developing Countries," by Bryant Robey et al., in the December 1993 *Scientific American;* and the roundtable discussion "World Population Policy" in the September 1997 issue of *Politics and Life Sciences.*

For information on world population, check out www.worldometers.info. It has all the latest statistics and some population clocks that show the world population as it increases. Kind of scary.

10

THE NATURE OF THE GROUP

*Arranging Our Families
and Organizing Our People*

CHAPTER CONTENTS Primate Societies • Marriage and Family • Kinship • Kinship Terminology • Organization above the Family Level • Contemporary Issues: Why Don't Bilateral Societies Have Equality between the Sexes? • Summary • Questions for Further Thought • Notes, References, and Readings

One of the biggest obstacles facing the anthropologist is **ethnocentrism.** All people are ethnocentric, which means that we feel our particular cultural system is the "correct" one and that our way of doing things is the "right" way. And indeed they are. If every person on earth didn't live within and rely on some sort of cultural system, human life as we know it would not exist. Without some set of agreed-on ideas and practices, our social fabric would come unraveled. You *should* think your culture is the right one for you.

The problem arises when we make value judgments about a different culture based on our own cultural ideas or, worse, when a society forces its culture on another. As discussed earlier, anthropologists strive not to analyze the cultures we study from the anthropologist's own perspective.

We have to practice, in other words, cultural relativity. We have to try to get inside the heads of other people, to see things from their perspective. We have already talked about the idea of worldview and about different sorts of economic systems. You should now understand something about the worldview of egalitarian societies, for instance, even though you are part of a class society.

In this chapter we'll look at one of the most complicated facets of a culture's worldview. It deals with our family relationships, something basic to our lives both as individuals and as a species. For most societies, family relationship, or **kinship,** is the basis for social organization in general. As you might expect by now, not every society looks at kinship the way we in most of North America do. But learning about kinship systems that differ from your own will bring you closer to understanding and being able to practice cultural relativity.

ethnocentrism Making value judgments about another culture from the perspective of one's own cultural system.

kinship Your membership in a family and your relationship to other members of that family. May refer to biological ties, but in anthropology usually refers to cultural ties modeled on biological ones.

AS YOU READ, CONSIDER THE FOLLOWING QUESTIONS:

1. What do we know about the social organization of nonhuman primates, and can this shed any light on human societies?

2. What different types of marriage do we find in human societies, and how might this variation be explained?

3. What kinds of variations do we find in descent lines, and how do these correlate with other cultural variables?

4. What are some of the variations in kinship terminology, and how does such terminology relate to other aspects of a cultural system?

5. How are different cultural systems organized above the family level?

PRIMATE SOCIETIES

As noted in Chapter 5, primates are social creatures that recognize and respond to one another as individuals. Primate societies are made up of the collective relationships among individuals, and an individual may hold a particular status relative to others in the group. This can differ widely from species to species, of course, but a common social characteristic, at least among the anthropoid primates (see Figure 5.3), is a strong bond among individuals that are closely biologically related—that is, among members of some biological family unit.

For example, in some baboons the social center of the troop, and the subgroup that ties generations together, is made up of related females. These females form alliances with one another that help ensure their own reproductive and child-rearing success and the passing on of their genes via the reproductive success of their close relatives, who share many of those genes (Figure 10.1).

In chimpanzees, perhaps the strongest social bond is that between mother and infant. This is not unusual for mammals, but for these apes, with their large, complex brains and the amount they need to learn to

FIGURE 10.1

A family of olive baboons in Kenya—a group of related females and their young—focuses on the oldest female (*far right*). Such family units form the core of baboon troops.

become functioning adults, the mother-infant bond is particularly long-lived and important. The nature of that interaction can have a lasting effect on a chimp's life. Poor treatment by the mother, for example, often makes a chimp a poor mother herself when she bears young. Chimps, in other words, *raise* their young, and the family bonds that result may last a lifetime.

Members of this chimp family unit may, throughout their lives, protect and care for each other, especially during illness and injury. Offspring often remain close to their mothers for many years, helping them in their old age. Older daughters help their mothers with younger babies. Males have been known to help brothers in their competition for dominance.

In bonobos there is even a stronger and longer-lasting mother-son bond. Sons may stay with and travel with their mothers well into their adulthood. There is also a strong bond between brothers.

Interestingly, this sense of caring and bonding can extend outside the actual biological family unit. Offspring are important to the group as a whole, and adult bonobos may risk their own welfare to come to the aid or protection of an *unrelated* youngster threatened with harm. This is true of baboons as well. Bonds among adult females are a focus of bonobo society, and those females are not necessarily related to one another. In chimps, bonds among unrelated males are important. Once, according to Jane Goodall, an adolescent male chimp adopted an unrelated youngster that had been orphaned. In a sense, then, some primates have extended the concept of family beyond just easily recognized biological relationships.

But in all cases there is some recognition of and importance given to relationships between individuals that *are* related. In other words, kinship in many primates—although not formalized as among humans—is more than just the temporary, instinctive bond between mother and dependent young. It is an integral part of the larger social order.

In the human primate, the social system in most cultures is based on family. One's place in society is influenced, if not determined, by one's membership in a family and one's specific relationships to other members of that family. And the basic biological relationships of family are interpreted and translated by culture into an almost bewildering array of kinship systems.

MARRIAGE AND FAMILY

From Family to Kinship

For most of human evolutionary history, and for recent foraging groups, *society* was synonymous with *family*. Social units were made up of small groups of nuclear families that were no doubt related—several biological brothers and their wives and children, for example, with perhaps some grandparents. Social interaction was thus based on family relationships, and these would have been rather obvious and easily kept track of. After all, such groups consisted of relatively few individuals, and the intimacy with which they lived meant that biological events—births, deaths, even sexual relations—were known about and observed.

As food production made possible larger populations, social interactions got more complex. Now there were more people, more goods and services being produced and passed around, and more than just a few biological families. There were groups other than close relatives to interact with. There was a need for some sort of leader or overseer to handle interactions within the group and between multiple groups. A new social organization was required—one based not on natural groupings but on cultural ones, ones that could be geared to the specific needs and desires of the population and cultural system concerned.

But must such a social system be created from scratch? Does a group just dissolve all existing social relationships and make up new ones? Hardly. For there already *is* a model for organizing a society: the family relationships around which less complex societies were arranged. What apparently happened was that food-producing societies, needing new and varied schemes of organization, created *cultural variations on biological themes*. What family you belonged to, your place in that family, and where your family line fit relative to other family lines still determined your place in society. But the system, even though it looked like and used the terminology of biological relationships, was a cultural one. It may have ignored some biological relationships. It may have created categories that crosscut actual biological groups, or it may have lumped, under one name, people of quite distinct biological identities. The model is from biology, but the specific features are cultural.

The base of any kinship system remains the nuclear family—two or more parents and their offspring. Anthropologists have devised diagrams to represent this unit and its extensions (Figure 10.2). In these diagrams, triangles represent males, females are circles, and an equal sign means marriage. A vertical line indicates *descent,* the offspring from a marriage. A horizontal line means *sibship,* brothers and sisters.

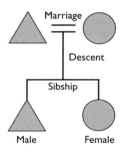

FIGURE 10.2
A basic nuclear family with one husband, one wife, and two children, a boy and a girl.

Variations of Marriage

Number of Spouses The number of spouses one may have varies from culture to culture and is the criterion for the two basic types of family. In sheer numbers, the majority of people in the world today live in societies where marriage involves just one of each spouse, the practice called **monogamy** (*mono,* "one"; *gamy,* "marriage"). But in some societies a person may have more than one spouse. The general term for this is **polygamy** (*poly,* "more than one"). Obviously, there are two versions of this. If a man has several wives it is **polygyny** (from the Greek *gyne,* "woman"). If a woman has several husbands—a rare occurrence—it's **polyandry** (from the Greek *andros,* "man"). Polygamous families are obviously more complex than monogamous ones. Co-wives or co-husbands have relationships among themselves that can sometimes be contentious; children have half-siblings (same mother, different fathers; or same father, different mothers); and there are simply more people in the family to deal with.

monogamy A marriage unit made up of one husband and one wife.

polygamy A marriage system that allows multiple spouses.

polygyny A marriage system with one husband and multiple wives.

polyandry A marriage system with one wife and multiple husbands.

Frequency of Marriage Patterns   Now, those of us from monogamous societies no doubt think of that system as the normal and correct one, and for us it is. But the statistics show something else. In a survey of 565 world societies, only about 25 percent were strictly monogamous, that is, never allowing multiple, simultaneous marriages. You can literally count the number of polyandrous societies on the fingers of one hand—only 4, or less than 1 percent, in the same survey. So, while most *people* now live in monogamous societies, most *societies* (no matter how many people live in them) are polygynous; they account for over 70 percent of societies in the survey. What explains this statistic?

In Chapter 9, we noted a correlation between marriage pattern and subsistence pattern—monogamy tends to be practiced in foraging, complex agricultural, and industrial societies. Polygyny is associated with horticultural, pastoral, and nonindustrial agricultural societies (see Table 9.1). I believe a basic answer lies in these correlations. In horticultural, pastoral, and nonindustrial agricultural societies, the family is the basic economic unit. Whether the family is relatively self-sufficient, as in horticultural groups, or involved in a more complex trade network, as in nonindustrial agricultural groups, the family is the unit of production. Thus, the more adult members in the family, the more workers there are. When one wife is limited in her work by pregnancy or caring for a young child, multiple wives mean that there are still other adult women to share the work. Moreover, polygyny enhances the reproductive potential of the family (Figure 10.3).

Now, an obvious objection arises here: Don't such families make things harder on themselves, economically, by having the additional children that multiple wives would produce? If there were fewer mouths to feed, two adult workers in the family would probably suffice. Remember, however, that the fairly low rate of infant mortality (death within the first year of life) that we take for granted is a recent phenomenon of industrialized societies with adequate nutrition and medical care. For most people throughout most of human history, infant mortality has been much higher. So, to have enough children who will grow up to perpetuate the family—and the society—each household must increase its *potential* reproduction, acknowledging that a fair number of the children born will not survive to adulthood. Thus, the prevalence of horticultural and nonindustrial agricultural societies in human history accounts for the statistical popularity of polygyny.

Why, however, doesn't the same hold true for industrial and foraging societies? In industrial societies, production becomes more dependent on nonhuman energy. Fewer people can produce more food than in the other types of subsistence. (Recall that less than 3 percent of the United States population lives on farms. The food we eat is produced by a tiny proportion of the people.) In a sense, the individual, rather than the family, is now the *basic economic unit*. Moreover, with better nutrition and medical care, more children live to reach adulthood. Very large families would, in most cases, put a strain on a family's economics.

FIGURE 10.3
Johnny Bungawuy, a native of Arnhem Land in northern Australia, with seven of his eleven wives and some of his children who accompanied him on a successful hunt for a pelican. These people belong to a foraging society that practices polygyny, a common marriage system in northern Australia, where food resources are abundant.

In foraging societies, the whole society is the basic economic unit. Sharing is the focus. Production on the level of the nuclear family is less important than production on the societal level. And because foraging societies depend on naturally occurring resources, they are aware of the strains that greater populations could place on their subsistence. Recall that many foraging societies, even given infant mortalities, require methods of limiting their births. More adult providers in the family would gain them nothing—in fact, it would *cost* them since adults consume more resources than children do. Anyway, in small societies, polygyny might be difficult, since there would hardly be enough "extra" women to go around.

What about polyandry? Why is it so rare? The answer is simple. Although a family of one woman with several husbands would provide a larger family workforce, it would offer no greater reproductive potential than would a monogamous family. Polyandry is found where land is scarce and property is inherited through men. So as not to break up land holdings, several brothers may marry the same woman. Property is kept intact and within the family. Several polyandrous societies are found in Tibet, where arable land is at a premium.

KINSHIP

Families, of course, are not isolated units. They are strung together horizontally to include persons we refer to as aunts, uncles, and cousins (Figure 10.4). This is the **extended family**. Families are also strung together vertically over time to include grandparents and other ancestors. The dimension over time is the **descent line**. In Figure 10.5 the female (shaded) is a daughter in one nuclear family. When she marries,

extended family Nuclear families linked by blood, generally ones that inhabit the same location.

descent line Nuclear families that are connected over time.

FIGURE 10.4
Horizontal extension of a nuclear family—the extended family. The married couple in the center have two children, one of each sex. Each parent has two siblings, one of each sex, each of whom also has two children, one of each sex. For simplicity's sake, the spouses of the parents' brothers and sisters—and their relations—have been left out.

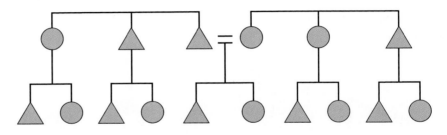

FIGURE 10.5
A simple descent line with nuclear families linked by the female, who is a daughter in one nuclear family and a wife and mother in the other.

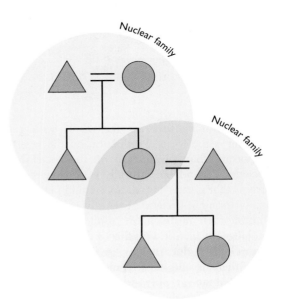

she becomes part of two connected nuclear families, the one in which she is a daughter and the one in which she is a wife and mother. The same would hold true for her mother and her daughter, and so on. It is in the descent line that we see some of the most interesting variations in basic social organization.

Types of Families

Bilateral Families   If you were asked to which descent line you belonged, you'd probably answer both your father's and your mother's. True, you may carry your father's last name, there may be some legal matters that emphasize your ties to one side over the other, and you may feel more personally connected to one side; but in general social and cultural terms, your place in your family is as the product of, and as a member of, both sides. We call this system **bilateral** ("two-sided").

bilateral A kinship system in which an individual is a member of both parents' descent lines.

Patrilineal system   Matrilineal system

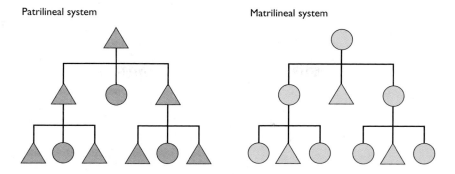

FIGURE 10.6
The members of a patrilineage and of a matrilineage.
In a patrilineage, females
may be members but cannot
pass on their membership
to their offspring. In a
matrilineage, males may be
members but cannot pass
on their membership to
their offspring. In some
patrilineal societies, wives
become members of their
husband's lineage as well.

A bilateral system appears to make biological sense. But not every society arranges kinship relationships to reflect biology. A bilateral system doesn't fill the cultural needs and outlook of every society. Indeed, most societies organize descent lines in very different ways.

Unilineal Families Most kinship systems, about 60 percent, are **unilineal** ("one line"). This means that an individual belongs to only one side of the family. Depending on the society, this is either the father's side, in a **patrilineal** pattern, or the mother's side, in a **matrilineal** arrangement (Figure 10.6). This does not mean that if you lived in a patrilineal society you wouldn't know who your mother was or that you wouldn't live with her, care about her, and have a special emotional and practical relationship with her. You would recognize your biological relationship with her and with members of her family. But if your whole society was organized according to kinship, for any function in which your place in society was important, you would be a member of your father's line, not your mother's. Important functions in this regard might include property ownership and inheritance, military alliances, leadership and other statuses, and potential marriage partners. In North American society, your place in the group is determined by your residence, occupation, and socioeco- nomic class. In most societies, though, it's which lineage you belong to.

In unilineal societies, membership in a lineage is inherited through the parent whose sex is the basis for the kinship system. In a patrilineage, you inherit family membership from your father; in a matrilineage, from your mother. You can pass on membership in the lineage only if you are of the corresponding sex. For instance, if I lived in a matrilineal society, I would be a member of my mother's lineage, but my children would be members of my wife's lineage. I could not pass on membership in my lineage.

Frequency of Unilineal Societies Now, the obvious question: Why? Doesn't unilineality seem to violate logic? In fact, it makes sense in societies that continue to organize themselves using the kinship model but in which there are large populations with many family lines. If

unilineal A kinship system in which an individual is a member of only one parent's descent line.

patrilineal A unilineal kinship system in which an individual is a member of the father's descent line.

matrilineal A unilineal kinship system in which an individual is a member of the mother's descent line.

things such as your economic responsibilities, your political and military alliances, and your rights of inheritance are determined by who your relations are, it makes things a lot simpler by preventing relationships from having to be accounted for *in two directions*. Unilineality makes social organization based on kinship easier and more efficient. Just why each individual system originated and why it has its particular set of rules is another question. Remember, you can't always infer origin from current functional relationships. Nonetheless, some degree of overall social simplicity seems to be an important goal of unilineality.

Family Type and Cultural Systems

Can we draw any correlations between descent systems and other aspects of culture? Are there reasons why some groups are matrilineal and others patrilineal? And what about bilaterality?

Like monogamy, bilaterality is associated with foraging and complex agricultural and industrial societies—the technologically least and most complex types. For foragers, bilaterality makes obvious sense. It reflects their egalitarian outlook, and the practical implementation of egalitarianism is aided by social symmetry. Each person is equally related to both sides of the family. When meat is distributed along kinship lines, this symmetry results in that distribution being simple and equitable. Moreover, bilaterality allows individuals to maximize their kin network; one can find relatives in many if not most other bands within the society.

For complex societies, which are not organized by kinship, no manipulation of the biological categories is required. Kinship is a more personal matter, and so the biological relationships can serve as the model for the kinship system. (Remember, however, this does *not* determine emotional or psychological relationships, nor, necessarily, social norms. See the "Contemporary Issues" box in this chapter.)

In unilineal societies, the specific type of system seems correlated to economics, in a broad sense. Women perform most of the farming labor in most horticultural societies, so women tend to be the focus of the social structure, and these societies tend to be matrilineal. This establishes a stable network of kinship ties and helps provide a high degree of internal political stability.

However, horticulturalists in dense tropical forests often confront a shortage of resources. Farming labor can become more intensive, and competition and even internal warfare are not uncommon within such groups. In these cases, men become a social focus, and the societies tend to be patrilineal.

It should be noted that there are exceptions to these correlations. There are bilateral horticultural societies and unilineal foraging societies. The above generalizations should not be seen as cause-and-effect relationships but rather as models for how to think about and analyze the variations in kinship systems among human societies. As we have noted, culture is not a "thing" that responds unvaryingly to certain situations. Culture springs from the minds of people. As anthropologist Roger Keesing, a specialist in kinship, puts it:

> Cultures do not respond to pressures. Rather, individual human beings cope as best they can, formulate rules, follow and break them; and by their statistical patterns of cumulative decisions, they set a course of cultural drift.

It should also be noted that there are other descent systems besides the major ones just described. In some, an individual may choose to belong to either the father's or the mother's side. In others, one is a member of the mother's line for some purposes and the father's for others. These, however, are rare, so we will limit our discussion to the three major patterns.

Within the major types of descent organization, there is even more variation. Societies have different terminology systems for ordering the exact relationships among individuals. There are about half a dozen major systems. We will look at three to show the aspects that vary, how we study them, and what they can tell us.

KINSHIP TERMINOLOGY

What do you call the man who is your mother's husband and your immediate male ancestor? That may sound like a dumb question. You call him *father,* of course. And no one else shares that designation. But it's not a dumb question in anthropology, because the categories of family relationships differ from society to society, as does just about everything else.

Kinship terms are, of course, linguistic and vary greatly from language to language, so it would be unwieldy to describe systems using actual cultural terms. We can, however, diagram the systems using symbols. Two individuals who share the same category are symbolized by the same color. In a diagram of a North American family, for example, the color indicating your biological father would be shared by no one else, while the color for your first cousin could be shared by many.

Terms for members of one's family, furthermore, are relative to the point of view of a particular person. You call the man mentioned before *father,* but your mother calls him *husband.* Your *cousin Tom* is your uncle's *son.* So each diagram is viewed from one person's perspective, and we call that person EGO.

The Eskimo System

Let's begin with the system that should be easiest for us to understand. It's the Eskimo system, so named because it was described in studies of that group.

FIGURE 10.7
The Eskimo kinship system.

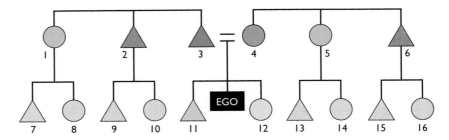

In Figure 10.7, two married individuals, 3 and 4, have three kids, 11, EGO, and 12. Each parent has two siblings, one of each sex, and each of these has two kids. For simplicity, we'll leave out the spouses of the parents' siblings. EGO is of no particular sex, so we can change "its" sex for different examples.

Notice that EGO's biological parents are indicated by colors found nowhere else on the diagram. This means that EGO calls them by terms used for them alone. The parents' siblings fall into two categories, one for males and one for females, but the same categories are used for both sides. In EGO's generation, there are again specific terms for EGO's biological siblings, distinguishing males from females. Finally, all the offspring of EGO's parents' siblings are called by the same term, here with no differentiation for sex (although many cultures using the Eskimo system do make a linguistic distinction).

Look familiar? It should. Just substitute English words for the colors: *father, mother, brother, sister, aunt, uncle,* and *cousin.* It would work for other languages as well, including Spanish, French, German, Russian, and many more.

The Eskimo system is found most often at both ends of the continuum of subsistence types. It tends to be used by foragers and by agricultural societies. Why? Look at what is emphasized by the terms: the nuclear family. Within that unit, people are specified. Outside that unit, people fall into a more limited number of categories with no distinction as to side of the family or, in the case of the English *cousin,* as to sex. In kinship terminology, *specificity indicates emphasis.*

The Eskimo system has a bilateral descent line with symmetrical sides of the family. It reflects an economic emphasis on the nuclear family, as in foraging groups, or a conceptual emphasis on the nuclear family as the only important recognized kinship unit, as in industrial societies. It allows the nuclear family to be set off and persons outside it to be equally important—or equally unimportant. So it works as well among the San as among twenty-first-century Americans.

The Hawaiian System

The Hawaiian kinship system is probably the simplest (Figure 10.8). In this system, persons are distinguished only by sex and generation. This

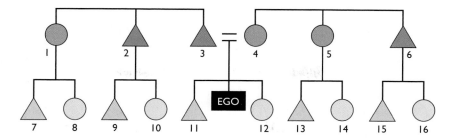

FIGURE 10.8
The Hawaiian kinship
system.

system is found in groups that have bilateral descent or in groups in which you are a member of either line or different lines for different purposes. Unlike the Eskimo system, also associated with bilaterality, the Hawaiian doesn't focus on the nuclear family but lumps nuclear family members and other close relatives into just a few broad categories. Societies that use this system usually comprise more people than do foraging groups. There is more emphasis on symmetry of the two sides. EGO's culturally defined relationships to a large number of people are thus fairly straightforward.

There is another aspect of kinship that is linked to terminology—the incest taboo, discussed in Chapter 7. Remember that mating between siblings and between parents and offspring is universally prohibited.* Although that taboo may have originated with reference to the biological meaning of those terms, in practice it relates to their cultural meanings as well. In other words, any person to whom you refer using the same term you use for your biological siblings or parents is the *same* as those people. The incest taboo would apply to them as well.

Look back at the Hawaiian system. Whom can EGO marry on the diagram? Nobody. Everyone on the diagram is the same as the members of EGO's biological nuclear family. EGO must find a mate outside his or her family line.

The Omaha System

The terminology systems used by unilineal societies are the most complex. The Omaha system, used by that Native American group as well as many other societies around the world, is a good example (Figure 10.9). It looks very strange at first, but if we take it one step at a time, it makes sense. First, for the moment, ignore persons 9, 10, 13, and 14. They're special, and we'll return to them shortly.

Having left those four out, you should notice that on EGO's father's side of the family there are more categories than on the mother's side. In

---

*Technically, this is called a rule of **exogamy** (literally, "marriage outside of") and refers to the unit of people outside of which one must find a marriage partner. A rule of **endogamy** ("marriage within") defines the group *within* which one must find a mate. The Hutterites are largely endogamous, for example.

exogamy Marriage outside a specified unit of people.

endogamy Marriage within a specified unit of people.

FIGURE 10.9
The Omaha kinship system.

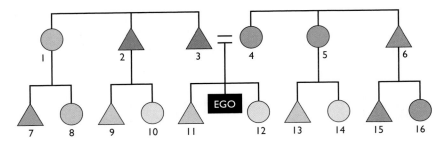

fact, all the members of EGO's mother's family (except 13 and 14—keep ignoring them!) are just male or female, regardless of generation. If we were to add more generations, the situation would still be the same. The color shared by numbers 4, 5, and 16, then, would translate into a word meaning something like "female member of my mother's lineage." Similarly, the color for 6 and 15 means "male member of my mother's lineage."

On the father's side, however, both sex and generation are specified. The color for 2 and 3, for example, means "male member of my father's line *in my father's generation.*" What this tells you is that the Omaha system is associated with patrilineal societies. As EGO, my important culturally defined relationships are with other members of my patrilineage. Thus, it is important for me to specify the categories into which they fall. I am not a member of my mother's patrilineage, though, so those individuals are not as culturally important to me. As a result, they are specified only by their sex.

It is important not to confuse personal recognition with cultural categories here. Certainly, if I were a member of a society using the Omaha system, I would know who those people on my mother's side were, and I would call them all by their personal names. My mother would not be a member of my patrilineage, but I would live with her while I was growing up and have close emotional ties with her. She would be my mother in every way we understand that term. The categories we're discussing refer to cultural relationships—various economic and social rights and responsibilities—that happen to be organized based on kinship.

Now add back those four relations you ignored earlier, and look at EGO's generation. The people in this generation fall into many different and asymmetrical categories. Numbers 15 and 16, as we noted, are simply a male and female on the mother's side. Numbers 7 and 8 are individuals with specific terms; we'll get back to them. Numbers 9, 10, 13, and 14, from *both* sides, are the same as EGO's biological siblings.

The Omaha system, as well as some others, makes a distinction between two kinds of children of your parents' siblings. We call them **parallel cousins** and **cross cousins.** Parallel cousins are children of same-sex siblings, your father's brother's kids or your mother's sister's

parallel cousins The children of your father's brothers or mother's sisters.

cross cousins The children of your father's sisters or mother's brothers.

kids. Here they are numbers 9, 10, 13, and 14. Cross cousins are your father's sister's kids and your mother's brother's kids, here numbers 7, 8, 15, and 16.

The origin of this distinction is debatable, but we may show one result—the application of the incest taboo. Numbers 9, 10, 13, and 14, sharing the same symbols as the biological siblings, clearly fall into the taboo category. This system also excludes *everyone* on the mother's side as a potential marriage partner to avoid combining descent lines that the unilineal system has separated; it also prevents marriage within one's own lineage. On the father's side, however, 7 and 8 could be acceptable marriage partners. They are neither a member of your mother's lineage nor yours. They are members of *their father's patrilineage*, that is, of number 1's husband. In other words, they are members of an unrelated lineage. Indeed, in some cultures with this system, the cross cousins on your father's side are the *preferred* marriage partners.

In actual practice, we have to look at each kinship system and see if we can discern the functional relationships involved. As with every other aspect of culture, there are no hard and fast rules. For instance, a few groups that use the Omaha system are matrilineal, so our neat analysis won't work for all unilineal systems.

There are more systems of terminology and subsystems within some of these three patterns. See the references at the end of the chapter for some sources. For the moment, if you're intrigued, consider the Crow system (named after another Native American group). It is the mirror image of the Omaha system and is associated with matrilineal societies. See if you can diagram it.

ORGANIZATION ABOVE THE FAMILY LEVEL

Within societies there are many organizing principles in addition to those based on the kinship model. For instance, in many societies there are **age sets**—groups of people born within some limited time range of one another. Age-set members remain associated for life and have certain special social and economic rights and responsibilities toward one another.

There are also associations based on gender. **Men's associations,** common in societies in the New Guinea highlands, are as important as any other social category for defining a person's social position and socioeconomic relationships with others (Figure 10.10). We also find various forms of military associations and associations based on occupation, ethnic affiliation, and region of birth.

Political Organization

As societies get larger and more complex, there is a need for other systems of organization. As anthropologist Elman R. Service puts it:

age sets A social unit made up of persons of approximately the same age.

men's associations A social unit made up of a society's men. Common in highland New Guinea.

FIGURE 10.10
Among the Gimi of Papua New Guinea, men and boys sleep in "men's houses" in the centers of their fenced-in compounds. Women and children are forbidden to enter the men's houses or even to walk on the paths leading to them. They live in smaller houses at the edges of the compounds.

political organization The secular, nonkinship means of organizing the interactions within a society and between one society and others.

Kinship . . . can integrate a society only up to a certain point in its growth. After that, the society must fission into separate societies if growth continues. . . . Only with the achievement of new integrative means can an increase in complexity keep pace with the growth.

The "new integrative means" he refers to is **political organization.** It serves the same functions as organization on the family level, but it involves more people and more complex interactions. According to Frank Vivelo, political organization

> refers to the means of maintaining order and conformity in a society. It concerns the allocation of power and authority to make decisions beyond the personal level, i.e., decisions which affect the group . . . as a whole. It provides structure through which decisions about social policy, and the implementation of social policy, are effected. In addition . . . [it] also concerns the way a society orders its affairs in relation to other groups.

As you should expect by now, the specific features of political organization vary enormously among different societies. We can,

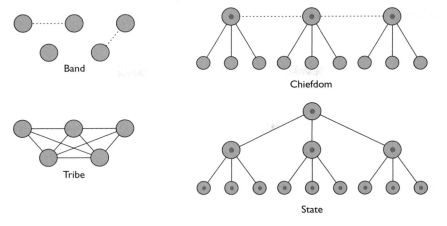

Band

Chiefdom

Tribe

State

FIGURE 10.11
Basic types of political organization. Bands are small autonomous units without formal leaders and with informal relationships with one another as the need arises (indicated by the dashed line). A tribe is a collection of bands, still without full-time leadership but with more formalized relationships among all the individual units (indicated by the solid lines). A chiefdom has formal, full-time leaders who rule over groups of individual units and interact among themselves in matters of concern to the entire society. A state requires centralized authority that coordinates and controls the interactions of the individual units, often through the leader of each unit. In reality, chiefdoms and states comprise more subunits than depicted here. A state system can consist of many layers of subunits such as towns, counties, and states, each of which has its own leadership structure.

however, categorize the variation into a few general types (Figure 10.11; see also Table 9.1).

Bands   Introduced in Chapter 9, **bands** are the simplest and, in a sense have no political organization at all. They are based on kinship and are characteristic of foraging societies such as the San and the Eskimo. As you recall, foraging societies are made up of small, autonomous, flexible units with no social stratification, although there are individuals who are informally more influential.

Tribes   Tribes are political organizations characteristic of horticultural and pastoral groups. Elman Service has referred to these as "collections of bands." The basic organization is still along kinship lines, but now those lines are combined into larger units—often called lineages or clans—and relations unite different kinship units and different residence areas such as villages. Tribes are essentially egalitarian, and there is no central authority, but the problems facing this larger group are generally more complex than those of a band society and so must involve decisions on the part of the tribe as a whole. The Yąnomamö and the Dani (see Chapter 14) are examples of tribes.

Chiefdoms   Chiefdoms are the next level of organization. There is still no *one* central authority over the whole society, but because there are more individual units making up the society, there are *numerous* central authorities, the chiefs, who lead groups of those individual units. Such an organization is found in less complex agricultural and large pastoral groups. The basis of organization may still be kinship, since the position of chief is often hereditary. Chiefdoms are socioeconomically somewhere in between egalitarian and class systems; there are social strata, but there is an attempt to smooth out inequalities through redistribution. Although foragers, the Kwakiutl are an example of a chiefdom (see Chapter 9).

band A small autonomous group, usually associated with foraging societies.

tribe A political organization with no central leader but in which the subunits may make collective decisions about the entire group.

chiefdom A political organization made up of groups of interacting units, each of which has a chief, or leader.

CONTEMPORARY ISSUES

Why Don't Bilateral Societies Have Equality between the Sexes?

It may seem contradictory that societies with bilateral descent lines display sexual inequalities. Doesn't the equal relationship of a person to both parents mean that the parents themselves are equal in social and cultural areas? Why, for example, does a wife take her husband's last name and children their father's? Doesn't this actually denote a patrilineal descent system?

In fact, type of descent line and the social and cultural relationships between the sexes are two different issues. American society is, indeed, bilateral, and yet it has traditionally been dominated by men. Women have only had the vote in the United States since 1920. Until relatively recently, far fewer women than men attended college, and if they did it was often a college solely for women. Those women who worked outside the household did so, to a great extent, in support services. Most of us picture a woman when we

use or hear the terms *nurse* or *secretary*. (Notice that the phrase *male nurse* is still common, as if men in that occupation were the overwhelming exception.) When the U.S. Senate and Congress meet in joint session, it is still a sea of male faces (and white male faces at that). Even the two women on the current Supreme Court make up only 22 percent of that body. There is still, in some occupations, a disparity in salaries between men and women doing the same work. But *patriarchal* is not *patrilineal*.

Descent systems are a reflection of broad, society-wide socioeconomic considerations. We can link the different systems (with exceptions, of course) to subsistence patterns. Bilaterality is found in foraging societies that are organized as symmetrical, egalitarian affiliations of fairly small numbers of nuclear families. In these cases, although there is a

---

States **States** are characterized by having one central authority. Complex agricultural and industrial societies consist of large numbers of people with complex interactions and living in numerous individual units. There is a clear need for all the individual units—even though each may have its own chief—to be integrated. Thus, we find kings, pharaohs, czars, and presidents in this type of system. The centralized authority itself may be complex and multifaceted, as is the federal government of the United States, with its three branches. There are many other modern-day examples of states. Well-known ancient examples include the Maya of Central America, Great Zimbabwe in southern Africa, Mesopotamia in Southwest Asia, and ancient Egypt.

Social organization, then, is a broad and complex topic. The general idea, however, is this: the organizing groups may sometimes be based on biological factors such as age, sex, and kinship. Nevertheless, the actual categories, the rules for membership, and all the ideals of behavior associated with the categories are cultural inventions geared toward addressing the needs of the group that uses them. It's in this light that we attempt to understand them.

state A political organization with one central authority governing all the individual units.

sexual division of labor, there is also a basic sexual equality. But bilaterality is also found in complex agricultural and industrial societies where cultural manipulation of biological categories is not necessary and where the family has a personal rather than an economic focus. The characteristics of such societies have given rise to at least the potential for inequalities in the relationships between men and women.

In urban and suburban settings especially, a more distinct division of labor evolved. Instead of all members of a household being involved in aspects of the same economic activities, the husband would leave the house to work. The wife, likely also a mother, would take care of home and children. The sexes were thus isolated from one another for large portions of the day, and women became isolated from public life. They still performed important labor, but it was not labor that generated income. Women thus became economically dependent on men and, as a result,

often lacked property and power. They became, in a sense, an underclass.

From this male-dominated socioeconomic situation, and from the efforts by men to directly maintain the power and wealth such a situation provided them, came the idea that women were "the weaker sex." Women in the United States, for example, were seen as unqualified for men's jobs, as incapable and not in need of formal education, and as needing extra physical protection and care. (Even into the twentieth century, some women were virtually confined to their beds during pregnancy.) Certainly, it was thought, women lacked the mental abilities for commercial or political leadership positions, and a woman doctor or scientist was considered an oddity.

Although the situation is far more equitable today, we are—in both our economics and our worldview—still working toward overall equality for men and women in this society. The fact that we organize kinship bilaterally does not require or guarantee that equality.

SUMMARY

All groups of living organisms require some mechanism to coordinate the actions of their members. For most living things, this mechanism is genetic. But with large-brained primates—creatures that rely on learned behavior for survival—group organization becomes more complex and variable. In anthropoid primates such as the baboon, chimpanzee, and bonobo, the identities, characteristics, and relationships among individuals are important in the establishment and maintenance of social organization.

In the human primate, the basis for social organization is, not surprisingly, the family, the basic reproductive and economic unit. For most human societies throughout most of our evolu-

tionary history, social organization has been based on kinship. But even when populations become large, complex, and composed of many biological kinship groups, the organizational structure may still be based on the biological model. Now, however, kinship units are culturally defined and may crosscut or lump biological categories, and so we see all manner of variation—in one's individual identity as a member of a kinship group and in the identity and number of potential marriage partners. These variations may be examined and understood under the assumption that the form of organization works for the people who practice it and is an integral part of their whole cultural system.

When societies become so large and complex that kinship alone can't operate to organize and coordinate them, broader forms of integration must be devised. These are political units. Although many of these still have kinship-based aspects, they are largely based on residence and socioeconomic interaction.

QUESTIONS FOR FURTHER THOUGHT

1. It's easy to say that we should apply cultural relativity in our studies of and dealings with other cultures. But putting it into practice is another matter. Thinking about the current world situation, with its many intercultural conflicts, how might cultural relativity be helpful? What are its limits? Are there times when it's *appropriate* to be ethnocentric?

2. As an exercise in appreciating other kinship systems, draw a kinship diagram for your family—include as many members, living and deceased, as you can*—and imagine (and redraw) it as if it were a patrilineal and then a matrilineal system. Next, use Omaha terminology and see how that would change how you view your family members and relationships.

3. Larger societies include groups whose organization can be categorized using the types of political systems discussed in this chapter (bands, tribes, chiefdoms, and states). What type, for example, might the Hutterites fall under? How about the church you belong to? your university? your extracurricular groups and clubs?

NOTES, REFERENCES, AND READINGS

Information on baboon social organization can be found in Linda Marie Fedigan and L. Fedigan's *Gender and the Study of Primates*, Barbara Smut's *Sex and Friendship in Baboons*, and Shirley Strum's *Almost Human*. For primate behavior in general, try *Patterns of Primate Behavior*, by Claude Bramblett, *The Nonhuman Primates*, edited by Phyllis Dolhinow and Agustín Fuentes, and *Primates in Perspective*, edited by Christine Campbell et al.

Although it is over thirty years old, I still find Roger Keesing's *Kin Groups and Social Structure* a useful general book on those topics. A good chart on the relationship between kinship and subsistence patterns is on page 134, and the passage I quoted is from page 140.

The survey I mentioned in conjunction with the percentages of cultures exhibiting different descent systems is George Murdock's *World Ethnographic Sample*. Information specifically about the topics of this chapter is in his *Social Structure*.

Descriptions of and discussions about the correlations between marriage, kinship, and subsistence pattern can be found in M. Kay Martin and Barbara Voorhies's *Female of the Species*.

Elman R. Service discusses the categories of political organization in *Profiles in Ethnology*, third edition. The passage I quoted is from page 3. The definition of political organization I quoted is from Frank Robert Vivelo's *Cultural Anthropology Handbook*, page 135.

For a detailed discussion of the rise of the state, see chapter 13 of Kenneth Feder's *Past in Perspective*.

---

*Some additional symbols might be helpful here:

⚰ deceased

◍ living elsewhere

≠ divorced

COMMUNICATION

Sharing What We Need to Know

When a honeybee finds a new source of food—flower pollen and nectar—she flies back to the hive. Within minutes more bees emerge and, amazingly, fly straight to the food. Their ability to do this is a result of what goes on in the hive after the first bee flies in.

Inside the hive, that bee does a dance, called a waggling dance, to communicate to the other bees the direction, distance, and identity of the food (Figure 11.1). First, because it's usually dark in the hive, she emits sound signals that help the other bees determine where she is and how she's moving. She then dances in a figure-eight pattern on a vertical surface of the hive; the angle of one line of the dance relative to the vertical is the same as the angle between the sun and the food source. The pace of her dancing tells how far away the food is; the faster she dances, the closer the food. At some point, the bees observing the dance emit sounds that vibrate the honeycomb. This causes the dancer to stop, and she gives the watchers small samples of the food so they know its taste, smell, and quality. After receiving the necessary information, the other bees fly out to find the food. They can find food just as easily on cloudy days as on sunny days because they can see ultraviolet light.

As amazing as this is, it's just one example of the many ways in which organisms communicate with other members of their species. We sometimes think that humans have the only communication system capable of transmitting such specific information, but as with other traits assumed to be unique to humans, that's not the case. The bee dance, as we'll discuss, has the rudiments of some features of human communication.

The goal of this chapter is to understand what human communication is and how it acts as one of our species' survival mechanisms. At the base of this understanding is the simple concept that communication is the way in which information from the nervous system of one organism is transmitted to that of another of the same species. It follows that a species' communication system reflects the species' nervous system and the nature of the information being communicated. A bee, for example, is built to perceive the location and nature of its food source, and it has evolved the ability to share that information with its fellow bees. As you might expect, as simple nervous systems evolved into brains, and as necessary information became more involved, communication systems became more complex.

A look at the specific features of the human communication system will show how this relationship between an organism's nervous system and its communication system works. Although the term is often used more broadly, I use **language** to refer solely to human communication by means of shared symbols in the form of sounds or their representations. (We also, of course, communicate in nonlinguistic ways, such as facial expressions.)

AS YOU READ, CONSIDER THE FOLLOWING QUESTIONS:

1. How do we define the human communication system, and what are its features?
2. How might our language ability have evolved?
3. What can studying the linguistic abilities of apes tell us about human language?
4. In what ways is a language related to the culture that uses it?

LANGUAGE

Recall from Chapter 4 that the makeup of the human brain allows us to have culture. Essentially, our neocortex can experience not only present events but also events from the past and even hypothetical and future events. The human brain can do this because it stores massive

language Human communication by means of shared symbols in the form of sounds or representations of sounds.

amounts of information—derived from experience through the sense organs—in such a way that all the individual pieces of data are separately filed but highly cross-referenced. Thus, they can be manipulated—taken apart, modified, and put together in a virtually infinite number of combinations. This ability not only lets us think about experiences but also enables us to make generalizations about them and derive abstract ideas and concepts from them. So our communication system must possess features that reflect these processes and make sharing our data and ideas possible. In humans, linguistic abilities are housed in a special area on the left side of the brain (see Figure 5.5), but the functions of that area are basically the same as those of the neocortex in general.

The Features of Language

First, we can talk about things that are not right in front of us, things that are not immediate stimuli—for example, the concepts we've been discussing throughout this book. This characteristic is called **displacement.** The subjects of our language can be displaced in time and space.

Second, in contrast to the communication systems of other species, our language is not made up of a series of individual signals, each with a single and specific meaning. Our ideas are expressed in units of meaning called *sentences,* which in turn are made up of smaller units called *words,* which themselves are made up of various combinations of *sounds.* This feature of language is called **duality of patterning.** Language operates on two levels. Individual sounds, **phonemes,** which themselves are meaningless, are strung together in various combinations that have meaning, proceeding from the smallest meaningful unit, the **morpheme,** to larger units such as words, sentences, paragraphs, and so on.

Duality of patterning makes possible the endless generation of new combinations of these units to express new experiences, new meanings, new ideas, and new concepts. This is called **productivity.** Just as we manipulate the thoughts in our brains, we manipulate the mechanism we use to share those thoughts. If we couldn't do that, we couldn't share, and culture, by definition, must be shared.

Finally, since we communicate abstractions, it would be impossible for our language to be made up of sounds that are iconic (that is, resemble the thing being talked about) or that are specifically linked to one meaning. Rather, our sounds and the units of meaning we combine them into are **arbitrary.** They are culturally agreed-on and shared symbols for facts, ideas, and concepts. That's why every language in the world can have a different linguistic symbol for the same thing. The Tswana, a southern African people, call one species of nut-bearing tree *mongongo* (and the word has been adopted into English). The San call the same tree //"*gxa* (the / is a dental click and the " a glottal flap).

displacement The ability to communicate about things and ideas not immediate in space or time.

duality of patterning Here, the two levels of human language: units of sound and units of meaning that those units of sound are combined to create.

phoneme A unit of sound in a language.

morpheme A unit of meaning in a language.

productivity Here, the ability of human languages to generate limitless numbers of meanings.

arbitrary Here, the fact that the features of human languages bear no direct relationship to their meanings but are agreed-on symbols.

Apply these features to the communication system of the bees. There is a degree of displacement, since the flowers are not right in front of the bee that is communicating information about them. She must remember their location for the few minutes it takes her to fly back to the hive and dance. Similarly, the bees receiving the message must remember it long enough to find the flowers. But the bees can't share information about last year's flowers or even yesterday's, and they can't communicate about food sources in the future. Neither is there duality in the bee's communication system. Each aspect of the dance has a meaning of its own, and that's it. Thus, there can be no real productivity. All the bees talk about is the direction, distance, and general type of food. Finally, the bee's communication system is not symbolic. The waggling dance is an analog in that the bee waggles at an angle relative to the sun and paces her dance in direct correlation to the distance. That's a lot different from saying, "Fly 300 yards at 10 degrees east of north." Those symbols have meaning only because we have agreed that they do.

Language Acquisition

Our languages must be learned. We are no more born knowing how to speak our native language than we are born knowing the rules of our culture. Languages use abstract, arbitrary symbols that allow people to speak about abstract concepts. Languages are passed on to future generations not in the genes but by cultural sharing. And language is facilitated through the use of artifacts—written words in literate cultures, as well as the spoken words themselves, which are also artifacts because they are created by people.

But there is a biological basis for language. We have to learn the features of our native language, but that learning itself has a biological component. Before you ever opened a grammar book in elementary school, you could already speak your native language with a great deal of fluency. You made mistakes, of course, and we all do, even through adulthood. But our linguistic mistakes were, and are, generally exceptions to the basic rules of our language's grammar.

What happens when we are children is that part of our brain is furiously working to take in data about our communication system and to formulate the generalizations about it that will enable us to use it. A child learns the rules of grammar not through repeated instruction but rather by hearing the language spoken and trying to speak it.

Consider the grammatical mistakes children make. They usually concern exceptions to the general rules—exceptions that must be specifically and individually learned. A child who says "Yesterday I seed a rabbit" in a language that normally forms the past tense by adding -ed is using logic and is actually demonstrating an understanding of a basic rule of English grammar.

There's some evidence that language-learning ability decreases with age. It becomes, for most of us, much harder to learn new languages once we're in our teens. Children deprived of human contact and thus of the opportunity to hear and use language have a very difficult time making up for the deficit later on. Language ability is part of our biological makeup and so, it seems, is the ability and process for learning it.

Descriptive Linguistics

The study of all the arbitrary pieces of human language is called **descriptive linguistics.** To give you an idea as to what is involved and how languages differ from culture to culture, let's just touch on some of the essentials of this field.

The basis for any language is the set of sounds it uses. These are its phonemes, and each language has its own phonemic inventory. Some of these sounds may be used in other languages as well, but some may be unique. For instance, the language of the San contains four phonemes that we refer to as clicks. They are real parts of the language. The difference between one click and another can mean the difference between one word and another.

Languages also differ in phonemic distinctions. Two of the most often cited examples involve phonemes in English and Chinese. The *t* phoneme in the words *tack* and *stack* are, to English speakers, the same. To a speaker of Chinese, however, they are different. Say them out loud and notice that the *t* in *tack* has a puff of air after it (called *aspiration*) but the *t* in *stack* does not. This difference in Chinese could alter the meaning of a word. On the other hand, the first phonemes in *lock* and *rock* are different to an English speaker but are just variations of the same phoneme to Chinese and Japanese speakers.

The arrangement of phonemes also differs among languages. For instance, the *mb* combination may appear in the final position of a word in English, as in *lamb,* but never in the initial position, as in *Mbuti* (say it with two syllables not three), the name of a Central African people. An initial *nkr,* as in *Nkrumah* (also two syllables), the name of the first president of Ghana, is also absent from English.

Phonemes don't have meanings themselves, but when combined with other phonemes, they form the basic meaningful units of language, called morphemes. A word is composed of one or more morphemes; it means something. But not all morphemes are words. The word *words,* for instance, is made up of two morphemes: *word,* with its obvious meaning, and *-s,* which means "make the preceding morpheme plural." A morpheme may come in several versions. The English morpheme that, as a prefix, makes the attached word negative, comes in four forms: *im-, in-, ir-,* and *un-,* as in *im*possible, *in*credible, *ir*responsible, and *un*reasonable.

descriptive linguistics The study of the structure of language in general and of the specific variations among languages.

Moreover, pitch and stress can act as morphemes, changing the meaning of a word or set of words. In Chinese there are four variations in pitch (the rise or fall of the voice) placed on a combination of phonemes basically pronounced *ma,* resulting in four different words. In Russian the difference between a statement and a question does not have to involve word order, as in English. The changes in pitch as you say the words of the sentence make the difference. Compare the following English and Russian sentences (the Russian is written phonetically, since that language uses a different alphabet):

I am going to the post office.
Am I going to the post office?

Ya idu nah pōtchtu. (statement)

Ya idu nah pōtchtu. (question)

Finally, morphemes are strung together to make up the unit of speech that conveys whole ideas, the sentence. Each language differs in its rules for the order of morphemes in a sentence. This is called **syntax.** For instance, if we want to negate the idea expressed in an English sentence, we usually put a negative morpheme in front of the appropriate word: *I don't love you.* In German, the negative morpheme *nicht* can go at the very end of the sentence: *Ich liebe dich nicht.* (The humorous construction, made famous in the movie *Wayne's World,* of putting *not* at the end of a sentence, as in *I love you . . . not!,* wasn't funny when that movie was translated into German.)

An example of the power of the rules of language—the rules that we generate as children even before we learn them formally—comes from linguist Noam Chomsky. He offered the following sentence:

Colorless green ideas sleep furiously.

Although it is nonsensical, we easily recognize the sentence as grammatically sound. All the morphemes and the words they make up are in the right places and order. Compare it to this version:

Furiously sleep ideas green colorless.

This one makes no more sense, but neither does it sound like an English sentence. Another famous example comes from *Through the Looking Glass,* by Lewis Carroll:

'Twas brillig, and the slithy toves
   Did gyre and gimble in the wabe;
All mimsy were the borogroves,
   And the mome raths outgrabe.

Don't bother consulting a dictionary; you won't find most of those words. But you may have thought they were real because the word structure and order followed the rules of English.

syntax Rules of word order in a language.

These, then, are the basic pieces of our language systems. Within certain rules, these pieces are broken up, shuffled around, and recombined to facilitate the communication of our thoughts—thoughts that themselves have been through the same kinds of manipulations.

At this point, two questions should come to mind: How did human language evolve? And why do human languages differ?

LANGUAGE AND EVOLUTION

How Did Language Evolve?

We can generalize and say that the characteristic features of human language make ours an *open* communication system. Because of its duality and productivity, human language is almost infinitely creative.

The communication systems of nonhumans, on the other hand—even of the nonhuman primates—are *closed* systems. That is, there are certain calls or other signs that have meanings, but those meanings are specific. For example, chimpanzees have a large repertoire of calls, facial expressions, and gestures, but these normally express emotional or motivational states such as fear, aggression, sexual stimulation, or excitement over, say, food or the presence of strangers (Figure 11.2). Thinking back to our discussion of the brain in Chapter 4, we might say that chimps communicate limbic-system functions—basic survival-oriented emotions. The chimps do not *name* things. Technically put, their communication system is not referential; it doesn't *refer* to something in the physical environment. Nor has anyone ever observed a chimp combining or stringing together calls to convey new meanings. There is, however, at least one exception. Studies of chimps and even some African monkeys show that danger calls may differ depending on the source of the danger, for example, whether it is on the ground (a leopard) or in the air (an eagle). Chimps also may specify the presence of a snake. If there's anything important enough to "talk" about specifically, it would be potentially lethal predators.

In terms of human evolution, the question now becomes, How did a closed call system, no doubt possessed by our ancestors, turn into an open system? Linguists Charles Hockett and Robert Ascher, in an article titled "The Human Revolution," propose a simple model (which I'm going to simplify even further here) of how this transition may have occurred. Hockett and Ascher suggest that some human ancestor found two closed calls to be appropriate for communicating a certain situation. But instead of using both calls, this innovative early hominid combined the calls, perhaps using part of each to make up a brand-new call that conveyed the meaning of both the old calls. Suppose the call for "food" is made up of the sounds *ABCD* and the call for "danger" consists of the sounds *EFGH*. Both calls would be appropriate, say, if a leopard were found standing over a newly killed antelope. Or, one could be "productive" and

FIGURE 11.2
A male chimpanzee displaying a "full open grin." This is a sign of excitement, often used by a high-ranking chimp when close to a subordinate.

use *ABEF,* meaning "food but danger too." This might make the combination *CDGH* mean "no food and no danger either," and *ABGH,* "food and no danger." The system is now open, and all the other calls and their parts may become phonemes that can be combined into various morphemes, which can, in turn, be combined into words and sentences. To be sure, it didn't happen this quickly and simply, but the development of language must have entailed a process very much like this.

When Did Language Evolve?

Until people started writing, only around 5,000 ya, language left no physical remains. We must rely on indirect evidence, and this comes in three forms.

FIGURE 11.3
Natural endocasts from South African australopithecines, showing the degree of detail possible. Notice the blood vessels, especially in the upper right cast. Such casts may also be made artificially and allow us to compare the brains of our ancestors with those of modern humans.

endocasts Natural or human-made casts of the inside of a skull. The cast reflects the surface of the brain and allows us to study the brains of even extinct species.

Brain Anatomy First, we know that the brains of living humans are asymmetrical—the right and left hemispheres are differently shaped and perform different functions. Language and the ability to use symbols correspond to the left hemisphere, and we know with some precision just which linguistic functions are located in which specific areas. By looking back in the fossil record, then, we might try to find at what point modern-looking brain structure appeared, especially those features and areas associated with language.

Fortunately, the inside of the skull reflects some of the features of the brain it once held. Natural **endocasts** and artificially produced endocasts of fossil skulls provide images of our ancestors' brains (Figure 11.3).

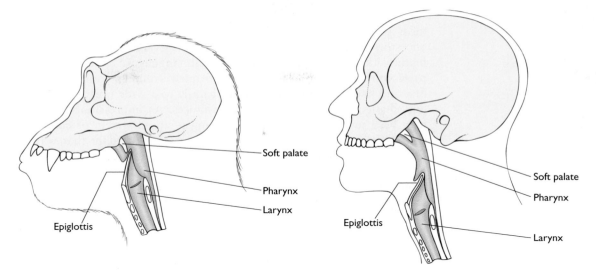

Soft palate

Pharynx

Larynx

Epiglottis

Soft palate

Pharynx

Epiglottis

Larynx

FIGURE 11.4
The vocal tract of a chimp compared with a modern human's. The high placement of the chimp's vocal tract makes it impossible for it to produce all of the sounds that are part of modern human languages.

What we find, however, doesn't really help answer our question. Asymmetrical brains and language-associated areas are found in all members of genus *Homo* and even in *Australopithecus*. Indeed, we know that chimp brains are also asymmetrical, even in some of the same ways as ours. Until we can discover just what these features were used for by our ancestors, brain anatomy can only hint at mental function.

Vocal Apparatus   A second type of evidence comes from the base of fossil skulls, which scientists use to reconstruct the vocal apparatus. Even though the vocal apparatus is made up of soft tissue, those parts are connected to bone. The shape of those bones is correlated to the shape of the larynx, pharynx, and other anatomical features (Figure 11.4).

Reconstruction work on australopithecines indicates that their vocal tract was basically like that of apes, with the larynx and pharynx high up in the throat. While this allowed them to drink and breathe at the same time (as human infants can do up to about eighteen months of age), it did not allow for the precise manipulation of air that is required for the sounds made by modern human languages. The early hominids could make sounds, but they would have been more like those of chimpanzees.

By the time of *Homo erectus*, however, vocal tracts were more like those of modern humans, positioned lower in the throat and allowing for a greater range and speed of sound production. Thus, *H. erectus* could have produced vocal communication with precise sound differentiation. Whether or not they were doing so, however, can't be inferred from this physical evidence.

Need   The third type of evidence is the least concrete but, to me, the most compelling at this time. We may ask, At what point did our ancestors have something to *talk about* that would require the complex features that characterize modern human languages? Here I come back to *Homo erectus,* who manufactured fairly complex tools, controlled fire, and had the ability to adapt culturally to a wide range of different and changing environmental circumstances. As impressionistic as this may be, I just can't imagine them using a closed system of communication given the kinds of information necessary to adapt that way. At the same time, I also see language as evolving, not suddenly changing. So I would imagine that could we hear *Homo erectus* talking, we would not recognize a thing about their communication system. The features of modern languages probably did not appear at their current level of complexity until later. So, in general, the question of just when language (as opposed to a closed communication system) evolved remains unanswered.

APES AND LANGUAGE

A different sort of linguistic research reminds us of the biocultural nature of human language—and reinforces our acknowledgment of the great apes as our closest relatives. Although chimpanzees, bonobos, gorillas, and orangutans lack an open communication system in the wild, several individuals from each of these species have been taught to communicate in a human language, with all the traits that term implies.

Researchers made numerous attempts in the past to teach chimpanzees to actually speak. These attempts were doomed, of course, because of the differences in vocal tracts and facial and tongue muscles between our two species. A chimp named Vicki, for instance, was trained in the 1950s to "speak" a few words—things like *mama, papa,* and *cup.* The vowels in her words, however, were merely puffs of air, and Vicki had to hold her lips together with her finger to make the *m* and *n* sounds.

Washoe: The Pioneer

Then, in 1966, a pair of psychologists, Beatrix and Allen Gardner, based their research on the recognition that not all humans are capable of speech and that therefore speech is no indication by itself of linguistic capabilities. They tried a new approach. They acquired a young chimp named Washoe and began to teach her American Sign Language (Ameslan). This is the language used by many hearing-impaired people, and it conveys information with every bit as much detail, efficiency, and nuance as the spoken word. Indeed, because people signing must look

a.

b.

c.

d.

FIGURE 11.5
A sentence in American Sign Language (Ameslan): "Good morning, have you had coffee yet?" This form of sign language, the most common, does not have a sign for all the words in the sentence and yet clearly conveys the meaning. Facial expressions and body language are important. (a) "Good"—fingers touch lips and then move forward. (b) "Morning"—left hand placed in crook of right arm; right arm moves upward (the sun coming up). (c) "Coffee"—motion of a coffee grinder. (d) "Yet"—palm faces back and hand is moved back and forth several times (being behind). The signer's expression and slightly tilted head make it obvious she's asking a question.

at one another, additional information can be transmitted through body language and facial expression (Figure 11.5).

Washoe passed away in 2007, at the age of 42, but spent her last years with four other chimps at the Chimpanzee and Human Communication Institute at Central Washington University. The resident chimps know and use hundreds of signs. They understand how word order can change the meaning of sentences. They combine words in varying ways to name new objects, for example, Washoe's "water bird" for *swan*. They are, thus, using a referential language. One of the chimps, Loulis,

FIGURE 11.6
A man teaches a chim-
panzee to sign "drink." The
chimp's signs are easily
recognized and interpreted
by speakers of American Sign
Language.

is Washoe's adopted son. He learned sign language from Washoe and the other chimps without human input. The chimps sign to each other when humans are not present. They also sign to themselves. They talk about objects and events that are not present and even about things in the future. Shortly after their special Thanksgiving dinner one year, one of the chimps started signing about a "food tree." He was referring to the fact that Debbi and Roger Fouts, directors of the institute, would soon put up a Christmas tree, which they decorate with edible goodies. When confronted with a new object, the chimps can categorize it according to attributes it shares with already-known objects. In short, they are using—although at the level of a small child—a real human language with all the traits that define that communication system.

Besides the chimps of Washoe's community, there are other chimps, bonobos, gorillas, and orangutans that sign (Figure 11.6) and yet others that communicate by using symbols on keyboards or shaped plastic tokens. Among the most notable are Koko and Michael, signing gorillas, famous for having and naming pet cats (Figure 11.7), and Kanzi, the bonobo that learned a symbolic keyboard language by watching his mother being taught. (Kanzi has also learned how to make stone flakes. He has used these flakes to cut the string around a box containing food.)

There were—and still are—a few researchers who claim that these apes are just mimicking their trainers and are not really generating language on their own. But most researchers feel that the data from these studies clearly show that apes have the mental capability to learn at least the rudiments of our species' unique communication system. As Koko puts it, "Fine person gorilla."

FIGURE 11.7
Koko, with Francine Patterson, signs "Smoky" in reference to her kitten Smoky.

Why Can These Apes Learn Language?

These studies, of course, bring up an obvious question. In the wild, the great apes use closed call systems. For what purpose, then, do they have brains capable of learning and using an open communication system, a trait we always thought was ours alone?

Remember that although our language ability is contained in one localized, specialized area of our brain, the basic "wiring" in that area is much the same as that throughout our brain. After all, the nature of the thoughts we transmit is reflected in the nature of the language. Given that the brains of apes have the same sort of wiring as ours, even if not as large and complex, it's not too surprising that they can be taught human linguistic behavior to some extent.

But why have they evolved such brains in the first place—brains that experience events and manipulate data? Simply put, apes lead complex lives. They live in social groups with elaborate personal relationships and interactions. They rely on learning in order to survive in their environments. As we see from the variation in behavior from one group of apes to another, they can alter their behaviors to fit their needs and develop forms of a behavior unique to their group and then pass on these traditions to future generations. They eat a wide range of foods and need to know where edible foods are, how to get them, when some foods become ripe, when some are bad to eat, and so on. Their brains have evolved to facilitate these adaptations. That they don't have a complex communication system means that they have no need to share some of these specific pieces of information beyond the unintentional sharing accomplished by imitation. Personal knowledge and sharing of emotional states suffice. But on an individual basis, they need brains with some of the basic abilities that, in one group of apes, would eventually evolve into the human brain. Thus, with proper training, motivation, and a stimulating environment, apes can be taught to use, and even come to intentionally use and generate, a form of our communication system.

LANGUAGE AND CULTURE

Language, of course, is a human cultural universal. But as with other cultural universals, language varies enormously from society to society. Can we explain this? What is the connection between language and culture?

The World's Languages

There are some 3,000 languages spoken in the world today. Some of these, like the cultures that use them, are becoming extinct as the modern industrial world spreads over the planet. No doubt a large number of languages we've never heard of have already become extinct.

As with cultures in general, languages are related to one another. They can be arranged taxonomically according to similarities and differences. A common ancestor language can give rise to several new languages. By comparing such things as rules of grammar, phonemic inventories, and, especially, vocabulary, we can begin to understand the evolutionary histories of languages—which ones gave rise to which other ones. We can draw family trees and even attempt to reconstruct hypothetical ancestral languages, such as Proto-Indo-European (Figure 11.8).

Classifying and reconstructing languages are difficult tasks, however, because language is fluid—it changes rapidly and is easily influenced. The French, for example, now commonly use such English derivatives as *le weekend*. American English, a Germanic-language, regularly uses words whose origins are French, Latin, Greek, Spanish, Celtic, Hebrew, Italian, and even Sanskrit. Japanese has many borrowed words from English, with the sounds translated to the closest Japanese sounds. Thus they enjoy the American national pastime *basu-boru*. Japanese workers

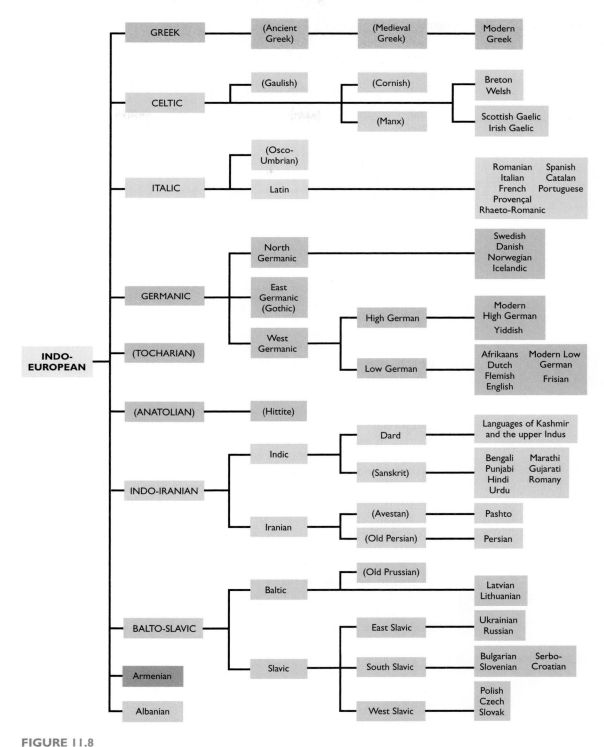

FIGURE 11.8

A family tree of Indo-European languages. The languages in parentheses are no longer spoken, although some may survive in written form.

FIGURE 11.9

Some words in Indo-European and non-Indo-European languages. (The words are rendered phonetically where the alphabet is different, as in Russian, or the language is not written, as in Fore.) Notice the similarities among the Indo-European words. These are cognates. (From Diamond 1992: 250)

Indo-European Languages						
English	one	two	three	mother	brother	sister
German	ein	zwei	drei	Mutter	Bruder	Schwester
French	un	deux	trois	mère	frère	soreur
Latin	unus	duo	tres	mater	frater	soror
Russian	odin	dva	tri	mat	brat	sestra
Old Irish	oen	do	tri	mathir	brathir	siur
Lithuanian	vienas	du	trys	motina	brolis	seser
Sanskrit	eka	duva	trayas	matar	bhratar	svasar

Non-Indo-European Languages						
Finnish	yksi	kaksi	kolme	iti	veli	sisar
Fore	ka	tara	kakaga	nano	naganto	nanona

often finish the day at *happii awaa*. My Japanese counterpart would now be sitting at his *konpyutaa*.

As a result, when trying to classify and reconstruct languages, a process known as **historical linguistics,** we use words that are less likely to change with contact between cultures or with the introduction of new technologies. These include words for body parts, numbers, and family relations. We call words that are related by descent **cognates** (Figure 11.9).

Most English speakers are familiar with the degree of linguistic variation in other Indo-European languages. Many of us have taken courses in one or more of these, and many of us speak another Indo-European language. But many of us lack an appreciation of the enormous variation found among languages around the world. I once heard a person describe someone else as being able to "speak African." It would probably amaze that person that there are some 800 languages spoken in Africa. On the island of New Guinea, which is smaller than Alaska, there may be (or at least have been in the recent past) as many as 1,000 distinct languages spoken.

These figures illustrate the importance of language to a culture and its people. Language is the most important way we learn our culture in the first place—and it is how we pass that culture on. To truly understand another language is to truly understand the culture it represents. And that's a monumental task.

Languages and Cultural Systems

Since the beginnings of anthropology, researchers have been trying to discover the relationships between a cultural system and the language its people speak. Can everything about a language—its phonemes, morphemes, rules of grammar—be related to the culture that it expresses?

historical linguistics The branch of linguistics that attempts to classify and construct a family tree of languages and to reconstruct extinct languages.

cognates Words that are similar in two or more languages as a result of common descent.

There have been many attempts to describe such relationships, and they have nearly all met with failure. There seems to be no practical reason why French has gutteral *r*'s and Spanish speakers roll theirs; why German can separate its negative morpheme *nicht* from the corresponding verb but English, a closely related language, cannot; and why clicks as phonemes are found mainly in southern Africa. Like genes, the specific features of languages seem to undergo flow, drift, and mutation—random changes not related directly to cultural adaptation.

Cultural Meanings What *is* connected to cultural systems directly, however, are the words themselves. What people call things tells us what sorts of categories they recognize. How they express ideas tells us how they view their world. We have already discussed one example of this—kinship terminology (Chapter 10). Although we used graphic symbols instead of actual words, our symbols (for example, see Figure 9.19) represented word usage, and the study of which relatives were called by what terms told us something about the cultures that practiced each system we described.

As discussed in Chapter 7, the phenomenon of grouping things according to a society's worldview is called folk taxonomy. The study of folk taxonomies is known as **ethnosemantics,** or "cultural meanings." As a classic but often misunderstood example, we can look at words for the white, crystalline matter that falls from the sky in winter. In English, we call it *snow.* We modify that word by adding an adjective, depending on our situation. Thus, when I look out on my snow-covered driveway, I wonder if it's a deep snow or a shallow snow or heavy or light snow. When I was a kid, I cared whether it was wet snow or dry snow, the former being better for snowballs and snow forts. Skiers listen for reports of powder or granular snow.

The Shuar (formerly called the Jivaro), an indigenous group in the forests of Ecuador, perhaps best known for their shrinking of human heads, are said to incorporate the phenomenon of snow into a single concept represented by a single term. It refers to the Andes Mountains, with which they are familiar but which play no direct role in their lives. The term includes the mountains, the snow, the idea of high altitude, and so on. In short, it means something like "the way it is up there."

At the other extreme are the peoples of the Arctic. An old interpretation from the early days of anthropology (and repeated through the years by many anthropologists, including me) held that the Eskimo had many separate words for different kinds of and conditions of snow, with no single root word for snow at all. That sounded good, but linguistic anthropologist Laura Martin has shown that the Eskimo do indeed have a root word for snow. Their way of modifying words, however, is so different from English that their snow words looked

ethnosemantics The study of the meanings of words, especially as they relate to folk taxonomies.

completely different to English-speaking anthropologists. Nonetheless, the point is that because snow is important to the Eskimo, they recognize and name many different types and conditions of snow. In other words, their categories—their folk taxonomies—for snow reflect the role snow plays in their lives. How best to travel, what game will be present for hunting, how cold the air is, how fast the wind is blowing—all these depend on or can, in part, be predicted by the nature and condition of the snow. For example, they have a word for falling snow and another for snow on the ground; one word for drifting snow and another for a snow drift; a word for snow that can cause avalanches; even a word for the bowl-shaped hollow in the snow around the base of trees (something many of us may never have even noticed). The words and categories of words that a language uses are intimately related to the environment, worldview, and cultural system of the society that uses the language.

Other folk categories have also been studied. Color terms, for example, vary greatly from society to society. Some groups, such as the Dani of New Guinea, have only two color terms, roughly corresponding to *light* and *dark*. In Western societies, we have dozens of recognized, agreed-on color terms. It's not that the eyes and brains of the Dani are different. All normally sighted humans see the same color spectrum. What's different is the cultural importance each group gives to distinguishing and naming the different sections of the visible spectrum. Explanations for this diversity are still being sought. It may have something to do with the nature of the group's environment. People living in areas with fewer natural colors—the Arctic or a desert—may have a simpler color taxonomy than, say, people living in a rain forest. It may also have to do with art styles. For a society whose art attempts to be realistic, it becomes important to recreate and name the great diversity of colors in nature.

Number systems, too, vary. The number system we recognize goes on counting forever. The Dani, on the other hand, recognize "one," "two," "three," and "many." Again, there is no perceptual or intellectual difference between us and them. It's just that within their cultural system, it is not necessary for them to tally or keep track of the specific number of anything beyond three. Don't assume, however, that one can easily account for all such differences by relating them to environments or overall levels of cultural complexity. Another highland New Guinea group, the Kapauku, count into the thousands. As with all cultural phenomena, the interrelationships can be obscure and complex, and with language they seem especially so.

Language History   Languages also have histories, and a language is related to the cultural history of a society. The Hutterites, for example, are trilingual. They originated in a German-speaking region, and their conservative outlook and lifestyle would predict that they would keep the language that was first used to communicate their thoughts and cultural ideas. Moreover, the German they use is High German, an old form. English is utilitarian. The Hutterites now live in English-speaking countries in North America. Their own language, with which they communicate information about everyday matters, has a practical history. It includes words derived from the languages common to the areas in which the Hutterites have lived during their nearly 500 years. I was able to pick out some German, Russian, and English in their vocabulary. For example, they called me *the fingerprint mensch,* a German-English mix. In fact, their language uses words and phrases not just from those major languages but from specific dialects of those languages.

Finally, languages vary according to the social contexts in which they're used. The field of **sociolinguistics** focuses on the way language differs by geographic region, class, gender, ethnic group, and social setting. For example, in the United States there are several words for the same food item: *hoagie, grinder, sub,* and *hero* are all regional names for a large sandwich.

So language is an intimate part of any cultural system. It is the mechanism whereby each of us, as a youngster, learns the basics of our cultural system, and it is the means we use to communicate to others—in the present and the future—the facts, ideas, and norms of our culture. One feature of a language—the words, their meanings, and their categories—is a reflection of the very basis of a cultural system, its worldview.

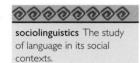

sociolinguistics The study of language in its social contexts.

SUMMARY

A communication system functions to transfer information from the nervous system of one organism to that of others of its species. It is therefore a reflection of the structure and function of that nervous system. Human communication—language—has features that enable us to share information and ideas that are cultural. The traits of human language reflect the features of our brain that make culture possible. Thus, human language is very different from the communication systems of even our closest evolutionary relatives.

We have only indirect evidence for when language evolved in hominids, but we can get a glimpse into how it evolved by comparing our communication system with that of the great apes and trying to determine under what circumstances a closed call system would have

evolved into an open symbolic language. The fact that under certain conditions apes can be taught to use a human language shows us again just how similar our species are in terms of mental abilities. At the same time, since the apes don't use such a system in the wild, these studies also show us how intimately connected language and culture are.

The specific connections between a particular language and the culture that uses it are not, as previously believed, on the level of sounds and grammatical structure. There are, however, direct connections between the worldview of a society, the words people use to talk about that world, and the categories into which those words are organized. On a broader scale, features of a language can reflect something about a society's cultural history.

CONTEMPORARY ISSUES

Are Written Languages More Advanced than Unwritten Ones?

The modern world would be inconceivable without written language. Today's global society relies on the accurate and efficient recording and sharing of massive amounts of information. All the world's major languages, and many less common ones, are now written. We usually refer to those that are not written as *preliterate*, as if literacy were the natural outcome of all language evolution and, thus, as if preliterate languages were somehow less than fully evolved—less complex, less accurate, less efficient. Is this the case?

First, we need to understand that there is no correlation between the complexity of a society and the complexity of its language. To be sure, complex modern industrial societies have larger vocabularies than small, isolated foraging groups. The *New Shorter Oxford English Dictionary* (abridged from the longer version by including only words in use after 1700 or that appear in the works of Shakespeare) still contains over half a million words. But that's because societies that use English have more things to name and more involved relationships to precisely describe.

That does not mean, however, that English is more complex than San or one of the thousand or so languages from the New Guinea highlands. Jared Diamond mentions, as just one example, that the language of the Iyau people of New Guinea uses variations in pitch to give a single vowel as many as eight different meanings. Other so-called primitive languages have grammatical rules that are far more complex than those of English and related languages and thus far more convoluted to nonnative speakers (such as the linguistic anthropologist trying to describe them).

Pidgin languages *are* much simpler than established languages. Pidgins arise when groups from two cultures come into intimate contact with one another—for example, colonists and native workers—and the two groups need to

QUESTIONS FOR FURTHER THOUGHT

1. Experimentation involving apes and language is not without controversy. Research some of the related literature or watch a video, such as "Can Chimps Talk?" from the *Nova* series, for different points of view on the subject. What do you think? Are the apes communicating in a form that has the characteristics of human language? If so, are there any ethical implications, for example, in how we treat these species?

2. There are many regional accents in the United States, and from these we can often identify a person's place of origin. (When I first went to college in Indiana, people immediately knew I was from New York.) Why do you think these accents developed as they did? Where did the distinct sounds come from? Is there any *one* "correct" American accent?

3. If you have had any experience with bilingual education, what do you think of such programs? Are there benefits or drawbacks to providing instruction in two or more languages? How do you think such instruction should be conducted? What place should dialects of English, such as so-called Black English Vernacular (BEV), have in U.S. education?

communicate. They concoct a crude and variable language that uses combinations of sounds and words from both standard languages. If, however, the next generations of the groups begin using the pidgin as their native language in more social situations than those in which the pidgin arose, they may find its simplicity inadequate. They will spontaneously expand the pidgin into a *creole*—a formal language with larger vocabulary, more complex grammar, and more consistency. Still less complex than established languages, creoles nonetheless have many of the attributes of those languages and may take on even more over time.

Now, what about writing? Writing is invented under very special circumstances. In fact, it appears to have been independently invented in only four locations: the Fertile Crescent of Southwest Asia, Mexico, China, and Egypt (and the last two are disputed by some authorities who say these cultures either borrowed writing from neighboring cultures or were inspired to invent it by example). What do these societies have in common? It was in these locations that food production first started and thus where we find the first large,

sedentary, stratified societies with cities and state political systems. It was these societies that first required writing for economic, political, and military record keeping and for disseminating important information. From these powerful societies, writing or the idea of writing spread to other populations.

But what about some large food-producing societies with complex political systems that did not have writing? These include the Inca of South America, the Hawaiians, large societies and states of sub-Saharan Africa, and the large North American societies of the Mississippi Valley. Were the four states that independently invented writing more evolved? Only in the sense that—because of a combination of geography, climate, availability of domesticable species, and timing—those four populations developed a need for writing as a result of that sociocultural outcome of food producing: the city-state. Writing, like so many other cultural innovations we've discussed, is the result of a need, not of some inevitable stage of progress toward which all cultures naturally move.

NOTES, REFERENCES, AND READINGS

An article on the communication of bees is "The Sensory Basis of the Honeybee's Dance Language," by Wolfgang Kirchner and William Towne, in the June 1994 *Scientific American*. Notice that these authors, as do many, use language and communication interchangeably. For some nice graphics, see also "The Buzz on Bees," by Jeffrey Kluger and Kristina Dell, in the November 6, 2006, issue of *Time;* and for more on the amazing behaviors of bees, see Edward O. Wilson's "How to Make a Social Insect" in the October 26, 2006, *Nature*.

For an overview of linguistics try A. R. Akmajian et al., *Linguistics*, and for anthropological linguistics, see Zdenek Salzmann's *Language, Culture, and Society.*

See Jane Lancaster's *Primate Behavior and the Emergence of Human Culture* for a detailed discussion of the differences between human language and the communication systems of other primates. The famous article by Charles Hockett and Robert Ascher, "The Human Revolution," is in *Current Anthropology*, volume 5.

A good summary of the status of the ape-language studies, focusing on Washoe and her community, is "Chimpanzee Sign Language Research," by Roger and Debbi Fouts, in Phyllis Dolhinow and Agustín Fuentes's *The Nonhuman Primates*. A more detailed treatment is Roger Fouts's *Next of Kin*. The linguistic achievements of Koko and Michael are discussed, with lots of pictures (including one Koko took of herself), in "Conversations with a Gorilla," by Francine Patterson, in the October 1978 *National Geographic*. An article about Kanzi and his linguistic and toolmaking abilities, called "Ape at the Brink," by Sue Savage-Rumbaugh and Roger Lewin, is in the September 1994 issue of *Discover*.

An interesting discussion of language families and their relationships to cultural and genetic groups is "Genes, Peoples and Languages," by L. L. Cavalli-Sforza, in the November 1991 *Scientific American*.

For the origins of English words, look in any dictionary or try a dictionary of foreign words and phrases such as that published by Oxford University Press. An interesting article about English borrowings into Japanese appeared in the April 4, 1999, *New York Times* titled "Help! There's a Mausu in My Konpyutaa!" by N. Kristof.

More on folk taxonomies can be found in Ronald Casson's *Language, Culture, and Cognition*. The technical article on Eskimo snow words is by Laura Martin in *American Anthropologist*, volume 88, number 2, and for a delightful description of those words and the conditions they describe, see *The Secret Language of Snow*, by Terry Tempest Williams and Ted Major.

The various connections between languages and history and discussions of language complexity can be found in Jared Diamond's *The Third Chimpanzee* and *Guns, Germs, and Steel*. The former includes a description of the reconstruction of Proto-Indo-European. Some of Diamond's other ideas in these books have been called into question, but his data on languages seem sound. For a critique, see the review of *Yali's Question* by Roger Ivar Lohmann in *Anthropological Quarterly* 79 (4).

12

MAINTENANCE OF ORDER

Making the Worldview Real

CHAPTER CONTENTS Religion • Variation in Religious Systems • Religion and Culture • Law • Summary • Questions for Further Thought • Contemporary Issues: How Do We Deal with Faith-Based Acts of Terror in Contemporary Global Society? • Notes, References, and Readings

Commercial television is not known for its profundity, but on occasion it does provide a memorable line. One of my favorites is from the comedy series *Taxi,* which ran in the 1970s and 1980s. In one episode, one of the employees of the Sunshine Cab Company asks Latka, a generic foreigner played by Andy Kaufman, why his upcoming wedding ceremony is so bizarre and complex. Latka answers that in his country there is a saying that what separates man from the animals is "mindless superstition and pointless ritual."

And, honestly, don't we often think of the beliefs and rituals of other peoples as mindless and pointless? We even have that view of some beliefs and rituals of our own culture—the ones that we don't happen to practice. It's a natural reaction, and there's a good reason for it.

We see the beliefs of others, and the ways in which they express those beliefs, as mindless and pointless because ours are so basic to us. Beliefs are important, however, because beliefs—as we discussed in Chapter 4—are a direct reflection of our worldview, our set of assumptions, attitudes, and responses that give rise to and hold together the cultural fabric of our lives. Except for personal survival, nothing is more important or more central to our existence.

Specific cultural expressions that reflect worldview can generally be termed **religion,** although in complex and multicultural societies, secular **legal systems** take the place of religious doctrine for setting formal rules for human behavior. Still, as we'll see, such legal systems are themselves often secular restatements of religious principles.

For a basic definition of religion, we can expand on that offered by anthropologist Edward Norbeck. Religion, he says, is a

> distinctive symbolic expression of human life [based on the supernatural] that interprets man himself and his universe, providing motives for human action.

Moreover, he sees the roles of religion

> as explanatory, and in many ways psychologically reassuring, and as socially supportive by providing validations for existence, motives for human action, and as a sanction for orderly human relations.

Religions, or legal systems that derive from them, are our way of making our worldview real. They provide us with a means for communicating our assumptions about the world. They give us a medium for

religion A system of ideas and rules for behavior based on supernatural explanations.

legal system A set of rules governing the behavior of individuals and institutions within a society.

formulating norms of behavior that correspond to the worldview. They provide a framework for putting those norms into action in our everyday dealings with one another and with the world around us. Furthermore, they are the way in which we impart our worldview to future generations. Little wonder, then, that *our* religion seems so natural and *theirs* so strange.

As with any facet of culture, however, our overriding assumption is that a religious system makes sense to the people who practice it. We already saw this when we compared some features of contemporary Eskimo religion with those of Southwest Asian religion from 10,000 ya. Let's now look more closely at religion and related cultural phenomena and see in what ways cultures are similar and different in their expressions of this important behavior.

AS YOU READ, CONSIDER THE FOLLOWING QUESTIONS:

1. How do we define religion? What are its functions? How might it have evolved?

2. What are some of the variable features of religious systems, and how might we explain this variation?

3. How may we study a religion as a part of the cultural system that practices it?

4. What are legal systems, and how do they function?

RELIGION

A Definition

Norbeck's definition indicates what religion does, but just what *is* it? Religions vary greatly from society to society, but the one trait they all have in common is the supernatural. Religion is a set of beliefs and behaviors pertaining to the supernatural.

By *supernatural* we mean something that is outside the known laws of nature and that involves some conscious *agent* who brings about real phenomena. That agent might be a god or might be a human, but the relationship between agent and result is beyond scientific investigation. There is, obviously, variation among cultures and within cultures as to which phenomena are treated scientifically and which supernaturally, and how. In North America, disease is typically treated scientifically within the medical community and by most citizens. There are, however, elements of the supernatural involved, from individual faith to institutionalized faith healing, prayer, and alternative (and scientifically unsubstantiated) forms of medicine.

The Fore of New Guinea (see Chapter 14) explain all illness, indeed all misfortune, as the result of sorcery, a supernatural explanation with other humans as agents. Yet they certainly would use practical methods to treat symptoms—binding and treating wounds, for example.

Not only is a belief in the supernatural universal among religions, but religion itself is a cultural universal. As with the other cultural universals we discussed in Chapter 7, the universality of religion requires an explanation.

The Basis of Religious Belief

A basis of religion can be found in our big brain that evolved as our species adapted by understanding its environment and by using that understanding to manipulate the environment for survival. The potential to understand, however, does not guarantee that everything will be understood. Some natural phenomena are within the intellectual grasp of humans, but others are not. These, however, also need to be explained— which is one place where forces outside of nature come in.

People need to feel some control over the circumstances of their worlds, even if only in the form of understanding those circumstances. So, when some natural phenomenon was beyond the reach of a people's practical knowledge, the supernatural was invoked. If the phenomenon seemed to be beyond the laws of nature, so then was the explanation. Thus all aspects of their world were put into concrete terms that could be communicated. The worldview, in other words, was made real.

Another proposed explanation for the origin of religious belief comes from our sense of "intersubjective engagement"—care about what others intend and feel. In other words, we think about "agents" of actions and we attribute "agency" to natural phenomena, feeling that some other being, or even some inanimate object, intentionally causes things to happen. We then attribute to these beings and objects, as Darwin suggested in *The Descent of Man*, the same feelings of justice and affection that we ourselves feel. Moreover, we tend to want to see purpose in phenomena, including our own lives, rather than some mechanistic explanation. These tendencies have been verified in studies of children but clearly extend into adulthood.

The universality of religion, then, is a result of our big, complex brain, which proves to be both a blessing and a curse. It gives us the ability and the desire to understand the world around us, yet we are acutely aware of the fact that we can't understand everything, including our own mortality (Figure 12.1; see also Figure 6.25)—a focus of much religious beliefs and ritual.

FIGURE 12.1
Rituals performed around death and burial are not just recent cultural phenomena. In this grave from the nearly 7,000-year-old site of Vedbaek in Denmark, a mother and newborn child were buried together. The mother's head was placed on a cushion of material decorated with snail shells and deer teeth. Similar materials were found around her waist, evidence of some sort of dress. Her child was buried with a flint knife (the blue object among the child's bones), as were all males in this cemetery, and was laid to rest on the wing of a swan. Although we can't know the exact meaning of these features, they clearly meant something.

Antecedents to Religion

As we have done throughout this book, we should ask again if there are any antecedents to human religion to be found among nonhumans. Are there any clues that some other creatures might even dimly ask some form of the questions that religions answer? There is one. Granted, it's open to interpretation, but it's also rather tantalizing since it comes from our closest relatives, the chimpanzees.

During a violent thunderstorm at the Gombe Stream Reserve in Tanzania, Jane Goodall observed what she called a "rain display" or "rain dance." At the height of the storm, several male chimps took turns running to the top of a hill and then hurtling down it screaming, jumping into trees along the route, tearing branches from the trees, and

FIGURE 12.2
An artist's depiction of a chimp "rain dance." As lightning flashes in the background, several males hurtle down the hill, swinging around trees and tearing off branches, while females and young watch safely off to the side.

waving them around (Figure 12.2). When one male reached the bottom, he returned to the top to start over, during which time the other males performed and a gallery of females and youngsters observed from the sides of the route. This was an uncommon event; Goodall saw it only a few times during her more than thirty years at Gombe.

Just what the rain dance means to the chimps is probably an unanswerable question. One is tempted, however, to imagine the dance as a reaction to the anxiety that the chimps feel toward what must, even for wild creatures, be a frightening phenomenon. Perhaps the chimps are trying to scare away the storm that is scaring them, recognizing an agency on the part of the storm as well as their own agency. If that's the case, their dance may be seen as having the rudiments of a religious ritual. Maybe, of course, they are just performing what animal behaviorists call a displacement activity, like our whistling in the dark. Or, as Goodall also proposes, perhaps all that running around just helps them keep warm.

Could human religion have started in a similar way—by some behavior aimed at influencing an unexplained phenomenon? Neandertal burials (see Chapter 6) probably had the objective of somehow influencing the event of death—either for the benefit of the deceased, if the burials demonstrated a belief in an afterlife, or for the emotional benefit of the living, if the burials simply showed a reverence for the physical remains of a member of the family and group. In either case, something beyond concrete, observable nature was being invoked.

The same can probably be said of the Upper Paleolithic cave art (Chapter 6). One hypothesis as to the meaning of this art is that it influenced natural phenomena such as fertility or hunting success. The recognition of some agent would seem to be a necessary component of such a perceived connection between art and nature.

VARIATION IN RELIGIOUS SYSTEMS

Let's look at the ways in which religious expression differs among cultures. Like any cultural expression, religion varies in how it is geared to individual culture systems and in how it changes to keep pace with them. There are, of course, as many specific religious systems as there are cultures, but we can get an overview by noting the variation in how religions deal with the supernatural.

Number of Supernatural Beings   We already discussed in Chapter 9 the distinction between monotheistic and polytheistic religions and the connection between these and some general types of worldview. Polytheism tends to be found in societies, such as the foraging San or Eskimo, that interact with their environments on a more personal level, where the people see themselves as one of many natural phenomena. Groups practicing polytheism tend not to have political systems with formal leadership. The supernatural reflects the natural in terms of social organization as well.

Monotheistic systems and *hierarchical* polytheistic systems (such as in ancient Egypt) are found in groups that have gained distinct control over their habitats—groups such as the early agriculturalists of Southwest Asia. These groups tend to have a hierarchical political system with formal leadership and full-time labor specialists.

Nonetheless, the dichotomy between monotheism and polytheism isn't always clear-cut. It has been said, for instance, that true monotheism is rare. For example, while Christianity has a single, all-powerful deity, that deity comes in three forms: the Holy Trinity of Father, Son, and Holy Ghost, or Holy Spirit. Moreover, the Virgin Mary is virtually deified by some Christian churches, and all sorts of angels and saints are included among Christianity's beings with supernatural powers, as is the devil.

Judaism, on the other hand, from which Christianity branched, is more truly monotheistic (although it also recognizes angels and the devil). The difference in the recognized number of supernatural beings between Judaism and Christianity probably can be traced to the wide spread of the latter and the diversity of the cultural systems that adopted it (voluntarily or otherwise), each system giving the basic religion a slightly different spin. Remember, worldview is generated by a combination of environment plus history.

FIGURE 12.3

FIGURE 12.3
The town of Sedona, Arizona, and the surrounding area are said to contain numerous vortexes, places with supernatural properties, specifically where energy is concentrated in such a way as to enhance one's psychic powers. At Boynton Canyon, believers have left offerings atop a tree stump at the supposed heart of a vortex. This vortex is said to help one recall past lives. (It didn't work for me.)

Categories of the Supernatural   The nature of the supernatural also differs among humankind's religions, and we can categorize three basic kinds of beliefs. The first is animism. It refers to the belief in a force possessed by a person, an animal, a place, or a nonliving thing (Figure 12.3). Charms, such as lucky rabbits' feet or New Age crystals, are examples. So are the sacred black and green stones venerated by the Dani of New Guinea. People can also possess such a force—for example, the San healers (see Figure 9.6). And many cultures have taboos against contact with certain objects, for example, the "unclean" foods listed in the Bible (see Chapter 14). They are said to have negative *mana* (from a Polynesian word).

The second kind is a belief in supernatural beings of human origin—ancestors and ghosts. Recall the importance of ghosts of the deceased for the San (Chapter 9). The lives of the Dani are very much ruled by the ghosts of their ancestors. Such supernatural beings are important among peoples for whom the kinship group is the major social, political, and decision-making unit. Thus, not only are living humans important, so too are the spirits of deceased humans. Again, the real and the supernatural reflect one another.

The third kind is belief in supernatural beings of nonhuman origin. These are beings who created themselves, or who always existed, and then made the world with all its creatures, including people. These beings may take the form of a single, all-powerful god or a number of individual spirits, such as those that control the natural features of the Eskimo's world. A culture, of course, may recognize a combination of these types of supernatural beings or forces. The San, for instance, have both human ghosts as well as spirits of natural phenomena. They also recognize two powerful gods who created everything in the first place and who generally keep things going.

Personalities of the Supernatural   Supernatural beings also differ in personality. Some are benevolent, some malevolent, some mischievous. This may be connected to how a group of people perceives their environment: Is it harsh, as for the Eskimo? Or is life fairly easy and predictable, as for the Dani? Indeed, for the horticultural Dani, basic subsistence seems so easy that their main supernatural beings, the ghosts of their ancestors, are known mostly for their mischievous deeds. The supernatural forces recognized by another New Guinea group, the Fore, are mostly malevolent, as we will discuss in Chapter 14.

It has also been suggested that the personality of the supernatural may correspond to a society's child-rearing habits. If they treat their children gently, their gods are gentle gods. If they are strict disciplinarians, the gods are to be feared. Notice how the Christian deity is referred to as "God the Father," and the followers as "His children" or "His flock." Gods are often linguistically classified as parents.

Intervention by the Supernatural   Also showing variation is the degree to which the supernatural intervenes in the daily affairs of people. Generally, the more important scientific knowledge is to a society, the less *direct* the influence of the gods is. Natural phenomena, including human actions, are attributed to natural forces. The degree and kind of intervention may also be related to the complexity of the social order. Especially where there are inequalities in wealth and power, rules for human behavior that are said to come directly from the supernatural may help to maintain the existing order (and, thus, the wealth and power of those who have it).

Religious Specialists   The kind of person who specializes in taking care of the religious knowledge and welfare of a people varies as well. Here we may define two basic categories. The first are part-time specialists, usually called on only in times of crises such as illnesses. They are often referred to as **shamans** (after a Siberian word). Shamans receive their powers directly from the supernatural; they are "chosen" for this position. They use trances and dreams to intervene with the spirits to correct sickness and other problems. This type of religious specialist is found in egalitarian and less complex horticultural societies where there are no full-time labor specialists and where religious knowledge, so vital to survival, is known and practiced by everyone. Only special situations, such as curing, require the extra help of shamans. The San healers would be an example.

shaman A part-time, supernaturally chosen religious specialist who can manipulate the supernatural.

FIGURE 12.4
A Catholic priest conducting a mass. He is a priest in the anthropological sense in that he has chosen his profession and has trained for it. Priests, unlike shamans, possess knowledge as opposed to supernatural powers.

priest A full-time, trained religious specialist who can interpret the supernatural and petition the supernatural on behalf of humans.

More complex cultures have **priests.** In anthropological terminology, priests are full-time specialists who train for their profession, learning what is passed down by their predecessors. They are the repository of religious knowledge and thus are the persons who know best what the gods say, how best to interpret their words, and how best to get in touch with the gods. Whereas shamans have real supernatural power, priests have knowledge of the supernatural. Put another way, priests tell us what to do on behalf of the supernatural, and shamans (often for a fee from a client) tell the supernatural what to do on behalf of us. Priests in the Catholic Church would be an example of priests in the anthropological sense (Figure 12.4).

With priests' knowledge often comes power of a more down-to-earth nature—political power. In some cultures it can be difficult to separate the political system from the religious system and political leaders from the religious ones. This was true for the ancient Aztecs of Mexico, for instance, and to a great extent for Europeans during medieval and Renaissance times.

FIGURE 12.5
Yąnomamö men take hallu-
cinogenic drugs almost daily.
One man blows a powder—
made from the leaves of a
plant—up the nose of
another. The Yąnomamö
believe the powder brings
them closer to important
beings in the spirit world.

Contacting the Supernatural   Finally, the ways in which people get in touch with the supernatural show variation. People may pray in a congregation or alone. The prayer itself may be individual or may involve group recitation of prescribed words. Some form of eating may be involved—everything from a feast to the taking of communion, the symbolic ingestion of the body and blood of Christ.

Sacrifice is a common way of pleasing the supernatural. The sacrifice may entail the actual killing of an animal or a human (the latter also found among the Aztecs), or it may involve some sort of abstinence, as some Christians practice during Lent and some Jews on the Sabbath.

Music, noise, and dance are also ways of attracting the attention of the gods or spirits, as is art—drawings or some symbol representing the supernatural. And in some cases, people feel closer to the supernatural during a transcendent experience, sometimes brought about by taking drugs. The Shuar of Ecuador and the Yąnomamö of Brazil do this (Figure 12.5). Such psychological states may also be brought on by fasting, exhaustion, or mutilation. Among the Dani, the female relatives of a person who has died have one or two fingers chopped off at the first joint. (All women, however, keep at least the thumb and first two fingers of one hand.) In James Michener's famous novel

Hawaii, there is a graphic description of a Hawaiian who mutilates himself following a relative's death. Walking on fire, self-flagellation with whips and chains, and piercing the cheeks with long skewers all fall into this category.

Magic is the use of rituals and paraphernalia to compel or manipulate the supernatural to act in desired ways (Prayer is a *petition* to the supernatural.) If such acts have evil intent, they are called **sorcery**. Magic and sorcery provide a sense of control over important matters. For example, the Fore of New Guinea (see Chapter 14) see disease as the result of sorcery. Such an explanation reflects the political and economic tensions, rivalries, and jealousies that are characteristic of Fore society. Thus, since diseases are caused by humans, other humans may take actions against those who invoked the diseases and so against the diseases themselves.

Witchcraft is often confused with sorcery and has many current vernacular definitions. Technically, witches are those with inherent powers that allow them to do harm without necessarily using magical paraphernalia. The witch is thus a supernatural being. "Witches" come in all sorts, from characters on TV shows such as *Buffy the Vampire Slayer* to followers of Wicca (who consider *themselves* "white"—that is, good—witches).

This, then, is what religion is and some of the general ways in which it varies from culture to culture. The richness of this variation, and the explanations for individual expressions within particular cultures, is a broad and complex topic. We may, however, take a closer look at one religion and see how some of its major features relate to the overall cultural systems of its followers and how these features have changed over time and space. We can then look at some of its variations.

RELIGION AND CULTURE

It's easier, in a way, to examine the religion of some "exotic" group of people, since we can analyze it from afar and remain culturally and emotionally detached. But whether we examine an exotic or familiar religion, the same anthropological ideas apply. To demonstrate this, let's discuss a religious tradition that many of us either practice or at least have some knowledge of—one that in a broad historical context helps make up the moral and ethical outlook of North American society. It's also a religion about which we have extensive written records. Let's look at Christianity.

The Origins of Christianity

From an anthropological perspective, Christianity must be viewed as a branch of Judaism, because that's how it originated. The first Jewish kingdom was founded by David (of David and Goliath fame) in Palestine

magic The use of ritual and paraphernalia to compel or manipulate the supernatural to act in desired ways.

sorcery Magical acts with evil intent.

witchcraft Traditionally, evil acts performed by individuals who possess inherent powers.

in the early 900s B.C. David was considered a messiah, which originally meant one who had great holiness and power. Shortly after David's death his kingdom was divided, and a few hundred years later it was conquered. There followed hundreds of years of oppression of the Jews by several other nations.

A result of this long period of colonialism and economic oppression was the development of the idea that someday, if the Jews kept their covenant with God, another messiah would come. This messiah would lead the Jews in military conquest over their oppressors. The idea peaked during Roman rule, which began in 40 B.C. During that time, a number of "messiahs" appeared and led groups of Jews in what the late anthropologist Marvin Harris calls guerrilla warfare against the Romans.

It was into this political environment that Jesus was born. He is seen today, of course, as a peaceful messiah, but there is good evidence that he was, in his time, part of the military messiah tradition.

Jesus was captured and crucified—the standard form of execution for such rebels, because it was slow and painful and provided a powerful warning to others. Death had ended the brief tenures of Jesus' predecessors, but a number of his ardent disciples claimed that rather than proving Jesus *wasn't* the promised messiah, his death was a test of his followers' faith. If they kept that faith, he would one day return. So, a small cult of Jewish Christians formed and began to spread, preaching this new variation of Jewish doctrine but still maintaining ties with the religion at large. Over the next thirty years (Jesus was killed in A.D. 33), the cult spread as far as Rome itself and was being taken up by some non-Jews.

Thus began a split between the Jews of Palestine and those outside the homeland. The separation became complete when, after the Jewish uprisings had become a serious problem for the Romans, Vespasian and his son launched a military campaign that culminated in the destruction of the temple in Jerusalem in A.D. 70 and the fall of the famous fortress of Masada in A.D. 73 (Figure 12.6). (You should remember Vespasian from the story of Maiden Castle in England.)

With the temple—the heart of Judaism—destroyed, connections between Jews and the Jewish Christians were severed. The Palestinian Jews had to cease, or at least not actively pursue, their messianic beliefs—for a time anyway. The Jewish Christians, though, responded differently, especially in other parts of the Roman Empire, including Rome itself. Jesus became a peaceful savior, bringing salvation not in this world but in the next—hardly a threat to the Romans. It was about this time that the first of the Gospels, the Book of Mark, was written to tell the story of Jesus and outline his teachings, confirming his emphasis on heavenly rather than earthly reward (although they retain some of his more militant statements). Differences between the new Christianity and Jewish tradition were formalized. The food laws from the Old Testament, for example, were ignored,

FIGURE 12.6
The Romans laid siege to the fortress of Masada (*left center*) for several months in A.D. 73, living in camps like the one near the cliff in the foreground. Finally, when it was clear they could hold out no longer, the 960 defenders of Masada chose suicide rather than surrender.

and circumcision was no longer prescribed. Christianity, as we recognize it today, had begun.

Numbers of communities banded together to await the Second Coming of Jesus and to preach the teachings of this new religion. Some of this early history is recounted in Acts of the Apostles in such passages as 2:44: "And all that believed were together, and had all things common." Sound familiar? It's the passage on which the Hutterites base their communal lifestyle. We can now see their lifestyle as descending directly from some of the first Christian communities.

The origin of Christianity, then, can be understood as a branching off from the long-standing traditions of Judaism, stimulated by a particular set of historical circumstances and the reactions of a group of people to them. The basic tenets of the religion are a reflection and an affirmation of a particular worldview—a view generated by all the aspects of the founding group's environment and history.

Over nearly 2,000 years, the basic idea of Christianity has spread throughout the world, has been adopted by many different societies, has developed all sorts of variations, and has undergone extensive historical change. There are now three major branches of Christianity: Roman Catholic, Eastern Orthodox, and Protestant, each, especially the last, with a number of subbranches. Let's look at two subbranches of Protestantism as further examples of the anthropology of religion.

Some Examples

The Hutterites   You recall that the Hutterites were founded as part of the Anabaptist movement of the early 1500s. The Anabaptists comprised many groups that repudiated infant baptism (hence the name), believed in a literal interpretation of the Bible (especially the New Testament), and disliked state-controlled religion.

At the time of the Anabaptist movement, an innovation in Europe was changing the way people could acquire information. Advances in printing had put the Bible in the hands of the common citizen. Now, for literate persons (mostly townsfolk and artisans) or persons who knew someone who could read, there was no need to rely on the church for knowledge about the content and interpretation of the Bible. Some people began to think for themselves about religious issues, and the Anabaptist ideas noted above were three important and common conclusions.

Such conclusions, however, were not viewed kindly by the mainstream Catholic and Protestant churches, which were, at the time, inextricably linked to the state. Repudiating infant baptism had been considered heresy for some time, but their "real" crime, of course, was their threat to the church's and state's hold over the religious lives—and, thus, the economic lives—of their subjects. Many of the religious

FIGURE 12.7
Torture and public burnings of witches and heretics, such as the Anabaptists, were common in Europe from the 1400s through the 1600s.

rebels were tortured and burned at the stake (Figure 12.7). Among them was Jacob Hutter, whose followers took his name in tribute.

Living communally and self-sufficiently, apart from society at large, was not an original part of the Anabaptist belief system, but it became necessary in the face of continual persecution. The self-sufficiency was possible since many of the people, as noted, were literate urban artisans and craftspersons. So the early Hutterite communities began to produce their own food and to manufacture their own houses, clothing, and other artifacts (Figure 12.8). The Hutterites' agricultural lifestyle, of course, has lasted to the present. So too has their craftsmanship. One still finds shoemakers, carpenters, and even bookbinders in a Hutterite colony.

The ideological basis for such economic and social communism was found, not surprisingly, in the Bible. The social system of the Hutterites—having "all things common"—is modeled after the communities of early Christians, who gathered together, separate from the larger society, to follow the teachings of Christ while awaiting his return, as the Hutterites do.

The Holiness Churches Now, compare the Hutterites' version of Christianity with that of another North American group. This branch is generally less well defined than the Hutterites and is quite variable, but we can focus on its most extreme form. It's called by a number of names depending on the region, but a common one is the Holiness Church, and its followers are known as the Holy Ghost People.

Holiness churches started in the first decade of the twentieth century in Tennessee and are now found mostly in Appalachia and the Southeast—Georgia, the Carolinas, Florida, Virginia, West Virginia, Kentucky, Tennessee, and Ohio. The basis for their form of Christianity comes from the Gospel of Mark, 16:17–18. Speaking to his disciples, Jesus says,

> And these signs shall follow them that believe; In my name shall they cast out devils; they shall speak with new tongues; They shall take up serpents; and if they drink any deadly thing, it shall not hurt them; they shall lay hands on the sick, and they shall recover.

The Holy Ghost People feel that if they believe strongly enough, the Holy Ghost enters their bodies. The manifestations of this are, as predicted in Mark, "speaking in tongues" (a babbling, rolling sort of speech whose meaning is thought to be intelligible only to others with the Holy Ghost), convulsive dancing and trancelike states, the ability to "lay hands on" the sick and cure them, and a "call" to handle venomous snakes or drink poison (Figure 12.9).

The snakes are local rattlesnakes and copperheads. The poison is a dilute strychnine or lye solution. The meaning of these acts, always performed at the height of the service, when the music is loud and many persons are manifesting the Holy Ghost, has to do with professing one's faith. "God," they are saying, "will protect me from this dangerous act, so strong is my belief. But if I die from it, that's God's will, and I will

FIGURE 12.9
This man, at a Holiness service, has been called by the Holy Ghost to show his faith by handling poisonous snakes.

accept it." Persons bitten by the snakes or who become very ill from the poison will not accept medical aid. At least twenty adherents are known to have died over the last eighty years from snakebites. Although the practice is outlawed in most of the states listed, it persists.

Besides these biblically sanctioned features, there are some others that characterize and distinguish Holiness Church services. There is often, for example, no formal minister. The leader is chosen much like the San choose the man who decides where to hunt. It is based on out-goingness, charisma, speaking ability, or, perhaps, just whoever gets up and starts. Sometimes, it's the person who has been bitten by snakes most often.

Moreover, what goes on during a service is often individual rather than group-oriented. People pray in their own words, kneeling if they want or standing, dancing, or lying down. Possession of the Holy Ghost is an individual matter. It doesn't happen to everyone, and for those to whom it does happen, how they manifest the experience is up to the Holy Ghost. A Holiness service can appear rather chaotic. There are quiet periods, such as when the collection plate is passed or when individuals "testify," telling personal stories about their experiences with the Holy Ghost. But during the height of the service, some participants play music, some pray, others dance or lay hands on the sick, and still others handle snakes or drink poison.

The Holy Ghost People's relationship with God is unique in Christianity. Most Christians' prayer is in the form of a request to God. But as one man puts it in a film of a Holiness service, these Christians feel that "if you believe, God is obligated to answer your prayer." God is still supreme and can do with His followers as He chooses, but a strong enough faith on the part of the people "obligates" God to them.

How may we interpret this somewhat unusual version of Christianity? The fact that the Holy Ghost People are Christians lies in the history of the culture to which they belong, but their specific practices can in part be accounted for in economic and social terms. The Holiness Church is largely a phenomenon of poor, rural Appalachia (although it has moved into urban areas with the migration of people). Appalachia is home to some of the poorest people in the United States. They are small-scale farmers, local merchants, or employees of coal-mining or other large companies. They don't, in other words, have the kind of control over their economic welfare that many Americans have—or think they have.

But the image of American affluence that comes across in books, magazines, and television is quite different from the lives led by people in poor, rural America. Having little more than this image with which to compare themselves, they may feel out of step with mainstream American life. The religious expression of the Holiness Church provides a sense of control. The practitioners of this religion have a oneness with God in the possibility that they may be possessed by the Holy Ghost, who can then choose to act through their bodies. In fact, simply by believing strongly enough, they can even obligate God to them.

Moreover, in an environment economically near the bottom of America's social stratification, the Holiness service is an opportunity for egalitarianism. There is no formal hierarchy. Everyone is important. Everyone expresses himself or herself as an individual. The only difference between people—the possession of the Holy Ghost—is a difference that can be equalized by strong belief. Possession of the Holy Ghost is open to all.

Finally, anthropologist Westen LaBarre suggests that the Holiness service may provide a mechanism for sexual expression. During a Holiness service, as depicted in the film *Holy Ghost People*, social interaction between members of the opposite sex (and not necessarily between recognized couples) includes much physical contact in the form of touching and dancing. The idea is to pass on and share the presence of the Holy Ghost. There is, of course, no overt sexuality, but the interaction may serve to provide an outlet for sexual identity and expression, which are normally repressed in a conservative society such as this.

As with most other cultural (and biological) behaviors, however, these practices developed gradually—in other words, they evolved—and their current functions don't necessarily account for their origins. Nor are people always consciously aware of those functions. In the case of the Holiness Church, though, the fact that it is a relatively new denomination and is still found in its place of origin lends support to the idea that, here, current functions are original functions.

From this brief examination of Christianity in general, and of two denominations in particular, you should have an idea of how anthropology looks at religion. First, we look for some general principles regarding what types of religions are found in certain types of cultures. Second, we examine specific religious traditions by delving into the cultural histories of the societies involved and into the people's reactions to the social, political, and economic situations woven into these histories. Religion is part of a cultural system that is intimately connected to all other parts.

But, it must be noted, this scientific approach does *not* make a religion any less real for those who practice it and is not intended to dismiss religious beliefs. So basic are religious beliefs to peoples' lives— as members of cultures and as individuals—that they cannot entirely be reduced to or explained by the objectivity of scientific investigation. The reality of religious beliefs operates at many levels.

If religion acts to provide motivations and sanctions for human actions, what about societies that are so populous, complex, technologically and scientifically elaborate, and multicultural (with religious pluralism) that no one religion can serve those society-wide functions? What maintains order in such societies?

LAW

We may lump other order-maintaining systems into a single category and call them legal systems. Legal systems define the premise on which human interactions in the society are based. They outline specific behaviors that correspond to this premise, and they provide rules for handling disputes about and transgressions of these behaviors. Although often secular, laws can be based on the religious principles that express the worldview of the culture in question.

Let's take as an example another familiar, as opposed to "exotic," culture—the United States. The basis of our legal system is found in Judeo-Christian religious tradition, the core principles of which are expressed by such ideas as "Thou shalt love thy neighbor as thyself" (Leviticus 19:18); "all things whatsoever ye would that men should do to you, do ye even so to them" (Matthew 7:12); and "Judge not, and ye shall not be judged" (Luke 6:37).

What is the essential premise of our legal system? Nowhere is it better stated than in the Declaration of Independence:

> We hold these truths to be self-evident, that all men are created equal, that they are endowed by their Creator with certain unalienable Rights, that among these are Life, Liberty, and the pursuit of Happiness.

The Constitution lays out the foundation of a government formed to

> establish justice, insure domestic tranquility, provide for the common defense, promote the general welfare, and secure the blessings of liberty.

In the first ten amendments, or Bill of Rights, the Constitution outlines some specific ideas aimed at protecting the rights named in the Declaration and at fairly punishing those who are accused of trespassing on the rights of others. Viewed in this way, our legal system is a translation of some basic Judeo-Christian religious principles into secular terms and the formulation of specific laws to implement those principles in the real world.

All this seems rather obvious and, for us, there seems no other system that could protect and ensure those rights. But there are. Although it would be accurate to say that all people seek to be alive, free, and happy, just how cultures define those ideals in practical terms differs greatly.

For the Dani of New Guinea, for example, the taking of human lives is a regular, formalized tradition that is central to their existence. The Dani have a system of ritualized warfare (which we will examine more fully in Chapter 14) that involves the killing of an enemy to placate the ghost of a slain member of one's own group. In return, the enemy must slay a member of the first group to placate the ghost of its member, and so on. These groups, it is important to understand, are groups *within* Dani society. And so important is this revenge cycle that a woman or child may be killed in place of a male warrior if too much time has passed without avenging a death.

Certainly, we in the United States are familiar with violence—from the level of individual acts to officially sanctioned wars. Still, it may be difficult for many of us to view the Dani's ritualized warfare with any degree of cultural relativity. How, we might ask, could a society condone the killing of its own members? We must remember, however, that there is a reason for their behaviors within their larger cultural system and that through it they are pursuing happiness as they define it—just based on a very different premise from ours. One might say (and I don't mean this sarcastically) that their premise is something like "do unto others what others did unto you." And their culture has persisted successfully for thousands of years.

The nature of legal systems differs among types of cultures. Band societies have no formal legal system or set of formal laws. Rather, behaviors that are disruptive to the group are dealt with through social pressure, group consensus, possible physical conflict, or splitting up of the group. Procedures may differ according to the particular situation.

As societies become more complex, legal systems and the laws they uphold become more formalized. In tribal societies, the focus is still on the maintenance of community relations, but there is often someone—a headman or council of elders—who presides over attempts to settle disputes or correct some transgression. In chiefdoms, more authority is placed in the hands of a leader, rules are more rigid, and specific punishments are recognized and applied.

In state societies, formal and complex legal institutions are required. Laws are codified and specific and are based on standards that relate to the whole culture; they can no longer vary according to each specific case.

SUMMARY

A worldview is an abstract set of assumptions about the conditions that are central to any cultural system. But worldview requires a mechanism to give it reality, to allow it to be transmitted among a people and to future generations, to answer questions about the world, to translate its assumptions into values that regulate human behavior, and to formulate rules of behavior that put those values into action. These are the functions of religion and secular legal systems.

Religion, distinguished from secular systems by its focus on the supernatural, is, like any facet of culture, highly variable from society to society. It is, however, a cultural universal, explained by our need for a way to understand the complex world around us and to coordinate our actions accordingly. Many features of the natural world can be explained scientifically. Many others, however, cannot; they require explanations that are beyond science. Religion also serves to regulate the various levels of human interaction— to tell us how to behave.

Religion, as one of several aspects of cultural behavior, has variables that correspond to other features of the related culture. Since history also affects worldview, we must look at the historical dimension of a religious system in order to understand its origins, basic characteristics, and meaning.

In many, if not most, societies, some of the rules guiding human behavior have evolved from strictly religious to more secular terms. In societies like our own, where the answers to worldview questions are largely scientific and rational, the vast majority of our basic rules are secular laws. Laws perform the same functions as religious systems, at least with regard to defining the premises for human action and outlining the specific actions that correspond to these premises. Laws also take care of disputes about those regulated actions and provide for the punishment of those who transgress them. Even where a society is regulated almost exclusively by a secular legal system, there is often at the basis of that system a religious tradition. The religious rules have been translated into secular ones.

QUESTIONS FOR FURTHER THOUGHT

1. In March 2002 a fire broke out in a public girl's school in Mecca, Saudi Arabia. Religious police prevented emergency personnel from rescuing the students because they were not wearing the head scarves and black robes required by strict Islamic law. Police beat some of the girls to prevent them from leaving the school and being seen in public. Fifty girls were injured, and fifteen died. Because this incident involved religious belief, is it beyond criticism? Should the anthropological concept of cultural relativity apply? If so, how? Does it matter that this act stemmed from *one interpretation* of Islamic scripture?

2. In 2004 a bill was passed in France to ban religious symbolism in public schools. Included were large crucifixes and yarmulkes, but the bill was aimed essentially at Muslim girls and their head scarves. Is

CONTEMPORARY ISSUES

How Do We Deal with Faith-Based Acts of Terror in Contemporary Global Society?

Religious freedom is certainly an important and major tenet of American ethics and laws. We laud other countries that follow that precept and castigate those that don't. Indeed, so strong is this ethic in our society that we tend to shy away from public criticism or even analysis of religious beliefs and practices. But are there limits to how much we should accept religious practices, especially those that claim absolute knowledge about the world and then act out directly against groups holding alternative religious views or no religious views at all?

As I write this, a serious global problem remains the threat from what we generally refer to as "terrorism." Although terrorism as a tactic is not confined to a specific group, geographic location, or historical period, many of the terrorist acts that are currently a focus of worldwide concern are committed by Islamic fundamentalists.* It is important to note that only a very small minority of Muslims practice such tactics. Indeed, many Muslims interpret the Koran as prohibiting such behavior. Yet the Islamic fundamentalists responsible for the 9/11 attacks, for example, resorted to terrorism based on *their* interpretation of the Koran. That is, they found justification for their beliefs and behaviors not in some external system of ethics loosely based on that book but on passages within it. Their acts, in other words, could not be divorced from the religion *as they saw it*, which they were following and upholding.

How is it possible to have such variable interpretations of one set of writings that are central to a religious system? Consider the Bible. Within that book there are passages that specifically sanction killing nonbelievers (Deuteronomy 13:7–11) and, at the same time, passages that tell us "thou shalt not kill" (Exodus 20:13). Likewise, Jesus says in one verse that he has come not "to send peace, but a sword" (Matthew 10:34) and in

another to "love thine enemies; do good to them that hate you" (Luke 6:27). To be sure, violent acts have been committed in the name of Judaism and Christianity (the Crusades, the Inquisition, witch burnings, to name a few), for which specific justification can be found in the Bible, depending on one's interpretation of particular passages.

And how is it possible that two branches of the same religion (Christianity) view secular matters so differently? Fundamental Protestantism specifically, and by definition, argues against the scientific evidence for evolution, while Roman Catholicism accepts the scientific verification of the theory.

It goes without saying that those responsible for terrorist acts must all be held accountable. But the above examples point out that, with regard to religiously motivated terrorism, we have to ask some tough and potentially unpopular questions: How accountable should we hold the religion *from which* the terrorists find guidance, justification, and motivation for their acts? Is one interpretation of a religion more valid, more acceptable, than another? If so, who decides? How can we uphold our vitally important ethic of freedom of belief while judging others' religious behaviors, which, one could argue, are based on that same freedom?

These ideas and questions are very abstract, yet this topic deserves in-depth discussion that is beyond the scope of this box. These are important matters. In the "Questions for Further Thought," I pose some questions that may help focus your consideration of these issues.

---

*The term *fundamentalism* was originally applied to nineteenth-century Protestant groups that believed in a strict and literal interpretation of the Bible, reacted against social and political liberalism, and rejected evolution. Fundamentalism now is used to describe any form of a religion that advocates strict adherence to traditional (fundamental) doctrines.

this a violation of the concept of freedom of religion? Or, given the recent history of terrorist acts committed by Muslim fundamentalists, could such legislation be considered a necessary precaution or at least an understandable reaction?

3. We read a good deal about faith-based politics over the course of the recent presidential campaign. In light of what seems to be a blurring line separating church from state, consider this question: Should religious faith be a basis for governmental decisions, even positive ones? If so, to what extent?

NOTES, REFERENCES, AND READINGS

My favorite work on the anthropology of religion is still Edward Norbeck's *Religion in Human Life: Anthropological Views*. It defines religion and its roles and gives numerous ethnographic examples. The passages I quoted are from pages 6 and 23.

A good collection of readings is Arthur Lehmann and James Myers's *Magic, Witchcraft, and Religion: An Anthropological Study of the Supernatural*.

A good article on the origins of religion is "On the Origin of Religion," by Elizabeth Culotta, in the November 6, 2009, issue of *Science*.

The chimpanzee "rain dance" is described in Jane Goodall's *In the Shadow of Man*. The quote is from page 67.

My discussion of the origins of Christianity is largely from Marvin Harris's *Cows, Pigs, Wars, and Witches: The Riddles of Culture*. Harris cites specific evidence for the original identity of Jesus as belong-ing to the military messianic tradition. Among this evidence are some passages from the Bible such as "Think not that I am come to send peace on earth: I came not to send peace, but a sword" (Matthew 10:34) and "he that hath no sword, let him sell his garment, and buy one" (Luke 22:36).

For more on the Hutterites, see the references cited in Chapter 1.

The Holy Ghost People are described and ana-lyzed in detail in "Serpent-Handling as Sacrament," by Mary Lee Daugherty, in the Lehmann and Myers book noted above and in Westen LaBarre's *They Shall Take Up Serpents*. The latter gets a little heavy on the sym-bolic, psychoanalytic side, but it's worth reading.

A controversial and thought-provoking discus-sion of the topic of the "Contemporary Issues" box, and much more, is *The End of Faith: Religion, Terror, and the Future of Reason*, by Sam Harris.

13

CULTURE CHANGE

Theories and Processes

CHAPTER CONTENTS The Processes of Culture Change • Understanding Cultural Evolution • Summary • Contemporary Issues: Can Anthropology Be Both a Scientific and a Humanistic Discipline in Today's World? • Questions for Further Thought • Notes, References, and Readings

It should be obvious by now that cultures are anything but static and unchanging. Although we can try to describe the interrelationships among the features of a cultural system at any given point in time (as we will do Chapter 14), many of those features are changing as we're studying and analyzing them. Culture change is the norm, not the exception. Think of the changes you've witnessed in your culture.

We have already noted some major changes and their effects—things such as the beginning of animal and plant domestication and the origin of cities. But culture change involves smaller changes as well. And any change alters the cultural system of which it is a part, because culture works *as a system,* with all its facets operating together and interacting with one another. (See Figure 4.4.)

How do cultures change? Are there any specific processes that account for changes in cultural systems? The answers to these questions can help us explain changes in the past, understand changes that are occurring now, and prepare us for changes in the future as the rate of culture change accelerates in the modern world.

AS YOU READ, CONSIDER THE FOLLOWING QUESTIONS:

1. What processes bring about change within a cultural system?

2. What are some of the major models that attempt to account for cultural evolution?

THE PROCESSES OF CULTURE CHANGE

Discovery and Invention

Every cultural creation—every new idea or new artifact—must start somewhere. Thus, at the base of all culture change are the related processes of **discovery** and **invention.** *Discovery* is the realization and understanding of some set of natural relationships. *Invention* refers to the creation of new artifacts and ideas that put the discovery to use. Discovery is knowledge; invention is application.

For example, discovery of the nature of fire was necessary before fire could be used for cooking, light, heat, and scaring away animals. The fact that flint struck with another rock would produce a spark or that wood rubbed against wood would produce heat had to be discovered before fire could be purposely made. Discoveries, of course, may

discovery The realization and understanding of a set of relationships. An addition to knowledge.

invention New creations. The application of discovered knowledge.

be intentionally sought after (since, as the saying goes, necessity is the mother of invention), or they may be accidental. I'm confident that the spark-producing qualities of flint were discovered as a by-product of knapping stone tools (see Figure 6.12).

Discoveries May Be Abstract Discoveries—additions to knowledge—may also be abstract. One may, for example, "discover"—in the sense of proposing an idea—that societies should be based on the premise that each person possesses the right to life, liberty, and the pursuit of happiness. Then one can invent a social system that implements that idea, that puts it into action in the complex, everyday, real world.

Discoveries Do Not Result in All Possible Applications A discovery may not always lead to all the inventions that outsiders would think of as its obvious applications. The applications of a discovery must fit within the existing cultural system. As a classic example, consider the wheel in Mesoamerica. The properties of the wheel—contrary to the common misconception—*were* discovered in the New World. The idea was just never put to use as it had been in the Old World, where it was used for wheeled vehicles, for harnessing water power, and for making pottery. The only known use of the wheel in the New World prior to European contact was for children's toys—clay animals with axles and wheels (Figure 13.1). Without domestic draft animals, there was no need to invent wheeled vehicles, and perfectly usable pottery was already being produced without potter's wheels.

A contemporary example is electric automobiles. They exist and they work well and don't pollute, but current limits on their range don't fit the driving needs of our society, and their fuel source is a major concern to the petroleum industry, which wields great political and economic power. So a perfectly good idea has not yet been widely adopted. Rather, hybrid (gasoline and electric) and biodiesel-fueled vehicles—culturally acceptable compromises—are now increasing in popularity.

Discoveries Must Coincide with Cultural Norms Sometimes a discovery is not accepted because it conflicts with some aspect of the cultural system. The conclusion by Copernicus, later verified by Galileo, that the earth was not the center of the universe violated mainstream religious interpretations of the Bible, which said that the earth did not move. The telescope, however, the instrument Galileo used to gather supporting data for this idea, was readily adopted for acceptable uses such as keeping track of the comings and goings of merchant vessels in the port of Venice. In a similar vein, when given a scientific explanation for the outbreak of a deadly disease, the Fore of New Guinea (see Chapter 14) were unable to understand the disease as

FIGURE 13.1
A clay toy with wheels, representing either a deer or a dog, from the site of Vera Cruz in Mexico and dated to about A.D. 500.

anything but the result of sorcery, a concept central to their worldview and cultural system.

Discoveries May Change the Culture   Once adopted, a new discovery and its initial applications become part of a cultural system and bring about changes within the system. We saw the profound changes that resulted from the invention of farming techniques (see Chapter 9). Or think about such things as the domestication of the horse, the invention of wheeled vehicles, and more recent innovations such as the production and harnessing of electricity, the understanding of atomic energy, and the inventions of the transistor (a small device for controlling the flow of electricity without the presence of a vacuum), the laser, and the microchip (a tiny integrated circuit with multiple transistors). As an exercise, count the number of items in your household with microchips and think about how they have changed life in modern times.

Diffusion

As indicated in the previous section, each society can discover and invent only so much. Thus the second basic process of culture change is the diffusion of discoveries and artifacts, the giving and taking of culture among different societies. Diffusion is thought to be responsible, on average, for 90 percent of a society's cultural inventory. As a result, societies isolated from outside contact change slowly. Those with greater opportunity for contact—and thus for borrowing—change more rapidly.

This emphasis on diffusion is sometimes hard to grasp because once an item is borrowed, it is modified and adapted by the borrowing culture and becomes a part of the cultural system. It becomes so firmly a part of that system that we don't realize that it may not have originated within that culture. A classic and often-quoted article by anthropologist Ralph Linton makes this point. Linton wrote "One Hundred Percent American" in 1937, so some of the references are a bit outdated, but the message is still clear. It follows a typical American man through the first part of his day. Here are excerpts:

> Our solid American citizen awakens in a bed built on a pattern which originated in the Near East but which was modified in Northern Europe before it was transmitted to America. He throws back covers made from cotton, domesticated in India, or linen, domesticated in the Near East, or wool from sheep, also domesticated in the Near East, or silk, the use of which was discovered in China. . . . He takes off his pajamas, a garment invented in India, and washes with soap invented by the ancient Gauls. He then shaves, a masochistic rite which seems to have been derived from either Sumer or Egypt. . . . On his way to breakfast he stops to buy a paper, paying for it with coins, an ancient Lydian invention. . . . As he absorbs the accounts of foreign troubles he will, if he is a good conservative citizen, thank a Hebrew deity in an Indo-European language that he is 100 percent American.

Cultural ideas and technologies are not, of course, always borrowed intact, nor is everything borrowed that *could* be borrowed. If, to take a hypothetical example, an indigenous American people from before European contact had seen wheeled vehicles, they may well have rejected the idea of incorporating them since they lacked domesticable large animals to pull them. Other items may be rejected because they conflict with religious or ethical beliefs. Anthropologists Carol and Melvin Ember point out that although the Japanese borrowed much from the Chinese, they never adopted the idea of binding women's feet because Japanese culture traditionally abhors any type of body mutilation. Clothing styles seem particularly open to diffusion (American jeans are sought after all over the world), but differences in standards of modesty cause many styles to be rejected. As immodest as some societies consider the clothing styles in the United States, I doubt whether we would ever adopt the male attire of many societies of the New Guinea highlands (see Figure 8.1).

Items that *are* borrowed are modified to fit the receiving society's cultural system. So central is wine in French culture that when American fast-food restaurants diffused there, wine was added to the menus.

English missionaries introduced the game of cricket to the Trobriand Islands (now part of Papua New Guinea) in the early twentieth century. The Trobrianders quickly made it their own, changing the rules, redesigning the equipment, and using the game as a substitute for intervillage warfare and for establishing alliances. And their team names, often sexual references, seemed quite contradictory to the English intent of using the game to "civilize" the natives.

Adaptation of borrowed items is often strikingly seen in religion. Because of the cultural and psychological importance of religion, people are obviously reluctant to give up their religious beliefs, even under pressure. Thus new beliefs are often incorporated into existing ones to produce a synthesis. This is called **syncretism.** Voodoo (or Voudou), for example, a religion of Haiti, derives from several West African cultural traditions and is heavily influenced by Catholicism. The great variety of specific beliefs and rituals within Christianity can be explained in part by the wide spread of that religion and the synthesis of basic Christian ideas with existing religious traditions of the cultures adopting, or forced to adopt, it. Many non-European expressions of Catholicism still include traditional local elements.

Acculturation and Revolution

Two other basic recognized processes of culture change are, in a sense, extreme forms of invention and diffusion.

Acculturation   Acculturation is defined as rapid diffusion under the influence of a dominant society. This may occur voluntarily or by force.

Examples of the latter are all too common. Native Americans, for instance, were quickly acculturated into the European-based society of the colonial powers and later the United States. As just one example, many Indians in the American Southwest still practice Catholicism and have Spanish surnames, a remnant of several hundred years of Spanish presence in the region (Figure 13.2). Throughout history, slaves were acculturated into the societies of their owners, and countries conquered during war were forced to take on at least some of the cultural aspects of their conquerors, although the conquerors were also influenced by the cultures they defeated. For example, when the European Christians conquered and ruled Islamic Spain from the eleventh through the fifteenth centuries, they found a wealth of written knowledge in science, mathematics, and philosophy, some of it passed down from classical Greece. This knowledge then entered and had a profound effect on Western Europe's history.

An example of more voluntary acculturation is the phenomenon of the *cargo cults.* A number of South Pacific island societies, from New Guinea to Fiji, came into brief contact with industrialized

syncretism The synthesis of existing religious beliefs and practices with new ones introduced from the outside.

acculturation Rapid diffusion of cultural items either by choice of the receiving society or by force from a more dominant society.

technologies during World War II. They liked what they saw and wanted to incorporate that technology along with foreign words and habits—which came to be generally called *cargo*, borrowing from the English word—into their cultural systems. Once the war was over, the islands were left pretty much as they had been, minus the actual

FIGURE 13.3
Some men from the island of Tanna in Vanuatu march with bamboo rifles and "U.S.A." painted on their chests in the hope that by mimicking the behavior of Western soldiers they can attract a messiah named John Frum, who will bring material goods.

cargo. To get the cargo back, some of these societies took on many of the trappings of Western culture as they remembered them. They began to use English words. They started to dress like and mimic the military personnel they had observed, sometimes marching and carrying rifles carved from wood (Figure 13.3). They worshiped sacred objects—old helmets, dog tags, and other military and personal items the Western military had left behind. They created gods to whom they prayed for the return of the cargo. One of these gods, on the island of Tanna in the Republic of Vanuatu, was named John Frum, another English borrowing.

Revolution Revolution is usually thought of in the context of a violent overthrow of an existing government—as in the American, French, and Russian revolutions. But a revolution can also refer to a radical change in other aspects of society. There are scientific revolutions. The discoveries of Galileo, Darwin, and Einstein come to mind—discoveries that radically and fairly rapidly changed the way

revolution Rapid and extensive culture change generated from within a society.

people thought. We have already noted some technological revolutions, such as the invention of the microchip. A revolution in the sense of a process of culture change can, I believe, be thought of as rapid invention—new ideas and applications from within a society (or borrowed and radically adapted from outside) that thoroughly alter that society.

In this sense, then, a revolution can also involve a strong cultural statement by a portion of a society that quickly affects and alters the society as a whole. The Protestant Reformation may be thought of in this way. Even the social changes we saw in the United States in the 1960s—trends toward greater individual freedom of expression—were a result in part of a strong statement by America's youth in conjunction with elements of its artistic and academic culture. The statement caught on and has affected our entire social and cultural system to the present.

All these processes should not be thought of as independent and separate, of course. As with other processes we've discussed (such as the processes of biological evolution), they can interact with one another. For example, the stimulus for an invention can diffuse from another culture, even if the invention itself does not. This, in fact, is known as **stimulus diffusion.** The French Revolution, for instance, was influenced in part by the success of the American Revolution. And in the early nineteenth century, a Cherokee named Sequoyah invented an alphabetic system for writing his language, stimulated by his knowledge that whites had a means for inscribing their language.

These are the processes that bring about changes in cultures. But we are still left with some major questions that bring us back to the topic of evolution, with which we began. In terms of the history of culture, can we perceive any overall trends? Are there any general rules of culture change, any particular direction that culture change takes? The search for answers to such questions characterized much of the early history of anthropology.

UNDERSTANDING CULTURAL EVOLUTION

By the last third of the nineteenth century, largely as a result of the work of Charles Darwin, the idea was reasonably well accepted that humans had evolved from other creatures and that our evolution had taken place over millions of years. Furthermore, because of extensive exploration over the previous 350 years, Western knowledge included information about the vastly diverse cultural systems that existed among the world's peoples. It became only natural, then, to attempt to explain this cultural diversity in terms of the new evolutionary

stimulus diffusion When knowledge of a cultural trait in another society stimulates the invention of a similar trait.

framework. In other words, if we had evolved biologically, we had certainly evolved culturally. As we discussed in Chapter 8, many early thinkers (including Linnaeus) attempted to account for racial variation in an evolutionary context. Why not account for cultural variation in general in a similar fashion, searching for the same sorts of trends and directions that were being proposed for biological change over time?

Classical or Unilinear Evolutionism One of the first schools of thought on this subject is associated with the English anthropologist Edward B. Tylor (1832–1917) and the American Lewis Henry Morgan (1818–1881). It is called **classical,** or **unilinear evolutionism.** The idea was that all societies pass through the same series of evolutionary cultural stages, which Morgan termed "savagery," "barbarism," and "civilization." The savage stage is characterized by foraging and the use of fire and the bow and arrow; barbarism, by domestication of plants and animals, pottery, and the beginnings of metallurgy; and civilization, by writing and the invention of phonetic alphabets. Each stage could be represented by existing societies; thus the obvious explanation for the diversity of culture was simply that some societies had progressed further along the series and that others had changed more slowly and were still in earlier stages.

While culture certainly has to evolve over time, there are problems with this early model. First, it required that all societies, as they evolve, independently invent the same innovations and artifacts and undergo parallel development through the stages. Influence among societies—that is, diffusion—was not part of the model. Second, it set up a predetermined and fairly simple scheme in which every culture was pigeonholed into one of the three stages according to a limited set of criteria. In this, the model failed to do justice to the wealth of cultural diversity and to the complexity of cultural evolution. Third, it assumed that the goal of cultural evolution—civilization—was the stage reached by the society to which the theorists belonged. It was, in short, quite ethnocentric, and in this regard it mirrored many of the studies of racial classification being conducted at the same time.

Diffusionism As if to answer the problem of too much focus on independent invention, the concept of **diffusionism** arose. We have discussed the importance of diffusion in culture change. But this school of thought, popular in the first decades of the twentieth century, *oversimplified* the process by claiming that cultural innovation arose in only a few centers of culture (or even just one) and then spread to the rest of the world. One group, enamored of ancient Egypt, supposed that Egypt had been the source of almost all cultural innovations except for the simplest of hunting tools. According to this group, everything we think of as

classical evolutionism A synonym for unilinear evolutionism.

unilinear evolutionism An outdated concept of cultural evolution that claims all societies pass through the same series of stages, from savagery to civilization.

diffusionism An outdated concept of cultural evolution that claims major cultural advances were made by one or a few societies and spread from there to all other societies.

complex culture—from artifacts to social institutions—was invented in ancient Egypt and diffused from there.

There were, however, less extreme schools of diffusionism. One, originating in Germany, proposed a number of early cultural centers from which cultural traditions spread in ever-widening circles. This is the *Kulturkreise* ("cultural circle") model. It explains the modern presence of "less advanced" societies by supposing that they failed to acquire the cultural innovations of the expanding circle as a result of being pushed into remote geographical regions by more advanced populations.

Diffusionism also suffers from the problem of being a predetermined scheme into which data are fit rather than one that allows the data to generate the models to be tested. Moreover, it's clear that culture is far too complex and variable to be accounted for by having spread from a small number of centers. Finally, diffusionism—just the opposite of unilinear evolutionism—doesn't give *enough* credit to independent invention. It assumes most peoples are not capable of coming up with new ideas and technologies, which apparently require an intellect found only among a few populations.

Historical Particularism   **Historical Particularism**, an American school, is associated with the famous Franz Boas (1858–1942), who attempted to overcome some of the objections to these other models. He rejected the idea of parallel development driven by some universal law of cultural evolution and focused on fieldwork, the accumulation of firsthand data about societies and their cultures (Figure 13.4). Moreover, Boas said this fieldwork should be (1) holistic, looking at all aspects of a culture and their interrelationships, and (2) relativistic, understanding a culture within the context of its cultural system. Boas was the first to formalize these concepts—of data collection, holism, and relativism—and make them important parts of anthropology.

With this approach, however, Boas implicitly rejected the possibility of *any* generalizations about culture and cultural evolution. Each culture, he said, could be understood and explained only by intensive study of its particular history (hence the name of the model). If there were similarities among cultures, they resulted from diffusion, trade, or represented similar cultural responses to similar environmental circumstances. In fact, the Boasians thought there was so much diffusion that it was difficult if not impossible to classify individual cultures. Instead, they developed lists of specific cultural traits that defined broad culture areas rather than looking at boundaries between individual societies.

Still, Boas advanced the study of cultural evolution by finding some middle ground between the simplistic and extreme focuses of the independent-invention and diffusionist schools—realizing *both processes were important*. He also proposed a relationship between culture and

historical particularism The American school of cultural evolution that rejected any general theory of culture change but believed that each society could be understood only in reference to its particular history.

FIGURE 13.4
Margaret Mead (*left*) doing fieldwork in Samoa in the 1920s. Mead is famous for her fieldwork as well as for being one of the first well-known women anthropologists. As her clothing suggests, she also advocated the idea of "participant observation" in fieldwork, meaning that the anthropologist could better understand a society and its culture by trying as much as possible to be a part of it.

environment, getting away from both the ideas of a unilinear evolution of all cultures regardless of environment and of the diffusion of cultural items without any sort of adaptive selection and modification by the receiving society. And, once again, it was Boas and his followers who made scientific data collection through field research, holism, and relativism part of the very identity of anthropology.

It is safe to say, however, that—no matter how one sees them specifically affecting cultural systems—invention and diffusion are the driving forces behind culture change. We may propose an analogy to the processes of biological evolution. Invention is like mutation—the source of new variation. Just as a mutation spreads through heredity and gene flow, so a new cultural innovation spreads through diffusion, either when the idea itself moves among societies or when the people migrate and carry the idea with them. But the success of a mutation is dependent on its adaptive value. If it is useful, it's selected for by natural processes of differential reproduction. If not, it is selected against. The same holds true for cultural innovations. They are not just blindly accepted. Rather, they undergo cultural selection with regard to their value to and fit within the new cultural system. The difference between the two sets of processes is that cultural innovation and selection include an element of conscious, purposeful thought, whereas biological mutations and natural selection are random, unconscious, and undirected. That added dimension—of human motivation, consciousness, and will—makes a big difference, as we will see in the next chapter.

SUMMARY

Cultures change at different rates and times, but change is inevitable for any society. Two basic processes bring about culture change. The first process is the interaction of discovery and invention—the addition of new knowledge about the world and the application of that knowledge through the creation of artifacts and ideas. Innovations are selected and modified to fit a society's existing cultural system.

Possibilities for innovation within any given society are limited. The second process of culture change—diffusion—is responsible for the majority of any society's cultural inventory and explains the diversity in level of complexity among societies. Diffusion is the process of cultural borrowing. Isolated societies, with limited exposure to the innovations of other groups, change slowly. Societies that live in areas with greater intercultural contact change more rapidly. As with innovations, potentially borrowed items are selected for their fit within the receiving

society's system. When borrowed, they are modified to fit the system.

Acculturation is rapid diffusion under the influence of a more dominant culture. This may take place by force, as in military conquest, or voluntarily, as with the cargo cults of the South Pacific.

Revolution is rapid invention—change from within a society that alters the whole social fabric. Revolutions may involve violent overthrows of existing governments or more peaceful cultural statements, such as religious revolutions or the changes seen in United States society that began in the 1960s.

Early theories of cultural evolution were often oversimplified models stressing one process of change—either independent invention or diffusion. Thanks in part to the Boasian school of thought, we now see that all the processes of change work together in complex ways that vary with each society's particular history.

CONTEMPORARY ISSUES

Can Anthropology Be Both a Scientific and a Humanistic Discipline in Today's World?

Let's begin with the answer to this question: Anthropology *can* be both scientific and humanistic, and, in today's world, it *must* be.

In Chapter 2, I indicated that one of the appeals of anthropology to many people, and one of its major contributions, is its humanism—its understanding of and concern for other peoples and their cultures and for humanity in general. Obviously, in the process of studying a society's culture, one comes to know its people in a profound way, and one recognizes—beyond all the striking differences—the essential similarities among all humans. I chose the Hutterites as subjects to help me answer a biological question. But during my brief fieldwork, I came to know many of them quite well, and I became deeply interested in their way of life, their attitudes, and their problems. I never thought for a second about living that life; it was foreign to many of my beliefs, habits, and likes. Nor did I get along with every Hutterite I met; some I was friendly with, some I never warmed up to, and I'm sure the feeling was mutual. But I went away with a better understanding of and a deep respect and concern for the culture and the people who practice it.

This phenomenon is true for most anthropologists, I believe. Certainly, it occurs among cultural anthropologists who study living peoples and cultures. But even archaeologists, who study cultures and peoples no longer living, can develop an intimacy with and respect for those societies. And many ancient societies still have identifiable living descendants with whom archaeologists can form professional and personal relationships. Indeed, even paleoanthropologists studying long-extinct species of hominids may still acquire a feel for their subjects, so detailed and personal is the nature of anthropological data. We can't, for example, help speculating how Lucy died 3.2 mya, because we feel some connection even across so many millennia. Her well-preserved bones conjure up a picture of her death on the shore of a body of water, with her corpse sinking into the thick silt at the bottom to slowly decay.

This intimacy with and concern for other peoples have motivated anthropologists to apply their knowledge (from their privileged positions as members of affluent societies) to address the concerns and problems of their subjects. Many peoples—especially those in isolated, poor, minority, or subservient societies—are at best ignored and at worst denigrated, exploited, and violently persecuted. No thinking person can ignore this, and anthropologists—immersed as they are in the lives of others—must confront it head-on. As a result, many anthropologists have lately focused on advocacy—speaking,

QUESTIONS FOR FURTHER THOUGHT

1. We mentioned fully electric cars as an example of an invention that has not yet been widely adopted into this culture. Think of another example, and explain why it won't be accepted.

2. Ralph Linton's 1937 article talked of items invented elsewhere that were adopted into American society. Name some *American* cultural items or ideas that have been adopted by other societies. How, if at all, have they been modified by these societies?

lobbying, and collecting money for people in the societies they have studied and come to know. (See, for example, the discussion of the San in Chapter 15.)

But the anthropology-as-advocacy approach has led to criticism. Anthropologists involved in these sorts of activities have been accused of abandoning anthropology as science. They are not, it has been said, advancing our knowledge of peoples, cultures, and humanity in general but rather have become politically oriented and, as such, let beliefs and opinions instead of facts influence how they describe and analyze a group of people and their culture.

For their part, some anthropologists whose focus is on advocacy for a particular group have characterized science as cold, detached, and dehumanizing and even a tool of the politically powerful to justify some social-economic-political status quo. As a result, there's something of a split within the discipline (sometimes actually reflected in the division of university departments) between science-oriented and advocacy-oriented anthropology, and the debate has taken on varied (and complex) philosophical dimensions.

Does this mean the demise of anthropology as we have known it, a field that has been called "not only scientifically important but intellectually bold and morally brave"? I certainly hope not, nor do I think this will be the outcome. But a solution rests with the realization that science and humanism can and should work together in this field, that they are not mutually exclusive, and that the free discussion of differences in philosophy and theory drives progress in knowledge and its applications.

The subject matter and methodology of anthropology make it uniquely qualified to speak with and for peoples of other cultures or subcultures in the face of extensive and accelerating change in the modern world. Indeed, anthropologists would be remiss if they did not apply their knowledge and skills in this way. At the same time, offering opinions on real, concrete matters without factual information to support them ranges from ineffectual to dangerous. If we are to provide a forum and voice for the people of other societies, we must do so with the best information at hand—and some of the best information about societies and their cultural systems comes from anthropology in its role as a scientific discipline. All the best intentions for another people will do them no good unless reality is taken into account, and as anthropologist Robin Fox says, "Science, with its objectivity . . . remains the one international language capable of providing objective knowledge about the world. And it is a language we can all use and share and learn." To not apply science—especially when that application can assist people in achieving the basic human right of exercising control over their lives—is arguably immoral. Thus the reconciliation of the scientific and humanistic roles of anthropology is a bold, brave, and important goal.

3. We live in a world where dissemination of and access to information is easier and faster than ever, thanks to the Internet, e-mail, and digitized data. What processes of culture change are involved here, and how do you think they will affect future societies?

4. British writer James Burke once predicted that the revolution in electronic data and communication would allow people to work more out of their homes and thus bring back the concept of the neighborhood. But it seems quite the opposite. What do you think?

NOTES, REFERENCES, AND READINGS

Ralph Linton's famous article appeared in *The American Mercury* (1937) and is reprinted in numerous collections of anthropological literature.

For some insight into the story of the electric car, watch *Who Killed the Electric Car?* produced by Sony Classics Pictures.

A good article on the much-misunderstood religion of Voodoo, with information about its syncretic nature, is "Voodoo," by Karen McCarthy Brown. It can be found in Arthur Lehmann and James Myers's reader, *Magic, Witchcraft, and Religion.*

A well-illustrated piece on the cargo cults is in the May 1974 *National Geographic,* titled "Tanna Awaits the Coming of John Frum," by Kal Muller.

For a comprehensive collection of pieces on anthropological theory, with commentary through introductions and extensive footnotes, see *Anthropological Theory: An Introductory History,* by R. Jon McGee and Richard Warms.

14

THE EVOLUTION OF OUR BEHAVIOR

Putting It All Together

CHAPTER CONTENTS "Of Their Flesh Shall Ye Not Eat" • Peaceful Warriors and Cannibal Farmers • Biology and Culture in Interaction • Contemporary Issues: Are Humans Naturally Violent? • Summary • Questions for Further Thought • Notes, References, and Readings

Anthropologists agree that all the facets of a cultural system are integrated—connected to one another by a complex web of interactions, both at any given time and over the course of time. I have tried to show this integration in the last five chapters by pointing out interrelationships within individual aspects of cultural adaptations and in examples of connections among cultural features.

Anthropologists agree, as well, that culture has two interacting roles: as the means by which we adapt to our natural environment and as the means by which we respond to our cultural environment itself. A cultural behavior, then, has both practical value and meaning.

Now we must try to put all these ideas together and see how they work when we look not just at individual aspects of a cultural system but at a cultural system as a whole. When we do this, we begin to find some disagreement among anthropologists. These disagreements are complex, but they focus on which role of culture is most important.

Some anthropologists emphasize the practical adaptive role of culture, maintaining that the ultimate explanation for cultural phenomena lies in the fulfillment of basic needs such as providing food, water, and shelter. Others focus on culture itself, stressing that cultural phenomena need be explained only by their meaning within a given cultural system. Put another way the debate focuses on the relationship between ideas and behavior. Does behavior guide ideas (the practical adaptive explanation), or do ideas guide behavior (culture as meaning)?

I believe that cultural phenomena fulfill many roles in a complex feedback system, far more complex than this either-or debate indicates. I will apply this idea to two cultural examples in the second section of this chapter. First, however, I think I can best demonstrate the integrated roles of culture by bringing back some ideas we've already covered and by looking, in detail, at two diverse explanations for a particular cultural expression. The proponents of these explanations are British anthropologist Mary Douglas and American anthropologist Marvin Harris. The topic of their debate—going back to that most basic of human concerns—is food, specifically the lists of clean and unclean foods from the Bible.

AS YOU READ, CONSIDER THE FOLLOWING QUESTIONS:

1. What are some of the ways anthropologists attempt to analyze and understand cultural behaviors within the context of specific cultural systems? How is the discussion of biblical food laws an example of such analysis?

2. How do the descriptions of the two New Guinea societies reflect the author's approach to cultural analysis?

3. In what general ways do culture and biology interact to produce human behavior?

"OF THEIR FLESH SHALL YE NOT EAT"

The Kosher Laws

Jews are forbidden to eat the flesh of swine (Figure 14.1). So, too, are Muslims. For these religions, pigs are considered unclean creatures: "Of their flesh shall ye not eat, and their carcasses shall ye not touch." But

FIGURE 14.1
Domestic pigs showing the cloven hoof. Because they have this feature and do not chew cud, they were placed in the category of prohibited foods among the ancient Hebrews.

TABLE 14.1 Summary of Biblical Dietary Laws

Food Group	Clean	Unclean	Stated Criteria for Prohibition
livestock and wild game	cattle sheep goats antelope deer	pigs hares hyraxes camels	animals that chew cud but lack cloven hoofs animals that have cloven hoofs but don't chew cud
water creatures	fishes with fins and scales	finless or scaleless fishes mollusks crustaceans	water creatures that lack fins and/or scales
birds	"clean" fowl (Deuteronomy 14:11)	flightless birds waterbirds birds of prey scavengers wading birds	apparently, any birds that swim, walk, wade, eat meat, or don't fly
insects	locusts* grasshoppers* beetles*	all other "creeping flying things" (Leviticus 11:23)	insects that walk *and* fly (the clean ones "leap")
other		weasels mice tortoises ferrets chameleons lizards snails moles anything that has already died	"creeping things" (Leviticus 11:29) creatures with paws

*Eventually, *all* insects were prohibited by rabbinical scholars.

pork is only one of a long list of foods considered unclean by the ancient Hebrews. (Pork is the only specific meat prohibited in Islam, although anything already dead or any animal sacrificed to another religion is also inedible.) You can find a long list of prohibited foods in both Leviticus 11:1–47 and Deuteronomy 14:1–21. Read them both, as each has some specific information not included in the other. It takes a little patience to sort out all the generalizations, so a summary is presented in Table 14.1. Hebrew food laws also include detailed guidelines for the preparation of foods (Figure 14.2)

FIGURE 14.2
A Kosher deli with separate sinks and utensils for meat and dairy products. The Hebrew food laws include rules about consistency, uniformity, and lack of confused categories. Thus, "Thou shalt not seethe [cook] a kid in his mother's milk" (Deuteronomy 14:21).

How do we explain these clean and unclean animal food sources? Using the pig as an example, we can discount the conventional wisdom that pigs are literally unclean because they are dirty and carry disease. They are, in fact, no dirtier than any other domestic animal, nor are they the only animal that can be a source of disease. The parasite usually associated with pigs, the trichina worm, is rare in hot climates, can be controlled simply with proper cooking, and was known no earlier than the nineteenth century—millennia after the lists of clean and unclean food had been created. Moreover, many of the other creatures labeled as unclean are perfectly fine, safe sources of food. There's obviously some other explanation.

Ideas Guide Behavior

Mary Douglas emphasizes the symbolic functions of cultural practices. Once beyond the obviously practical (things such as tools to acquire food and so on), the functions of most acts, she feels, are aimed at conforming to and thus reinforcing our basic assumptions about our world, our worldview.

Most of the taboos, Douglas feels, are aimed at preserving peoples' "holiness" (Leviticus 11:43–47), which she takes to mean wholeness, completeness, and consistency. "Holiness requires that individuals shall conform to the class to which they belong. And holiness requires that different classes of things shall not be confused."

It follows that food should be classified in such a way that the categories ("classes") are clear and that creatures conform to the characteristics that define their class. If they don't, they are not holy—and are thus unclean.

So, Douglas says, water creatures that lack fins and/or scales fail to conform to the criteria defining this class of organisms. Creatures that "go on all four" but that also fly are unclean because they fail to behave appropriately for legged land creatures, which should be jumping or walking. Animals with "paws," she says, are unclean because they have "hands instead of front feet" and so "perversely use their hands for walking." And all those "creeping" creatures are taboo because of their "indeterminate form of movement."

The list of unclean birds doesn't seem to work well with Douglas's interpretation. A raven is not fundamentally different from, say, some perching bird like a robin, which, I assume, would be acceptable to eat. Douglas addresses this by suggesting that the list may be poorly translated from Hebrew and Greek. If the list could be retranslated, she offers, we might find the unclean birds to be birds that can't fly or that swim and dive as well as fly and thus are "not fully birdlike."

So far, the lists of creatures that can and cannot be eaten or even touched serve an important symbolic purpose. They maintain the "holiness" of those who adhere to their principles; they remind them constantly of their relationship with God, from whom the rules are said to have come. "By rules of avoidance holiness was given a physical expression in every encounter with the animal kingdom and at every meal," says Douglas.

But Douglas's interpretation doesn't explain why the animals are categorized as they are in the first place. Who says creatures with fins and scales are the "proper" kind of water animal? Who decided that a huge number of insects don't conform to their category because they have feet but also fly? What's wrong with creeping? and paws?

And notice what's missing from the list: plants. Surely there are plants that are bad to eat or fail to conform to some taxonomic norm. Clearly, there's more to the story, and a clue can be found in Douglas's discussion of livestock.

Here, the criteria for cleanliness are clearly based on practical matters. Douglas says, "Cloven-hoofed, cud-chewing ungulates are the model of the proper kind of food for a pastoralist" because the rules are "*a posteriori* [after the fact] generalizations of their habits." In other words, the rules reflect what the people were already doing with regard to eating these animals. Behavior, in this case, was guiding ideas. And we must assume that with something as vital as food, what they were already doing had practical reasons behind it.

Behavior Guides Ideas

Marvin Harris is a cultural materialist, someone who sees cultural patterns not as "random or capricious" but as based on "practical circumstances" and "ordinary, banal, one might say 'vulgar' conditions, needs, and activities." People may do things for reasons that are symbolic on the surface, but beneath it all, their cultural practices originate in down-to-earth, "mundane," usually economic matters. Says Harris,

> Practical life wears many disguises. Each lifestyle comes wrapped in myths and legends that draw attention to impractical or supernatural conditions. These wrappings give people a social identity and a sense of social purpose, but they conceal the naked truths of social life.

Harris would agree with what Douglas said about the livestock—that the dietary laws are after-the-fact generalizations of already existing habits that revolved around the ecology of the area. A long-standing emphasis on farming in the area brought about ecological changes turning forests into grasslands, which themselves sometimes converted to deserts (Figure 14.3). This had the effect of making hunting a costly proposition in terms of nutrition returned for energy expended.

Thus the practical concern of cost versus benefit for sources of food was, according to Harris, at the heart of the matter. People stopped hunting for wild creatures, especially those that provided little meat and were hard to catch. They were also careful about the animals they herded; such animals had to be useful alive (for work, milk, and fertilizer) as well as on someone's dinner plate. Otherwise, the cost in energy was too high.

The emphasis on farming also explains why plants were not given clean and unclean labels. Raising plants was so central that there was no need for any formal reinforcement of the habits or reminders about which plants to grow and which to avoid. That information was a given.

This explains the famous prohibition against eating pork. Although pigs are a good source of leather and meat, they are difficult to herd. They cannot digest cellulose and thus are not grazing animals suited to the natural flora of Southwest Asia. In fact, their digestive system is much like our own (part of the reason fetal pigs are often dissected in biology labs), so they actually compete with humans for the same food sources. Finally, they are hard to raise in hot, dry climates because they don't sweat. Because they need an external source of moisture to cool their bodies, they will roll in mud or even their own excrement if no other source is available—the origin of the notion that they are especially dirty. It was, in short, not a good idea for the peoples of Southwest Asia to raise pigs. Although they did at one time (archaeologists have found bones of domestic swine), they gradually stopped doing so as the area's ecology changed. This must also explain the Muslim prohibition.

FIGURE 14.3
View of the Gaza Strip, along the Mediterranean Sea, taken from a space shuttle. Years of grazing and climatic changes have removed much of the vegetation and turned the area into desert. Note particularly the very light strip along the shore. North of the clearly defined border between the Egyptian Sinai and southern Israel, irrigation has allowed farming, as seen by the dark fields. Assessing the costs versus benefits of raising different foods in such ecological conditions helps explain the biblical dietary laws.

What about animals that *were* herded—sheep, goats, and cattle? All these animals can thrive under the ecological conditions of Southwest Asia and can, because they are naturally herding animals, be easily controlled. They serve functions other than as sources of food. They all provide milk. Sheep have wool. Cattle can be used for agricultural work and, when dead, as a source of meat and leather. The benefits of herding such species outweigh the costs.

Hunted animals were also considered clean or not depended on the same basic criterion: cost effectiveness. Wild deer, oxen, and antelope have long been successfully hunted (see Figures 6.31 and 6.32) and provide a good deal of meat. Hares and hyraxes, on the other hand, are harder to find and kill and are not worth the effort.

To round out this part of the list, we have the camel, an animal so useful for transportation and other work that to eat it would have been detrimental in terms of energy efficiency. The same could be said for the horse and donkey. The latter was widely used in the area, but neither is included in the lists, although Harris says that rabbinical scholars have normally added them to the unclean list. Their use alive was so important that eating them was out of the question—so much so that it may simply have not been necessary to list them. (The Koran specifically releases Muslims from the prohibition against eating camel flesh. Many Islamic pastoralists used the camel for long trips through desert areas and, in an emergency, eating camel might have been the only means of survival. A prohibition would have been decidedly counterproductive.)

Birds such as eagles and vultures (both unclean) were hard to catch and would not have provided much nutrition for the effort. (I'll bet they're not very tasty either.) Many of the prohibited birds are birds of prey or scavengers. They eat other animals, including ones that are already dead. The eating of carrion is prohibited by both the Bible and the Koran, probably because of the potential ill effects of eating decaying flesh. (It is true that our earlier ancestors were scavengers. They certainly could have eaten already dead animals with impunity, but I also imagine some of them suffered for it.)

Harris also applies the inefficiency of most hunting to explain the taboo against finless, scaleless aquatic animals such as clams, eels, and shrimp—which were not common in the interior of Southwest Asia. Nor would animals with "paws" and those "creeping" things have been very energy-efficient sources of food.

Neither would most insects. But those that were edible—locusts and grasshoppers, especially—were big, meaty bugs that were most abundant and easily captured when they were swarming and eating people's crops. There was surely some practical sense in eating these insects, and folks did (Figure 14.4).

A Synthesis?

We seem to have two distinct points of view here: Douglas, who feels the explanation for the laws lies in their symbolic and organizing value, and Harris, who thinks the laws stem from practical considerations. I think they are both right and that each emphasizes a different aspect of the same story. When you read their arguments carefully, you see that they realize this as well.

Harris explains the origin of the laws as religious expressions of preexisting practical habits. Douglas acknowledges that in the passage I quoted about the cloven-hoofed, cud-chewing ungulates. But the fact that the laws are expressed in terms of loose zoological categories labeled "clean" and "unclean" may be explained by the need for people to order their world in a way that makes sense culturally and symbolizes basic cultural ideas. The categories are folk taxonomies (see Chapter 7).

FIGURE 14.4
A farmer in Burkina Faso in West Africa raises a horde of locusts from a tree whose vegetation might have fed livestock. A locust swarm in Somalia in 1958 is said to have measured 400 square miles and numbered 40 billion insects capable of eating 80,000 tons of food plants a day.

Now, once the laws were in place, serving to codify and maintain certain practical habits, they also functioned to remind people of their identity and relationship with the supernatural, even after their practical functions were no longer important. Harris says:

> Food taboos and culinary specialties can be perpetuated as boundary markers between ethnic and national minorities and as symbols of group identity independently of any active ecological selection for or against their existence. But I don't think such beliefs and practices would long endure if they resulted in the sharp elevation of subsistence costs.

In short, Harris and Douglas do not really hold contrary views on the analysis of cultural phenomena. Rather, they each emphasize a different process in what amounts to a complex feedback loop. For another example, consider that although Islam and Judaism arose from the same general geographic area and share much history and many beliefs, Islamic dietary laws are much less restrictive than Jewish ones. Muslims can, for instance, eat shellfish; Jews who keep kosher cannot. Many Jews have held on to this prohibition, even those who live in areas where shellfish are easily obtained and not a health risk. For cultural reasons, the symbolism of the prohibition is more important than material concerns. The Muslims did not carry over this restriction (although, recall that they did with the pork taboo) for reasons that may involve practicality (the presence and abundance of shellfish in coastal areas) or symbolism (to differentiate their beliefs from Jewish tradition) or some combination of both. Specific cultural systems are explained by the specific and complex histories and environments of the societies in question.

To summarize: It makes sense that many, if not most, cultural behaviors originate for practical reasons. If a society can't satisfy its basic biological needs, symbolism and meaning become irrelevant. Once basic behaviors are in place, they become part of an integrated, meaningful, complex cultural system. In Harris's words, behaviors guide ideas. Then, however, the ideas generated by those practical behaviors become integral parts of the cultural system and of the lives of the people who practice it. Those ideas, then, guide behavior. Of course, both these processes are always in operation within any cultural system at any given time and over time. Both these directions of influence must be looked for and considered when we attempt to understand a system of culture, be it someone else's or our own.

Now, how does this work when we look at more than just a society's dietary laws? As examples, let's examine more closely two fascinating stories from New Guinea and see how this all goes together.

PEACEFUL WARRIORS AND CANNIBAL FARMERS

That both my examples come from New Guinea does not mean that the analytical process I've described is applicable only to peoples from this large island in the western Pacific. It can be applied to any culture. It's just that these two examples are among my favorites and are two you are not likely to forget (Figure 14.5).

The Dani

The Dani, whom I've mentioned several times, live in the western half of New Guinea called West Papua, now a part of Indonesia. The lives of the Dani have, of course, changed over the last several decades as industrial societies and technologies have increasingly invaded their once isolated mountain valley. The Dani I'll describe are the Dani of the late 1950s and early 1960s, when anthropologists first extensively studied them and before outside contact had changed forever a way of life they had led for thousands of years. I'll speak in the ethnographic

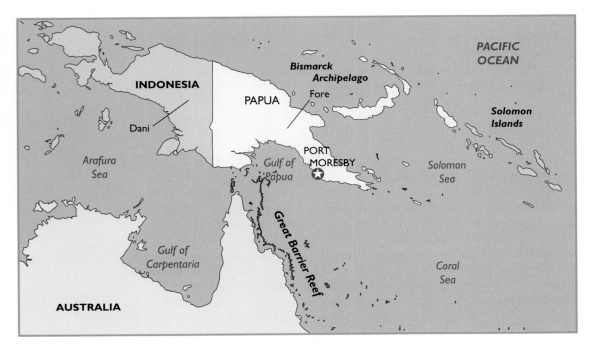

FIGURE 14.5
Map of New Guinea locating the Dani and Fore.

present. My information comes largely from ethnographic studies by anthropologist Karl Heider.

There are about 100,000 people who speak the Dani language, but the group we're concerned with, about 50,000 individuals, lives in the Grand Valley of the Balim River, an area of about 250 square miles. The Dani are horticulturalists, using digging sticks and human labor to break ground and plant, care for, and harvest their crops. They use an extensive system of ditches that have four functions: to bring water to crops, drain excess water away from crops, serve as a barrier to protect crops from pigs, and make compost.

Their major crop, making up perhaps 90 percent of their diet, is the sweet potato. Almost their only source of meat comes from domestic pigs. In contrast to Southwest Asia, highland New Guinea is an ideal place for pigs—it's not too hot, there's plenty of moisture, and because of the successful sweet potato farming, there's plenty of food for both pigs and people. New Guinea had little natural game to begin with, and much of that has been hunted out.

In general, the Grand Valley is a nice place to live. The average year-round temperature is about 70° Fahrenheit, and there is plenty of rain. Although there are seasonal fluctuations in rainfall and temperature, there is essentially a year-round growing season. The elevation is high enough so that tropical diseases are uncommon. One might think that people in such a place would live happy, peaceful lives. Happy,

FIGURE 14.6
A Dani war dance.

perhaps; indeed, Heider describes the people themselves as "gentle" and "nonaggressive." But peaceful, hardly. For the Dani are continually at war, and not with outsiders but with one another.

The Grand Valley Dani are divided into about twelve alliances, which are subdivided into a total of about fifty confederations. There has existed, for how long no one knows, a state of ritual war between various alliances. The motivation is the placation of ghosts. The ghost of a person slain in warfare demands revenge. This requires that the life of an enemy be taken in return. That death, of course, requires revenge as well, making the cycle self-perpetuating.

The opportunity to take lives is provided by large battles (Figure 14.6). These take place, by mutual agreement, on a no-man's-land between alliance territories, usually only on days when the weather is nice. The weapons used are bows and arrows and 13-foot spears. These weapons are not particularly well made, and an alert warrior can usually see them in flight and avoid being hit. When a man is killed or badly wounded, however, the battle ceases, for there is concern that no more than one life be taken in revenge, even in response to multiple deaths. The battle has the appearance of a huge game, though one with very high stakes.

If several of these battles fail to result in the required death, the group needing the kill may resort to ambush. Here, an unwary woman or child may be the victim and serve the purpose of revenge as well as a warrior in battle. When a person has been killed, all other activities cease and both sides perform rites: one a dance of joy that their ghost has been avenged, the other a funeral with all the display of emotion one would expect, especially if the deceased is a child.

On reading about the Dani or watching Robert Gardner's marvelous film *Dead Birds* (so called because the Dani see themselves as birds, which are mortal, as opposed to snakes, which shed their skins and so are immortal), many people see such a cycle of death as incongruous given the relatively "temperate" (as Heider says) conditions of their environment and personalities. Why do people who seem to have no real economic hardships and who feel normal emotions of grief and sorrow have a cultural practice that ensures that a violent death takes place on a regular basis? Moreover, the men seem obsessed by war and death, as most of their daily activities are centered on watching for the enemy, making weapons, and weaving bands decorated with shells that are traded only at funerals. How can we explain such a cultural system? Follow Figure 14.7 as we address this.

FIGURE 14.7
Holistic summary of Dani warfare.

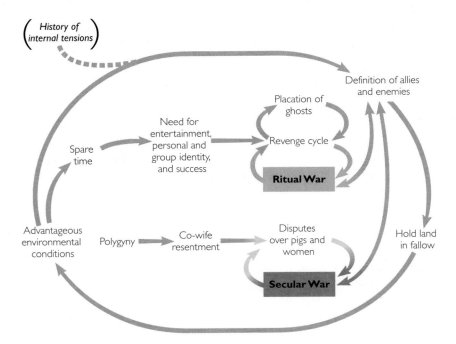

You should know that the ritual battle is not the only kind of war the Dani fight. They also have periodic secular wars. These are fairly rare, occurring maybe every ten years. They are so rare, in fact, that Heider didn't know of their existence when he first studied the Dani. These wars take place for secular reasons, usually arguments over wives or pigs (both are commodities and signs of status to the polygynous Dani) or some other matter that gets out of hand and cannot be resolved peacefully.

Secular wars are usually fought between confederations within an alliance, because it is between such groups that potentially contentious economic and social issues arise. Secular wars are not played by rules. The idea is to kill members of the enemy confederation and to take their goods and land. The last such war took place in 1966, when some 125 people, of both sexes and all ages, were massacred. It was this war that prompted the Indonesians, who had taken over West Papua (known then as Irian Jaya) from the Dutch in 1963, to step up their attempts to pacify the Dani.

War, as most of us normally think of it, is thus possible within the Dani cultural system and has obviously been part of it. While these secular wars are few and far between, the ritual wars are continual. It almost appears as if the ritual war fills in the time between "real" wars—and, to an extent, I think that's the case.

The ecological conditions of the Grand Valley make basic subsistence a fairly easy task. With relatively little labor, the Dani can grow sweet potatoes in sufficient quantities to feed everyone, and this vegetable seems to be nutritious enough to make up the bulk of their diet. The pigs, raised and cared for with little labor, provide additional sustenance. The majority of the food-related labor, in fact, is done by women and children. The men usually break ground for a new garden, the hardest work involved, but after that women do the farming. Children are largely responsible for the pigs. The men, as a consequence, have lots of spare time.

Now, don't get the idea that the men dreamed up this elaborate game to relieve their boredom. It's not that simple. It's more accurate to say that an important *current function* of the ritual war, and part of the reason it has persisted, is that it gives the men something to do. It provides a focus for their daily lives. It gives them a social and personal identity. It's exciting. But this is not why it *originated*.

The ritual war derived from some already existing behavior—namely, the secular wars—and the secular war came about for some down-to-earth practical reasons. Over maybe tens of thousands of years, the Dani were able to spread out over this temperate, isolated valley and easily raise pigs and grow sweet potatoes. The population increased. Almost naturally some units of this population—depending on many variables—had more arable land than others, grew more sweet potatoes, had more pigs. Perhaps some men had more wives than others. A sense of "mine "and "thine" arose, and social inequalities developed. Conflicts could easily arise over these factors as well as over matters of relative power, influence, and social status. Polygyny itself carries the seeds of tensions, because the common phenomenon of **co-wife resentment** can sometimes cause one wife to go back to her parental village, which in turn creates ill will between her husband and her kinsmen.

In other words, these conditions, and the Dani's reactions to them, set the stage for a worldview where tension and potential conflict are normal (or at least not abnormal) states of affair. Territories are established, statuses are acknowledged, and wealth is unequally distributed—all things we don't see among egalitarian foragers, who may act violently toward one another but not on the scale of warfare.

So, the ritual war has derived from—is an extension of, a symbol of, a metaphor for—the secular conflicts and the conditions that brought them about. The exact relationship and history we'll probably never know. But the ritual war caught on, in part because of its identity as a derivative of the other tensions and conflicts and in part because it fills the time and provides a major theme for Dani life. It may even serve to maintain readiness for a potential secular war, a "war game" as we use the phrase.

The importance of the ritual war is evidenced by its justification within the Dani religious system. It is not just a frivolous game but a vital part of their worldview and most deeply held beliefs. Recall the cultural feedback loop described earlier in this chapter: ideas guide behaviors, and in turn behaviors guide ideas. In the case of the Dani:

> The tensions and secular wars (*behavior*) gave rise to the revenge cycle for the ghosts of the slain (*idea*) which guided the ritual war and its central place in Dani culture (*behavior*).

Are any other relationships in operation here? During the ritual war, a no-man's-land exists between rival factions. This land is not planted, although when alliances shift (confederation and alliance membership is not stable) it may be farmed once again. After a secular war, there is usually much shifting of people, alliance membership, and land. This shifting allows areas of land to lie fallow for a time, which lets the nutrients build back up, which in turn may add to the overall success of Dani farming. Whether the Dani are aware of this is unclear, nor do we know whether it really makes a difference. But it's one area of possible investigation.

Another economic relationship exists as well. Tension and war are justifications for ceremonies—funerals as well as feasts—that help strengthen alliance relationships. Ceremonies are not only important symbolically but are also events during which food is consumed and goods are exchanged. Pigs, for example, are normally eaten only in some ceremonial context. Ceremonies, then, serve as a means of wealth redistribution—of both symbolic shell bands and pig flesh.

co-wife resentment Tension among the wives of one man in polygynous societies, often caused by the differing statuses of those wives.

One would think that when the Dutch and then the Indonesians pacified the Dani and put an end to the warfare cycle in the early 1960s, the whole of Dani society would have unraveled, lacking such an integral part of their culture. Something with so many interrelationships and to which the Dani devoted so much time and concern must be something they couldn't do without. But that's not what happened. The Dani took the imposed change quite calmly. The men continued to sit in watchtowers, guarding against an enemy attack that would never come. They found other occasions to eat pigs. They carried their weapons and wore their finest battle garb for fights that would never happen. Taking away the actual war made little difference to them.

What we see here, then, is a complex interaction of ideas and behaviors that evolved over many years and resulted in the manifestation of Dani culture in the early 1960s. (And what I've outlined is only part of the story; see Karl Heider's book for more detail.) Although we have been able to see how all the aspects of Dani culture *can* interact, we can't know for certain how they really do and did interact. Obviously, the calm with which the Dani accepted pacification tells us there's something else involved. The above analysis is only a hypothesis that requires testing. Because of the changes to Dani life, such testing may be impossible. At any rate, it is by observing, describing, and proposing relationships between ideas and behaviors that we may begin to approach the understanding of individual cultural systems and of culture in general.

The Fore

For a second example, let's move to the eastern half of New Guinea—now the largest part of the independent nation of Papua New Guinea—and another society I've mentioned elsewhere in this book, the Fore (*fo-RAY*). Again, I use the ethnographic present.

There are about 14,000 people who consider themselves Fore. Our discussion, however, centers largely on a subgroup, the South Fore, who number about 8,000. Like the Dani, the Fore are horticulturalists and pig keepers. Also like the Dani, their major crop is the sweet potato, although they grow a greater variety of minor crops. The Fore also do more hunting than the Dani.

As with any culture, the Fore exhibit a set of cultural features that makes them unique. But when first extensively studied, they exhibited another distinction as well—a disease found occasionally in surrounding groups but heavily concentrated among the South Fore. They call the disease *kuru,* and we have adopted that name. It is a degenerative disease of the central nervous system. Its symptoms follow an almost unvarying pattern, starting with loss of balance and followed by loss of motor coordination, slurred speech, abnormal behavior (such as uncontrollable laughter), and finally complete motor incapacity and death. It takes on average a year for this sequence to progress (Figure 14.8).

FIGURE 14.8
A Fore woman in the terminal phase of kuru, supported by her husband. She can no longer sit up unaided and, although she appears to be smiling, has lost control of her facial muscles.

When kuru was first discovered among the Fore, its cause was a mystery, and it displayed a strange distribution. Between 1957 and 1968 there were 2,500 deaths from kuru in the area, about 80 percent of them among the South Fore. The most common victims by far were adult women, in whom it was nearly eight times as frequent as in adult men. Children of both sexes were the next most common victims, followed by elderly men. There was clearly a lot to explain.

The first problem was to discover the cause of the disease. At first, because of its isolated nature, kuru was thought to be genetic. But there is no genetic mechanism that would account for the distribution of the disease among the Fore. Anyway, it was too frequent to be genetic. A disease that is 100 percent lethal would have been selected out of existence, except for isolated new cases, long ago.

A clue came from veterinary medicine. It was reported that a similar disease called *scrapie* was known among sheep and goats that deteriorated brain tissue. This led to further investigation.

We now know that kuru is caused by prion proteins. Prions are normal proteins in the nervous tissue that sometimes fold up in an abnormal configuration. In this form they trigger the same folding up of the normal proteins, which then build up in and eventually destroy brain tissue. The condition is called *spongiform encephalopathy*. Expressions

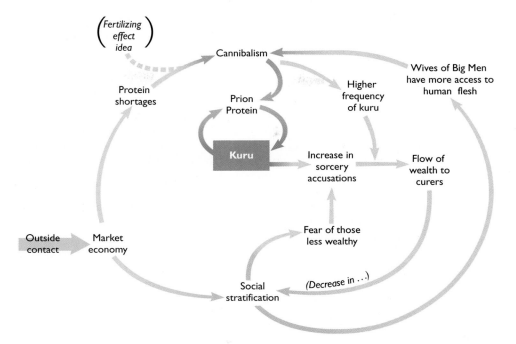

FIGURE 14.9
A holistic summary of the kuru phenomenon among the Fore.

of this disease include mad cow disease in cattle, scrapie in sheep and goats, and Creutzfeldt-Jakob disease and kuru in humans. Although the trigger for the abnormal shape of the protein may come, not surprisingly, from a genetic mutation, the frightening thing about prions is that they can be transmitted *across* species. Moreover, they are very hard to destroy. In the late 1980s and early 1990s, mad cow disease spread throughout England, presumably because cattle there were fed meal that contained the remains of other domestic animals. Even though these remains were cooked and processed into meal, the prions survived and were passed to other cows through ingestion. Dating from the mid-1990s, at least ninety-one cases of Creutzfeldt-Jakob in England, France, and Ireland can be traced to human consumption of infected beef. In other words, these are all essentially the same disease.

Since people the world over may get the disease, why was it so concentrated among the Fore? How was it being passed from one person to another, and why in such an odd pattern? The answer, first proposed by anthropologists Shirley Lindenbaum and Robert Glasse, was cannibalism, which was largely practiced by women, who shared the human flesh with their children and, sometimes, with elderly men. Consuming the flesh of someone who died from kuru, even though the flesh was cooked, passed the prion proteins on to others. Because they practiced **endocannibalism,** the disease was concentrated and found almost exclusively among the South Fore (Figure 14.9).

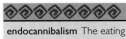

endocannibalism The eating of human flesh from members of one's own society.

Why were they practicing cannibalism, and why was it mostly the women who practiced it? Fore cannibalism seemed to have been practiced for reasons somewhere between ritual and nutrition. The Fore seek to acquire a "fertilizing" effect from the bodies. As Lindenbaum states, "Dead bodies buried in gardens encourage the growth of crops. In a similar manner human flesh, like pig meat, helps some humans regenerate. The flesh of the deceased was thought particularly suitable for invalids."

But when we step back and look at broader relationships, we may see this practice as having a more material origin. It appears to have been taken up by women—in the relatively recent past, an idea borrowed from some surrounding societies—to supplement their diet in what was fast becoming a protein-poor society where men, who dominate Fore society, had first access to the small supply of wild game and pigs that were available. So, indeed, cannibalism here does seem to have a nutritional function at its origin.

Why was the society becoming protein-poor? Complex economic changes brought about by the Australian government (which controlled Papua New Guinea from 1906 to 1975) had turned these former foragers and horticulturalists into settled farmers, with an emphasis on the sweet potato and the pig, as well as on cash crops such as coffee. This way of life, and the larger, more sedentary populations it produced, had gradually depleted the forests and the game they contained, making protein increasingly scarce. Moreover, now that they were part of a larger, money-oriented economic system, these fairly egalitarian people began to exhibit stratification in both wealth and status. In this environment, for the reasons noted, cannibalism arose and quickly became part of the Fore cultural system, endowed with symbolic meaning. Again, we see the mutual influences of behaviors and ideas. In a tragic coincidence, then, the practice of cannibalism transmitted and increased the frequency of a devastating disease, which otherwise would have affected only the few individuals in whom the abnormal protein occurred.

But this cycle caused even more changes. The Fore explain serious diseases as the work of sorcerers, people who for one reason or another bear a person ill will and act to cause that person harm (see Chapter 12). As kuru increased, the Fore began to fear that their women would all die and that they as a society would perish, and they naturally explained this in terms of the acts of many powerful sorcerers. Who were these sorcerers? People who were not faring well in the new economic stratification. So the increase in kuru coincided with the coming of economic differences and rivalries. In addition, it seems as if the wives of the "Big Men"—those with the most power and wealth—had more access to human flesh than the wives of the less powerful, with the result that kuru was more frequent among families of the Big Men, who, then, naturally saw themselves as being victimized by those of lesser status and wealth. The invocation of sorcery to explain the disease thus made perfect sense within the Fore cultural system.

Finally, to whom did the Big Men turn to try to counteract this sorcery? To their own sorcerers, of course, who did not come cheaply. Thus, the wealth of the Big Men began to pass to others in the form of fees to the counter-sorcerers or bribes to the accused sorcerers themselves. Lindenbaum calls this an example of redistribution, which acted to even out some of the differences in wealth and status.

These two examples from New Guinea and the brief analysis of the biblical food laws show the intimate connection not only among different aspects of cultural systems but also between culture and biology. We had to understand the biology of pigs, for example, and the nature of a bizarre anomalous protein in order to explain cultural phenomena and the cultural systems of which they are a part. But are there any more direct connections between biology and culture? Just how much influence does biology have over our actions?

BIOLOGY AND CULTURE IN INTERACTION

The Question of Altruism

On the cold, stormy evening of January 13, 1982, during the Washington, DC, rush hour, Air Florida flight 90 out of National Airport apparently iced up during takeoff and moments later crashed into the Potomac River, killing seventy-eight people. Only a handful of the plane's passengers survived, and one of them probably owes her life to a young man named M. L. Skutnik.

Skutnik, a government worker, was stopped in the traffic jam resulting from the crash. He was watching the rescue operations when he noticed a woman survivor in the water unable to grab on to a lifeline. Removing his coat and shoes, he dived into the icy Potomac and saved her life.

In June of the following year, Kansas City Chiefs running back Joe Delaney saw three young boys in trouble out in the water of a Louisiana lake. Delaney jumped in to help them. Others came to their aid, but unfortunately, two of the boys drowned. So did Delaney, who couldn't swim.

In July 2004, Kathleen Imel was driving down a street in Aloha, Oregon, when she saw two pit bulls chasing 7-year-old Joshua Pia Perez. By the time Imel, 51, reached the boy in her car, he was being mauled by the larger of the two dogs, weighing approximately 70 pounds. Imel then ran to the boy and tried unsuccessfully to scare off the dogs. As a last resort, Imel shielded the boy with her body until neighbors, and later police, arrived to help. Imel and the boy survived, but both suffered multiple severe wounds to their faces and bodies that required surgery.

These heroic deeds fall into a category of behavior called **altruism**— acts performed for the benefit of others with no regard for one's own welfare. The question that comes immediately to mind is why anyone would perform such an act. Why did these individuals do what they did?

altruism Acting to benefit others while disregarding one's own welfare.

Perhaps they were responding to learned cultural ideals. There would, however, have been no retribution—legal or moral—if they hadn't acted. Under the circumstances, their deeds were extremely dangerous. No one and nothing was forcing them to act. No one would have blamed them if they hadn't. Perhaps, though, what they did was an automatic response to some biological instinct, coded somehow in their genes. But one of the strongest instincts is surely that of personal survival, and all these people put their lives at risk (and Delaney lost his) for people they didn't even know. Perhaps, then, their deeds involved some complex interaction between culture and biology.

Nature and Nurture

Such questions are part of a larger issue that has long been debated in many scholarly areas. There are two extreme points of view on the subject, which we call **biological determinism** and **cultural determinism** or, more simply, "nature versus nurture." The first position holds that much human behavior is biologically determined, though, of course, mediated by culture. The second purports that humans are born pretty much as behavioral "blank slates" and that culture then "writes in" everything that needs to go on those slates. These extremes are rarely held today, although there are those who lean in one direction or the other. As so often occurs in such cases, evidence points to an interaction of biology and culture, a middle ground between the nature and nurture extremes. But let's first examine the extremes.

Cultural Determinism Is Untenable The nurture, or cultural determinism, school of thought is clearly untenable. It posits, to use a computer metaphor, that we arrive in this world like computers with internal hardware but nothing programmed. But one can't load data into a computer without the appropriate application software. If the human brain were not already "programmed," for example, to learn language, no amount of exposure to language would result in a person's being able to speak.

This point of view also implies that at some point in our evolution we left behind our biological heritage and became something qualitatively different. But, obviously, we carry the anatomical and physiological imprints of our evolutionary past. Why not the behavioral ones as well, even if only in terms of general behavioral themes?

Biological Determinism Is Untenable A strict nature, or biological deterministic, point of view is also untenable, but for more complex reasons, and real or perceived support of this position is what has generated the controversy around this question.

It's obvious, and uncontroversial, that the behavior of non-culture-bearing species is programmed in their genes in a complex

biological determinism The idea that human behaviors have a biological basis with minimal influence from culture.

cultural determinism The idea that human behaviors are almost totally the result of learned cultural information, with few or no instinctive responses.

FIGURE 14.10
A prairie dog acting as a sentinel, giving what animal behaviorists call a jump-yip, a signal meaning "all clear."

series of stimulus-response reactions. The nest-building behavior of the weaver ants I described in Chapter 4 is an example. It has even been shown that social behaviors can be biologically based and, thus, explained by the operation of natural selection—even behaviors that may benefit the group rather than the individual.

Take altruism, for example, which—in its broad definition—seems to exist in nonhuman species. In some mammalian species such as ground squirrels and prairie dogs, certain individuals act as guards or sentinels, watching for predators while the others forage (Figure 14.10). If a predator is sighted, the sentinel gives an alarm call and the others literally hit the dirt. In some species the sentinel is at more risk than the others. How, then, could such behavior have been selected for if it might lead to *less* chance of passing on one's genes?

Kin Selection as an Example The proposed answer is a phenomenon called **kin selection.** If the members of such a mammal group are closely related, they share many of their genes. As a result, the fitness of a set of genes (and, thus, the adaptiveness of the phenotype) is measured not only by the reproductive success of the individual but also by the reproductive success of all those possessing the gene. (See the description of baboon

kin selection Promoting the passing on of one's genes by aiding the survival or reproduction of one's close kin.

behavior in Chapter 10.) Thus, any behavior that aids the passing on of the gene in question is selected for. This would include any behavior that benefits the related group as a whole, even if it might not necessarily benefit particular individuals. Over time, a set of genes for sentinel behavior will increase in frequency because, at any given time, some individuals possessing those genes will perform guard duty and, even if they are eaten and lose their opportunity to pass on any more genes, they will have helped save the lives of many related individuals who share the genes.

Biology and Human Behavior

So, complex behaviors in other species can be accounted for in terms of natural selection and the other processes of biological evolution. The problem arises when such reasoning is applied to humans. Could there be a similar biological basis for our behaviors? An area of study, variously known as **sociobiology, evolutionary psychology,** or **behavioral ecology,** has suggested that this is possible—that certain typical human behaviors arose and became part of our behavioral repertoire because they conferred a reproductive advantage to those possessing them. In other words, because these behaviors had a genetic basis, they developed through the mechanism of natural selection.

One reaction to this model came from those who interpreted "biologically based" to mean "biologically determined," that is, that this idea implied severe limits on human free will and thus on the power of culture. Other objections were more political. They claimed that the idea was racist and sexist, or at least potentially promoted racism and sexism. The reasoning behind such accusations was that if human behaviors are genetically determined, then the *differences* in human behaviors lie in genetic differences, and so the two sexes and people from different populations, being genetically different, can thus be seen as unequal on a very basic biological level.

But there are scientific, as well as political, objections to an extreme "nature" viewpoint. Essentially, this model implies that our behaviors are all aimed at maximizing our reproductive success. It can even be seen as implying that cultural variations on these behaviors have evolved for that reason. Some of the more popular versions of this idea assume that people, in performing some behavior, are at some level still aware of the biological advantage that may have selected for the behavior in the first place. But not all cultural behaviors and ideas are aimed at reproductive success. Polyandry, for example (see Chapter 10), is hardly the best method for passing on a maximum number of one's genes. Rather, there are important and complex *cultural* reasons for this variation on the family model.

To give another example, journalist Robert Wright, in his book *The Moral Animal,* posits that infanticide may be the result of a "mental

sociobiology The scientific study that examines evolutionary explanations for social behaviors within species.

evolutionary psychology A synonym for sociobiology.

behavioral ecology A synonym for sociobiology.

organ that implicitly calculates when killing a newborn will maximize genetic fitness." In noncultural creatures, this may be the case. Lions kill biologically unrelated offspring so they can mate with lionesses and produce cubs that will inherit their genes. But in humans infanticide is not always done with *this* calculus anywhere in mind. People kill infants to maximize *something,* and so clearly the potential to kill one's offspring is there, but what's maximized is not always, and maybe never, one's genetic fitness. For example, the Yąnomamö of Brazil and Venezuela traditionally killed female infants. The reason was their emphasis on male warriors. Because of tension and competition among Yąnomamö villages, the very survival of each village depended on the ability to defend and conduct offensive war, which was a vehicle for procuring land for farming and hunting. So women had to give to their husbands and their villages new potential warriors, and a first-born daughter or the second of two daughters born in a row was commonly killed. The benefit was symbolic. In fact, it was actually counter-productive genetically, since Yąnomamö villages often had, as a result, a shortage of marriageable females, and so another reason to go to war was to steal women to provide wives. The behavior was important, and it was *culturally* selected for, but there's no logic in thinking it evolved in any biological sense.

Can these two extreme views be reconciled? In fact, I've already discussed two examples at length in Chapter 7: marriage and the incest taboo. We may come "preprogrammed" with some general behavioral themes or potentials—such as the attraction and bonding between males and females and the avoidance of mating with immediate family members. These may, in our evolutionary past, have been so important adaptively (in maximizing reproductive potential) that they channeled and placed strict limitations on our behavior. But then the web of relationships that makes up a cultural system provides the motivating factor for how specific versions of those themes are expressed and explains the specific function of those expressions. Culture, as in the case of inbred ancient Egyptian royalty, can reverse the behavioral norm. But these cultural expressions may still be seen—in all their rich diversity—as variations on behavioral themes that were selected for before we became the cultural primate. In this way, biology and cultural systems interact.

Altruism Revisited

Now, what about Skutnik, Delaney, and Imel? Is this model applicable to their deeds of heroism? Perhaps the *fact* that they were able to spontaneously place their own lives at risk to help fellow species members is based on some ancient biological program similar to the noncultural one that programs individuals in other species to act as sentinels for their group or to defend their young. But those behaviors evolved to

CONTEMPORARY ISSUES

Are Humans Naturally Violent?

Perhaps the most common question regarding a biological basis for our species' behavior concerns violence. A brief glance at human history—or simply a look at today's newspaper—could easily convince you that the answer to the above question must be yes. Although most people probably go through their entire lives without committing a truly violent act, the frequency of human violence and the intensity of some violent acts—from individual murders to the genocide of millions—certainly make it seem reasonable that aggression is part of our species' behavioral repertoire. Although most of us can suppress or rechannel our aggressive tendencies, those tendencies can, under sometimes inexplicable circumstances, be expressed. The biological basis for violence has been the premise of numerous popular and even scientific works, perhaps the most famous (or infamous) of which were *African Genesis* (1961) and *The Territorial Imperative* (1966), both written by playwright-turned-amateur-anthropologist Robert Ardrey. They are better written than most examples of the genre, but their arguments are typical.

Based on the accepted fact that humans are the products of an evolutionary history, Ardrey claims that the violent acts humans commit toward one another can be traced to our descent from apes that were "armed killers"—that is, our australopithecine ancestors whom he characterizes as roaming the savannas of Africa with weapons, killing other animals for food and, on occasion, killing one another in defense of their territories. An instinct for violence is thus, he said, in our genes, and it is expressed by war and other aggressive acts that seem at times to have

become a hallmark of our species. Indeed, Ardrey claims that war, territoriality, and competition have led to the great accomplishments of civilization but that, at the same time, "civilization is a compensatory consequence of our killing imperative; the one could not exist without the other." This is because civilization is also a natural result of evolution that acts to sublimate and inhibit our "inherent talent for disorder."

As further evidence of the instinctive nature of human aggressiveness, Ardrey offers the observation that we *also* possess instinctive behaviors that seek to limit aggression, much like the submissive behavior of dogs and wolves or the threat gestures of some nonhuman primates—behaviors that make the point of showing who's boss without bloodshed. A good example is "that innate aggressor, the athlete . . . [who] accepts and absorbs the rules and regulations of his sport without, in many cases, benefit of a registerable IQ." Aggression, competition, and violence are so much a part of our biology, says Ardrey, that we can't do without them, so we also have evolved ways of inhibiting them to keep "within the bounds of danger." Oftentimes, however—whether in athletic competition or the waging of war—we go well beyond those bounds. So, by such arguments, violence is a natural behavior because it makes Darwinian sense—having been selected for because it conferred such a powerful reproductive advantage for early hominids that it became part of our species' behavioral repertoire.

Are we biologically capable of violence? Of course; humans commit violent acts. Might violence have a specific biological component?

Scientists have demonstrated correlations between tendencies toward violence in some individuals and imbalances in important brain chemicals. But is violence something we have inherited from our evolutionary past because it was naturally selected for and still makes sense in terms of enhancing one's reproductive success? We have already discussed this issue with regard to other human behavioral themes, but let's look specifically at this one. It is an important issue, and arguments such as Ardrey's can be quite persuasive.

The first problem with Ardrey's idea is that he lumps diverse acts together under one category. Killing something for food—which he claimed our remote savanna ancestors did, and which is an aggressive act—is *not* necessarily the same as the planned genocide of other members of one's species because of ethnic, religious, or political differences. A hunting instinct has very different origins, immediate motives, and functions from conscious and planned murder.

Even if we could consider all examples of human aggression as the same, there is no evidence that the australopithecines were "armed killers" (and the evidence was slim when Ardrey was writing). They did not make stone tools, there is no evidence of other tools (much less weapons as Ardrey claims), and if they ate any meat, they scavenged it. Nor is there evidence of any territorial homicide.

Second, such ideas assume that even if a connection existed between a behavior and reproductive success, that connection has existed over the millions of years the behavior was passed along in our evolution and still exists now. As we discussed with the issue of infanticide or the more benign practice of polyandry, there are presumably *reasons* for these behaviors, but the reasons may have nothing to do

with reproductive success. They can be explained as parts of cultural systems, and both their functions and the motives underlying them may have nothing to do with reproduction. In fact, they can be counterproductive in this regard. Certainly murder seldom serves to promote the passing on of one's genes.

Throughout our evolutionary history and at any point in that history, biology and culture have interacted in complex ways. But seeking to explain specific cultural phenomena as the result of naturally selected behaviors that maximize reproductive success both oversimplifies the complexity of natural selection and minimizes the nature of cultural systems and the power of cultural motivations.

Acts of aggression expressed by human beings need to be examined and dealt with as cultural phenomena. We may have the biological potential to commit violent acts against members of our species, and the basis for that potential may lie within some basic instincts— unsurprising and uncontroversial things like self-preservation or protection of family members. But these acts (except for those clearly the result of neurological or neurochemical defects) are triggered by cultural ideas and ideals. They are responses of human beings as members of cultural systems—as individuals or groups of individuals interpreting and responding to their world and worldview. As a result, we gain nothing by oversimplifying the source of human violence (since the reasons for violence are embedded deep within cultural systems) nor by adopting some fatalistic, pessimistic viewpoint that all violent acts are expressions of some ancient genetic program that we're stuck with.

promote the passing on of one's genes, even if they are in the body of a related individual. The three people mentioned didn't even know the people whose lives they tried to save.

Maybe, as with the case in the kibbutzim (see Chapter 7), culture has fooled Mother Nature. Those three heroes may have been among those who take seriously the cultural idea that we're all brothers and sisters or that we should treat others as we would be treated. Naturally, none of them felt the same about all people, but their belief in a moral abstraction may have been enough to trigger an altruistic response and lead to what, by adaptive criteria, were irrational acts—but acts full of positive cultural meaning.

SUMMARY

Culture consists of both ideas and behaviors. One area of debate within anthropology focuses on the direction of the influence between the two. Some feel that behaviors give rise to and guide ideas; others say that ideas give rise to and guide behaviors. An examination of cultural phenomena shows that the influence is in both directions. Practical behaviors become translated into ideas that become part of integrated, holistic cultural systems. Ideas then influence behaviors, since behaviors must meet practical needs as well as remain consistent with and help maintain the cultural system itself. This mutual influence can be demonstrated more persuasively when entire cultural systems (or at least large portions of them) are examined.

A long-standing question in anthropology and other human-oriented disciplines relates to the relative influences of biology and culture on human behavior patterns. As with the issue

above, there have been two extreme views. One claims that culture creates minor modifications in some biologically based and naturally selected-for behaviors. The opposite view says that biology has little or no real influence and that human behaviors are entirely cultural. Again, examining behaviors seems to show a complex interaction between biology and culture. While the immediate motivation for and function of our behavior patterns relate to their place within our cultural systems, those general patterns themselves may have been selected for in our precultural stage because they conferred an adaptive—that is, a reproductive—advantage. Variations in behavior patterns such as marriage, incest taboo, and language are explained by variations in cultural systems. That there *is* marriage, incest avoidance, and the ability to produce symbolic language have, at their base, a biological explanation.

QUESTIONS FOR FURTHER THOUGHT

1. Can you think of another set of dietary laws that might be examined using the model from this chapter? How about the Hindu prohibition against eating cows?

2. Some extreme acts of violence in the world today—such as the 9/11 attacks and suicide bombings in the Middle East—force us to look again at the question of innate human violence. These acts seem to defy what is perhaps the *most* innate human behavior—self-preservation. Analyze these behaviors in light of this chapter's discussion.

NOTES, REFERENCES, AND READINGS

The debate over the direction of influence between ideas and behaviors in culture is discussed in Marvin Harris's book *Theories of Culture in Postmodern Times,* in which, among other things, he evaluates an extreme nature position on the influence of biology.

Mary Douglas's model of cultural analysis can be found in her *Purity and Danger: An Analysis of Concepts of Pollution and Taboo.* The discussion here is from her chapter "The Abominations of Leviticus." Marvin Harris's ideas on cultural materialism are detailed in his technical *Cultural Materialism: The Struggle for a Science of Culture* and more entertainingly in *Cows, Pigs, Wars, and Witches: The Riddles of Culture* and *Cannibals and Kings: The Origins of Cultures.* The quotes I use are from page 5 of *Cows, Pigs, Wars, and Witches* and pages 202 and 206 of *Cannibals and Kings.*

For more information about the Dani, see Karl Heider's *Grand Valley Dani: Peaceful Warriors.* Be sure to see Robert Gardner's movie *Dead Birds,* which is available through a number of academic film rental organizations. The story of the Fore and kuru is detailed in one of the best examples of holistic anthropology available, Shirley Lindenbaum's *Kuru Sorcery: Disease and Danger in the New Guinea Highlands.* The quote I used is from page 22. A more recent piece, which also talks interestingly about some aspects of scientific research, is "Fieldwork in the South Fore: The Process of Ethnographic Inquiry,"

by Robert Glasse and Shirley Lindenbaum. A more up-to-date discussion of kuru, related diseases, and prion proteins (with a graphic description of Fore cannibalism) is *Deadly Feasts,* by Pulitzer Prize–winning author Richard Rhodes.

Still a good book on the Darwinian basis of animal behavior, and the book that started the modern nature-nurture controversy through its application of sociobiological ideas to human behavior, is Edward O. Wilson's *Sociobiology: The New Synthesis.* A collection of works on all sides of the debate, and on the debate itself, is Arthur Caplan's *The Sociobiology Debate,* which is now out of print but worth looking for. A new collection on all aspects of human behavioral evolution is *The Biological Basis of Human Behavior: A Critical Review,* by Robert Sussman. Robert Wright's recent argument for a biological basis for specific human behaviors is *The Moral Animal: Evolutionary Psychology and Everyday Life.*

For a different interpretation of some altruistic-looking behavior among animals, see "Selfish Sentinels," by Daniel Blumstein, in the June 4, 1999, issue of *Science,* page 1633.

For an extreme nature, or biological determinist, point of view on human violence, see *African Genesis* and *The Territorial Imperative,* both by Robert Ardrey. The quotes used in the "Contemporary Issues" box are from pages 355 and 359 of the former and page 317 of the latter.

15

ANTHROPOLOGY IN TODAY'S WORLD

Problems and Contributions

CHAPTER CONTENTS   Change in the Modern World • Applying Anthropology • The Human Species Today • The Human Species in the Future • Contemporary Issues: What Kinds of Careers Are There in Anthropology? • Questions for Further Thought • Notes, References, and Readings

Anthropology is often seen as dealing with the past or with so-called exotic cultures. But as you should understand by now, it deals very much with the present, with one's own culture, and with the global "village" our world has become.

The societies we have touched on in this book have, of course, changed since anthropologists first visited and described them. Those that remain are all very much a part of our global society with all its benefits and problems, and anthropology not only studies ongoing changes in them but also plays a part in helping societies through such changes. There are other ways in which anthropology may be applied as well, as we will discuss in this chapter.

Because anthropology studies the human species as a whole, we may legitimately ask where our species is now and where it might go in the future.

AS YOU READ, CONSIDER THE FOLLOWING QUESTIONS:

1. What has happened to some of the societies we've studied in this book?

2. How can anthropological knowledge be applied to modern concerns, such as overpopulation and the depletion of natural resources?

3. What is the status of our species today, and what can we say about our species' future?

CHANGE IN THE MODERN WORLD

Although culture change, as described in Chapter 13, may be the norm, it can present problems, especially during the process of acculturation or when a society is trying to realign and maintain its system in the face of change. Such situations are, of course, more common as our world becomes effectively smaller. Let's look at recent changes in some of the societies we've discussed as just a few representative examples.

The Hutterites

In the summer of 1983, ten years after my first visit to two Canadian Hutterite Bruderhofs, I went to two American Bruderhofs, and the differences I perceived between the Canadian and American Hutterites—and the difference of a decade—were striking.

It had been said, and it was my impression (although based on a small sample), that the American Hutterites tended to be a little less open and a little more suspicious of outsiders than those in Canada. This may be in part because during World War I many U.S. Hutterites who resisted the military draft because of their pacifist beliefs were jailed as draft resisters. In fact, two Hutterites died in prison as a result of maltreatment. In addition, the Hutterites felt that how their colonies were taxed in the United States was unfair. As a result, most Hutterites moved to Canada, where they were not drafted and where some tax arrangements were made. (Since then, the United States has made similar accommodations. About 29 percent of all Hutterite colonies are now in the United States.)

The modern world has brought changes to the Hutterite way of life. The colonies depend on the income acquired from the sale of produce and, to a lesser extent, handmade goods and services such as the repair of farm equipment. Hutterites must be, and are, well versed in the mainstream market system. That system, however, is becoming increasingly complex, as is farming and the technologies needed to support it. As a result, the Hutterites require more information, enough to warrant changing their educational practices.

Until recently, Hutterite youths received standard schooling within the colony from an outside licensed teacher until they were old enough to legally drop out. With the need for more education, Hutterites now go to school through grade twelve. This need, in turn, has led to a desire to have their own licensed teachers. Some young people are also acquiring vocational degrees as well as college degrees in some of the technological skills required to maintain the colonies' self-sufficiency.

At the same time, the Hutterites must try even harder to keep the outside world from influencing their young people too much and threatening the very continuation of their culture. The young man who became my informant had, in fact, left the colony for a time to attend college. He had no plans to return following graduation but found himself unable to adapt to the kind of individualized existence found on the outside and missed the security of colony life. After a few years he returned. His sister, however, had left and married a non-Hutterite. One of his brothers had also left, and a second brother, whom I met—with styled hair, jeans instead of homemade pants, and Nike running shoes—struck me as at least a potential candidate for leaving. Even the young man himself, although he had returned, married, and had a son, was different from other Hutterites (Figure 15.1). He had an extensive library that reflected his continued interest in worldly matters outside the concerns of most colony members. A Bible and a few works by Hutterites are the usual extent of a member's reading material.

Because keeping young people in the colony means the survival of the culture, the Hutterites were reluctant to talk about how many people had left. Although I could get no hard data, I had the distinct impression that the case of this one family was not unusual. After over

400 years of successfully maintaining their separation *from* the world while still being *in* it, they are now confronting a situation where that kind of separation seems impossible. On their solution to this problem rests their very future.

One approach—and, in a way, one they have always used—is to let in just enough of the outside world to maintain the financial success that sustains their independence and to keep their young people from feeling too out of touch and different from mainstream culture. Sending some young people to college is part of this approach. And, recently, a group of Hutterite high schoolers in Manitoba created a Web site with extensive data about the lives, history, and beliefs of the society. There is a saying in anthropology that cultures change just enough so they don't have to change profoundly. That seems true of the Hutterites and is, I think, along with their devout religious beliefs, a key to their longevity.

The Dani

By contrast, the Dani have not had the luxury of exercising much control over changes in their society. By the time Karl Heider visited the area in 1970, the Indonesian government had stopped the warfare, and there was, in their territory, an army and police post (inside which the Dani were not permitted to carry their weapons), a first aid station, a landing field, a Catholic mission, a school, and even tourists. Today, a major road, the Trans-Irian Highway, connects the north and south coasts of the country, running through the Grand Valley town of Wamena. That town, not even mentioned on the earliest

FIGURE 15.2
A Dani man in traditional dress tries to warm himself in the evening chill amidst the shops and traffic of modern Wamena, West Papua.

maps of the region, now has a population of 10,000 (Figure 15.2). Mining and logging companies are changing the face of much of the landscape. Although the Dani try to cling to old ways—some still dress in the traditional style—they are now involved in trading rice, cattle, fish, and coffee; leading tourists on treks; selling, as Heider puts it, "garish tourist artifacts"; and worshiping at Christian churches. A Dani Baptist deacon is quoted as telling his congregation, "There is no fighting. You don't have to hunt or garden. Everything good comes to you." That remains to be seen.

The San

The San have experienced what anthropologist Richard Lee calls "directed social change." In 1960 the San of Namibia, then a country under the control of South Africa, were settled in an area set aside for them as part of South Africa's apartheid (racial separation) policy. Some of the men worked on road gangs or in workshops, but many were unemployed—a concept that would have made no sense to them just a few years before. Women spent their time with household chores, and the children were supposed to go to school, but absenteeism was high. Everyone was fed by the government. Boredom, alcoholism (alcohol was an important item the government made available in their stores), and violence increased.

Starting in 1966 some native peoples of Namibia began fighting for independence from South Africa under the South-West African People's Organization (SWAPO). To combat SWAPO, the South African government not only sent in its own troops but also recruited locals, including the San (Figure 15.3). Induced by good wages (up to $500 a month), the San enlisted in large numbers for a war that few really understood and that involved the killing of an "enemy" made up of some of their fellow Namibians. Raids were even made over the border into neighboring Angola. Besides the obvious dangers of warfare and the further divisions among the indigenous peoples, the pouring of large sums of money into the lives of the San led to social stratification of a once-egalitarian people, with the consequent resentments and conflicts. Alcoholism and violence further increased. In one two-year period (1978–1980), Lee recorded seven homicides—a huge number for a people who had been relatively peaceful for years.

Namibia's attainment of independence in 1990 was initially a mixed blessing for the San, according to Lee. Many former soldiers were back home with nothing to do. Once-protected San land was

FIGURE 15.3
San soldiers.

being eyed enviously by cattle herders, many of whom moved onto the land before legal restrictions were enacted (those restrictions resulted from the work of a foundation set up by anthropologists and an indigenous farmer's cooperative and union). Additional problems, however, came from within, as this traditionally egalitarian society had to elect leaders, own and divide land, and speak as a whole people rather than as small family groups. Clearly, gaining independence after thirty years of colonialism proved problematic. Lee, however, says the San's new empowerment is "a modest basis for optimism." More on the San in a bit.

There are many other examples of change as the rich diversity of the world's peoples and their cultures encounter the global village, global economy, and global ecosystem our planet is fast becoming. What role can anthropology take in the modern world?

APPLYING ANTHROPOLOGY

There is nothing wrong, of course, with knowledge for its own sake, and anthropology has inarguably added to our understanding of our species through its holistic scientific studies. Some of this understanding might be merely interesting, but much of it can be applied to helping societies—including ours—cope in today's complex, fast-changing world.

Anthropology has shown how science—often stereotyped as being concerned only with chemicals, heavenly bodies, and atoms—can be applied to an understanding of the evolution and nature of human behavior. As we confront differences in beliefs and behaviors among societies, as well as disturbing increases in anomalous behaviors—violence, to name an obvious example—such potential understanding is of great importance.

The nature of relations between the sexes and the multitude of ideas and attitudes regarding gender are a clear focus of anthropology's contribution. We now have an understanding of the difference between sex and gender, the relationship between those two categories, and the cultural variations that exist. We can shed some light on what have often been considered deviations from normal sexual and gender behavior and place them in cultural contexts, the better, perhaps, to address issues of sexual discrimination and abuse.

Anthropology has shed light on health issues, including the nature and causes of variation in disease frequency among societies and the different ways societies categorize and think about diseases. The application of this understanding to AIDS—its origin, spread, and attitudes about its victims in different societies—is an obvious example. By comparing the health of modern industrial peoples with that of foragers, or even extinct populations, we may even be able to suggest some ways we could alter our lifestyles for better health.

Forensic anthropology is a growing specialty. Its techniques have been applied to solving crimes, identifying accident victims, and disclosing war crimes.

In a broad perspective, anthropology has provided insight into historical trends, giving us the potential to make general predictions about what circumstances might lead to what results. The archaeological record, for example, has shown why farming originated and what benefits and problems resulted from that change in subsistence. The more we understand the past, the better we can understand the present and guide the future.

With the world's societies in increasing interaction with one another, anthropology offers a perspective with both ethical and practical applications. Knowing what culture is, how it operates, and why it varies helps us understand—on a profound level—cultures other than our own. Indeed, when we better understand our *own* culture from an anthropological perspective, we better understand others. This has obvious humanistic relevance, but it is also important from a practical perspective. Conducting international business, for example, requires that businesspeople have an understanding of and sensitivity to cultural differences, particularly as they relate to their own cultures. Multinational corporations frequently hire anthropologists as consultants on such matters.

One of anthropology's most important contributions has been its investigation of the nature of biological diversity and the cultural phenomenon of racial classification. Understanding what race is—and what it is not—goes a long way toward eventually addressing burdening social problems caused by a lack of such understanding.

As the increasing world population puts further pressure on resources and our ability to govern and serve our peoples, anthropology can aid in the dissemination of family planning information and technologies. For many cultures, the idea of limiting one's family is unnatural, even if it might make sense. Understanding another society's traditional views on this matter can be vital to introducing its people to relevant information and techniques.

In a world where conflict and war are so commonplace that we are almost inured to it, understanding the cultural reasons for violent conflict is essential. Wars are fought for a multitude of reasons. To be able to discern the reasons for a specific conflict is a requirement for dealing with and, hopefully, ending that conflict with negotiation rather than with more violence.

Finally, although change is inevitable and no society is immune to change, most societies feel that they should have some say in the speed, direction, and nature of the changes affecting them. This, of course, is not always the case. Some dominant cultures deny subservient cultures any voice in what happens to them. In other cases, imposed change may be well meaning but misguided due to a lack of knowledge about the other culture and, thus, about the potential results of change. Anthropology can make a tremendous contribution by using its understanding of other peoples to help give them a voice and to help predict and guide changes as they take place. To finish bringing the story of the San up to date, let's use them as an example.

As changes to the San's way of life were imposed from the outside and were taking place within San society, the simple accumulation of basic anthropological knowledge was important. Without documentation and basic data about the indigenous culture, members of the outside cultures were unable to help or understand the San.

Some anthropologists became advocates for the rights of these (and other) peoples. The Nyae Nyae Development Foundation of Namibia was founded in 1998, and is still in operation, to lobby nationally and internationally to preserve land rights for the San and to raise funds for that purpose. Much of its work involves communicating information about the San to relevant agencies.

Other anthropological researchers focused on helping the San themselves to apply their traditional ideas to the new situations confronting them. Having, in a way, a dual perspective—as members of a multicultural, international, industrial society and as scientists with a holistic knowledge of their subjects—anthropologists are uniquely able to serve as advocates. Translation into and from indigenous languages is just one of many services anthropologists provide. Their dual cultural perspective enables them to be, perhaps, more accurate than other translators.

Anthropologist and filmmaker John Marshall, who began documenting the lives of the San in the 1950s, notes that the anthropologist also plays the role of listener or "cultural therapist" as the people themselves discuss and try to confront change. Much like some psychological analysts, the anthropologist can, without interfering or coercing, suggest different perspectives and give the people in question what is perhaps their most powerful weapon—knowledge.

The application of anthropology in these ways is not without its controversies (see the "Contemporary Issues" box in Chapter 13). But the application of anthropological knowledge in today's world attracts many people to the discipline and has become a growing specialty within the field. (See the "Contemporary Issues" box in this chapter.)

THE HUMAN SPECIES TODAY

There are two general criteria for evaluating the success of a biological species. One, obviously, is reproductive success. Reproductive success is, after all, the measure of species adaptation and the factor that drives natural selection. The second criterion is longevity—how long the species has maintained an adaptive fitness that allows it the chance to perpetuate itself.

In strict numerical terms, we are clearly reproductively successful. Our population is over 7 billion and counting. We're projected to reach 9.3 billion by 2050. But there's another variable in reproductive success besides sheer numbers. A species can be *too* reproductively successful and then risks running out of space and resources, as well as undermining those behaviors that have evolved to maintain social order among its members. Successful species have mechanisms for limiting their total population relative to existing environmental conditions. Sometimes this is simply a matter of an increased death rate as a result of some abnormal environmental variable—lack of food or water, a climate that is too hot or too cold, and so on. Sometimes it's more subtle, as when environmental disruptions lead to interruptions in mating behavior or reproductive physiology.

But our species manipulates environmental variables through our intelligence and culture. We can protect ourselves from the elements, find alternative sources of food, migrate to new areas, and deal with some injuries, illnesses, and handicaps in ways that eliminate them as impediments to reproduction. These steps all sound good on the surface—but they have consequences that, even today, we sometimes do not fully appreciate. First, of course, we run the risk of producing too many people for the resources at hand. It can be convincingly argued that we have already done this. True, there are many people in the world today for whom the necessities of life are readily and easily available. Indeed, many resources go to waste in affluent societies. But there are even more people on this planet who do not receive adequate food, water, and shelter. In some cases, of course, this is due to political situations rather than lack of availability. After all, there are homeless and underfed people in the wealthiest of nations. But, in broad perspective, if large numbers of the species do *not* have access to adequate resources, those resources are effectively *not* available. If there's not enough to go around, for whatever reason, we've run out. In ecological terms, we've reached our **carrying capacity**.

The second consequence is that each time we manipulate the environment in the face of depleted resources and increased population, we have to intensify that manipulation—hunt more animals, farm more land, use more water, divert sources of water to new locations, use more wood and other raw materials to construct more shelters, and so on. Over time the environment is affected and can be irrevocably disrupted with the result that alternative resources and space are increasingly less available. And with reduced availability, we have greater need to further intensify our manipulation of the environment. Eventually, something has to give.

This consideration brings up the matter of species longevity. The relationship between a species' evolutionary health and how long it has been around is, of course, relative to the nature of the species. For some species of bacteria, with a generation turnover time of one hour, a short

carrying capacity The maximum population of a species allowed by existing environmental conditions and resources.

tenure on earth can indicate success. For a large species with a long generation time, a longer time in existence is required to say the species has been successful. By the most liberal of definitions (see Chapter 6), our species is 2 million years old—not a long period for a large mammal with a generation time of decades—so it would be premature to say humans are successful based on the time we've been around.

But even time itself is not a good measure. To be considered adapted, a species must be in some equilibrium with its environment—extracting enough to survive but not extracting so much that it depletes the resources it needs and thus, in the end, adversely affects itself. Since we began farming, we have increasingly taken more out of the environment than we have put back. We don't trap solar energy like green plants. We don't provide a food source for other creatures except decomposers like bacteria and fungi, and some of our funerary practices, such as embalming and cremation, even deprive those organisms. Rather, we have altered the natural ecology of much of the planet, including, through our waste products, changing the very chemical makeup of the land, water, and atmosphere. We have brought about the extinction of many species. Indeed, the rate of extinction over the past few hundred years appears to have been more rapid than that during any of the five previous mass extinctions (for example, the one 65 mya that included the dinosaurs). This has led some to refer to the last century or so as the "sixth extinction." While the causes of some previous extinctions are still being debated, that of the current one is clear—it's us.

So, one could conclude that—although many of us live relatively healthy, safe lives with adequate nutrition, water, and shelter—the species as a whole is not in the best state of health. What can we say about the prognosis?

THE HUMAN SPECIES IN THE FUTURE

If we are to extrapolate into the future, we must (as we noted in Chapter 13) understand the nature of change, and we must appreciate the inevitability of change. To think about change in a broad perspective, we must understand the concepts of contingency and constraint.

In the early 1980s, I wrote the following:

> Considering our current situation, we can see ourselves standing on the edge of a lush Eden of scientific, technological, medical, and social advances that make all our lives longer and happier. Or we might be poised on the edge of a cliff, below us a deadly cauldron—a polluted, violent, nuclear nightmare.

When I wrote that, tensions between the former Soviet Union and the United States were high. There was serious talk of a global nuclear war—and the stockpiles of nuclear weapons in some half-dozen countries were the equivalent of 20 billion tons of TNT, about 1.6 million times the power of the bomb that destroyed Hiroshima in 1945. At my university, there was a faculty-student group whose focus was to educate themselves and others about the threat of and results from nuclear war. Our "bible" was Jonathan Schell's *The Fate of the Earth,* a book that painted a grim picture of the world after a nuclear conflict as "a republic of insects and grass," two groups of organisms that seem to be little affected by nuclear radiation. Other problems, of course, existed, but in the mid-1980s they seemed to pale before the vision of a world devastated by nuclear war. We dreamt, as did Schell in his book, of how different the world would be if that threat, which we had lived with for nearly forty years, could be lifted. At the time, it seemed like no more than a dream.

A decade later, I had a glimpse of what that world was like. In the early 1990s the Soviet Union collapsed and with it the imminent sense of worldwide nuclear holocaust—what we used to term the "unthinkable," because, truly, it was impossible to conceive of, there being no prior experience with anything of that magnitude. We have now, of course, replaced it with the "thinkable"—that is, the possibility that any of a number of current violent conflicts and tensions could result in the localized use of nuclear arms. For that, because of Hiroshima and Nagasaki, we do have a reference point. And such a limited conflict could easily spread.

And even if nuclear weapons are not part of the picture, we are still beset with local but sometimes terribly bloody wars. As I write in the winter of 2012–2013, there conflicts in Sudan, Somalia, Chad, Syria, Mali, Pakistan, and of course, Iraq and Afghanistan.

Although environmental problems—pollution, extinction, destruction of the rain forests, and global climate change (so-called global warming)—are still very much with us and have, in fact, gotten worse, they have been joined by a newly realized problem. As our population expands and as we move into new areas—especially in the tropics—we are coming into greater contact with other species that carry diseases to which they are immune but that prove deadly to us. HIV, the virus that causes AIDS, came from a West African population of chimpanzees that had evolved the ability to carry the virus without being adversely affected. Another strain of HIV came to humans from a species of African monkey. AIDS is the leading cause of death in sub-Saharan Africa, where in 2009 there were 22.5 million people with HIV/AIDS. The disease is spreading rapidly, especially in populous countries such as India, China, and Brazil. Hanta virus from rodents, ebola virus from an as-yet-unknown source, and campylobacter, a bacterium from chickens, are other examples of pathogens that have recently jumped from other species to ours with serious consequences. We discussed in Chapter 14 still another example of an **emerging disease,** the prion protein disorders, which are also transmitted between species.

emerging disease Any of a group of diseases, of various causes, that have newly appeared or are rapidly expanding their range in the human species.

The point is that, even in the mid-1980s, these specific changes were largely unforeseen. We might have assumed, based on twentieth-century history and facts about the possession of nuclear weapons, that *if* the Soviet Union collapsed the imminent threat of all-out nuclear war would be ended. But who could have guessed with any certainty that the Soviet Union would collapse and that conflict would flare up among the former Soviet-controlled countries and the former Soviet republics? Could we have predicted that within a few years a number of deadly diseases would emerge, one of which is now changing the demographics of a whole continent? Who would have thought that with the threat of nuclear war between the superpowers virtually eliminated, we would face a new worry, terrorism, which could conceivably involve small nuclear weapons?

The reason these things, so familiar to us now, were unpredicted just two decades ago is that history is contingent. That is, each event is dependent on the series of events that preceded it. Historians and evolutionary scientists engage in reconstructing contingent series of events to explain why the world is as it is. But, as Stephen Jay Gould puts it, we explain "in retrospect what could not have been predicted beforehand." A change in any preceding event will change the events that follow, but because so many interacting events are involved, we have little predictive ability to foresee *how* a particular change will alter subsequent events. Thus each specific sequence of events in history is unique and unrepeatable, although, in hindsight, each makes sense.

So, can we say *anything* with confidence about our species' future? Or is history an "anything goes" situation? Are all conceivable paths and outcomes possible?

Despite the contingent nature of history, there are constraints and limitations that lead to general trends. Let's take examples from biological evolution. So far as we know, among the countless millions of species that evolved on this planet, only one small group possesses the consciousness required for complex abstract conceptualizing and a language capable of sharing such concepts. If some past events had been different, a species like ours might not have evolved.

On the other hand, once the basic vertebrate body design appeared, a certain limited set of features evolved independently in three lineages of vertebrates that adapted to an aquatic life—fishes, cetaceans (whales and porpoises), and ichthyosaurs (extinct marine reptiles)—because that basic shape is obviously a very good way to propel a creature through the water. We see here a basic general trend in evolution, although we might still say that trend—the vertebrate body plan—was a unique event.

How may we apply this to the future of the human species? In trying to predict our future, we are clearly limited in making specific forecasts. Look, for example, at how difficult it is for economists to predict exactly what will happen with global monetary trends. Regarding human beings, their psychologies, and their cultural systems—in all

CONTEMPORARY ISSUES

What Kinds of Careers Are There in Anthropology?

If you have found the topics in this book interesting, or even if you are already an anthropology major, you may still be wondering what one can do with a degree in the field. Pursuing a career in something interesting is one thing; putting food on the table and a roof over one's head is something else.

Most working anthropologists do what I do. They have at least a master's degree or, more likely, a doctorate and teach in a college or university while researching and writing. Although a PhD takes at least four additional years of schooling, and often longer, teaching is a career I can heartily recommend.

Even, however, with an advanced degree, there are many other nonacademic careers open to anthropologists. Among these are work in research institutions, government agencies, multinational businesses, consulting firms, social service agencies, environmental organizations, human rights programs, cultural resource management firms, historical commissions, medical examiners' offices, health departments, biomechanics companies, and many more.

What if a bachelor's degree is your goal? Are careers using your anthropology background still available? Absolutely. Many of the organizations listed above have entry-level positions with on-the-job training, often with additional schooling financed by the company, and opportunity for advancement. And because of the breadth of this field, there are applications of anthropological knowledge that we probably haven't thought of. Organizations just need to be shown that the ideas, methods, and conclusions of anthropology can be of value to their activities. Careers using your background are limited only by your imagination.

A great place to get more information and some very practical advice is *Careers in Anthropology*, second edition, by John T. Omohundro.

their rich variety—it seems as if almost anything is possible. And yet the past has shown us trends that do provide us with predictive ability. We know, for example, that despite our intellect and our ability to understand and manipulate our environments and their resources, we are constrained by our biology and by certain biological and ecological laws. The natural resources of the planet are limited. Just as medieval alchemists could not turn lead into gold, we cannot make more basic resources, at least not without using up others. Eventually something will run out. The planet has a carrying capacity for each species, even ours. And we have data, at relatively small scales, for what happens when things do run out. History provides us with many examples of famine and the resultant starvation and war. We might reasonably expect, given our expanding global population and the limitations of the earth's resources, to see these events increase in magnitude.

But the purpose and value of prediction—even if it is limited to general trends with specific events being so contingent as to be unpredictable—is not to be able to foretell doom and destruction. The value of understanding those general trends is to be able to, as the cliché says, learn from the past—if only we pay heed to its lessons and try to apply them.

Knowledge, in the modern world, is accumulating at a frustrating rate. It is becoming more and more difficult to stay current in one's own field, let alone be minimally conversant even in related fields. We are seeing an increasing specialization in scientific and other scholarly disciplines. Nonetheless, we must maintain an appreciation for the holistic perspective and encourage holistic and multidisciplinary approaches—because the real world doesn't divide itself into nice, neat categories. In this regard, anthropology—with us as its subject and holism as its central principle—can be in the forefront as we face the challenges at the edge of the future.

QUESTIONS FOR FURTHER THOUGHT

1. Focus on some current problematic situation in the world and think about how, to what extent, or even *if* anthropology could contribute to the solution of that situation.

2. Do you agree that, objectively, our species is not in particularly good health? If so, what, if anything, do you think we can do about it? If not, why not?

3. Finally, consider how the knowledge of anthropology you now have has changed your view of the world. Do you see the world at all differently? Do you think this knowledge will be useful even in an occupation not specifically related to anthropology? If so, in what way(s)?

NOTES, REFERENCES, AND READINGS

Have a look at the Hutterites's Web site, www .hutterites.org.

For an idea, with pictures, about how the Dani and their country have changed over the last decades, see the third edition of Karl Heider's *Grand Valley Dani* and three articles in *National Geographic:* "Netherlands New Guinea" (May 1962), by John Scofield; "Two Worlds, Time Apart: Indonesia" (January 1989), by Arthur Zich; and "Irian Jaya" (February 1996), by Thomas O'Neill. The quote from the Dani deacon is from page 24 of the last article. For an account of the first outside contact with the Dani, see *Lost in Shangri-La* by Mitchell Zuckoff. It's a great adventure story.

Richard Lee's *The Dobe Ju/'hoansi*, third edition, has several chapters on the recent changes to beset the San and includes additional information about how anthropologists are offering help. And see www .kalaharipeoples.net for updates on the San.

A good collection of articles about applications of anthropology is *Applying Anthropology: An Introductory Reader*, eighth edition, edited by Aaron Podolefsky and Peter Brown.

For introductions to applied anthropology as a new subfield within the discipline see *Applied Anthropology: A Practical Guide*, by Erve Chambers, and *Applied Anthropology: An Introduction*, by John van Willigen. An up-to-date and timely discussion of the nature, importance, and application of anthropology and its holistic approach is in Marvin Harris's *Theories of Culture in Postmodern Times.*

For an introduction of cultural anthropology with a specifically global or world-system approach, try *Cultural Anthropology,* sixth edition, by Emily A. Schultz and Robert H. Lavenda.

On the idea of the "sixth extinction," see Richard Leakey and Roger Lewin's book of that name. The story of humankind's changing relationship with the environment is covered in *Dominion: Can Nature and Culture Co-exist?* by Niles Eldredge.

The threat of a global nuclear war is greater than it has been in twenty-three years according to the Doomsday Clock (www.thebulletin.org), where it is now five minutes to midnight. This makes all the more frightening and relevant Jonathan Schell's *The Fate of the Earth.*

On emerging diseases, see *Virus X,* by Frank Ryan, and *Viral Sex: The Nature of AIDS,* by Jaap Goudsmit.

On the topic of global warming, see the movie *An Inconvenient Truth,* or read Al Gore's *An Inconvenient Truth: The Planetary Emergency of Global Warming and What We Can Do about It.* For an even broader view, try *Worldchanging: A User's Guide for the 21st Century,* edited by Alex Steffen.

In this chapter, I related my view as to the relative importance and interaction of contingency and constraints in evolution and history. This topic, however, is still a matter of intense debate, with the major opponents being Stephen Jay Gould for contingency and Simon Conway Morris for constraints. Gould's description of contingency in evolutionary history is nicely covered in an article called "Eight Little Piggies" in his book by the same name. The quote is from page 77. Detailed arguments in the debate are in Gould's *Wonderful Life* and Conway Morris's *The Crucible of Creation,* and nice summaries of their points of view are in the December 1998–January 1999 issue of *Natural History,* "Showdown on the Burgess Shale."

Glossary

acculturation Rapid diffusion of cultural items either by choice of the receiving society or by force from a more dominant society.

adapted When an organism has physical traits and behaviors that allow it to survive in a particular environment.

age sets A social unit made up of persons of approximately the same age.

agriculture Farming using animal or mechanical labor and complex technologies.

alloparenting shared care and provisioning of the young by other group members.

altruism Acting to benefit others while disregarding one's own welfare.

animistic The belief in supernatural powers of people, animals, places, and objects.

anthropology The holistic, scientific study of humankind.

arbitrary Here, the fact that the features of human **languages** bear no direct relationship to their meanings but are agreed-on symbols.

arboreal Adapted to life in the trees.

archaeology The subfield of anthropology that recovers evidence of the human cultural past and reconstructs past cultural systems.

artifact Any object that has been consciously manufactured. Usually refers to human-made objects but now includes some items made by other primates.

artificial selection Selection for reproductive success in plants and animals that is directed by humans. Also called selective breeding.

balanced reciprocity Giving with the expectation of equivalent return. See **generalized reciprocity.**

bands Small autonomous groups, usually associated with **foraging** societies.

behavioral ecology A synonym for **sociobiology.**

belief systems Ideas that are taken on faith and cannot be scientifically tested.

bifacial A stone tool that has been worked on both sides.

bilateral A kinship system in which an individual is a member of both parents' descent lines. See **unilineal.**

biocultural Focusing on the interaction of biology and culture.

biological anthropology The subfield of anthropology that studies humans as a biological species.

biological determinism The idea that human behaviors have a biological basis with minimal influence from culture.

bipedal Walking on two legs.

brachiating Moving using arm-over-arm swinging.

bulb of percussion A convex surface on a flake caused by the force used to split the flake off. Rarely found in a natural break.

carrying capacity The maximum population of a **species** allowed by existing environmental conditions and resources.

caste A system of socioeconomic stratification in which the **strata** are closed and a person's membership is determined at birth.

catastrophism The idea that the history of the earth and its life is accounted for by a series of global catastrophes.

chiefdom A **political organization** made up of groups of interacting units, each of which has a chief, or leader.

chromosome Strands of **DNA** in the nucleus of a cell.

civilization A culture with an agricultural surplus, social stratification, labor specialization, a formal government, rule by power, monumental construction projects, and a system of record keeping.

cladistics A classification system based on order of evolutionary branching.

class A system of socioeconomic stratification in which the **strata** are open and a person may move to a different stratum.

classical evolutionism A synonym for **unilinear evolutionism.**

cline A geographic continuum in the variation of a trait.

codify To arrange systematically. To put into words and other symbols.

cognates Words that are similar in two or more **languages** as a result of common descent.

co-wife resentment Tension among the wives of one man in **polygynous** societies, often caused by the differing statuses of those wives.

cross cousins The children of your father's sisters or mother's brothers.

cultural anthropology The subfield of anthropology that focuses on human cultural behavior and cultural systems and the variation in cultural expression among human groups.

cultural determinism The idea that human behaviors are almost totally the result of learned cultural information, with few or no instinctive responses.

cultural relativity Studying another culture from its point of view without imposing our own cultural views.

culture Ideas and behaviors that are learned and transmitted. Nongenetic means of adaptation.

deduction Suggesting specific data that would be found if a hypothesis were true. Works from the general to the specific. See **induction.**

dependency Here, the period after birth during which offspring require the care of adults to survive.

descent line Nuclear families that are connected over time.

descriptive linguistics The study of the structure of **language** in general and of the specific variations among languages.

diffusion The movement of cultural ideas and artifacts among societies. Cultural borrowing.

diffusionism An outdated concept of cultural evolution that claims major cultural advances were made by a few or a single society and spread from there to all other societies.

discovery The realization and understanding of a set of relationships. An addition to knowledge. See **invention.**

displacement The ability to communicate about things and ideas not immediate in space or time.

diurnal Active during the day.

division of labor The apportioning of a society's jobs to specific individuals, for example, designating men's and women's job roles.

dominance hierarchy Social ranking based on individual differences.

duality of patterning Here, the two levels of human **language:** units of sound and units of meaning that those units of sounds are combined to create.

ecofact An unmodified natural object used as a tool.

ecology The science that studies the network of relationships within environmental systems.

egalitarianism The practice of not recognizing, and even eliminating, differences in social status and wealth.

emerging disease Any of a group of diseases, of various cause, that have newly appeared or are rapidly expanding their range in the human **species.**

endocannibalism The eating of human flesh from members of one's own society.

endocasts Natural or human-made casts of the inside of a skull. The cast reflects the surface of the brain and allows us to study the brains of even extinct species.

endogamy Marriage within a specified unit of people.

estrus In nonhuman mammals, the period of female fertility or the signals indicating this condition.

ethnocentrism Making value judgments about another culture from the perspective of one's own cultural system.

ethnographic analogy Interpreting archaeological data through the observation of analogous activities in existing societies.

ethnographic present Speaking of a society as it was in the past but using the present tense.

ethnography The area of anthropology that describes a cultural system, usually based on fieldwork within a society.

ethnosemantics The study of the meanings of words, especially as they relate to **folk taxonomies.**

evolution   In biology, the idea that **species** change over time and have a common ancestor.

evolutionary psychology   A synonym for **sociobiology.**

exogamy   Marriage outside a specified unit of people.

experimental archaeology   The process of understanding ancient skills and technologies by reproducing them.

extended family   Nuclear families linked by blood, generally ones that inhabit the same location.

fission   Here, the splitting up of a population to form new populations.

folk taxonomy   A system of classification based on the relationships among cultural categories for important items and ideas.

foraging   Another name for the hunter-gatherer subsistence pattern.

forensic anthropology   A subfield of anthropology applied to legal matters. Usually involved in identifying skeletal remains and assessing the time and cause of death.

fossils   Remains of life-forms of the past.

founder effect   Genetic differences between populations produced by the fact that genetically different individuals established (founded) the populations.

gametes   The cells of reproduction, which contain only half the **chromosomes** of a normal cell.

gamete sampling   The genetic change caused when genes are passed to new generations in frequencies different from those of the parental generation.

gender   The culturally defined categories and characteristics of men and women.

gene flow   The exchange of genes among populations through interbreeding.

gene pool   All the **alleles** in a population.

generalized reciprocity   Giving with no expectation of equivalent return. See **balanced reciprocity.**

genes   Technically, those portions of the **DNA** molecule that code for the production of specific **proteins.**

genetic drift   Genetic change based on random changes within a species' **gene pool;** includes **fission** and the **founder effect,** and **gamete sampling.**

glaciers   Massive sheets of ice that expand and move.

grooming   Cleaning the fur of another animal; an activity that, in primates, also promotes social cohesion.

haft   To attach a wooden handle or shaft to a stone or bone point.

hand axe   A **bifacial,** all-purpose stone tool, shaped somewhat like an axe head.

historical archaeology   The **archaeology** of a society that has written records.

historical linguistics   The branch of linguistics that attempts to classify and construct a family tree of languages and to reconstruct extinct languages.

historical particularism   The American school of cultural evolution that rejected any general theory of culture change but believed that each society could be understood only in reference to its particular history.

holistic   Assuming an interrelationship among the parts of a subject.

hominid   Modern humans and African apes and their direct ancestors. The term previously referred to humans and human ancestors only, under a phenetic taxonomy.

horticulture   Farming using human labor and simple tools such as digging sticks and hoes.

hunter-gatherer   A subsistence pattern that relies on naturally occurring sources of food.

hypothesis   A proposed explanation for a natural phenomenon.

incest taboo   A cultural rule that prohibits sexual intercourse or **marriage** between persons defined as being too closely related.

indigenous   Native; refers to a group of people with a long history in a particular area.

induction   The process of developing a general explanation from specific observations. See **deduction.**

industrialism   Sometimes recognized as a subsistence pattern; characterized by a focus on mechanical sources of energy and food production by a small percentage of the population.

infanticide   The killing of infants.

inheritance of acquired characteristics   The incorrect idea that adaptive traits acquired during an organism's lifetime can be passed on to its offspring.

intensive foraging   Hunting and gathering in an environment that provides a very wide range of food resources.

invention   New creations. The application of discovered knowledge. See **discovery.**

kin selection   Promoting the passing on of one's genes by aiding the survival or reproduction of one's close kin.

kinship Your membership in a family and your relationship to other members of that family. May refer to biological ties, but in anthropology usually refers to cultural ties modeled on biological ones.

labor specialization When certain jobs are performed by particular individuals.

language Human communication by means of shared symbols in the form of sounds or representations of sounds.

legal system A set of secular rules governing the behavior of individuals and institutions within a society.

Levallois A tool technology in which uniform flakes are struck from a prepared core.

limbic system A portion of the brain involved in emotions such as fear, rage, and care for the young.

linguistic anthropology The subfield of anthropology that studies language as a human characteristic and attempts to explain the differences among human languages and the relationships between a language and the society that uses it.

magic The use of ritual and paraphernalia to compel or manipulate the supernatural to act in desired ways. See **sorcery.**

market system Where **money** is used for exchange in place of goods and services; it operates on a supply-and-demand basis with a profit motive for suppliers.

marriage A set of cultural rules for bringing together a man and a woman (usually) to create a family unit and for defining their behavior toward one another, their children, and society.

matrilineal A **unilineal** kinship system in which an individual is a member of the mother's **descent line.** See **patrilineal.**

melanin The pigment largely responsible for human skin color.

melanocytes Specialized skin cells that produce the pigment **melanin.**

men's associations A social unit made up of a society's men. Common in highland New Guinea.

microliths Small stone flakes, usually used as part of a larger tool such as a sickle.

money A symbolic representation of wealth. Used for exchange in place of actual products or services.

monogamy A marriage unit made up of one husband and one wife.

monotheistic Refers to a religious system that recognizes a single supernatural being.

morpheme A unit of meaning in a **language.**

Mousterian A toolmaking technology, associated with the European Neandertals, in which flakes were carefully retouched to produce diverse tool types.

mutation Any spontaneous change in the genetic code.

natural selection Evolutionary change based on the differential reproductive success of individuals within a species.

neocortex A portion of the brain involved in conscious thought, spatial reasoning, and sensory perception.

niche The environment of an organism and its adaptive response to that environment.

nocturnal Active at night.

nomadic Refers to societies that move from place to place in search of resources or in response to seasonal fluctuations.

nuclear family The family unit made up of parents and their children.

olfactory Refers to the sense of smell.

opposability The ability to touch the thumb to the tips of the other fingers on the same hand.

ovulation The period when an egg cell matures and is capable of being fertilized.

parallel cousins The children of your father's brothers or your mother's sisters.

pastoralism A subsistence pattern characterized by an emphasis on herding animals.

patrilineal A **unilineal** kinship system in which an individual is a member of the father's **descent line.** See **matrilineal.**

phenetics A classification system based on existing phenotypic features and adaptations.

pheromone A chemical substance secreted by an animal that conveys information and stimulates behavioral responses.

phoneme A unit of a sound in a **language.**

physical anthropology The traditional name for **biological anthropology.**

Pleistocene The geological time period, from 1.6 mya to 10,000 years ago, characterized by a series of advances and retreats of polar and mountain **glaciers.**

political organization The secular, nonkinship means of organizing the interactions within a society and between one society and others.

polyandry A marriage system with one wife and multiple husbands.

polygamy A marriage system that allows multiple spouses. See **polygyny** and **polyandry.**

polygyny A marriage system with one husband and multiple wives.

polytheism A religious system that recognizes multiple supernatural beings—technically, multiple gods.

postpartum sex taboo The practice of prohibiting sex for a certain period of time after a woman gives birth for purposes of limiting the birthrate.

prehensile Having the ability to grasp, especially by wrapping the hand or foot around an object.

prehistoric archaeology Archaeolgy of a society prior to written records.

pressure flake Taking a flake off a core by pushing a wood, bone, or antler tool against the stone.

priest A full-time, trained religious specialist who can interpret the supernatural and petition the supernatural on behalf of humans.

primate A large-brained, mostly tree-dwelling mammal with three-dimensional color vision and grasping hands. Humans are primates.

productivity Here, the ability of human **languages** to generate limitless numbers of meanings.

prognathism The jutting forward of the lower face and jaw area.

protocultural A behavior having most but not all of the characteristics of a cultural behavior.

pseudoscience Scientifically testable ideas that are taken on faith without scientific evidence to support them or even when tested and shown to be false.

quadrupedal Walking on all fours.

races In biology, the same as **subspecies.** In culture, categories that classify and account for human diversity.

racism Judging an individual solely on his or her assigned racial affiliation, based on the assumption that all members of a "race" possess specific characteristics. Prejudice and discrimination based on such a belief.

rank Refers to a society that strives for equal distribution of goods and services through the use of recognized, often temporary, status differences. See **redistribution.**

R-complex (Reptilian complex) A primitive portion of the brain involved in self-preservation behaviors such as mating, aggressiveness, and territoriality.

redistribution The central collection of surplus goods and their dispersal to people in need of them.

reification Translating a complex set of phenomena into a single entity such as a number. IQ test scores are an example.

religion A system of ideas and rules for behavior based on supernatural explanations.

revolution Rapid and extensive culture change generated from within a society.

savannas The open grasslands of the tropics, usually with reference to the plains of Africa.

science The method of inquiry that requires the generation, testing, and acceptance or rejection of hypotheses.

scientific method The formal process of conducting scientific inquiry.

sedentary A human settlement pattern in which people largely stay in one place year-round, although some members of the population may still be mobile in the search for food and raw materials.

semispecies Populations of a **species** that are completely isolated from one another but have not yet become truly separate species.

sexual dimorphism Physical differences between the sexes of a species not related to reproductive functions.

shaman A part-time, supernaturally chosen religious specialist who can manipulate the supernatural.

social stratification The presence of acknowledged differences in social status, political influence, and wealth among the people within a society.

society A group of organisms living together in an ordered community. In the case of humans, a group with a shared culture.

sociobiology The scientific study that examines evolutionary explanations for social behaviors within **species.**

sociolinguistics The study of language in its social contexts.

sorcery Magical acts with evil intent. See **magic.**

speciation The evolution of a new **species.**

species A group of organisms that can produce fertile offspring among themselves but not with members of other groups.

state A **political organization** with one central authority governing all the individual units.

stereoscopic Three-dimensional vision; depth perception.

stimulus diffusion When knowledge of a cultural trait in another society stimulates the invention of a similar trait.

strata The layers of rock and soil under the surface of the earth. Also the socioeconomic levels within a society.

stratigraphy   The study of the earth's **strata**.

subsistence pattern   How a society acquires its food.

subspecies   Physically distinguishable populations within a **species**. The concept, as a formal **taxonomic** unit, is falling from use.

symbol   Something that stands for something else, with no necessary link between the symbol and its meaning.

syncretism   The synthesis of existing religious beliefs and practices with new ones introduced from the outside.

syntax   Rules of word order in a **language**.

taxonomy   A classification using nested sets of categories of increasing specificity.

theory   A general idea that explains a large set of factual patterns.

tribe   A **political organization** with no central leader but in which the subunits may make collective decisions about the entire group.

uniformitarianism   The idea that present-day geological processes can also explain the history of the earth. Can be applied to biological change as well.

unilineal   A kinship system in which an individual is a member of only one parent's descent line. See **bilateral**.

unilinear evolutionism   An outdated concept of cultural evolution that claims all societies pass through the same series of stages, from savagery to civilization.

witchcraft   Traditionally, evil acts performed by individuals who possess inherent powers.

worldview   The collective interpretation of and response to the natural and cultural environments in which a group of people lives. Their assumptions about those environments and the values derived from those assumptions.

Bibliography

Akmajian, A., R. Demers, A. Farmer, and R. Harnish. 1991. *Linguistics*. 3rd ed. Cambridge, MA: MIT Press.

Allard, W. A. 2006. Solace at surprise creek. *National Geographic* 209 (June): 120–47.

Appleman, P., ed. 1979. *Darwin: A Norton Critical Edition*. 2nd ed. New York: Norton.

Ardrey, R. 1961. *African Genesis: A Personal Investigation into the Animal Origins and Nature of Man*. New York: Dell.

———. 1966. *The Territorial Imperative*. New York: Dell.

Attenborough, D. 1979. *Life on Earth*. Boston: Little, Brown.

———. 1984. *The Living Planet*. Boston: Little, Brown.

———. 1990. *The Trials of Life: A Natural History of Animal Behavior*. Boston: Little, Brown.

Baird, R. M., and S. E. Rosenbaum. 1991. *Animal Experimentation: The Moral Issues*. Buffalo: Prometheus Books.

Balikci, A. 1970. *The Netsilik Eskimo*. Garden City, NY: Natural History Press.

Barley, N. 1986. *The Innocent Anthropologist: Notes from a Mud Hut*. Prospect Heights, IL: Waveland.

Benedict, R. 1934. *Patterns of Culture*. New York: Mentor.

Blumstein, D. T. 1999. Selfish sentinels. *Science* 284 (4 June): 1633–34.

Bowen, E. S. (L. Bohannon). 1964. *Return to Laughter*. Garden City, NY: Anchor Books.

Bowlby, J. 1990. *Charles Darwin: A New Life*. New York: Norton.

Brace, C. L. 2005. *"Race" Is a Four-Letter Word: The Genesis of the Concept*. New York: Oxford University Press.

Bramble, D. M., and D. E. Lieberman. 2004. Endurance running and the evolution of *Homo*. *Nature* 432: 345–52.

Bramblett, C. 1994. *Patterns of Primate Behavior*. 2nd ed. Prospect Heights, IL: Waveland.

Brown, K. M. 1987. Voodoo. In *Magic, Witchcraft, and Religion: An Anthropological Study of the Supernatural*, ed. A. C. Lehmann and J. E. Myers. Mountain View, CA: Mayfield.

Calvin, W. H. 1996. *How Brains Think: Evolving Intelligence, Then and Now*. New York: Basic Books.

Campbell, C. J., A. Fuentes, K. C. MacKinnon, M. Panger, and S. K. Bearder, eds. 2007. *Primates in Perspective*. New York: Oxford University Press.

Caplan, A. L. 1978. *The Sociobiology Debate*. New York: HarperCollins.

Casson, R. W. 1981. *Language, Culture, and Cognition: The Anthropological Perspectives*. New York: McMillan.

Cavalieri, P., and P. Singer, eds. 1993. *The Great Ape Project: Equality Beyond Humanity*. New York: St. Martin's Griffin.

Cavalli-Sforza, L. L. 1991. Genes, peoples and languages. *Scientific American* (November): 104–10.

Cavalli-Sforza, L. L., P. Menozzi, and A. Piazza. 1994. *The History and Geography of Human Genes*. Princeton: Princeton University Press.

Chagnon, N. A. 1974. *Studying the Yąnomamö*. New York: Holt, Rinehart and Winston.

Chambers, E. 1989. *Applied Anthropology: A Practical Guide*. Prospect Heights, IL: Waveland.

Clapp, N. 1998. *The Road to Ubar: Finding the Atlantis of the Sands.* Boston: Houghton Mifflin.

Cohen, J. E. 1996. Ten myths of population. *Discover* (April): 42–47.

Conway Morris, S. 1998. *The Crucible of Creations: The Burgess Shale and the Rise of Animals.* Oxford: Oxford University Press.

Conway Morris, S., and S. J. Gould. 1998/1999. Showdown on the Burgess Shale. *Natural History* 107 (10): 48–55.

Coon, C. S. 1967. The Origin of Races. New York: Knopf.

Culotta, E. 2009. On the origin of religion. *Science* 326: 784–87.

de Waal, F. B. M., and F. Lanting (photographer). 1997. *Bonobo: The Forgotten Ape.* Berkeley: University of California Press.

Deetz, J., and E. S. Dethlefsen. 1967. Death's head, cherub, urn and willow. *Natural History* (March).

Dethlefsen, E., and J. Deetz. 1966. Death's heads, cherubs, and willow trees: Experimental archaeology in colonial cemeteries. *American Antiquity* 31: 502–10.

Dethlefsen, E., and J. Deetz. 1967. Death's head, cherub, urn and willow. *Natural History* 76 (3): 29–37.

Dettwyler, K. A. 1994. *Dancing Skeletons: Life and Death in West Africa.* Prospect Heights, IL: Waveland.

Diamond, J. 1991. Curse and blessing of the ghetto. *Discover* (March): 60–65.

———. 1992. *The Third Chimpanzee: The Evolution and Future of the Human Animal.* New York: HarperCollins.

———. 1997. *Guns, Germs, and Steel: The Fates of Human Societies.* New York: Norton.

Dolhinow, P., and A. Fuentes, eds. 1999. *The Nonhuman Primates.* New York: McGraw-Hill/Mayfield.

Douglas, M. 1966. *Purity and Danger: An Analysis of Concepts of Pollution and Taboo.* Middlesex, Eng.: Penguin.

Eldredge, N. 1995. *Dominion: Can Nature and Culture Co-exist?* New York: Henry Holt.

Entine, J. 2000. Taboo: Why Black Athletes Dominate Sports and Why We're Afraid to Talk About It. New York: Public Affairs.

Fagan, B. M. 1989. *The Adventure of Archaeology.* Washington, DC: National Geographic Society.

Fausto-Sterling, A. 1993. The five sexes. *The Sciences* (March–April): 20–24.

———. 2000. The five sexes, revisited. *The Sciences* (July–August): 18–23.

Feder, K. L. 1994. *A Village of Outcasts: Historical Archaeology and Documentary Research at the Lighthouse Site.* Mountain View, CA: Mayfield.

———. 1999. *Lessons from the Past: An Introductory Reader in Archaeology.* Mountain View, CA: Mayfield.

———. 2004. *Linking to the Past: A Brief Introduction to Archaeology.* New York: Oxford University Press.

———. 2004. *The Past in Perspective: An Introduction to Human Prehistory.* 4th ed. Mountain View, CA: Mayfield.

———. 2006. *Frauds, Myths, and Mysteries: Science and Pseudoscience in Archaeology.* 7th ed. New York: McGraw-Hill.

Feder, K. L., and M. A. Park. 2007. *Human Antiquity: An Introduction to Physical Anthropology and Archaeology.* 5th ed. New York: McGraw-Hill.

Fedigan, L. M., and L. Fedigan. 1988. *Gender and the Study of Primates: Curricular Module for the Project on Gender and Curriculum.* Washington, DC: American Anthropological Association.

Forbes, H. M. 1927. *Gravestones of Early New England and the Men Who Made Them: 1653–1800.* Princeton, NJ: The Pyne Press.

Forte, M., and A. Siliotti, eds. 1996. *Virtual Archaeology: Re-creating Ancient Worlds.* New York: Harry N. Abrams.

Fortey, R. 1998. *Life: A Natural History of the First Four Billion Years of Life on Earth.* New York: Knopf.

Fossey, D. 1983. *Gorillas in the Mist.* Boston: Houghton Mifflin.

Fouts, R. (with S. T. Mills). 1997. *Next of Kin: What Chimpanzees Have Taught Me about Who We Are.* New York: William Morrow.

Fouts, R. S., and D. H. Fouts. 1999. Chimpanzee sign language research. In *The Nonhuman Primates,* ed. P. Dolhinow and A. Fuentes. New York: McGraw-Hill/Mayfield.

Galdikas, B. 1995. *Reflections of Eden: My Years with the Orangutans of Borneo.* Boston: Little, Brown.

Gladwell, M. 2007. None of the above. *The New Yorker* (December 17): 92–96.

Glasse, R., and S. Lindenbaum. 1992. Fieldwork in the South Fore: The process of ethnographic inquiry. In *Prion Diseases of Humans and Animals*, ed. S. B. Prusiner, J. Collinge, J. Powell, and B. Anderson. West Sussex, Engl.: Ellis Horwood Limited.

Goodall, J. 1971. *In the Shadow of Man*. Boston: Houghton Mifflin.

———. 1990. *Through a Window: My Thirty Years with the Chimpanzees of Gombe*. Boston: Houghton Mifflin.

Goodman, A., D. L. Dufour, and G. H. Pelto. 2000. *Nutritional Anthropology: Biocultural Perspectives on Food and Nutrition*. Mountain View, CA: Mayfield.

Gore, A. 2006. *An Inconvenient Truth: The Planetary Emergency of Global Warming and What We Can Do about It*. New York: Rodale.

Goudsmit, J. 1997. *Viral Sex: The Nature of AIDS*. New York: Oxford University Press.

———. 1983. *Hen's Teeth and Horse's Toes*. New York: Norton.

———. 1989. *Wonderful Life: The Burgess Shale and the Nature of History*. New York: Norton.

———. 1993. *The Book of Life: An Illustrated History of the Evolution of Life on Earth*. New York: Norton.

———. 1993. *Eight Little Piggies*. New York: Norton.

———. 1996. *The Mismeasure of Man*. Rev. and exp. New York: Norton.

Greene, J. C. 1959. *The Death of Adam*. New York: Mentor Books.

Gregor, T. A., and D. R. Gross. 2004. Guilt by association: The culture of accusation and the American Anthropological Association's investigation of *Darkness in El Dorado*. *American Anthropologist* 106 (4): 687–98.

Harris, M. 1974. *Cows, Pigs, Wars and Witches: The Riddles of Culture*. New York: Vintage Books.

———. 1977. *Cannibals and Kings: The Origins of Cultures*. New York: Random House.

———. 1979. *Cultural Materialism: The Struggle for a Science of Culture*. New York: Random House.

———. 1999. *Theories of Culture in Postmodern Times*. Walnut Creek, CA: Altamira Press.

Harris, S. 2004. *The End of Faith: Religion, Terror, and the Future of Reason*. New York: Norton.

———. 2006. *Letter to a Christian Nation*. New York: Knopf.

Heider, K. 1997. *Grand Valley Dani: Peaceful Warriors*. 3rd ed. Fort Worth, TX: Harcourt Brace.

Herrnstein, R. J., and C. Murray. 1994. *The Bell Curve: The Reshaping of American Life by Difference in Intelligence*. New York: Free Press.

Hester, T. R., H. J. Shafer, and K. L. Feder. 1997. *Field Methods in Archaeology*. 7th ed. New York: McGraw-Hill/Mayfield.

Hockett, C. F., and R. Ascher. 1964. The human revolution. *Current Anthropology* 5: 135–68.

Holden, C. 2004. Peering under the hood of Africa's runners. *Science* 305: 637–39.

Hostetler, J. A. 1974. *Hutterite Society*. Baltimore: Johns Hopkins University Press.

Hrdy, S. B. 2009. Meet the alloparents. *Natural History* (April): 24–29.

Jablonski, N., and G. Chaplin. 2002. Skin deep. *Scientific American* (October): 74–81.

———. 2012. *Living Color: The Biological and Social Meaning of Skin Color*. Berkeley: University of California Press.

Jensen, A. R. 1969. How much can we boost IQ and scholastic achievement? *Harvard Educational Review* 39 (Winter): 1–123.

Johanson, D., and J. Shreeve. 1989. *Lucy's Child: The Discovery of a Human Ancestor*. New York: William Morrow.

Johanson, D. C., and M. A. Edey. 1981. *Lucy: The Beginnings of Humankind*. New York: Simon and Schuster.

Keesing, R. M. 1975. *Kin Groups and Social Structure*. New York: Holt, Rinehart and Winston.

Kennedy, K. A. R. 1976. *Human Variation in Space and Time*. Dubuque, IA: W. C. Brown.

Kirchner, W. H., and W. F. Towne. 1994. The sensory basis of the honeybee's dance language. *Scientific American* (June): 74–80.

Kluger, J. and K. Dell. 2006. The buzz on bees. *Time* (November 6): 56–57.

Kottak, C. P., J. J. White, R. H. Furlow, and P. C. Rice. 1997. *The Teaching of Anthropology: Problems, Issues, and Decisions*. New York: McGraw-Hill/Mayfield.

Kristof, N. 1999. Help! There's a mausu in my konpyutaa! *New York Times* (April 4): WK4.

LaBarre, W. 1962. *They Shall Take Up Serpents*. Minneapolis: University of Minnesota Press.

———. 1995. *The Sixth Extinction: Patterns of Life and the Future of Humankind*. New York: Doubleday.

Lancaster, J. 1975. *Primate Behavior and the Emergence of Human Culture.* New York: Holt, Rinehart and Winston.

Lee, R. 1993. *The Dobe Ju/'hoansi.* 3rd ed. Fort Worth, TX: Harcourt Brace.

Lehmann, A. C., and J. E. Myers, eds. 1993. *Magic, Witchcraft, and Religion: An Anthropological Study of the Supernatural.* Mountain View, CA: Mayfield.

Lemonick, M. D., and A. Dorfman. 2009. A long-lost relative. *Time,* October 12, 42–45.

Lenkeit, R. 2007. *Introducing Cultural Anthropology.* 3rd ed. New York: McGraw-Hill.

Lewontin, R. 1982. *Human Diversity.* New York: Scientific American Books.

Lieberman, D. E. 2009. *Homo floresiensis* from head to toe. *Nature* 459: 41–42.

Lindenbaum, S. 1979. *Kuru Sorcery: Disease and Danger in the New Guinea Highlands.* Mountain View, CA: Mayfield.

Linton, R. 1937. One hundred per cent American. *The American Mercury,* 40.

Lohmann, R. I. 2006. Field methods. In *Encyclopedia of Anthropology,* ed. H. J. Birx. Thousand Oaks, CA: Sage.

———. 2006. Review of *Yali's question: Sugar, culture, and history. Anthropological Quarterly* 79(4): 755–761.

Lopez, B. 1986. *Arctic Dreams: Imagination and Desire in a Northern Landscape.* New York: Bantam Books.

Macauly, D. 1979. *Motel of the Mysteries.* Boston: Houghton Mifflin.

Mann, C. C. 2009. Chagnon critics overstepped bounds, historian says. *Science* 326 (September 11): 1466.

Marks, J. 1995. *Human Biodiversity: Genes, Races, and History.* New York: Aldine de Gruyter.

———. 2002. *What It Means to Be 98% Chimpanzee: Apes, People, and Their Genes.* Berkeley: University of California Press.

———. 2006. Save the apes from the ape rights activists! *Anthropology News* 47(9): 4–5.

Marshack, A. 1975. Exploring the mind of ice age man. *National Geographic* 147 (1): 64–89.

Martin, L. 1986. Eskimo words for snow: A case study in the genesis and decay of an anthropological example. *American Anthropologist* 88 (2): 418–19.

Martin, M. K., and B. Voorhies. 1975. *Female of the Species.* New York: Columbia University Press.

McGee, R. J., and R. L. Warms, eds. 1996. *Anthropological Theory: An Introductory History.* Mountain View, CA: Mayfield.

McGrew, W. C. 1998. Culture in nonhuman primates? *Annual Review of Anthropology* 27: 301–28.

Meier, R. J. 2003. *The Complete Idiot's Guide to Human Prehistory.* New York: Alpha Books.

Mettler, L. E., T. G. Gregg, and H. E. Schaffer. 1988. *Population Genetics and Evolution.* Englewood Cliffs, NJ: Prentice Hall.

Mielke, J. H., L. W. Konigsberg, and J. H. Relethford. 2006. *Human Biological Variation.* New York: Oxford University Press.

Miner, H. 1956. Body ritual among the Nacirema. *American Anthropologist* 58: 503–7.

Mithen, S. 1996. *The Prehistory of the Mind: The Cognitive Origins of Art, Religion and Science.* London: Thames and Hudson.

Molnar, S. 1992. *Human Variation: Races, Types, and Ethnic Groups.* 3rd ed. Englewood Cliffs, NJ: Prentice Hall.

Montagu, M. F. A., ed. 1964. *The Concept of Race.* New York: Collier Books.

———. 1997. Man's Most Dangerous Myth: The Fallacy of Race. 6th ed. Walnut Creek, CA: Altamira.

Moran, E. F. 2000. *Human Adaptability: An Introduction to Ecological Anthropology.* Boulder, CO: Westview.

Muller, K. 1974. Tanna awaits the coming of John Frum. *National Geographic* 145 (5): 706–15.

Murdock, G. P. 1949. *Social Structure.* New York: Macmillan.

Nanda, S. 1999. *Neither Man nor Woman: The Hijras of India.* Stamford, CT: Wadsworth.

Nanda, S., and R. L. Warms. 1998. *Cultural anthropology,* 6th ed. Belmont CA: West/Wadsworth.

Norbeck, E. 1974. *Religion in Human Life: Anthropological Views.* New York: Holt, Rinehart and Winston.

Omohundro, J. T. 2001. *Careers in Anthropology.* 2nd ed. Mountain View, CA: Mayfield.

O'Neill, T. 1996. Irian Jaya. *National Geographic* 189 (2): 2–33.

Park, M. A. 1982–1983. Palmistry: Science or hand-jive? *Skeptical Inquirer* 7 (2): 21–32.

———. 2013. *Biological Anthropology.* 7th ed. New York: McGraw-Hill.

———. 2010. *Biological Anthropology: An Introductory Reader.* 6th ed. New York: McGraw-Hill.

Passingham, R. 1982. *The Human Primate.* New York: Freeman.

Parker, I. 2007. Swingers. *New Yorker* (July 30): 48–61.

Patterson, F. 1978. Conversations with a gorilla. *National Geographic* (October): 438–65.

Pennisi, E. 2009. Tales of a prehistoric human genome. *Science* 323: 866–71.

Pfeiffer, J. E. 1982. *The Emergence of Humankind.* 3rd ed. New York: Harper and Row.

Podolefsky, A., and P. J. Brown, eds. 2006. *Applying Anthropology: An Introductory Reader.* 8th ed. New York: McGraw-Hill.

Raby, P. 2001. *Alfred Russel Wallace: A Life.* Princeton, NJ: Princeton University Press.

Rachels, J. 1990. *Created from Animals: The Moral Implications of Darwinism.* Oxford: Oxford University Press.

Reddy, G., and J. Nanda. 2005. Hijras: An "alternative" sex/gender in India. In *Gender in Cross-Cultural Perspective,* ed. C. B. Bretell and C. F. Sargent. Upper Saddle River, NJ: Pearson, Prentice Hall.

Relethford, J. H. 2003. *Reflections of Our Past: How Human History Is Revealed in Our Genes.* Boulder, CO: Westview.

Rhodes, R. 1997. *Deadly Feasts.* New York: Simon and Schuster.

Rice, P., and A. Paterson. 1985. Cave art and bones: Exploring the interrelationships. *American Anthropologist* 87: 94–100.

Ridley, Mark. 1996. *Evolution.* 3rd ed. Cambridge, MA: Blackwell Science.

Ridley, Matt. 1999. *Genome: The Autobiography of a Species in 23 Chapters.* New York: HarperCollins.

Robey, B., S. O. Rutstein, and L. Morris. 1993. The fertility decline in developing countries. *Scientific American* (December): 60–67.

Rollin, B. 1992. *Animal Rights and Human Morality.* Rev. ed. Buffalo: Prometheus Books.

Rowe, N. 1996. *The Pictorial Guide to the Living Primates.* East Hampton, NY: Pogonius Press.

Ryan, F. 1997. *Virus X: Tracking the New Killer Plagues out of the Present and into the Future.* Boston: Little, Brown.

Sagan, C. 1977. *The Dragons of Eden: Speculations on the Evolution of Human Intelligence.* New York: Ballantine Books.

Salzmann, Z. 1993. *Language, Culture, and Society: An Introduction to Linguistic Anthropology.* Boulder, CO: Westview.

Sarich, V. and R. Miele. 2004. Race: The Reality of Human Differences. Boulder, CO: Westview.

Savage-Rumbaugh, S., and R. Lewin. 1994. Ape at the brink. *Discover* (September): 91–98.

Schadewald, R. 1981–1982. Scientific creationism, egocentricity and the flat earth. *Skeptical Inquirer* 6 (2): 41–48.

Schell, J. 1982. *The Fate of the Earth.* New York: Knopf.

Schultz, E. A., and R. H. Lavenda. 1998. *Cultural Anthropology: A Perspective on the Human Condition.* New York: Oxford University Press.

Scofield, J. 1962. Netherlands New Guinea. *National Geographic* 121 (5): 584–603.

Service, E. R. 1978. *Profiles in Ethnology.* 3rd ed. New York: HarperCollins.

Sharer, R. J., and W. Ashmore. 1993. *Archaeology: Discovering Our Past.* 2nd ed. Mountain View, CA: Mayfield.

Shepher, J. 1983. *Incest: A Biosocial View.* New York: Academic Press.

Shreeve, J. 1994. *Erectus* rising. *Discover* (September): 80–89.

Sloan, C. P. 2006. The origin of childhood. *National Geographic* 210 (November): 148–59.

Smith, J. M. 1984. Science and myth. *Natural History* 93 (11): 10–24.

Smuts, B. 1985. *Sex and Friendship in Baboons.* Hawthorne, NY: Aldine de Gruyter.

Steffen, A., ed. 2006. *Worldchanging: A User's Guide for the 21st Century.* New York: Abrams.

Stinson, S., B. Bogin, R. Huss-Ashmore, and D. O'Rourke, eds. 2000. *Human Biology: An Evolutionary and Biocultural Perspective.* New York: Wiley-Liss.

Stringer, C. B., and R. McKie. 1996. *African Exodus: The Origins of Modern Humanity.* New York: Henry Holt.

Strum, S. 1987. *Almost Human.* New York: Random House.

Sussman, R. W. 1999. *The Biological Basis of Human Behavior: A Critical Review.* Upper Saddle River, NJ: Prentice Hall.

Tattersall, I. 1993. *The Human Odyssey: Four Million Years of Evolution.* New York: Prentice Hall.

———. 2009. *The Fossil Trail: How We Know What We Think We Know about Human Evolution.* 2nd ed. New York: Oxford.

Teitelbaum, M., ed. 1976. *Sex Differences: Social and Biological Perspectives.* Garden City, NY: Anchor Books.

Tierney, P. 2000. *Darkness in El Dorado: How Scientists and Journalists Devastated the Amazon.* New York: Norton.

Toth, N. 1985. The Oldowan reassessed: A close look at early stone artifacts. *Journal of Archaeological Science* 12: 101–20.

Trefil, J., and R. M. Hazen. 1995. *The Sciences: An Integrated Approach*. New York: Wiley.

Vaidyanathan, G. 2011. The cultured chimpanzees. *Nature* 476: 266–69.

van Willigen, J. 1986. *Applied Anthropology: An Introduction*. South Hadley, MA: Bergin and Garvey.

Vivelo, F. R. 1978. *Cultural Anthropology Handbook: A Basic Introduction*. New York: McGraw-Hill.

Weiner, J. 1994. *The Beak of the Finch: A Story of Evolution in Our Time*. New York: Knopf.

Wetherington, R. K. 2012. *Readings in the History of Evolutionary Theory: Selections from Primary Sources*. New York: Oxford.

Wheeler, M. 1943. *Maiden Castle*. London: Society of Antiquaries of London.

Whiten, A., and C. Boesch. 2001. The cultures of chimpanzees. *Scientific American* (January): 60–67.

Williams, T. T., and T. Major. 1984. *The Secret Language of Snow*. San Francisco: Sierra Club/Pantheon.

Wilson, E. O. 1975. *Sociobiology: The New Synthesis*. Cambridge, MA: Harvard University Press.

———. 1992. *The Diversity of Life*. Cambridge, MA: Harvard University Press.

———. 1998. *Consilience: The Unity of Knowledge*. New York: Knopf.

———. 2006. How to make a social insect. *Nature* 443: 919–20.

Wolpoff, M., and R. Caspari. 1997. *Race and Human Evolution*. New York: Simon and Schuster.

Wong, K. 2005. The littlest human. *Scientific American* (February): 56–65.

Wrangham, R. 2009. *Catching Fire: How Cooking Made Us Human*. New York: Basic Books.

Wright, R. 1994. *The Moral Animal: Evolutionary Psychology and Everyday Life*. New York: Vintage.

Zich, A. 1989. Two worlds, time apart: Indonesia. *National Geographic* 175 (1): 96–127.

Zuckoff, M. 2011. *Lost in Shangri-La*. New York: HarperCollins.

Photo Credits

CHAPTER 1 Opener: © William F. Keegan; 1.2: © Momatiuk/Eastman/ Woodfin Camp and Associates; 1.4 (top & bottom): Michael A. Park; 1.6 (tl): © William F. Keegan; 1.6 (tr): © Phyllis Dolhinow; 1.6 (bl): © Irven DeVore/Anthro-Photo; 1.6 (br): © Enrico Ferorelli; 1.7 (tl): © Raymond Hames; 1.7 (bl): Courtesy Sharon Hutchinson; 1.7 (br): © Mel Konner/Anthro-Photo; 1.8 (tl): © Kenneth L. Feder; 1.8 (tr): © William F. Keegan; 1.8 (bl): Courtesy Terry del Bene; 1.8 (br): Margaret Conkey examining the paintings at the cave of Le Reseau Clastres (Ariège, France). Photo by Jean Clottes

CHAPTER 2 Opener and 2.3: © Photo Library/Science Source

CHAPTER 3 Opener: © Gerald Lacz/ Animals Animals; 3.3: © Julia Margaret Cameron/National Portrait Gallery, London; 3.6: © Photo Library/Science Source; 3.7: Neg. # K12654, Courtesy Department of Library Services, American Museum of Natural History; 3.8: © Gerald Lacz/Animals Animals

CHAPTER 4 Opener: © Gordon Wiltsie/National Geographic/Corbis; 4.1: © Gregory G. Dimijizn, M.D./ Science Source; 4.2: © Jane Goodall/ National Geographic Society Image Collection; 4.3: © Steve Gaulin/ Anthro-Photo; 4.5: © Gordon Wiltsie/ National Geographic/Corbis; 4.6 (left): © Erich Lessing/Art Resource, NY; 4.6 (right): © Richard T. Nowitz; 4.7 (All): © Kenneth L. Feder; 4.10: © English Heritage. NMR Aerofilms Collection

CHAPTER 5 Opener: © Frans Lanting; 5.6, 5.8, 5.9, 5.10, and 5.11: © Noel Rowe/alltheworldsprimates. org; 5.12: © Frans Lanting; 5.13: Michael A. Park; 5.14: © Stewart Halperin/Animals Animals; 5.15: Library of Congress Prints and Photographs Division (LC-DIG-ppmsca-18945)

CHAPTER 6 Opener: Courtesy Comité Départmental du Tourisme de la Dordogne; 6.3: © Bone Clones. www.bonesclones.com; 6.7: Neg. # 4744(6) Courtesy Department of Library Services. American Museum of NaturalHistory. Photo by D. Finnin/C. Chesek. 6.9: © Alan Walker/National Geographic Society Image Collection; 6.10: © The National Museums of Kenya; 6.11: © Eric Delson; 6.12 & 6.13: Michael A. Park; 6.15: © David L. Brill/Brill Atlanta; 6.18 (top left): © Boltin Picture Library/The Bridgeman Art Library; 6.18 (top & bottom right): © Kenneth L. Feder; 6.23: © John Reader/Science Photo Library/ Photo Researchers; 6.24: © Kenneth L. Feder; 6.25: © Phototheque du Musée de l'Homme, Paris, M. Lucas, photographer; 6.26 (left & right): © David L. Brill/Brill Atlanta; 6.27: © Kenneth L. Feder; 6.28: Courtesy of the Peabody Museum of Archaeology and Ethnology, Harvard University, 2005.16.318.38; 6.29: Neg. # 39686. Photo by Kirschner. Courtesy Department of Library Services. American Museum of Natural History; 6.30: Neg. # 2169(2). Courtesy Department of Library Services. American Museum of Natural History; 6.31: Michael A. Park; 6.32: Courtesy Comité Départmental du Tourisme de la Dordogne

CHAPTER 7 Opener: © Hisham Ibrahim/Photographer's Choice/Getty; 7.1: Michael A. Park; 7.2: © Richard Baker/In Pictures/Corbis; 7.3: © Noel Rowe/Pictoral Guide to the Living Primates; 7.4 (top left): © Daniel Dempster Photography/Alamy RF; 7.4 (top right): © Richard & Susan Day/ Animals Animals; 7.4 (bottom left & right): © Alán Gallegos/AG Photograph; 7.5: © CNRI/SPL/Science Source/Photo Researchers; 7.7 (top left & right & bottom left): © Noel Rowe/ Pictoral Guide to the Living Primates; 7.7 (bottom right): Michael A. Park; 7.9: © Dr. Serena Nanda; 7.10: © Jerry Cooke/Photo Researchers; 7.11: © Richard T. Nowitz

CHAPTER 8 Opener and 8.1: © George Steinmetz; 8.3: © Stephen Krasemann/Getty; 8.9: © The Granger Collection, New York; 8.10: Neg. # 338768. Photo by J.W.

Index

Bold page numbers indicate definitions.